Beyond the Borders
of the Law

Published in Cooperation with the
William P. Clements Center for Southwest Studies,
Southern Methodist University

Beyond the Borders of the Law

Critical Legal Histories of the

North American West

Edited by
Katrina Jagodinsky and
Pablo Mitchell

UNIVERSITY PRESS OF KANSAS

Published by the University Press of Kansas (Lawrence, Kansas 66045), which was organized
by the Kansas Board of Regents and is operated and funded by Emporia State University,
Fort Hays State University, Kansas State University, Pittsburg State University, the University of Kansas, and Wichita State University.

Library of Congress Cataloging-in-Publication Data

Names: Jagodinsky, Katrina, editor. | Mitchell, Pablo, editor. | William P. Clements Center for
    Southwest Studies, sponsoring body.
Title: Beyond the borders of the law : critical legal histories of the North American west /
    edited by Katrina Jagodinsky, Pablo Mitchell.
Description: Lawrence, Kansas : University Press of Kansas, 2018. | Includes bibliographical
    references and index.
Identifiers: LCCN 2018027419
    ISBN 9780700626786 (hardback)
    ISBN 9780700626793 (paperback)
    ISBN 9780700626809 (ebook)
Subjects: LCSH: Law—West (US)—Congresses. | Borderlands—West (US)—Congresses. |
    BISAC: LAW / Legal History. | HISTORY / United States / 19th Century. | HISTORY /
    United States / 20th Century.
Classification: LCC KF361.A2 B49 2018 | DDC 349.78—dc23.
LC record available at https://lccn.loc.gov/2018027419

British Library Cataloguing-in-Publication Data is available.

Printed in the United States of America

10 9 8 7 6 5 4 3 2 1

CONTENTS

Part III: Legal Borderlands of Justice and Reform

PREFACE

PABLO MITCHELL

A friend of mine, an immigration scholar, once told me that immigration is the result of failure, that immigrants leave their homes because their home countries have in one way or another failed them. There's a lot of truth in this; for some immigrants, it's the only reason they leave their homes and brave dangerous crossings and new lands. Historians too can be moved by failure, inspired to embark on their own far-flung journeys by home disciplines that provide less and less sustenance—as new methods and approaches seem to be ignored or one generation too faithfully begets another—and only slim hope for the future.

Like immigrants, however, historians can be driven by hope as well as loss and despair. There is an optimism in immigration, an opportunity that comes from leaving home and embarking on the new and novel. A similar form of optimism propels this volume as well. Like most decent ideas, *Beyond the Borders of the Law* owes its origins to another good idea. Brought together by Crista DeLuzio and David Wallace Adams for their 2009–2010 Clements Center symposium "On the Borders of Love and Power," Katrina Jagodinsky and I discovered a shared interest in both Borderlands history and Western legal history. We also, perhaps most importantly, shared a sense that each of those vibrant fields seemed not to have met each other, much less gotten to know each other very well. Maybe it was the lingering influence of the Love and Power workshop, but it seemed, as we had our initial conversations about this project, that these two fields might kind of hit it off, might actually be kind of good for each other.

Encouraged by the high spirits and wisdom of Andrew Graybill and Sherry Smith of the Clements Center, we thus set about planning the symposium. We invited a handful of scholars doing precisely the kind of work that we hoped would draw the fields together to participate in the workshop and hoped to entice several others to join us in this critical journey into and through the legal borderlands. Borderlands historians, legal historians, and historians well-versed in critical theory would of course be welcome, but so too would be those formally trained in and practicing the law, lawyers with an eye toward both legal history and the intricacies and subtleties of law and its many borders. From an outstanding set of proposals that were submitted in response to our call for papers, we selected participants who could speak to topics and time periods including Native history, the US-Canada and US-Mexico borders, regions from Texas to Alaska and Montana to California, and a chronology that stretches from the mid-nineteenth century to the near present. The chapters that follow are what have come of this sentiment that Western legal history and Borderlands history are better with each other than they are apart.

Beyond the Borders of the Law has been warmed by the suns of many scholars. One of the most important intellectual contributions to the scholarship of this volume has been Gloria Anzaldúa's insistence that the borderlands is a place of creativity and possibility as well as a land of despair and diminishment. We have as much to learn, she suggests, from the margins—the margins of empires, of territories, of languages, of cultures, even of ourselves and our own mottled, fearful, frayed edges—as we have to gain from our knowledge of the center and the stable and the more easily governed. Borderlands spaces are often unsettling locales where the tried-and-true can prove unwieldy and alkaline. New languages are required in border regions (new *lenguas,* to follow Anzaldúa's lead), new skills, new approaches and intimacies.

The rich novelties and adaptations of the borderlands are widespread. In the borderlands where the United States and Mexico meet, Mexican culture was no less transformed by its *frontera* than the United States was, and is, continuously renewed by its own border crossers. It is tempting to credit this creative, generative possibility of the borderlands, along with the untold dangers and deprivations, to the absence of governing bodies and empowered authorities. Indeed, the lawless West is one of the most enduring of American myths. As it happens, there is a curious twist in the myth of lawlessness: the more law there is, the less there seems to be. In fact, there was an abundance of law in the West, as there is in all borderlands regions, an overlapping of claims and jurisdictions and domains, a legal supersaturation rather than a watered-down skimpiness. Overflowing with law rather than law-less, legal borderlands can appear especially disorienting, with law and justice unevenly, even capriciously, enforced.

These overlapping legal systems (state, tribal, municipal, federal, transnational, international) never fit perfectly together and are always to some extent misaligned, sometimes with gaping omissions, sometimes with more subtle faults and cracks. Inequities of race and gender and other asymmetries of power add deeper perils to these uncertain legal terrains and in many respects those entering the borderlands bereft of power and resources tend to find fewer benefits in its liminal spaces and engaging hybridity. But even while barred from full citizenship, the most marginalized border dwellers could in fact prove quite capable of turning these cracks and fissures to their own advantage. In fact, one of the most remarkable features of the borderlands is the extent to which dispossessed individuals and communities could take the law, as it were, into their own hands and exhibit sophisticated and savvy legal maneuvers.

The chapters that follow reflect these broader themes of the creativity of the borderlands, the overabundance of law in the borderlands, and the surprising legal acumen of disenfranchised border dwellers. These themes flow beneath and inform each of the three sections of this volume: Legal Borderlands of Race and Gender, Legal Borderlands of Property and Citizenship, and Legal Borderlands of Justice and Reform. Exceptional in their own right, the essays in each section also reflect the volume's overarching interest in drawing Western legal history into more sustained conversation with Borderlands history.

Coeditor Katrina Jagodinsky's introductory essay argues that critical Western legal histories most accurately characterize law in the North American West, advocating for an increased standard of critical inquiry in the field and inviting senior and junior scholars alike to participate in the revitalization of Western legal history. Taking the reader through the variety of texts we might see as Western legal history, Jagodinsky shows how the field has paid some attention to race and gender. The chapters in the first section, by Sarah Deer, Jeffrey Shepherd, and Alicia Gutierrez-Romine, provide even more nuanced approaches, giving flesh to the intersections of race and gender that Anzaldúa and other borderlands scholars have highlighted for decades in their work.

Although focused on the turn of the twenty-first century, Deer's chapter on the Violence Against Women Act places current violence directed at Native women within a broader, centuries-long context of a US settler-colonial state that has repeatedly targeted Native communities, and particularly Native women. In this way, Deer vividly introduces readers to the perils of life in the borderlands, especially in spaces of overlapping laws and legal jurisdictions and the potentially devastating effects of legal ambiguity, and is thus for us a powerful way to start the volume.

In the next chapter, Jeffrey Shepherd focuses on the Blackfoot Confederacy, which spanned much of the present-day Montana-Alberta Plains region, and explores the array of legal boundaries and borders that Blackfoot bands encountered around the turn of the twentieth century. He describes the hardening of the US-Canada international border and the enforcement of reservation boundaries, while at the same time highlighting the border and boundary crossings by Blackfoot people: families visiting each other across the line, band members registering on tribal rolls in both the United States and Canada, and Blackfoot adoption of fluid yet contradictory notions of status, blood, and citizenship.

Alicia Gutierrez-Romine's chapter moves south and focuses on women and abortion along the US-Mexico border. In 1953 a California higher court reversed the conviction of two men charged with violating California's abortion statute by arranging abortions in Mexico for American women. Although abortions were illegal in California and Mexico, the decision opened a new path for women seeking abortions in the West and a lucrative abortion industry emerged south of the border. As women crossed a national border to procure abortions in Mexico, they highlighted failures of the American medical and legal systems. Gutierrez-Romine's chapter documents the terrible effect that these failures had on women's lives as well as the legal, medical, and physical borderlands surrounding abortion before *Roe v. Wade.*

Resource law (laws governing, for instance, water, oil, timber, coal, gold, and uranium use or extraction), laws of property and ownership, and laws of citizenship and exclusion are some of the most venerable and valuable subfields in the Western legal tradition. The essays by Dana Weiner, Tom Romero, and Brian Frehner in the second section of the volume suggest that, properly nudged, these subfields can speak to broader themes as well.

Dana Weiner uses disputes over land rights to open a window onto black Californians' fight for legal rights in the face of crushing discrimination before and after the Civil War. Weiner offers an important discussion of race, citizenship, and property rights. Like the subjects of many of the essays in this volume, African Americans in California refused to concede to exclusion and second-class status and proved canny and persistent claimants of both property in California and full membership in society.

Drawing two prominent, yet often disconnected, themes in Western history into direct conversation, Tom Romero examines in the following chapter the turn-of-the-twentieth-century connection between water and immigration law and policy. In Romero's compelling account, the rise of hydraulic society and laws governing water use in the West, one of the key events in the history of the region, and indeed in the history of the nation, appears to play a powerful role in regulating immigration and determining the flow of agricultural labor into the West.

Similarly, natural resources are for Brian Frehner an important set of legal borderlands. Frehner examines the decisions by significant numbers of Chickasaw and Choctaw citizens in Oklahoma to permit non-Indian companies to extract valuable resources, such as coal, from their lands. Frehner's account also speaks to intimate relationships in the borderlands with profiles of important intermarried families in Oklahoma and highlights the often ambiguous nature of citizenship and belonging that can emerge in spaces of overlapping legal authority and jurisdiction.

The law's all-too-familiar cast of characters (lawyers and defendants, judges and juries) can also expand from a borderlands perspective. The essays in the final section bring new legal actors and institutions into the spotlight, prompting us to reconsider the legal knowledge of Native Alaskans and Mexican immigrants and their families as well as the genealogies of federal prisons and detention facilities, desegregation movements, and racial conservatism.

The courtroom, the most iconic of legal spaces, is at the center of Andrea Geiger's exploration of clashes between Indigenous legal tradition and colonial law in late nineteenth- and early twentieth-century Alaska. Geiger's chapter considers the courtroom as a site of cultural contact and colonial encounter, paying close attention to the intricacies of legal cases filed in Alaska's territorial courts, where Indigenous people were prosecuted for exercising traditional rights—but where they also turned for protection of those rights, sometimes against members of other Indigenous communities.

Extending this discussion of national borders to incarceration and mass imprisonment in the West, Kelly Lytle Hernández examines the criminalization of unlawful entry into the United States in the 1930s, which sent tens of thousands of Mexican citizens to federal prison. Mexicans imprisoned for violating US immigration laws in fact constituted the second largest prisoner population during the decade (behind liquor law violators) and, in turn, the federal government built three prisons in the US-Mexico borderlands to incarcerate Mexico's unlawful border crossers. The chapter explores the unique programs that the US Bureau of Prisons developed during the 1930s to rehabilitate Mexico's unlawful border crossers, educating them to appreciate Mexican culture, excel in the Mexican economy, and never again violate US immigration laws by unlawfully returning to the United States.

In the next chapter, Allison Powers Useche examines charges of police violence, land theft, and involuntary servitude filed before the US-Mexico Claims Commission by Mexican nationals living in the American West. In the 1920s and 1930s, these claimants forced the Claims Commission to address the problem of how to deal with state actions that complied with constitutional requirements but violated international law. Useche uncovers forgotten moments of struggle over the limits and possibilities of international law to address structural injustices within the US legal system.

Another legal case, *Keyes v. School District No. 1*, is at the center of the final chapter, by Danielle Olden. After a group of multiracial parents filed suit against the Denver school system, alleging that school officials purposely segregated students, the *Keyes* case became, in 1973, the first de facto school segregation case heard by the US Supreme Court. Although scholars have long described *Keyes* as the first northern school desegregation case, Olden locates the case within Denver's ambiguous physical borderland between "the North" and "the West." She explores the educational consequences of the court's decision in favor of the plaintiffs, a decision ordering racial balance and racial classification of schoolchildren throughout the city. The chapter brings to the surface debates about racial formation and "common sense" understandings of race, ethnicity, and culture as Denver residents tried to articulate, negotiate, and adjudicate racial identity.

Among the most enduring of borderlands conventions is a wariness of, if not weariness with, convention. Our mea culpas will thus appear here at the beginning of the volume, rather than at its end. Inspired to fill gaps and absences in the fields of Western legal history and borderlands history, we have convened, through invitation and acceptance alike, an assembly of work that, despite its merit, has omissions and missed opportunities of its own. Most glaring for scholars like us who are indebted to and inspired by the work of Evelyn Nakano Glenn, Nayan Shah, Moon-Ho Jung, and Grace Peña Delgado, is the failure to include an essay on Asian Americans in the legal borderlands. Many of the themes and topics central to the study of Asian Americans in the West—such as the link between law and sexuality, especially in the work of Nayan Shah, and the persistent, and inspiring, assertion by ordinary Asian immigrants and Asian Americans, especially Chinese and Japanese workers, of their legal rights in US courts—would have undoubtedly enriched this volume and strengthened it significantly. While the chapters in this volume begin the hard work of drawing the fields of Borderlands history and Western legal history into conversation, this absence, and the other absences that readers will undoubtedly discover, are reminders that there is still hard work ahead.

ACKNOWLEDGMENTS

This collection would have been impossible without generous institutions and the good cheer, patience, and thoughtfulness of a wide range of colleagues. We are indebted to the William P. Clements Center for Southwest Studies at Southern Methodist University, especially Ruth Ann Elmore, Andrew Graybill, Sherry Smith, and Neil Foley. At the University of Nebraska–Lincoln, we received tremendous support from Carroll R. Pauley Memorial Fund, Office of Research and Development, Department of History, College of Law, Institute for Ethnic Studies, College of Arts and Sciences, Department of Political Science, and Center for Great Plains Studies. We are grateful to Melynda Seaton and the Great Plains Art Museum in Lincoln, Nebraska, who linked our conference to a stunning exhibition by Indigenous artists with interests similar to our own. James Garza, Margaret Jacobs, John Wunder, Evelyn HuDeHart, and Carol Weber were gracious participants in workshops and were our hosts in Lincoln and Dallas.

The contributors to this collection not only wrote outstanding essays in their own right; they also read and thoughtfully discussed each other's chapters. Working with them has been one of the best professional experiences of both of our careers. We have been exceedingly fortunate to work with Kim Hogeland of the University Press of Kansas. Kim generously attended both workshops, where we discussed each essay in detail, and carefully read and commented on several versions of each essay. As coeditors, Katrina and I relied on her sharp analysis, gentle prodding, and good sense throughout this process. The anonymous readers who gave their time to this manuscript also offered much food for thought, and we appreciate their insights and questions. As we worked together on final revisions, we all benefited tremendously from the careful and kind work of copy editor Deborah Bruce-Hostler and the efficient wrangling by managing editor Kelly Chrisman Jacques at the University Press of Kansas. We are grateful to everyone there for their help in executing this volume.

Pablo would like to thank his family, especially Beth McLaughlin, Ruby Mitchell, and Tayo McLaughlin, as well as his friends and colleagues at Oberlin College. Katrina thanks her husband, James Chamberlain, writing partners Margaret Huettl and Megan Prins, and the mentors past and present who have shared their time so freely.

Into the Void, or the Musings and Confessions of a Redheaded Stepchild Lost in Western Legal History and Found in the Legal Borderlands of the North American West

KATRINA JAGODINSKY

> Borders are set up to define the places that are safe and unsafe, to distinguish *us* from *them*. A border is a dividing line, a narrow strip along a steep edge. A borderland is a vague and undetermined place created by the emotional residue of an unnatural boundary. It is in a constant state of transition. The prohibited and forbidden are its inhabitants. *Los atravesados* live here: the squint-eyed, the perverse, the queer, the troublesome, the mongrel, the mulato, the half-breed, the half dead; in short, those who cross over, pass over, or go through the confines of the "normal."
>
> Gloria Anzaldúa, *Borderlands/La Frontera: The New Mestiza*

Introducing the Introduction

Wet behind the ears at my first American Society for Legal History conference in 2014, I listened with rapt attention as keynote speaker Patty Limerick asked: "Is western history legal history?"[1] Limerick answered in the affirmative, citing the many ways in which law had defined the North American West. By the time I heard Limerick speak in downtown Denver's Tenth Circuit Court of Appeals, the wheels behind this anthology had already been set in motion, and I was excited to be working among historiographic heroes who have helped me to reflect upon my own engagement with legal history.

Those of us who teach Western history courses can count the legal acts Limerick recited on our fingers and toes: the 1784 Land Ordinance, the 1787 Northwest Ordinance, the 1790 Trade & Intercourse Act, the 1803 Louisiana Purchase, and every treaty between American Indians and the federal government on one hand; the Missouri Compromises of 1820 and 1850, the Oregon Treaties of 1818 and 1846, and the series of legal maneuvers from the 1819 Adams-Onis Treaty and Texas Independence to the US-Mexican War and the 1848 Treaty of Guadalupe Hidalgo on the other hand. With our fingers accounted for, we can look to our toes to remember the Indian Removal Act of 1830 that paved the way for the establishment of Indian Territory in 1834, California Statehood in 1850, and the Kansas-Nebraska Act of 1854, the Homestead and Pacific Railroad Acts of 1862, the Chinese Exclusion Act of 1882, the Allotment or Dawes Act of 1887, the 1898 Newlands Resolution incorporating the Territory of Hawaii, and every Organic Act that transformed a western territory into an American state between 1803 and 1958.

The following chapters add even more judicial and legislative acts of creation and destruction to this list, and together they stand as the basic framework of American laws shaping the past and present of the North American West as we know it. Pablo Mitchell and I, intrigued by this legal landscape and inspired by the works we read in histories of gender and sexuality, race and ethnicity, borderlands studies, and critical race theory, wanted to gather those we had seen working with such strands, and the Clements Center Symposium model seemed an ideal venue for our ambitions. We reached out to others we knew through Western and legal history and launched a conversation about our desire to showcase, and make more visible, the scholarly community working on the North American West. The legal borderlands model allowed us to share a conceptual framework while we sought to demonstrate the extent to which the North American West has been, and continues to be, a profound site of overlapping and overreaching legal structures and practices steeped in articulations of race, gender, and power.

As defined in a 2005 special issue of *American Quarterly*, legal borderlands are both those mandarin legal texts that define and regulate geopolitical borders and the ambiguities or contradictions creating liminal zones within the law.[2] This concept seemed to us to be the most promising vehicle for applying the tenets of borderlands studies and critical race theory to Western legal histories. And so, the scholars in this volume have taken up the legal borderlands banner, some finding the device remarkably useful in deconstructing the tired and obstructive lawless West archetype, and others straining the limits of its utility as they seek to explicate a region characterized by lawful disorder and contradiction.

Clearly, we agree with Limerick that Western history is legal history. And yet, despite a number of important exceptions, Western legal history has failed to deliver on the promise of this premise. In fact, the very question Limerick posed in her 2014 address reveals that the divide between Western and legal histories remains both institutional, as a problem of leadership and membership, and intellectual, as a problem of unrealized potential. Others likely have their own assessments of Western legal history as a field, namely those who consider themselves its practitioners, but we contend that the most powerful histories of law in the North American West cross disciplinary and institutional boundaries and are as likely to be cultural or conceptual as they are to be statutory and statistical. Even if our focus might be on topics typical of Western legal history—federal Indian policy, water and natural resource law, or immigration policy—we are scholars who pivot our work toward the legal borderlands framework that originated in the interdisciplinary school of American studies.

Critical legal history, critical race theory, legal borderlands, and New Western history are by now mature concepts that have not permeated the Western legal history field. Critical works in Western legal history abound— this essay and this volume will cite many of them—and yet, few of those authors describe their work as critical or even as Western legal history. For wayfaring scholars seeking an intellectual community, this contradiction makes it difficult to assert or claim an academic identity.

This essay is a redheaded stepchild's intellectual autobiography disguised as historiography; a set of questions passing as answers that reveal the void in Western legal history. If you haven't thought about Western legal history much lately, or you can't quite put your finger on a Western legal historian, then you, too, have found the void. If you are a reader fully content with Western legal history, well, pull your boots on. My own disappointment with the scholarship branded as Western legal history sent me seeking solace elsewhere and through that journey, I came to legal borderlands. In sharing my own conversion story here, I am calling out to a community of intellectual pushers and pullers; of angry and empathetic scholars; of those who explore history, and the law, and the West, and are as often disturbed as they are enchanted. Collectively, we invite readers to join a field of border crossers following the lead of Gloria Anzaldúa and Patricia Limerick, reclaiming the freckles and bruises of scholarship not fully sponsored in Western or legal history, often inspired by New Western and borderlands history, but somehow still its own.

It All Started Somewhere: The Legacy of Borderlands Crossed in 1987

Enjoying Limerick's 2014 American Society for Legal History address in the US district courtroom reminded me of my own family history of courtroom appearances ranging from felony and misdemeanor charges to marriage ceremonies and custody disputes. I had only recently been hired at the University of Nebraska–Lincoln and still navigated the academy without grace, often feeling keenly the "emotional residue" of passing beyond the borders of my class. Securing my place in Limerick's audience, where I remained unsure whether I was "us" or "them," required the generosity of my mentors and the characteristic stubbornness and spite my fellow gingers often disclaim. Limerick's words also took me back to my simultaneous reading in 2001 of *Legacy of Conquest* and *Borderlands/La Frontera* during undergraduate studies at Lawrence University. Although I didn't read their foundational works until nearly fifteen years after their publication, I felt immediately each author's significance.[3]

Only seven years old when *Borderlands/LaFrontera* and *Legacy of Conquest* came out in 1987, I watched the country fly by out the window of an old, wood-paneled station wagon my mother had fondly named "Big Beauty," as she and her boyfriend, a Vietnam veteran turned vegan, drove us from my San Diego, California, birthplace to Tigerton, Wisconsin. When I read Limerick's work more than a decade later, her inclusion of personal recollections of a changing West throughout her essays spoke to me deeply. Crossing natural and unnatural borders as we drove from California to Wisconsin, we trespassed unknowingly on the Hopi reservation and instead of being evicted we were invited to stay for a rodeo that remains the only one I've ever attended. In Arkansas, I found the accents as difficult to decipher as the Jamaican antiapartheid anthems I heard on my mother's reggae records. As the people we encountered seemed simultaneously more and less like me, I learned that whiteness meant something different depending on the demographic ratio of the room, the county, the state. When we arrived in Wisconsin and I started second grade that fall, it was a shock to see only white children on the playground and hear only English spoken in the classroom in contrast to the San Diego daycare and grade schools I had attended. Although I could not express it at the time, I felt that a great violence had occurred and feared that outsiders—myself included—did not last long in that place. That we had moved to a town familiar to my mother and lived among family and friends helped to ease my fears, certainly, but the eerie feeling of transgression never left me, nor did my habit of questioning a shared identity based on skin color alone. Anzaldúa's simultaneous critique and defense of the community who raised her was intimately recognizable to me as an uneasy member of a rural and white majority who turned on its own most vulnerable as often as it targeted others. Without collapsing the stark and powerful distinctions between *La Frontera* and the Great Lakes, between being teased about red hair and being teased about red skin, my childhood of constant transition and feeling more mongrel than normal made me particularly receptive to Anzaldúa and other anticolonial writers of color then and now.

More than the shared experience of observing national histories through a personal lens, Limerick's focus on the ongoing twentieth-century debate over nineteenth-century Western expansion as conquest or progress also resonated in the violent conflicts over mining and the "Wisconsin Walleye War" over off-reservation treaty rights that unfolded during my adolescence. Just as my mother had taken me to anti–death penalty vigils and feminist film festivals in San Diego, she brought me to Wa-Swa-Gon Treaty Association meetings to support Ojibwe spearfishers and their families, and to Green Party rallies to shout down Kennecott mining executives who touted job creation statistics and other economic incentives in northern Wisconsin.[4] Although I attended public high school after Wisconsin Act 31 mandated that "schools are required to teach American Indian studies at least three times throughout a student's K-12 career" and that the state provide instruction on American Indian treaty rights, the fact remained that the majority of my neighbors regularly and confidently expressed vehement epithets against Native people and treaty rights advocates—like myself and my family. Hearing taunts from poor and wealthy white neighbors alike, some of whom sent their children to the same school I attended, made it clear to me that inequality bore many faces well before I knew the terms decolonization and intersectionality. Finding myself *en el otro lado* more often than not throughout my adolescence, I came early to the conclusion—Limerick and Anzaldúa's, too—that we were living in the legacy of ongoing white and male conquest.

It is these experiences that I took with me when I enrolled at Lawrence University—a private liberal arts school in central Wisconsin—as a low-income student who benefited tremendously from the counseling and support of the Upward Bound program. Perhaps not surprisingly, I also took with me a keenly honed sense of inadequacy and self-loathing that first-generation students and redheaded stepchildren seem to exude in abundance. A few hard knocks made it clear that I did not have the patience or persistence required of biology majors, and I too easily overindulged in the navel-gazing English majors can be known for, eventually making my way into the history department as a junior with a mediocre GPA, a smart mouth, and a few bad habits. Although I had seen firsthand the work of anticolonial activists in southern California and northern Wisconsin, I did not know that I had already been traversing legal borderlands and training with experts in decolonization and hybridity until I began to read the literary works of Paula Gunn Allen, Gloria Anzaldúa, and Joy Harjo alongside the classic postcolonial and postmodernist works of Judith Butler, Jacques Derrida, Frantz Fanon, Michel Foucault, Clifford Geertz, and Antonio Gramsci, while taking notes on remarkably compelling lectures in American history from Jerald Podair, an advisor who had already enjoyed a career in law. Even as my undergraduate mentors in history and English patiently taught me how to read and write critically, opening a world to me that I had never imagined, it was an internship at the D'Arcy McNickle Center for American Indian and Indigenous Studies at the Newberry Library in Chicago that would direct my subsequent academic trajectory. From the staff there, I learned that American Indian studies was its own field, an interdisciplinary mecca, and I began reading all that I could to prepare myself for graduate applications, starting with Vine Deloria Jr.'s critiques of academic and historical colonialism and Ward Churchill's (pre-ethnic fraud controversy, mind you) portrayal of Indigenous rights claims in the larger frame of the civil rights movement.[5]

This largely haphazard pursuit to become quickly acquainted with anticolonial Western histories is how I came to read both *Borderlands/La Frontera* and *The Legacy of Conquest* in 2001. Like Limerick's critique of Western history, Gloria Anzaldúa's prose took me back to the 1987 road trip that pulled me out of the US-Mexico borderlands and landed me squarely in the Great Lakes borderlands that starkly divided Native and non-Native. More so than Limerick's historical essays, Anzaldúa's personal narrative echoed my own intimate encounters with white male supremacy and sexual intimidation. Repeatedly throughout my childhood and adolescence I had seen domestic violence and social stigma used to silence women who spoke out against interpersonal, political, and racial inequalities. Seeing how these methods of sexual and racial dominance worked in my own life made me an avid reader of scholars who recounted and challenged similar patterns in their own personal and national histories. With this frame of mind and overlapping interests in Western history, feminist narratives, and federal Indian law, it was only a matter of time before I would encounter the work of Robert A. Williams.[6]

The Western historians reading this essay need no introduction to Patricia Limerick, and if they are lucky, they also need no introduction to Robert A. Williams and his stunning work on the foundational anti-Indian tenets of colonial-era diplomacy and early American democracy. To be honest, I don't remember now which of his works I read first, but I read fast and deep. His searing revelations of racism embedded within the construction of American legal ideology stunned me. Williams's work also led me to David Wilkins, who, like Gramsci and other critical scholars following his legacy, emphasized that the law created confusion and violence in the North American West rather than resolving lawlessness or disorder.[7] Seeing these authors as part of a community of scholars writing Western legal history because I did not yet know the parameters of that field, I applied their work to my understandings of history, law, and the West as I looked for graduate schools, still unaware that my dependence on books and teachers as an escape from the poverty and dysfunction I grew up in were characteristic of my class.

Where It Went from There: Sore Thumbs and Ivory Towers in Indian Country

Given the directions my undergraduate readings had gone, it is perhaps no surprise, then, that I would apply for graduate school at the University of Arizona, where Williams teaches Federal Indian Law and Critical Race Theory, and where I would get to work with K. Tsianina Lomawaima and Luci Tapahonso in the American Indian Studies program that Vine Deloria Jr. built. I read Sherman Alexie's "Unauthorized Autobiography of Me" in the first semester of that program. To Alexie's questions, "Have you stood in a crowded room where nobody looks like you? If you are white, have you stood in a room full of black people?" I could not only answer "yes," I could also answer that I had sometimes found white faces frightening.[8] I also read Joy Harjo's work that first semester and found tremendous truth and comfort in her claim that "the world begins at a kitchen table." Harjo's lyric verses, blended with Anzaldúa and Limerick's borderlands and wests, affirmed the importance of women's intellectual and intimate configurations of the past.[9]

Imagining myself part of their literary community, I sought classrooms and kitchen tables where I stuck out like a sore thumb because I had more often heard the truth about oppression and power spoken there. Fifteen years after moving from California to Wisconsin, I had returned to the Southwest, where I was grateful to hear Spanish and Diné more often than the epithets I heard so often in the Midwest.

Even amid such accomplished scholars and mentors at the University of Arizona, I had a long way to go before I could fully appreciate the depth and breadth of legal borderlands. Despite my early childhood in San Diego, which included frequent trips to Tijuana with my Spanish-speaking mother, fifteen years in rural Wisconsin had convinced me that border towns were those that surrounded tribal reservations as well as those divided by international boundaries. I had crossed borders onto reservations regularly, becoming well acquainted with the especially heightened and visible anti-Indian racism that slowly faded, but never fully disappeared, further away from tribal lands. Two additional years in an American Indian studies program reinforced my perception that Indian Country is in fact North America's largest internal borderland—extending beyond the United States into Canada and Mexico.[10]

My graduate training in American Indian studies also emphasized the important shift from postcolonial critiques to decolonizing methods, a conceptual and practical reorientation that borrows from postcolonial scholarship and history but insists that nation-states like the United States have yet to abandon colonial strategies in an effort to deny Indigenous autonomy. Readers ought to recognize the vital interventions of scholars like Linda Tuhiwai Smith and those who came after her, but I also found deeper appreciation for the work of poets like Paula Gunn Allen, who theorized the woman-centered politics in Indigenous communities I had known as a child; Joy Harjo, who marked the continuum between historical and contemporary struggles and values among Native people; and Simon Ortiz, who described the powerful ruptures marked by reservation boundaries. Because American Indian studies is an interdisciplinary program, I read these literary works alongside the critical histories of Thomas Biolsi, whose work singled out the heightened racism along reservation borders that I had personally observed, and Keith Basso, who highlighted the unequal power dynamics between Indigenous and academic histories. K. Tsianina Lomawaima's studies of federal Indian education policy underscored the importance of empathy and scrutiny when reading colonial archives, while Devon Mihesuah's broad range of scholarship made clear the importance of Native women's contributions to anticolonial knowledge in the past and present and warned against broad generalizations that mask the peculiarities of individual experience.[11]

I finished the master's program ready to spread the twinned gospels of decolonization and peoplehood, but only to the choir, and it had not yet fully occurred to me just how poorly I fit in, in some parts of both Indian Country and the ivory tower, neither "us" nor "them" in either place. Less out of place then among Indians than elsewhere, I began designing and teaching American Indian studies courses at Tohono O'odham Community College, an hour outside of Tucson. For two years, I enjoyed multilingual classrooms and shared committee meetings run by tribal elders. In this environment, there was no dividing line between academic and activist history, and the courses I taught remained interdisciplinary, so I had little cause to think about the boundaries between fields that other graduates of a master's program might more readily have identified. Instead, I thought almost constantly about the politics and optics of my role as a redheaded stepchild teaching American Indian studies in a tribal college. Thrilled, but also daunted, by the opportunity to teach anticolonial histories and methods among such a receptive audience of students and colleagues, many of whom had been living decolonization before they read about it, certain moments marked me indelibly. Listening to women talk about the networks they had built, and had sometimes seen torn down, to protect themselves and one another from border-crossing abusers made it impossible for me to separate violence from the law. Being pressed by an elder to define sovereignty in local terms made it obvious that such terms and concepts must be interrogated to ensure that they hold real, rather than merely rhetorical, power. Hosting decolonization and Native feminism workshops with tribal speakers who are now faculty on a variety of campuses made it clear that I had missed an

important lesson addressed in Gloria Anzaldúa's invitation to white allies: I
was trying to help when I should have been following.

> Many women and men of color do not want to have any dealings
> with white people. . . . Many feel that whites should help their own
> people rid themselves of race hatred and fear first. I, for one, choose
> to use some of my energy to serve as mediator. I think we need to al-
> low whites to be our allies. Through our literature, art, corridos, and
> folktales we must share our history with them so when they set up
> committees to help Big Mountain Navajos or the Chicano farmwork-
> ers or *los Nicaraguenses* they won't turn people away because of their
> racial fears and ignorances. They will come to see that they are not
> helping us but following our lead.[12]

What does this journey through the ivory towers of Indian Country have
to do with legal borderlands of the North American West? With Anzaldúa
or Limerick or any of the chapters that follow? They are, collectively, what
sent me back into the ivory tower, back into graduate school. Because I
knew that my role was not to occupy a position at the front of a room full
of Indians, inverting the experiences Alexie describes in "The Unauthorized
Autobiography of Me," but to do the work Anzaldúa described, not only
following the lead of queer and critical scholars like her but also learning
how to speak to my own people and join the legacy of door-busting Western
historians like Patricia Limerick. In many ways, it was a painful decision
to leave TOCC and the American Indian studies discipline, but it brought
me to a new community of scholars who had already been working at the
intersections of New Western history, critical legal studies, and borderlands
for nearly two decades.

Not quite sure what I was getting myself into, I applied to the history
PhD program at the University of Arizona, intending to train in Western
history and write a dissertation about Native women. I began coursework
in 2006 as an unfunded student. Coming in without the stamp of approval
that a funding package provided reinforced my sense that I was somehow
outside the fold. Despite my uneasy feeling, I failed to realize that this ges-
ture communicated the department's utter lack of confidence in my prospects and proceeded with the confidence of someone accustomed to uneasy
feelings. Some readers know that this is a common experience for today's
first-generation graduate students. In the American Indian studies program
my status as first-generation and unfunded was not unique; in a history

PhD program, the differences felt more obvious. Already inclined to read and write histories that called attention to unequal power dynamics, I now felt very keenly that I also engaged such inequalities through my own position within academia. Sensitive to the politics of the archives, classrooms, and texts that I navigated throughout the doctoral program, I came to rely heavily on my dissertation committee—all of whom navigated their own set of politics in the academy—and the scholarship of other border-crossing historians.

My doctoral training gave me the benefit of reading a broad array of the rich histories of the West spurred by both the New Western and borderlands history movements of the late 1980s and the critical turn in legal history of the same era. Unmistakably, my earlier concentration in federal Indian law, history of Indian education, and Native literature framed my view of borderlands, history, and law in the North American West. As it became clear that my dissertation would be a legal history of Native women in the North American West and would bear the imprint of scholars like Anzaldúa, Limerick, and Williams, my wise advisor Roger Nichols pointed out that I had better start reading Western legal history in earnest, and not just by accident or whim. Somehow, I still managed to get lost on the way there.

What is obvious to some is not always obvious to me, and so for quite some time after this initial directive from my advisor I thought I was reading Western legal history when in fact I was not. To me, Western legal history simply meant a historical focus on law in the North American West, so the scholars I read first were in fact critical legal scholars, critical race theorists, or the colleagues and descendants of Limerick and the New Western history school. Even when I read the work of Native feminists critiquing the law, it seemed like Western legal history to me. As I made my way through the doctoral program between 2006 and 2011, I took up the readings in borderlands, legal, and Western history that my coursework and research required. Although I often read them out of order, sometimes for teaching and sometimes for research, occasionally for pleasure and usually under pressure, I began noting gulfs in the field the way you can feel but not name the rifts among relatives at a family reunion.

First, There Was New Western History

Limerick displayed a particular sort of redheadedness when she rejected the influence of Frederick Jackson Turner's frontier thesis—a teleological, but also strangely pessimistic and nostalgic, ethnocentric narrative of Europeans becoming American as they likewise transformed Western wilderness into civilized communities—that had permeated histories of the North American West since he first offered it in 1893. Limerick called for a reorientation of the field in *Legacy of Conquest* and distilled a growing sentiment among her colleagues and students who acknowledged the histories of conquest and dispossession that Turner's progress narrative obscured.[13] Limerick asked Western historians to reconsider what was significant, distinctive, even exceptional about the North American West without borrowing Turner's answer that white, masculine, and agrarian progress characterized the Western past. She and her New Western history cohort launched a generation of scholarship that challenged assumptions about progress and destiny, inviting critical insights from Western history's many subfields that have repopulated the North American West with histories of Native and newcomer; male, female, and transgender; multilingual and illiterate; working class and robber-baron.

It is the framers and descendants of the New Western school of thought who also included legal analysis in the histories that I read voraciously during doctoral coursework and dissertation research. In addition to those already mentioned and some who appear in this volume, Brad Asher, Timothy Braatz, James Brooks, Sarah Carter, Miroslava Chávez-García, Evelyn Nakano Glenn, Laura Gómez, Linda Gordon, Karl Jacoby, Martha Menchaca, Adele Perry, and Vicki Ruiz all published studies that revealed the hegemonic idiosyncracies of the law in the borderlands of the North American West in ways that squarely turned the Turnerian West on its head and were, to me, quite obviously Western legal histories.[14] Of course the list here is incomplete, but it is representative of a wave of scholarship that highlighted legal forms of violence, subjugation, and displacement through a shared focus on race and gender in North American borderlands. They are the studies that Sarah Deer and Jeff Shepherd's chapters in this volume build on to consider Indigenous women's sexual vulnerability and Blackfoot bordercrossers' criminality. They are the scholars who give context to the racialized distribution of land and resources that Dana Weiner, Tom Romero, and Brian Frehner refer to in their chapters on black Californians' quest for citizenship and land rights, on concerns over the tandem restriction of immigration and water in Colorado, and on resource extraction among Oklahoma Choctaw and Chickasaws.

The hitch is that I followed the footnotes to critical race theory before continuing into Western legal or even borderlands history, and like so many others before me who had personally encountered inequality, I was converted. As I sought opportunities to hear these scholars present at historical conferences and read more into their intellectual genealogies, it slowly became clear to me that none of them claimed a home in Western legal history. What surprised and unsettled me even more is that some of them only occasionally claim Western history as their home field. For a student struggling to define herself within academia, tracing the disciplinary bounds of cross-disciplinary scholars proved both inspiring and fatiguing.

Critical Race Meets the North American West

With such praise already bestowed on Robert A. Williams in this essay, and as the graduate of an interdisciplinary program focusing on race and ethnicity, it should come as no surprise that I would frame my view of the North American West through the lens of critical race theory (CRT). CRT offers two particular tenets that address professional encounters with law in the North American West and are directly expressed in the legal borderlands framework. First, and perhaps most obviously, CRT points to race, racism, and racialism as fundamental factors in the legal and historical articulations of power and authority in American society. Most social and legal historians whose work has evolved in the wake of the critical race school argue that race is a socially constructed and historically contingent category that has been and continues to be assigned value that works to justify or obscure inequality. Most elegantly stated by Richard Delgado and Jean Stefancic in their multiple editions of *Critical Race Theory: An Introduction*, this finding builds on the anticolonial scholarship of figures like Albert Memmi and Frantz Fanon, both crucial in linking the law to the assumption of race-based colonial and national power.[15] CRT theorists, especially in the interventions of Kimberlé Crenshaw, point to multiple identity platforms working to shape individual and communal encounters with hegemony and power through the concept of intersectionality, illustrating that religion, gender, and class (among other categories) have complicating effects on racial and ethnic identity and status. Second, in another innovation Crenshaw models forcefully in her introduction to the foundational anthology, CRT theorists insist on the use of storytelling and personal narratives to enhance analytical and scholarly studies of race, racism, and racialism.[16] This very essay puts that method to use, as do many of the Western and borderlands histories concerned with the work of decolonization and antiracism that are cited in these pages. Combined with the assumptions of critical legal scholars—many of whom today simply regard themselves as good legal historians rather than a subgroup within the field—CRT tenets focusing on the omnipresence of racialized laws governing inequality, as well as the importance of critical storytelling as an analytical framework, are fundamental components of the legal borderlands frame put forward in the essays compiled in the 2005 special issue of *American Quarterly* and in this volume.[17]

In the North American West and in many other regions, border makers and legislators have focused on racial and ethnic boundaries to justify division and dispossession with varying strategies, according, for instance, to the sexual, linguistic, and class orientations of borderlands dwellers. For this reason, a CRT view of the North American West has always seemed relatively straightforward to me, especially given my own experience with regional identify shifts over the course of my childhood and career. Anzaldúa's poetic personal history of the political and cultural fault lines dividing the US-Mexico border is perhaps the most widely read and foremost example of an interdisciplinary application of critical race studies in the context of the North American West. In the thirty odd years since Anzaldúa's volume, published in the same year as Limerick's foundational work, many scholars have followed suit, historians and sociologists among them. Antonia Castañeda and Martha Menchaca wrote critical borderlands histories and historiographies of race and gender that applied critical race concepts to legal structures of inequality even if they didn't focus exclusively on the law.[18] Their intersectional models for interrogating race and gender in borderlands histories remain vital in my own conceptualization of legal borderlands and heavily influenced the critical stance of my own works.

Although they didn't limit themselves to the US-Mexico borderlands, or even to the North American West, Ian Haney López, Evelyn Nakano Glenn, and Peggy Pascoe's works on legalized racial inequality proved that combining critical race and critical legal precepts generated powerful legal histories.[19] The studies by Ned Blackhawk, Katherine Benton Cohen, Grace Peña Delgado, Laura Gómez, Karl Jacoby, Pablo Mitchell, Nayan Shah, Jeffrey Shepherd, and Coll Thrush that followed did focus on the North American West explicitly and continued to reveal the legal structures— some more explicitly and critically than others—that shaped white and patriarchal supremacy over the course of the nineteenth and early twentieth centuries, exposing the important cultural, environmental, and legislative work required to maintain racial and gender inequality in North American legal borderlands.[20] With these authors keenly in mind, I continued to think Western legal history was a thriving intellectual home for scholars linking New Western and critical legal history to write about marginalized survivors of the legacies of conquest. Andrea Geiger's chapter on Alaska Natives in territorial Alaskan courts, Kelly Lytle Hernández's essay on the US Bureau of Prison's peculiar treatment of Mexican border crossers, Allison Powers Useche's study of the US-Mexico Claims Commission's review of Mexican worker's violent mistreatment, and Danielle Olden's analysis of the fallibility of racial measures employed in *Keyes v. School District No. 1* are superb studies working in the wake of this literature.

Trained directly in Native, Western, and women's history, but only tangentially in legal history, I entered into critical legal history as a field distinctive from CRT by accident. As I rounded out my dissertation reading, I saw through Peggy Pascoe's work that histories of black women's antebellum and reconstruction-era challenges to slavery and other forms of legal inequality might be more informative to my understanding of Native women's nineteenth-century legal claims than the federal Indian law literature. The exciting trail of footnotes and additional graduate courses in comparative women's history introduced me to Kathleen Brown, Laura Edwards, Ariela Gross, Linda Kerber, Tiya Miles, and Jennifer Morgan.[21] These women's antiracist legal scholarship stressed the CRT recognition that law served to uphold white male supremacy as they also chronicled black and Indigenous women's resistance to such legal inequalities.

As I continued to pursue my own reading and scholarship, it became easy to link these works to those of Native feminists, the intellectual descendants of scholars I had read earlier in my master's degree training. Luana Ross has written the most powerful summation of Native feminism I have ever read, and other scholars like Sarah Deer, Jennifer Denetdale, Mishuana Goeman, Dian Million, Audra Simpson, and Heidi Stark have demonstrated that colonialism operates in the present and past as a particularly gendered tool of dispossession and violence and that sovereignty, if perceived as a Western and imposed construct without regard to Indigenous forms of gender, law, and order, cannot resolve the problem of ongoing settler colonialism in North American and global contexts.[22]

Reading each of these authors in conversation with one another, I imagined myself working within a very promising landscape of borderlands, critical, legal, and Western histories. All of these connections affirmed the earlier work of Antonia Castañeda and others demanding a "decolonization of western women's history," and so I continued to read and write with a fool's confidence.[23] Daft enough to assume I'd been reading Western legal history while enjoying the works cited above, I had to admit with embarrassment that I did not know the scholars my advisor named when he asked how I was doing on my Western legal history readings. As a good mentor should, Roger Nichols chastised and then charged me to read their works. Confronting genuine Western legal history felt much to me like meeting biological relatives who shared obvious and sometimes surprising resemblances without also inspiring affinity or attraction. It was a lonely feeling.

Although carefully researched and firmly stated, this scholarship by authors who fully embraced the Western legal history banner failed to consider the multiple categories of identity at play in courtrooms and capitols throughout the North American West, neglected to point out the statutory and social factors restricting marginalized actors' entry into those sites of power, and drew conclusions about equity and opportunity that assumed law and its practitioners operated without prejudice, coursing steadily toward equality for Westerners even as individual members of society violated the law to ensure their own dominance. Often about Indians or Mexicans, sometimes about women, and almost always focused on violence, much of this literature could be found guilty of the charges made in Richard Delgado's two-part essay on "Imperial Scholars": these authors mostly cited one another and, with a few exceptions, failed to acknowledge the impressive work of women and scholars of color working on law in the North American West. They rarely chronicled Western legal histories of minority rights claims with any consideration of anticolonial or CRT insights that had clearly been established by the time I was reading and they were publishing in 2010.[24] Such studies tend to offer judicial biographies, celebrating the deliverance of justice that frontier courts established or exposing the corruption and weakness of territorial law and order. Others elucidate the technical applications of particular statutes and tout the significance of remarkable cases, which is helpful in defeating the notion of a lawless West but not always helpful in illuminating the selective implementation of law and inconsistencies across the bench. Works that demonstrate this combination of careful research, inclusion of women and nonwhite actors, and a reluctance to offer a critical analysis of the legal system or the ways in which law codifies race and gender inequalities include Gordon Bakken's *Women Who Kill Men: California Courts, Gender, and the Press,* which finds that the law upheld justice for women who were defendants despite jurists' gendered biases; Clare V. McKanna's *Homicide, Race, and Justice in the American West, 1880–1920*, which argues that the West was a violent place and that defendants of color fared poorly in Western courts; and Bill Neal's *From Guns to Gavels: How Justice Grew Up in the Outlaw West*, which concludes that the turn of the twentieth century brought increased reliance on courts of law rather than contests between men to settle Western disputes.[25]

If you've been paying attention thus far, you should congratulate yourself for such stamina, but you should also see coming from a mile away that such works would not satisfy me or anyone else who had already benefited from the other scholars cited here. My advisor and I would agree that where their work directly overlapped with mine, I would need to take them into account, but that otherwise my own proclivities could guide my continued reading and so we plugged on to the defense. Clearly, we succeeded and in spring of 2011, I graduated, but even in my dissertation defense we could not decide which subfield my work occupied: Native, Western, or women's history. All of those things at once, I insisted, and have since learned the publishing pitfalls of attempting. That no one asked whether it was a legal history indicates how far I still had to go before defining or claiming that elusive category for myself.

Becoming Found in the Legal Borderlands of the North American West

Offered an overwhelming and empowering postdoctoral fellowship at Southern Methodist University's Clements Center for Southwest Studies, I sidestepped the Western legal history field once again and dipped more deeply into the borderlands studies that have now matured into a vibrant field of scholars with a range of specializations from nation-state formation to interracial intimacy to border crossing and policing. Among the many confessions buried in this essay is that my early dissertation focus on Indigenous and Latina studies and my narrow interest in the Southwest had shielded from my view borderlands scholarship on the Pacific Northwest and a growing critique of borderlands histories concentrating so squarely on the nation-state. Some authors had been part of my Western history training: Andrés Reséndez and Samuel Truett, for instance. Some books I had already read for their contributions to Western women's history: *Writing the Range* and *One Step Over the Line*, particularly, but I now also turned to those concerned with borders as a historical frame.[26] In tandem with histo-riographic borderlands essays undoubtedly familiar to readers, I found that borderlands historians offered a wide range of options for someone seeking to apply anticolonial, critical, and feminist precepts to legal histories of the North American West. So, once again, I found myself floundering awk-wardly in new historiographies that should not have been new to me at all and I felt the familiar flush of embarrassment and frustration that redheaded stepchildren know well. Thankfully, I found strong role models like Pablo Mitchell willing to share their wisdom with grace, and this is ultimately the turn that led me to legal borderlands.

Steve Aron and Jeremy Adelman's 1999 essay asserts a firm limitation on borderlands as those zones marked by international boundaries. Those authors insist that without political context, "borderlands" loses meaning as a category of analysis and could become interchangeable with frontiers or otherwise diluted by misapplication.[27] To fully consider such claims, I reread Andrés Reséndez and Samuel Truett, and followed up with Brian DeLay and Juliana Barr. I appreciated these authors' efforts to articulate cultural and gendered, as well as political, aspects of the US-Mexico border-lands. Reséndez pointed to the border as a site where individuals of varying racial-ethnic backgrounds forged their national identities creatively; Truett connected borderlands politics to metropolitan influences and revealed bor-der dwellers' resistance to political boundaries that failed to reflect their per-sonal cartographies of self-interest. DeLay exposed the shifting racial-ethnic and national alliances and animosities that allowed Americans to push the US-Mexican boundary further south and culminated in the military defeat of Comanches who had successfully manipulated the borderline as a shield and sword for over a century. Barr showed the importance of Indigenous women's roles in colonial border crossings and exchange.[28] Although each of these works seemed to begin their studies with Aron and Adelman's as-sertion that political boundaries anchor borderlands histories, my readings left me more convinced that borderlands dwellers, including those who oc-casionally strayed far from national boundaries, carried their border charac-teristics with them well beyond the dividing lines that Anzaldúa described as open wounds. After also turning in this phase of my readings to the clas-sic borderlands frameworks that Herbert Bolton established and David We-ber refined, I remain convinced that their interpretations also leave room for this personal, as well as political, definition of borderlands.[29]

As I continued working on my book, looking for evidence to answer the question of how Indigenous women confronted the legal regimes Americans imported into Indian Country in the nineteenth century, I became more convinced of the utility of borderlands as a way to explain the personal boundaries between Indian women and newcomer citizens, the political boundaries between Indian and non-Indian lands, and the legal boundaries between Indianness and non-Indianness. Because many Indigenous women's legal claims stemmed from their crossing borders between Indian and non-Indian circles and between Indian and non-Indian lands, it seemed clear that the consequences of these personal choices stemmed from the political borders that transected their lives. Native women's legal histories reveal that Aron and Adelman's insistence on the fundamentally political significance of borders remains relevant, while Jameson and Anzaldúa's insistence on the personal and psychic aspects of border crossings also yields critical insights. Following the lead of those who have written expertly on the gendered and racialized cartographies of social and political borderlands, I have come to see the value in applying a familiar concept from women's history—the personal is political—to argue that where borderlands are concerned, the political is also personal.[30] It is in the personal histories of borderlands dwellers that I am most able to appreciate the political nature of borders. Alicia Gutierrez-Romine's chapter on border-crossing abortion seekers models this dynamic beautifully. Expanding our conception of border zones to include the personal nature of national boundaries reveals the lines demarcating home and enemy territories, native and foreign lands and lives, the safe from the unsafe.

Reading Elizabeth Jameson's 2005 address at the annual meeting of the Pacific Coast Branch of the American Historical Association helped me comprehend the distinction between borders and borderlands:

National borders separate nations; their borderlands are places where social relationships cross those borders. Social borders erect social barriers, like those of race, for instance, while a parallel social borderland might be a zone or place where people of different races meet. Borders and borderlands can have multiple meanings; their significance usually differs for the various people they divide or connect. A border, for instance, can function both to exclude and protect. A national border can prevent certain people from entering a country; a social border can prevent people of different races or the same sexes from marrying each other. But borders can also function positively, to protect identity.[31]

I'm not sure I've managed to follow all eight of the rules she offered for dancing through borderlands history, but I gained from Jameson's essay, and the works her footnotes pointed me toward, the confidence to see borderlands as permeating the lives of the women I've written about, even if some of them never crossed a national boundary.

With the luxury of time I did not fully appreciate in my pre-tenure-track years, I read on. My pursuit of borderlands historiography took me from the US-Mexican border to the US-Canadian border in an essential series of anthologies.[32] I appreciated these authors' efforts to characterize borderlands histories in ways that highlighted identity—just as Anzaldúa had in her writings. Ken Coates suggested that "the study of borderlands presents a useful opportunity to examine the question of national (or regional) identity in its most highly focused form."[33] Andrew Graybill and Benjamin Johnson characterized borderlands scholarship in four modes: "works that interrogate the implications of border-making for indigenous peoples," studies that "focus on the cross-border migrations of non-Aboriginal peoples [and] emphasize the exceptional permeability of the US-Canadian boundary," those that "examine the relationship of the border to the natural world that it bisects, a division no less capricious to ecosystems than to human populations," and a "collection of studies [that] analyze the impact of the border on the formation of national identity."[34] In their collection, I especially appreciated essays that demonstrated borderlanders' construction of fluid identities and showed borders to be "places and ideas suited for cultural, intellectual, social, and political histories."[35]

In turning away from Western legal history as a field that just didn't feel like home, I began to appreciate a more broadly defined conceptualization of borderlands as personal and political spaces that are more like zones than boundaries because they seemed more accurately to reflect the women whose histories make up my first book.[36] Having Jeffrey Shepherd, Alexandra Harmon, and James Brooks as guest reviewers of my manuscript at the Clements Center proved especially helpful in making borderlands a recognizable frame in that project, even though my methodological thinking continues to evolve. If I am honest, I have to admit that I'm not actually satisfied with the way my first book considers or frames borders as a concept, mostly because it is still something I am working through, as this essay demonstrates. Certainly, some scholars crave a more narrowly defined borderlands approach focused on national and political borderlands and rooted more explicitly in the Spanish borderlands of the Bolton school, but there are also those who have established a tradition of scholarship emphasizing the cultural and personal aspects of borderlands history. In fact, such a combined approach is exactly what legal borderlands and this volume offers.

Having gained deep appreciation for the benefit of applying intersecting historical insights to a borderlands frame, a continued search for interdisciplinary approaches to borderlands is what brought me to the legal borderlands school, announced in that 2005 special issue of *American Quarterly* like manna from heaven. Broken into sections entitled "Law's Borders," "Borders of Identity," "Borders of Territory," and "Borders of Power," the essays demonstrated a powerful range of analysis that the legal borderlands frame allows, which this anthology expands upon. That I was reading the special issue at the same time Kelly Lytle Hernández gave a guest lecture at Southern Methodist University to accept the William P. Clements Prize for her book *Migra! A History of the U.S. Border Patrol* made it impossible for me to overlook the connections between legal borderlands and borderlands historiography in the making.[37]

On first reading, guest editors Mary Dudziak and Leti Volpp's introduction shot through me like a bolt of lightning and I was born again. Together, they tackled the definition of legal borderlands: "We might start with the role of law in borderlands that are geographic spaces. Borderlands can be contact zones between distinct physical spaces; they can be interstitial zones of hybridization. They can constitute spaces that challenge paradigms and that therefore reveal the criteria that determine what fits in those paradigms."[38] Dudziak and Volpp continued in characterizing the many facets of the legal borderlands concept: "Borderlands can also function not as literal physical spaces but as contact zones between ideas, as spaces of ideological ambiguity that can open up new possibilities of both repression and liberation. Legal borderlands can be physical territories with an ambiguous legal identity, such as US territories where the Constitution does not follow the flag."[39] The editors explained that the inherent ambiguity of legal borderlands "seems to render them sites of abnormal legal regulation, placing them on the edge of the law. But we can also draw upon the idea of legal borderlands to demarcate ideological spaces or gaps, holes in the imagining of America, where America is felt to be 'out of place,' contexts in which, in spite of American ideals of democracy and rights, violations of the law are routinized, such as in the space of the prison," or the reservation, as some of our contributing authors explore in following chapters.[40]

What especially rang true for me as one still unsure about what was so dissatisfying about Western legal history was Dudziak and Volpp's critique that "the supposition that these spaces are exceptional, rather than the norm, enables the continued belief that 'the story of America is the story of the rule of law,' for stories of the violation of the rule of law are explained through their location in those physical spaces or their placement in those ideological gaps."[41] The chapters that follow make this tenet unmistakably clear. This application of the legal borderlands concept to argue against an assumption that law brings order and that the history of the North American West can be explained as a pursuit toward the rule of law seemed to articulate exactly my dissatisfaction with conventional Western legal histories that described disorder and injustice as anomalies increasingly resolved through the emergence of the nation-state and the hardening of political boundaries at the close of the nineteenth century.

All Hat and No Cattle: Distinguishing between Critical and Western Legal Histories

When I joined the Department of History at the University of Nebraska–Lincoln in 2012, I slowly began to return to the foundational debates and guidebooks I had skimmed while dissertating and I did what I assume all new faculty do in order to resolve lingering concerns: I taught what I did not fully understand. It would turn out for me that teaching the void in Western legal history proved more fruitful than simply contemplating that terrain, and I am grateful to the many undergraduate and graduate students who have participated in the discussions and exercises that propelled my own understanding. This reflective and exploratory process prompted me to reach out to Pablo Mitchell to partner in building this volume and occupied my thoughts as I attended Patty Limerick's 2014 address at the Denver meeting of the American Society for Legal History. It also helped me to realize that the skepticism between critical and Western legal historians is mutual. Neither cohort is tremendously impressed with the other, it would seem.

What Western legal historians were putting down by 1988 that I did not pick up until nearly fifteen years later was a consensus on the legal arenas that characterized the North American West and therefore constituted the parameters of Western legal history. Defining Western legal history for the first time in an essay generated from a 1987 meeting of the minds hosted at Pepperdine University's School of Law, John Phillip Reid described three areas of inquiry: (1) studies that applied general principles of American legal history to the North American West; (2) legal histories particular to the West, such as "law of the Mexican borderlands, law of the Indian Territory, law on the California and Oregon trails, law of the cattle drives, law in the gold mining camps, the suppression of Mormon polygamy, and . . . water law"; and (3) depictions of a shared legal culture "directing, guiding, and even motivating nineteenth-century Americans," Reid's own area of interest.[42] Readers should observe that our own chapters and notes draw on many of these histories as we examine topics familiar to Western legal historians.

Written just a year after *Borderlands/La Frontera* and *Legacy of Conquest*, Reid's characterization of Western legal history nonetheless overlooked the problem of law as a system of power and conquest and embraced the Turnerian vision of rugged individualism reshaping an unoccupied frontier that so many other Western historians had already begun to turn against, making his field appear more resistant to revision than its practitioners would turn out to be. Although early Western legal historians embraced the law and society formulation of the law most commonly associated with Lawrence Friedman and his intellectual descendants—the law as reflective of society—they did not, broadly speaking, apply critical legal scholars' interrogatory approach to the law.[43] And some members, Gordon Bakken most notably, explicitly rejected the critical legal studies school on more than one occasion.

At the 1990 American Society for Legal History conference, Bakken outlined two problems in Western legal history and took a shot at critical legal scholars in the audience: "First, historians as well as present-day politicians have been ineffective in separating myth and reality. Second, on a historiographic level, professional historians have become mired in ideology, whether blinded by advocacy for Indians, Hispanics or Mormons, or strident attack upon these groups. . . . When Critical Legal Studies migrates beyond the Great Muddy, I am sure that it will do little to change this general condition."[44] Lawrence Friedman, Marion Rice, Christian Fritz, David Langum, and Harry Scheiber also joined Bakken on that roundtable. Friedman added his concern that Western legal history is perceived as "narrow and parochial." He urged scholars of law in the North American West to "think of [themselves] . . . as a legal historian, plain and simple."[45] It is true that much of Western legal history has suffered from an overzealous pursuit of exceptionalism and regionalism, which might explain why legal historians outside of the North American West have been slow to incorporate our favored region in their otherwise rigorous scholarship. If many Western legal historians remained Turnerian in their visions of the West as a region devoid of legal culture and practice prior to American settlement, then it is also understandable that New Western historians would turn away from such studies.

If nothing else, Bakken's disdain for critical legal history proves the arrival of that method in the North American West, and yet, many Western historians struggle to define this approach to legal study succinctly. In *Stanford Law Review*'s 1984 special volume on critical legal studies, Robert Gordon distilled the assumptions and practices critical legal historians had developed over the previous decade.[46] He offered "a seed catalogue or a *Pocket Guide to the Common and Exotic Varieties of the Social/Legal Histories of North America.*"[47] Critical legal scholars blur the boundaries between law and society to argue that the law shapes and reifies social conditions. They argue that the law constitutes consciousness, or the assumption that what is legal is also right, thus demonstrating the cultural and ritual importance of law to determine natural order. Critical legal histories assert that the law is indeterminate and contradictory, or that the law is a "slippery sucker" as I like to tell my legal history undergrads, and scholars of law in the North American West can no doubt relate countless examples to affirm this precept. Critical legal historians argue too that the law is dialectic and present at all levels, borrowing a sort of history-from-below perspective from social historians to show that common and marginalized historical actors bring to bear their own legal perspectives and customs on the hegemonic systems shaped by elites and vice versa. Finally, critical legal projects ask a central question—"How does the law serve interests?"—that indicates their rejection of a benevolent or universal theory of law that suggests law is an objective and independent system that is applied equally to all. The contributors to this volume exhibit each of these precepts in their studies of legal borderlands in the North American West.

Readers might recognize some of these critical assumptions as rooted in the insights of Fanon, Foucault, Gramsci, and others and might wonder why familiar critiques of the law and hegemony require such extensive exposition. As recently as 2012, Southern legal historian Laura Edwards pointed out that few historians have in fact taken up these critical legal approaches to the legal regimes they write about: "Historians who are not legal historians tend to stumble when it comes to matters relating to law and the legal system . . . while critical tools brought them to legal sources, they did not always use those tools in their analyses of law and legal institutions." She suggested that "we need to transform our view of law and history—and put them together in new ways," resulting in a lingering formalism in historians' view of the law despite critical analysis in other areas of history.[48] Speaking in regard to American legal historiography generally, Edwards described my own inkling that "the conceptual transformation proposed in [Gordon's 1984 essay] has yet to materialize."[49]

I would argue the delayed "conceptual transformation" Edwards described is especially apparent in Western legal history and that without this critical transformation the scholars I so deeply admire will remain hesitant to claim affiliation with Western legal history. Historians who are otherwise deeply trained in the critical and sophisticated methods of other subfields often come to the legal archive accidentally and may not think of those sources in strategic ways. John Wunder noted this problem in his 1997 essay on the state of Western legal history ten years after its first organizing symposium: "One of the greatest myths in the writing and reading of American history is that legal history requires an understanding or training nearly impossible to attain. All too many historians of the American West have bought into this mythology, which consequently allows them to avoid the legal dimensions of human actions."[50] Perhaps not all scholars avoid the law so explicitly, but many superb Western historians who are critically minded do not apply legal evidence as effectively as they could even when it would serve their argument.

If archival misgivings might bar critical scholars from engaging Western legal history more directly, it is the reluctance—sometimes overt resistance—on the part of otherwise well-intentioned Western legal historians to critically read the law and its structures that puts Western legal history out of step with other scholarly dialogues. The trajectory toward a greater understanding of the expansion of American legal culture into the North American West and a search for the distinctive in Western legal history that scholars in the field put forward in the last decade of the twentieth century could hardly have appealed to anyone working in critical race studies, New Western, or critical legal history. And yet, the field showed promise, occasionally expanding its range as it slowly shed its Turnerian skin. That opportunity appeared in the watershed anthology *Law for the Elephant, Law for the Beaver*, published in 1992.[51] John Reid threw down what Gordon Bakken called a "substantial scholarly gauntlet" in his lead essay, "The Layers of Western Legal History." In conjunction with "The Beaver's Law in the Elephant's Country: An Excursion into Transboundary Western Legal

History," a companion article published the previous year in *Western Legal History*, these essays offered a refined articulation of Reid's vision of Western legal history, which described the potential for a comparative view beyond American borders and employed the term "transboundary" to describe many of the phenomena discussed in this volume as "legal borderlands."[52]

Predisposed to a critical view of legal history by the time I first read *Law for the Elephant*, it was nonetheless affirming for me to read authors like Richard Maxwell Brown, Hamar Foster, John Wunder, and others in the collection who defined Western legal history as not only a particular subfield but also a sophisticated and worthwhile area of study. Reading *Law for the Elephant* allowed me to see an opening for the critical insights I first learned from Robert A. Williams's work and the distinctive West I had encountered in Patty Limerick's and others' work. Of the essays most compelling to me in *Law for the Elephant*, Wunder's stood out for its focus on anti-Chinese violence in the North American West.[53] The combined attention to archival detail and systemic racism taught me the importance of reading territorial legal transcripts—not necessarily treaties, or even legislation, but local court records—with a critical methodology.

Perhaps because the community of Western legal historians remained divided in its stance toward other shifts in legal and Western history, *Law for the Elephant* went out of print while Western legal historians pursued further studies affirming the rule of law and the rise of law and order to tame the Wild West. In his 1997 essay, Wunder also asked whether there was "in fact a New Western *Legal* History, and, if so, does it represent a clear break from the past? Have American legal historians and New Western history proponents collaborated, or are they on parallel paths? And, finally, might there be something 'old' about the new legal history of the American West?"[54] He offered an overview of debates in Western legal history and suggested that "there is no clear direction of Western legal history, but it is obvious that the New Western History has begun to penetrate the debate" and "that a New Western Legal History exists."[55] Like Friedman before him, Wunder urged readers to take more care in acknowledging their fledgling field because "there is, after all, drama to this story of law in the American West, and there is a general readership that wants to know about it."[56] Everyone in this volume agrees with that sentiment.

Writing ten years later, in 2007, Gordon Bakken surveyed the state of the Western legal history field at twenty years old, raising questions about the nature of law in the American West that would also make it clear certain answers were unwelcome. Borrowing Limerick's title phrase, Bakken suggested that "there was something in the soil in the West that made law different" and offered a review of promising scholarship examining law in the Western histories of mining, water policy, American Indians, Chinese immigration, women and gender, urbanization, environmental change, organized labor, and criminal justice, even as he took a swipe at critical legal historians when he paraphrased Howard Lamar: "Are the American people, particularly those who people the West, law-minded, as John Phillip Reid found on the overland trail, or is the law a tool of capitalistic oppression, as the critical legal studies school would have us believe?" Bakken concluded that "there is a lot to be done, but the field is now firmly established."[57]

Without applying analytical frameworks such as critical legal history, many territorial histories and judicial biographies chronicle important events but ultimately explain little about the dynamics of power and order in the North American West. Bakken's disdain for theory is shared by many in his field, and much of the current Western legal scholarship is centered on characterizing the emergence of American legal tradition in the West, in elucidating but not interrogating many of the laws and opinions listed at the opening of this essay, and in tracing the peculiarities of Western legal history. While each of these studies fulfills their aim of chronicling the law, few consider the law itself as the object of scrutiny or seek to uncover the ways in which the law—and not merely its flawed human practitioners—has orchestrated inequality.

Nonetheless, some of the authors active in *Western Legal History* (*WLH*) and working across the professional boundaries dividing Western and legal scholars have offered promising works. Although this collection of essays fails to include coverage of legal histories particular to Asians in the North American West, such studies have appeared regularly in that journal since its first 1988 volume. Contributors to *WLH* have focused occasionally, if not always robustly, on gendered legal histories, while coverage of federal and state Indian policies and Native critiques of such laws has been consistently strong, and editors have always noted the importance of Spanish-colonial influence on legal practices in the Southwest while making room for studies of Latino and Chicano legal strategies. If there is often a teleological view of the rule of law and state formation in *WLH* articles, there are also many useful studies on the emergence of territorial and state jurisdictions and juridical practices that we all depend on in our own work. *WLH* is in the hands of a new editor after nearly twenty years and continues to publish a broad range of articles in the diverse subfields Wunder and Bakken noted. It has only recently become searchable through HeinOnline, and historians less familiar with that legal research database rarely consult or cite its volumes. In the shift to digital scholarship, that journal will hopefully reach its intended audience as it chronicles the rich legal histories of women, noncitizens, and racial-ethnic shapers of the North American West. Junior scholars should take note of the journal's annual Jerome I. Braun Prize for best article when they consider venues for their work.

Bakken saw a bright future for Western legal history when he wrote in 2007, but there are signs the field has diminished in the decade since then, Limerick's 2014 address at the American Society for Legal History among them. Other than the scholars gathered in this volume and the articles appearing in *Western Legal History*, there is little evidence of a lively dialogue between scholars in the Western History Association and the American Society for Legal History that began in 1987. Perhaps eschewing critical studies proved detrimental, since both of those organizations have effectively mainstreamed the innovations New Western and critical legal historians made in that decade. Where the University of Nebraska Press and the University of Oklahoma Press both once offered series in Western legal history, there is no longer an active series in that subfield. Bakken passed in 2015, mourned by many in our profession who felt the gift of his mentorship and constant support of junior scholars, but his foundational contributions to Western legal history will be remembered through his impressive bibliography. If Bakken proved unwilling to apply critical insights, there is still plenty of room for scholars to benefit from his foundational studies and expand the implications of the work he started. This volume takes up some of that landscape.

The persistent void between critical and Western legal histories is also tied to the too-early passing of Peggy Pascoe, whose 2009 book *What Comes Naturally* and the articles that preceded it exhibited all of the promise of an integration of critical legal studies and Western legal history and whose death a year later left a vacuum of mentorship that we continue to suffer from.[58] In stark contrast to Bakken's approach, Pascoe described the legal system imposed in the North American West as one steeped in white supremacist thinking and challenged contemporary scholars convinced that color-blindness offered a solution to racism and racialization in her prize-winning study of miscegenation law throughout the American South and West in the nineteenth and twentieth centuries. Still mourned by many and irreplaceable to all, Pascoe and her work might have been in the audience's mind during Limerick's keynote at the 2014 Denver American Society for Legal History conference, modeling for audiences the merits of blending critical and Western legal histories that the legal borderlands frame promises. Despite the promise of Pascoe's work for Western legal history, she is most widely cited among historians of race and gender who only tangentially identify as legal scholars. Many of the scholars in this volume are working steadily in the wake of Pascoe's intellectual leadership.

Pascoe and Bakken's scholarship covered the same terrain with a much different scope, Pascoe openly embracing critical legal precepts and Bakken frequently mocking them. What both scholars shared is a concern with close readings of the Western legal archive; they differed in their view of the law and its role in constructing or mediating inequality. Bakken's autobiographical "Disclosure Statement and Acknowledgments" helps to explain his belief in law and order as one rooted in a midwestern and upwardly mobile Norwegian family history (our grandparents, it would seem, were very similar) and a view of legal history that reflects his training in the program Willard Hurst built in Wisconsin.[59] Retaining the structural view of the law that Hurst's school of thought espoused is paramount to invoking a Turnerian view of the West. Bakken's works, and those who share his and Hurst's realist view of the law, demonstrate a conviction that the law resolves the inequalities society creates. Pascoe's work is more theoretically informed, challenging not only the notion that law is an objective and teleological force but also the assumption that gender and race are neutral or natural categories.[60] Pascoe left no "disclosures" behind for us as Bakken did, but colleagues knew that Pascoe's personal experiences shaped her work as much as Bakken's or the work of any of the rest of us. According to Estelle Freedman, Pascoe's "Western origins have infused everything she writes, as has her feminism."[61] The tensions between Bakken and Pascoe's works are, as the scholars in this collection would agree, as much personal as they are political. They reflect the tensions in our collective fields, between those who favor Anzaldúa or Bolton, between those who are satisfied with recognizing a diverse West and those who still see a divided West, between those who apply theory and those who avoid it. We are the malcontents on the one side and the well intentioned on the other. We are not strangers to one another; we share conferences and review one another's work all the time. We all agree about the value and range of Western legal history, but many of us disagree about its meaning and utility. For some of us, this is a comfortable state of being.

Such tensions demonstrate to many what Western legal history is and is not, and redheaded stepchildren are nothing if not familiar with disputes between those they hold dear. My orientation to the occasionally tumultuous, but always thorough, Western legal history field did not convince me to join its gospel choir, but I nevertheless learned much about where and how to read the legal archives of the North American West more strategically and thoroughly from the field's proponents. It is in those archives that I hope to spend the remainder of my career with the ghosts and heroes cited in this essay.

Lest these last few pages seem to suggest an insurmountable rift in the blended family of Western historians concerned with race, gender, law, and order, readers should look forward to a set of essays that demonstrate the rich inheritance of ideas and training we collectively bear as the descendants of scholars whose legacies we embrace and resist. This volume is the result of a critical turn from the Western legal history fold thirty years after its founding. It is an indictment of that field's slow integration of the critical insights that we share as like-minded scholars seeking illuminating discussions of the law in the North American West. Our shared goal in navigating the void in Western legal history is to clarify the historical, intellectual, personal, and political landscape of legal borderlands rather than shrink from its vastness. Perhaps we are the blended family, gathered together in its thirtieth family reunion and still getting to know one another across conferences and publications; or perhaps we will remain "*los atravesados*: the squint-eyed, the perverse, the queer, the troublesome, the mongrel, the mulato, the half-breed, the half dead . . . those who cross over, pass over, or go through the confines of the 'normal.'"[62] Either way, we have gathered here between these pages to lay down the law.

Notes

Epigraph: Gloria Anzaldúa, *Borderlands/La Frontera: The New Mestiza* (Aunt Lute, 1999), 24–25.

1. Patricia Limerick, unpublished keynote address, American Society for Legal History Conference, Denver, CO, November 2014.
2. Mary L. Dudziak and Leti Volpp, introduction, "Legal Borderlands: Law and

the Construction of American Borders," *American Quarterly* 57, no. 3 (Sept. 2005).

3. Anzaldúa, *Borderlands/La Frontera;* Patricia Nelson Limerick, *The Legacy of Conquest: The Unbroken Past of the American West* (New York: W. W. Norton, 1987).

4. Patty Loew and James Thannum, "After the Storm: Ojibwe Treaty Rights Twenty-Five Years after the Voigt Decision," *American Indian Quarterly* 35, no. 2 (Spring 2011): 161–191. Larry Nesper, *The Walleye War: The Struggle for Ojibwe Spearfishing and Treaty Rights* (Lincoln: University of Nebraska Press, 2002).

5. Vine Deloria Jr., *God Is Red: A Native View of Religion* (Golden, CO: Fulcrum, 2003; 30th anniversary edition) and *Red Earth, White Lies: Native Americans and the Myth of Scientific Fact* (New York: Scribner, 1995) are my personal favorites of his vast bibliography. Ward Churchill, *Struggle for the Land: Indigenous Resistance to Genocide, Ecocide, and Expropriation in Contemporary North America* (Monroe, ME: Common Courage, 1993).

6. Robert A. Williams, *The American Indian in Western Legal Thought: The Discourses of Conquest* (New York: Oxford University Press, 1992). See also the more recent *Like a Loaded Weapon: The Rehnquist Court, Indian Rights, and the Legal History of Racism in America* (Minneapolis: University of Minnesota Press, 2005), and his tremendously inspiring article "Vampires Anonymous and Critical Race Practice," Symposium: Representing Race, *Michigan Law Review* 95, no. 4 (February 1997): 741–765.

7. David Wilkins and K. Tsianina Lomawaima, *Uneven Ground: American Indian Sovereignty and Federal Law* (Norman: University of Oklahoma Press, 2001); David Wilkins and Vine Deloria Jr., *Tribes, Treaties, and Constitutional Tribulations* (Austin: University of Texas Press, 2000). For his works focusing on Western violence, see Richard Slotkin, *Regeneration Through Violence: The Mythology of the American Frontier, 1600–1800* (Middletown, CT: Wesleyan University Press, 1973) and *Gunfighter Nation: The Myth of the Frontier in Twentieth-Century America* (New York: Atheneum, 1992).

8. Sherman Alexie, "The Unauthorized Autobiography of Me," in *Here First: Autobiographical Essays by Native American Writers*, Arnold Krupat and Brian Swann, eds. (New York: Modern Library, 2000).

9. Joy Harjo, "Perhaps the World Ends Here," *The Woman Who Fell from the Sky* (New York: W. W. Norton, 1996), 68.

10. Lauren Benton's work has since convinced me that those borderlands are a global phenomenon, but that realization came to me slowly and I did not read her work until 2011. Lauren Benton, *Law and Colonial Cultures: Legal Regimes in World History, 1400–1900* (New York: Cambridge University Press, 2001), and *Legal Pluralism and Empires, 1500–1850* (New York: New York University Press, 2013) speak to legal questions relevant to the North American West even though they focus on global empires.

11. Linda Tuhiwai Smith, *Decolonizing Methodologies: Research and Indigenous Peoples* (New York: Zed, 1999); Paula Gunn Allen, *The Sacred Hoop: Recovering the Feminine in American Traditions* (Boston: Beacon, 1986); Joy Harjo, *A Map to the Next World: Poems and Tales* (New York: W. W. Norton, 2001); Simon Ortiz, *Woven Stone* (Tucson: University of Arizona Press, 1992); Thomas Biolsi, *Deadliest Enemies: Law and the Making of Race Relations on and off Rosebud Reservation* (Berkeley: University of California Press, 2001); Keith Basso, *Wisdom Sits in Places: Landscape and Language Among the Western Apache* (Albuquerque: University of New Mexico Press, 1996); K. Tsianina Lomawaima, *They Called It Prairie Light: The Story of Chilocco Indian School* (Lincoln: University of Nebraska Press, 1994) and *"To Remain an Indian": Lessons in Democracy from a Century of Native American Education* (New York: Teachers College Press, 2006); Devon Mihesuah, ed., *Natives and Academics: Discussions on Researching and Writing About American Indians* (Lincoln: University of Nebraska Press, 1998) and *American Indigenous Women: Decolonization, Empowerment, Activism* (Lincoln: University of Nebraska Press, 2003).

12. Anzaldúa, *Borderlands/La Frontera*, 107.

13. Susan Armitage, "'The Legacy of Conquest,' by Patricia Nelson Limerick: A Panel of Appraisal Authors: Donald Worster, Susan Armitage, Michael P. Malone, David J. Weber and Patricia Nelson Limerick," *Western Historical Quarterly* 20, no. 3 (August 1989): 303–322; 307.

14. Brad Asher, *Beyond the Reservation: Indians, Settlers, and the Law in Washington Territory, 1853–1889* (Norman: University of Oklahoma Press, 1999). Timothy Braatz, *Surviving Conquest: A History of the Yavapai Peoples* (Lincoln: University of Nebraska Press, 2003). James Brooks, *Captives and Cousins: Slavery, Kinship, and Community in the Southwest Borderlands* (Chapel Hill: University of North Carolina Press, 2002). Sarah Carter, *Aboriginal People and Colonizers of Western Canada* (Toronto: University of Toronto Press, 1999). Miroslava Chávez-García, *Negotiating Conquest: Gender and Power in California, 1770s to the 1880s* (Tucson: University of Arizona Press, 2004). Evelyn Nakano Glenn, *Unequal Freedom: How Race and Gender Shaped American Citizenship and Labor* (Cambridge: Harvard University Press, 2002). Linda Gordon, *The Great Arizona Orphan Abduction* (Cambridge: Harvard University Press, 1999). Martha Menchaca, *Recovering History, Constructing Race: The Indian, Black, and White Roots of Mexican Americans* (Austin: University of Texas Press, 2001). Adele Perry, *On the Edge of Empire: Gender, Race, and the Making of British Columbia, 1849–1871* (Toronto: University of Toronto Press, 2001). Vicki Ruiz, *From Out of the Shadows: Mexican Women in Twentieth-Century America* (New York: Oxford University Press, 1998).

15. Richard Delgado and Jean Stefancic, *Critical Race Theory: An Introduction* (New York: New York University Press, 2001).

16. Kimberlé Crenshaw et al., eds., *Critical Race Theory: The Key Writings That Formed the Movement* (New York: New Press, 2010, 2nd edition).

17. Kimberlé Crenshaw et al., eds., *Critical Race Theory: The Key Writings That Formed the Movement* (New York: New Press, 1995). Thanks to Tom I. Romero II for directing me to the powerful discussion of critical race theorists' interventions and the often problematic co-optation of critical race theory within the legal studies and legal history community. See Richard Delgado, "The Imperial Scholar: Reflections on a Review of Civil Rights Literature," *University of Pennsylvania Law Review* 132 (1984): 561–578, and "The Imperial Scholar Revisited: How to Marginalize Outsider Writing, Ten Years Later," *University of Pennsylvania Law Review* 140 (1992): 1349–1372.

18. Antonia Castañeda's essays have recently been compiled in Linda Heidenreich and Antonia Castañeda, eds., *Three Decades of Engendering History* (Denton: University of North Texas Press, 2014). Martha Menchaca, *Recovering History, Constructing Race: The Indian, Black, and White Roots of Mexican Americans* (Austin: University of Texas Press, 2001).

19. Peggy Pascoe, *What Comes Naturally: Miscegenation Law and the Making of Race in America* (New York: Oxford University Press, 2009). Evelyn Nakano Glenn, *Unequal Freedom: How Race and Gender Shaped American Citizenship and Labor* (Cambridge: Harvard University Press, 2004). Ian Haney López, *White by Law: The Legal Construction of Race* (New York: New York University Press, 1996/2006).

20. Ned Blackhawk, *Violence Over the Land: Indians and Empires in the Early American West* (Cambridge: Harvard University Press, 2008). Katherine Benton Cohen, *Borderline Americans: Racial Division and Labor War in the Arizona Borderlands* (Cambridge: Harvard University Press, 2009). Karl Jacoby, *Shadows at Dawn: A Borderlands Massacre and the Violence of History* (New York: Penguin, 2008). Coll Thrush, *Native Seattle: Histories from the Crossing-Over Place* (Seattle: University of Washington Press, 2007). Laura Gómez, *Manifest Destinies: The Making of the Mexican American Race* (New York: New York University Press, 2008). Pablo Mitchell, *Coyote Nation: Sexuality, Race, and Conquest in Modernizing New Mexico, 1880–1920* (Chicago: University of Chicago Press, 2005). Jeffrey Shepherd, *We Are an Indian Nation: A History of the Hualapai People* (Tucson: University of Arizona Press, 2010).

21. Kathleen Brown, *Good Wives, Nasty Wenches and Anxious Patriarchs: Gender, Race and Power in Colonial Virginia* (Chapel Hill: University of North Carolina Press, 1996). Laura Edwards, *Gendered Strife and Confusion: The Political Culture of Reconstruction* (Champaign: University of Illinois Press, 1997). Ariela Gross, *What Blood Won't Tell: A History of Race on Trial in America* (Cambridge: Harvard University Press, 2010). Linda Kerber, *No Constitutional Right to Be Ladies: Women and the Obligations of Citizenship* (New York: Hill & Wang, 1998). Tiya Miles, *Ties That Bind: The Story of an Afro-Cherokee Family in Slavery and Freedom* (Berkeley: University of California Press, 2005). Jennifer Morgan, *Laboring Women: Reproduction and Gender in New World Slavery* (Philadelphia: University of Pennsylvania Press, 2004).

22. Luana Ross, "From the 'F' Word to Indigenous/Feminisms," *Wicazo Sa Review* 24, no. 2, Native Feminism (Fall 2009): 39–52. Jennifer Denetdale and Mishuana Goeman served as guest editors for the special issue of *Wicazo Sa Review* on Native Feminisms. Their introduction is extremely helpful in outlining the field: guest editors' introduction, "Native Feminisms: Legacies, Interventions, and Indigenous Sovereignties," *Wicazo Sa Review* 24, no. 2, Native Feminism (Fall 2009): 9–13. That special issue's theme is most recently revisited in Joanne Barker, ed., *Critically Sovereign: Indigenous Gender, Sexuality, and Feminist Studies* (Durham, NC: Duke University Press, 2017). Sarah Deer also appeared in that 2009 *Wicazo Sa Review* special issue and then published her monograph, *The Beginning and End of Rape: Confronting Sexual Violence in Native America* (Minneapolis: University of Minnesota Press, 2015). Dian Million introduced her "Felt Theory" in the 2009 volume of *Wicazo Sa Review* and in a special issue of *American Quarterly* that also focused on Indigenous feminism the year before: "Felt Theory," *American Quarterly* 60, no. 2, Native Feminisms Without Apology (June 2008): 267–272. That volume included articles from many of those who also participated in the *Wicazo Sa Review* forum as well as Audra Simpson, whose recent monograph is *Mohawk Interruptus: Political Life Across the Borders of Settler States* (Durham, NC: Duke University Press, 2014). Another integral thinker in Native legal studies is Heidi Stark, coeditor with Jill Doerfler and Niigaanwewidam James Sinclair of *Centering Anishinaabe Studies: Understanding the World through Stories*, which includes her chapter "Transforming the Trickster: Federal Indian Law Encounters Anishinaabe Diplomacy," (East Lansing: Michigan State University Press, 2013), 259–278.

23. Antonia Castañeda, "Women of Color and the Rewriting of Western History: The Discourse, Politics, and Decolonization of History," *Pacific Historical Review* 61, no. 4, Western Women's History Revisited (November 1992): 501–533. For a retrospective on Castañeda's call for decolonization, see Margaret D. Jacobs, "Getting Out of a Rut: Decolonizing Western Women's History," *Pacific Historical Review* 79, no. 4 (November 2010), 585–604.

24. Delgado, "The Imperial Scholar," 561–578, and "The Imperial Scholar Revisited," 1349–1372.

25. Gordon Bakken, *Women Who Kill Men: California Courts, Gender, and the Press* (Lincoln: University of Nebraska Press, 2009); Clare V. McKanna, *Homicide, Race, and Justice in the American West, 1880–1920* (Tucson: University of Arizona Press, 1997); Bill Neal, *From Guns to Gavels: How Justice Grew Up in the Outlaw West* (Lubbock: Texas Tech University Press, 2008).

26. Andrés Reséndez, *Changing National Identities at the Frontier: Texas and New Mexico, 1800–1850* (New York: Cambridge University Press, 2004). Samuel Truett, *Fugitive Landscapes: The Forgotten History of the U.S.-Mexico Borderlands* (New Haven: Yale University Press, 2006). Elizabeth Jameson and Susan Armitage, eds., *Writing the Range: Race, Class, and Culture in the Women's*

West (Norman: University of Oklahoma Press, 1997). Elizabeth Jameson and Sheila McManus, eds., *One Step Over the Line: Toward a History of Women in the North American Wests* (Edmonton: University of Alberta Press, 2008).

27. Jeremy Adelman and Stephen Aron, "From Borderlands to Borders: Empires, Nation-States, and the Peoples in between in North American History," *American Historical Review* 104, no. 3 (June 1999): 814–841.

28. Reséndez, *Changing National Identities*. Truett, *Fugitive Landscapes*. Juliana Barr, *Peace Came in the Form of a Woman: Indians and Spaniards in the Texas Borderlands* (Chapel Hill: University of North Carolina Press, 2007). Brian De-Lay, *War of a Thousand Deserts: Indian Raids and the U.S.-Mexican War* (New Haven: Yale University Press, 2008).

29. Herbert Eugene Bolton, *The Spanish Borderlands: A Chronicle of Old Florida and the Southwest* (New Haven: Yale University Press, 1921). Albert Hurtado, *Herbert Eugene Bolton: Historian of the American Borderlands* (Berkeley: University of California Press, 2012). David Weber, ed., *The Idea of Spanish Borderlands* (New York: Garland, 1991). David Weber, *The Spanish Frontier in North America* (New Haven: Yale University Press, 2009). David Weber, "The Spanish Borderlands, Historiography Redux," *History Teacher* 39, no. 1 (November 2005): 43–56.

30. Those not already cited who influence me most directly include: Sylvia Van Kirk, *Many Tender Ties: Women in Fur-Trade Society, 1670–1870* (Norman: University of Oklahoma Press, 1980). Sarah Deutsch, *No Separate Refuge: Culture, Class, and Gender on an Anglo-Hispanic Frontier in the American Southwest, 1880–1940* (New York: Oxford University Press, 1987). Grace Peña Delgado, *Making the Chinese Mexican: Global Migration, Localism, and Exclusion in the U.S.-Mexico Borderlands* (Redwood City: Stanford University Press, 2012). María Montoya, *Translating Property: The Maxwell Land Grant and the Conflict over Land in the American West, 1840–1900* (Lawrence: University Press of Kansas, 2005).

31. Elizabeth Jameson, "Dancing on the Rim, Tiptoeing through Minefields," *Pacific Historical Review* 75, no. 1 (February 2006): 1–24; 5.

32. Not quoted here but also included in this set of anthologies is Samuel Truett and Elliott Young, eds., *Continental Crossroads: Remapping U.S.-Mexico Borderlands History* (Durham, NC: Duke University Press, 2004).

33. John M. Findlay and Kenneth S. Coates, *Parallel Destinies: Canadian-American Relations West of the Rockies* (Seattle: University of Washington Press, 2002), 6.

34. Andrew Graybill and Benjamin Johnson, eds., *Bridging National Borders in North America: Transnational and Comparative Histories* (Durham, NC: Duke University Press, 2010), 15–16.

35. Graybill and Johnson, *Bridging National Borders*, 24.

36. Katrina Jagodinsky, *Legal Codes and Talking Trees: Indigenous Women's Sovereignty in the Sonoran and Puget Sound Borderlands, 1854–1946* (New Haven: Yale University Press, 2016).

37. Kelly Lytle Hernández, *Migra! A History of the U.S. Border Patrol* (Berkeley: University of California Press, 2010).

38. Dudziak and Volpp, "Legal Borderlands," 595–596.

39. Dudziak and Volpp, "Legal Borderlands," 596.

40. Dudziak and Volpp, "Legal Borderlands," 596.

41. Dudziak and Volpp, "Legal Borderlands," 596.

42. John Phillip Reid, "Some Lessons of Western Legal History," *Western Legal History* 1, no. 1 (Winter/Spring 1988): 5–6, 17. John Wunder, "What's Old about the New Western History?" Part 3: Law, *Western Legal History* 10, no. 1 & 2 (Winter/Fall 1997): 96.

43. Lawrence M. Friedman, "The Law and Society Movement," *Stanford Law Review* 38, no. 3 (February, 1986): 773. Friedman described "the study of law and society, by whatever name," as "something of a stepchild in the law school world." The law and society movement Friedman described then is now a mainstream school of thought in legal history practice, as perhaps legal borderlands can become.

44. Gorden Bakken, in "Western Legal History: Where Are We and Where Do We Go From Here?" *Western Legal History* 3, no. 1 (Winter/Spring 1990): 115–116.

45. Friedman, "The Law and Society Movement," 118.

46. Robert Gordon, "Critical Legal Histories," *Stanford Law Review* 36, 1/2 (1984): 57–125.

47. Gordon, "Critical Legal Histories," 58.

48. Laura Edwards, "The History in 'Critical Legal Histories': Robert W. Gordon. 1984. Critical Legal Histories. *Stanford Law Review* 36: 57–125" in *Law and Social Inquiry* 37, Issue 1 (Winter 2012), 187–199, 195, 197.

49. Edwards, "The History in 'Critical Legal Histories," 187–199, 189.

50. Wunder, "What's Old About the New Western History?" 92.

51. John McLaren, Hamar Foster and Chet Orloff, eds., *Law for the Elephant, Law for the Beaver: Essays in the Legal History of the North American West* (Pasadena, CA: Ninth Judicial Circuit Historical Society, 1992).

52. John Reid, "The Layers of Western Legal History," in McLaren et al., *Law for the Elephant, Law for the Beaver: Essays in the Legal History of the North American West* (Pasadena, CA: Ninth Judicial Circuit Historical Society, 1992), 23–73, and "The Beaver's Law in the Elephant's Country: An Excursion into Transboundary Western Legal History," *Western Legal History* (Summer/Fall, 1991): 149–202. Gordon Bakken extended Reid's casting of Western legal history in his anthology on the topic: Gordon Bakken, ed., *Law in the Western United States* (Norman: University of Oklahoma Press, 2000).

53. John R. Wunder, "Anti-Chinese Violence in the American West, 1850–1910," in *Law for the Elephant, Law for the Beaver: Essays in the Legal History of the North American West*, John McLaren et al., eds. (Pasadena CA: Ninth Judicial Circuit Historical Society, 1992), 212–236.

54. Wunder, "What's Old About the New Western History?" 87–88.

55. Wunder, "What's Old About the New Western History?" 101, 112.

56. Wunder, "What's Old About the New Western History?" 114.

57. Gordon Bakken, "Western Legal History: The State of the Field," *Western Legal History* 20 no. 1–2 (Winter/Fall 2007): 4, 5, 29.

58. Pascoe, *What Comes Naturally*. Peggy Pascoe, "Race, Gender, and Intercultural Relations: The Case of Interracial Marriage," *Frontiers: A Journal of Women Studies* 12, no. 1 (1991): 5–18; "Miscegenation Law, Court Cases, and Ideologies of 'Race' in Twentieth-Century America," *Journal of American History* 83, no. 1 (June, 1996): 44–69.

59. Gordon Bakken, *The Mining Law of 1872: Past, Politics, and Prospects* (Albuquerque: University of New Mexico Press, 2008), ix–xxx.

60. Peggy Pascoe, *Relations of Rescue: The Search for Female Moral Authority in the American West, 1874–1939* (New York: Oxford University Press, 2000).

61. Estelle Freedman, introduction, *Frontiers: A Journal of Women Studies* 31, no. 3 (2010): 2.

62. Anzaldúa, *Borderlands/La Frontera*, 24–25.

Part I
Legal Borderlands of Race and Gender

1

Enforcing Colonial Boundaries in the Twenty-First Century

Settler Anxiety and the Violence Against Women Act

SARAH DEER

As a non-Native man, I do not feel secure stepping onto the reservation now.

Kevin Cramer

North Dakota congressional representative Kevin Cramer spoke these words to a room of tribal leaders in 2013 while explaining his concerns about the federal Violence Against Women Act (VAWA), which had just been signed into law.[1] His audience was no doubt surprised that "stepping onto the reservation" posed some kind of threat to a congressman.[2] Why would a congressman—or any white man, for that matter—fear the reservation boundaries that the federal government itself originally created to confine and isolate Native people?

Representative Cramer's statement is revelatory because it makes the subtext of federal Indian relations into the text and boldly states the racism that underlies the federal-tribal relationship as manifested in the long, ignominious history of federal law, practice, and procedure.[3] Unpacking Representative Cramer's statement about tribal authority reveals that this same anti-Indian impulse was still a significant motivating force in 2013 when the Violence Against Women Act (VAWA 2013) amendments were negotiated. These amendments proposed to change the prohibition against tribal prosecution of non-Indians, expanding the scope of tribal criminal authority to include people (of all races) who commit crimes of domestic violence in Indian country. As such, the congressional debates over tribal jurisdiction implicated larger questions of tribal authority and sovereignty, as well as settler-colonial anxiety and paranoia about being held accountable by tribal nations. As Patrick Wolfe explains, settler colonialism "destroys to replace."[4] The logic of settler anxiety is understood as irrational fear of indigenous people as they present obstacles to the ultimate goals of settler society.

One of the most ironic aspects of Representative Cramer's statement is that the security and safety of *Native women* on reservations was the impetus of the VAWA legislation. By "flipping the script" and making the law about him (and other non-Native men), Representative Cramer's statement seems callous and misplaced. His statement represented the culmination of anti-VAWA rhetoric by other lawmakers invoking a fundamentally anti-Indian worldview fueled by irrational paranoia about tribal authority.

The legislation aimed to provide more protection to victims in Indian country. Even a cursory review of the literature on tribal communities reveals there has been little semblance of criminal justice in Indian country since the American government began ruling over tribal nations. In short, Native people have been at the mercy of predators.

Because of a bizarre patchwork of federal laws, tribal authority to govern the actions of non-Indians is gravely limited. Non-Indian criminals can only be punished by the state or federal government, but these governments have historically expressed little to no interest in meting out punishments for crimes committed in Indian country. Native people who are attacked, abused, kidnapped, raped, or even murdered by a non-Indian cannot rely on their tribal government for justice. Native women, children, and Two-Spirit (Native LGBT) people have been hit hardest by this lack of legal protection by their own government. Native victims of crime simply have not had the option of turning to their tribal governments for intervention. Instead, they must turn to a government that has historically been openly racist and contemptuous of their need for protection and justice. Seneca scholar Mishauna Goeman suggests that we consider "the ways that gendered and sexualized violence has multiple connections that spread out on vertical and horizontal scales."[5] Indeed, the incoherent rules for tribal jurisdiction serve to trap Native women in violent situations that make it dangerous to live safely within the boundaries of tribal reservations.

Unfortunately, because these arbitrary legal barriers have been established and implemented by the federal government, *only Congress* can remedy these problems. But seeking such changes in Congress has proven challenging, if not impossible. Historically, Native people's quest for justice has been complicated by the obstructionist position of the US government and an interlocking system of interest groups and elected representatives who appear motivated largely by racism and ignorance. For their part, Native women and their allies have spent the last twenty years in an intensified effort to address the edifice of racism and neglect that characterizes federal Indian law in this country.[6] While Congress has occasionally made initial steps to address the jurisdictional problems, these efforts have been limited to minor tweaks to federal Indian law.

Federal and state lawmakers (as well as other special interest groups) have employed rhetoric that ignores or deflects the fundamental problems and fails to articulate real solutions. This chapter historicizes the dysfunctions of federal Indian law with regard to Native women and children and then examines how lawmakers talk about these legal issues. The rhetoric used by federal lawmakers represents the boundary between safety and anarchy for Native people.

The national problem of violence against Native women is a complex one, partly for geographic reasons. Native women in the United States live in a wide variety of settings. Most Native people live in urban settings and off-reservation rural settings governed exclusively by the Anglo-American legal system. Some Native people live or work in or near a "border town" (a town or city just across the tribal boundary) and while they may live on the reservation and have access to tribal courts, when they travel across the border, they are governed by the settler court system of state and federal authorities. Other Native people live on "checkerboard reservations" of trust land where territorial jurisdiction questions are particularly complicated because non-Indians own land within reservation boundaries. These checkerboard reservations typically contain hundreds of internal boundaries—where even neighboring plots of land might fall under completely different jurisdictional schemes. As a result, nearly every aspect of contemporary tribal existence is complicated by bizarre geopolitical boundaries. It is in this intersection that victims of crime struggle for justice.

When tribal nations have sought federal law reform to simplify or consolidate power into a coherent scheme, they often face lawmakers and jurists who implicitly or explicitly claim that tribal nations should not be trusted with such power. Moreover, the basis for contemporary objections to the restoration of tribal authority is often racialized by lawmakers who invoke stereotypes about Native people to justify their settler arrogance.

Tribal nations, then, must counter both racism and settler colonialism when engaging with the federal government. This chapter seeks to explicate the development of these arguments in the context of VAWA 2013.

Settler Colonialism and Violence against Women

VAWA 2013 represents a recent effort to address a long-standing historical problem. The well-documented history of violence against Native women by non-Indians goes back centuries, including the enslavement and rape of Native women as an explicit part of the colonial settlement project in North and South America. Rape and murder were two of the most common weapons used to destroy tribal cultures, dating back to the time of first contact with Europeans.[7] Women and children were often targets for military conquest that was accompanied or was shortly followed by settler violence, which has continued to this day.[8]

Part of the reason for the increased rates of gendered violence can be explained by the worldview of settlers. Transplanted European legal systems were founded on assumptions of rule by wealthy male landowners. European women had virtually no political rights in such systems. Women were not able to vote, own property, divorce, or consistently seek remedies for the harm they experienced.[9] Preconquest Native communities, by and large, were more egalitarian than European societies based on anthropological accounts and oral histories of Native people. Native women, for the most part, did not suffer from the same kinds of sexism and patriarchy that European women faced prior to conquest.[10]

The infusion of patriarchy into North America combined with the expanding settler state resulted in widespread violence. In fact, the violence experienced by Native people has colored nearly every aspect of the settlement of North America and the establishment of the United States. Columbus and his entourage enslaved Native people almost immediately and claimed dominion over the population pursuant to the European "doctrine of discovery." Sexual violence became embedded in the Native slave trade.[11] The most obvious form of violence is manifested in military conflicts, where killing is the goal. But the violence experienced by Native people came from many sources, including so-called massacres that dot the landscape of American history. In some regions, Native people were targeted en masse by bands of self-proclaimed militias, who operated outside the bounds of law. In his book-length treatment of the 1871 Camp Grant massacre in Arizona,

Karl Jacoby notes, "the true magnitude of the violent encounter with the indigenous inhabitants of North America remains unacknowledged even today."[12] Violence was not always part of an organized, concerted effort. For example, merchants and traders posted on or near Indian reservations committed isolated acts of violence against Native women and children—usually with no accountability. Native women who were married to non-Indians "commonly suffered extensive violence."[13]

The Western frontier was particularly violent for Native women as geopolitical boundaries were destroyed and rebuilt. During major settling events such as the land rush in Oklahoma and the gold rush in California, white men sought to capture both land and women.[14] In the gold rush period, for example, it became commonplace for white men to kidnap Native women and children for sexual slavery. The United States usually failed to intervene—likely because the erasure of Native women's bodies was necessary for completing the colonial project. But all Native people—men, women, and children—were targets for violence. In many conflict zones, such as the Southwest and Plains in the mid-nineteenth century, the word "exterminate" was readily deployed by many Americans, including militia leaders and newspaper editors.

Throughout the nineteenth century, Native women were often victimized by individual members of the military who were posted at forts that later became reservations. When tribal governments tried to intervene, they were rebuffed, ignored, and even punished. Even the establishment of reservation boundaries was designed to deflect blame for these actions. Jack Norton explains that "the white man's ultimate solution to the clear evidence of brutality was not to reflect upon the criminality of his own behavior[;] he reacted instead by creating reservations in order to isolate the original inhabitants, and effectively take their land."[15]

By the early twentieth century, nearly all Native people in the United States were living in dismal poverty because the colonial project had all but destroyed traditional subsistence models without establishing any alternative viable tribal economies. Several twentieth-century federal policies sought to continue the project of erasure as a "solution" to the poverty within the boundaries of reservations. For example, during the so-called termination era of the 1950s, federal policy encouraged tribal nations to disappear—purportedly for their own good.[16] In the post–World War II era, federal government policies encouraged Native people to leave the reservations, dissolve their tribal governmental structures, find jobs in the cities, and assimilate into the multicultural melting pot of the United States. Many Native people did move to the cities, creating what we know as "urban centers" of Native people today. Amid these relocations, Native women and children had little access to social services or shelter programs and were vulnerable to non-Indians who committed acts of violence. There is little documentation of these initial violent encounters in urban centers subsequent to relocation—quite simply, because no one was tracking this dynamic. Prostitution became one outgrowth of Native women's experience in the cities due to poverty and exploitation.[17] Survival sex was sometimes the only way for these women to survive in this new environment. Native women were simply not protected by any laws—state or tribal.

Despite centuries of violence perpetrated against Native people by non-Natives, there was no quantitative documentation of the extent of this violence until the very end of the twentieth century. In 1999, the US Department of Justice released a small, almost unnoticed report that would likely have not received much attention were it not for the victim advocates throughout Indian country who immediately saw their reality printed on the pages of a federal document. Titled "American Indians and Crime," the small Bureau of Justice Statistics leaflet contained a series of statistics drawn from several federal sources indicating that Native people experience the highest rates of interpersonal violence in the nation.[18] In addition, the report indicated that most of the perpetrators (70 percent) of violent crime were non-Native. This rate of interracial violence is a striking anomaly in American criminology—most violent crime in this country can be characterized as intraracial—but violence from nontribal members is the norm for Native people throughout the United States.

Since the initial release of "American Indians and Crime," the federal government has released additional reports and data—which invariably come to the same conclusions as the initial 1999 report: violence is a part of everyday life for Native people, and much of the violence is committed by non-Indians. A 2004 update to "American Indians and Crime" concluded that close to 60 percent of Native victims of violence described their attackers as white.[19] Other reports continued to explicate the gendered dynamic of these interracial crimes. For example, the National Violence Against Women Survey yielded data showing that Native women experience the highest rates of sexual violence in the nation at 34 percent—leading to a mantra in the Native women's movement that "more than one in three Native women will be raped in their lifetime."[20]

Unlike most Americans who are victims of violent crime, Native women most often suffer at the hands of men who are not members of their own race. Many who are skeptical about such statistics do not realize that over 50 percent of Native women are married to non-Indians and that tribal communities include many non-Indians who live or work with Native people.[21] The most recent federal data on victimization, released in May 2016, again affirms the rate of non-Native violence perpetrated against Native people: 55.5 percent of Native women reported a history of intimate partner violence—a rate far exceeding that of the rest of the American population. Native women also reported that 90 percent of intimate partner violence was committed by someone who was non-Native.[22]

Many tribal nations and victim advocates quickly learned that these statistics could be used as leverage for legislative legal reform projects. The data about interracial crime, in particular, served as concrete proof that the existing criminal justice scheme was ineffective, establishing justification for law reform. But prior to VAWA 2013, there had never been a true formal interruption of the colonial project of non-Native violence against Native people—no national effort to stem the tide of violence and no major policy changes that would have acknowledged the pain and suffering of the victims. The real cause of this contemporary crisis can be explained, in part, by the bizarre framework of criminal justice operating on Indian reservations today.

Jurisdiction: Boundaries of the Law

The next step in articulating a cohesive critique of anti-VAWA rhetoric like that expressed by Representative Cramer requires a rudimentary understanding of contemporary criminal jurisdiction on Indian reservations. Today, the federal government formally recognizes over 560 tribal nations.[23] Each of these tribal nations has its own unique, painful history as well as unique aspects of resilience and perseverance that have sustained their existence despite the multiple efforts to extinguish them.

The law is a dynamic field where diverse groups constantly advocate for different positions, and in the arena of tribal law, this conflict of views is especially stark. Tribal attorneys and advocates refer to something called "inherent sovereignty"—the principle that tribal nations retain core components of precolonial sovereignty that emanate from their status as nations. Tribal nations often refer to this inherent sovereignty as dating to "time immemorial," dating back thousands of years.

Despite these articulations of inherent sovereignty, contemporary tribal nations are explicitly restricted in the kinds of power they can exercise because of unilateral jurisdictional limitations imposed by the federal government. While tribal nations continue to exercise some forms of criminal authority in the twenty-first century, there are external limits and controls placed on the operation of the criminal justice system that are outgrowths of federal and state efforts to restrict the overall power of tribes. Note that none of these restrictions or limitations are a result of requests from tribal nations. Indeed, these limits and boundaries are the product of colonial power and control, reflected in federal laws and cases that never truly considered the perspective of the tribal nations they disempowered.[24] While the full panoply of federal laws that restrict and constrict the power of tribal governments is beyond the scope of this chapter, this section provides a cursory overview of the jurisdictional nightmare that is federal Indian law.[25]

OLIPHANT V. SUQUAMISH

The tribal jurisdiction provisions of VAWA 2013 were designed to address gaps created by *Oliphant v. Suquamish Indian Tribe*, a 1978 decision of the US Supreme Court that stripped the power of tribal courts to prosecute non-Indians.[26] In *Oliphant*, the US Supreme Court ruled that tribal governments, by virtue of their "dependent" status on the United States, lack inherent jurisdiction over criminal acts committed by nonmembers.[27] But the verbiage of *Oliphant* expounds beyond the initial concern of tribal nations as "dependents"—as Mark Rifkin points out, the decision is partly predicated on the "racist image of needing to save whites from the dangers of Indian savagery."[28]

Oliphant established a bright-line rule. No matter what a non-Indian does, he or she cannot be held criminally accountable by the tribe. Southern Ute citizen Diane Millich's story is the prototypical domestic violence scenario left in the wake of *Oliphant*. She spoke of her experience at the presidential signing of VAWA in 2013:

> When I was twenty-six years old I dated a non-Indian, a white man. After six months we were married. My non-Indian husband moved into my house on the reservation. To my shock, just days after our marriage, he assaulted me. After a year of abuse, and more than a hundred incidences of being slapped, kicked, punched, and living in horrific fear, I left for good.

During that year of marriage, I called the police many times. I called our Southern Ute tribal police department, but the law prevented them from arresting and prosecuting my husband because he was non-Indian. The county sheriff could not help me because I am a Native woman and the beatings occurred on tribal reservation land.

After one beating, my ex-husband called the tribal police and the sheriff's department himself, just to show me that no one could stop him. All the times that I called the police and nothing was done only made my ex-husband believe he was above the law and untouchable.

My ex-husband told me, "you promised us until death do us part, so death it shall be." Finally he arrived at my office armed with a gun. I am alive today only because my coworker pushed me out of harm's way and took the bullet in his shoulder. For this crime, he was finally arrested. But because he had never been arrested for any of the abuse against me, he was treated as a first-time offender.[29]

Ms. Millich's story exposes the deep irony in Representative Cramer's statement about his "security." While Cramer's statement indicates fear of tribal nations, it also expresses the epitome of settler-colonial arrogance—to be allowed to live in a community and yet be above the law. The logic of *Oliphant* only makes sense in the context of settler colonialism. In other contexts, Anglo-American law rarely seeks to deny a government the right to protect its own people.

Concurrent Authority — The White Man's System Will Protect You

Many lawmakers and opponents of tribal sovereignty minimize the harm done by *Oliphant* by pointing to the fact that the federal or state governments can prosecute non-Indian offenders in many cases. "Concurrent jurisdiction" is one curious outgrowth of federal Indian law. It means that two separate governments have autonomous authority over a criminal act and can act independently. So, in theory, both the tribe *and* the state or federal government can prosecute a particular crime. Most tribal governments in the lower forty-eight states share criminal jurisdiction with the federal government pursuant to the Major Crimes Act, while other tribes share criminal jurisdiction with the state where they are located due to Public Law 280 or a similar law, as discussed below. While opponents of tribal authority often point to the concurrent authority as the better solution to non-Indian crime, there has been a history of nonenforcement in many tribal communities dating back decades. Put simply, many of these cases fall through the cracks whether through deliberate indifference or institutionalized apathy. The failure of state and federal intervention in crimes committed by non-Indians has been documented by the federal government itself in a series of audits and investigations that conclude that the application of state or federal law is not working. Tribal nations have no way to mandate action from any government other than their own.

Major Crimes Act (1885)

During the 2012–2013 VAWA period, some Republican lawmakers put forth proposed legislation that purported to expand the role of the federal government in prosecuting crimes committed by non-Indians. But the federal government has enjoyed that authority since the late nineteenth century, and this has not stemmed the tide of non-Indian crime. Kevin Washburn, Chickasaw legal scholar and former assistant secretary for Indian Affairs explains, "as federal authority slowly expands, the [crime] problem only continues to grow."[30] It's important to understand the context in which the federal government came to have criminal authority on tribal lands in order to understand why the current system has been so problematic.

In 1885, Congress passed a law called the Major Crimes Act (MCA), which authorized the federal government to punish major crimes such as murder, rape, kidnapping, aggravated assault, burglary, or larceny committed by Indians in Indian country. Today, tribal nations retain their authority over those crimes as well (as long as they are committed by Indians). So, in theory, both the federal government and the tribal government can prosecute a violent crime committed by an Indian. But only the federal government can prosecute a non-Indian committing the very same crime.

Congress passed the MCA because it wanted the federal government to be able to prosecute problematic Indians and they needed a law to provide that power. The impetus for MCA emerged after a famous Indian law case called *Ex Parte Crow Dog*, which started as a homicide case in the lands of the Lakota people in the Dakota Territory at the end of the nineteenth century.[31] Two chiefs had a feud, and one man (Crow Dog) killed another (Spotted Tail). Under Lakota jurisprudence, Crow Dog was held accountable and ordered to provide material goods to Spotted Tail's family. Federal Indian agents thought the death penalty should have been imposed. Crow

Dog was not a great friend of white men, which made him a "bad" Indian. The federal government proceeded to prosecute him, but Crow Dog successfully argued to the US Supreme Court that the federal government lacked jurisdiction over him without a "hook" to allow federal authority. Crow Dog walked free, but Congress passed the MCA less than two years later.

Thus, the imposition of the Major Crimes Act was designed to punish Indians like Crow Dog.[32] It was not truly designed to protect the Native community, but rather to protect the power of the white community over the Native community. And, other than adding additional crimes to the list, the MCA has not really changed since 1885. In addition to being an affront to tribal self-determination, the system of federal crime control on reservations simply hasn't worked. For the most part, the history of policing reservations by the federal government is abysmal. It has been a low priority for the US Attorneys' offices for generations. Moreover, federal offices can be three or more hours away from the community where the crime has occurred. For decades, tribal nations were rarely told that the US attorney had decided not to prosecute a crime; it would just lay dormant forever.[33] As one might imagine, this under-prosecution has left many victims without recourse.

Public Law 280 (1953)

Not all tribes share the concurrent jurisdiction with the federal government. In the mid-twentieth century, Congress decided to approach crime on Indian reservations differently by delegating the federal authority over crimes to certain states. Passed by Congress in 1953, Public Law 280 affects approximately half of all Indian tribes, including all but one tribal government in Alaska. During the 1950s termination era, federal Indian policy shifted as federal officials sought to get out of the business of governing tribes and prosecuting crimes on reservations. To achieve that end, reservation boundaries needed to be completely dissolved, which would necessitate a shift from federal power to state power. Essentially, when reservations went away, Congress intended for the former reservation land to become absorbed into a state's political boundaries. Public Law 280 turned over enforcement of major crimes (e.g., murder, kidnapping, and rape) to particular states in which tribes resided. It was hoped that Native people would then just be assimilated into the state population, effectively dissolving the boundary and extinguishing the tribe and its political existence through assimilation rather than outright genocide. Congress started slowly—by delegating federal authority to six states—Alaska, Oregon, California, Nebraska, Minnesota, and Wisconsin.[34] It was thought that the project would eventually be expanded to all tribes. But Congress never expanded Public Law 280 (it might be thought of as a failed "pilot project") yet left the jurisdictional scheme in place for those tribes in the original bill.

Congress did not adequately consult with the tribes or the states before passing Public Law 280. Instead, it thrust the responsibility for law enforcement and prosecution on reservations onto the states but failed to provide any infrastructure or funds to support this transfer of power.[35] And, for tribes with contentious relationships with the state government surrounding them, this mandate was an unpleasant surprise.[36] According to many experts, crime rates increased in the years following Public Law 280.

Some tribal nations have no other option but to rely on the federal or state government for crime control because they lack the necessary infrastructure and resources to operate an effective contemporary criminal justice system. Without a stable, sufficient funding base, it is difficult to sustain a comprehensive criminal justice system. Other tribal nations choose not to exercise contemporary criminal authority because it clashes with customary forms of intervention. For this reason, there will never be one monolithic legislative "fix" that will solve the problem of non-Indian crime. Nonetheless, the activism leading up to the VAWA 2013 controversy was grounded in the philosophy that tribal nations should be able to exercise criminal authority over anybody within their territorial jurisdiction.

Congressional Rhetoric: Settler Anxiety and Maintenance of Boundaries

With the fundamental structure of tribal jurisdiction established, we return to Representative Cramer's irrational fear of tribal borders by exploring the legislation that created so much anxiety and fear on the part of many Republican men.

The VAWA story begins in 1994, when the original federal Violence Against Women Act was passed (in a bipartisan Senate vote of 95–4). The multifaceted legislation contains numerous provisions aimed at addressing gender-based crimes throughout the United States (not just Native communities), focusing on domestic violence, dating violence, sexual assault, stalking, and sex trafficking. VAWA is up for renewal approximately every five years. Beginning with the 2000 reauthorization, advocates for Native women began to press for additional changes in VAWA to better meet the needs of women living in tribal communities. These efforts have resulted in a "Tribal Title" in VAWA that addresses a variety of issues pertaining to Native women living in Indian country.[37] Additional improvements were made in VAWA 2005, again without much controversy.

When VAWA was up for renewal in 2012, advocates for Native women again proposed new provisions to address the continuing crisis of violence against women within the boundaries of Indian country. The provision that became the most controversial is the focus of Representative Cramer's statement: the restoration of tribal criminal jurisdiction over non-Indians who commit acts of domestic violence on tribal lands. This legislation has been framed as a "partial *Oliphant* fix" because it alters the unforgiving legal rule imposed by *Oliphant v. Suquamish*—at least for domestic violence cases. The federal legislation refers to this restoration as "special domestic violence criminal jurisdiction" (SDVCJ).[38]

During the months leading up to the passage of VAWA 2013, House Republicans demurred on the *Oliphant* fix and offered alternative legislation.[39] The alternative bill offered by opponents to the *Oliphant* fix, however, was to enhance and strengthen *federal* response to crime in Indian country. Some Republicans also disputed the accuracy of the reports showing high rates of violence committed by non-Indians but were not able to offer credible alternative data. As the debate continued, these lawmakers began to express considerable settler anxiety regarding tribal authority over non-Indians.

The rhetoric of the anti-VAWA Republicans in 2012 and 2013 is evidence that settler colonialism, privilege, and anti-Indian sentiment are still very much present in national discourse about tribal governmental power and reservation boundaries.[40] A series of comments made by congressional representatives, each of them white men, in objection to VAWA during the 2012–2013 legislative debates reveals that their rhetoric is centered in a privileged, procolonial framework that is fundamentally at odds with safety for Native women. In this section, I also consider contemporaneous blog posts and a law review article written by Paul J. Larkin, a senior legal fellow at the Heritage Foundation (a well-known conservative think tank), who also voiced opposition to the return of tribal authority over non-Indians. In analyzing these statements, I have grouped them into four categories: (1) racist rhetoric, (2) antisovereignty rhetoric, (3) constitutional objections, and (4) paternalist rhetoric. Each category requires the development of a distinct counterpoint.

CATEGORY I — RACIST AND DEHUMANIZING RHETORIC

One of the primary concerns about tribal jurisdiction seems to be connected to the fear of Indians sitting in judgment of white men. But why fear the judgment of Indians, unless Indians categorically are unable to be fair? White people have been sitting in judgment of Indian defendants in state and federal courts for well over a century, so it is certainly a double standard to protest the reverse. But the rhetoric in this section denigrates the ability of tribal people to be fair. Much of the rhetoric deployed by lawmakers in opposition to VAWA served to dehumanize Native people and exposed antisovereignty and racist assumptions about Native people.

The most obvious of these concerns were those made by Senator Grassley from Iowa. On February 20, 2013, Senator Chuck Grassley, a Republican, was speaking at a town hall in Iowa the week following his vote against VAWA 2013. One member of the audience questioned his vote. In explaining why he disagreed with the tribal provisions, he remarked, "So the idea behind [VAWA] is we'll try them in tribal court. But under the laws of our land, you got to have a jury that is a reflection of society as a whole, and on an Indian reservation, it's going to be made up of Indians, right? *So the non-Indian doesn't get a fair trial.*"[41]

Senator Grassley's statement combines legal ignorance with racial stereotypes. First, he fails to understand (or is being intentionally deceptive) that the US Constitution does not require that a jury be a "reflection of a society as a whole." The actual rule from the Sixth Amendment right to a jury requires that juries be drawn from the local state and district where the crime was committed and cannot exclude people on the basis of race. Mr. Grassley was probably referring to requirements created by the Supreme Court that defendants have a right to a jury that is "drawn from a fair cross section of the community." But this requirement does not mean that a white defendant is guaranteed to have a minimum number of white jurors. Of course, the opposite problem is presumably not a concern for Senator Grassley—namely that Native defendants in federal court rarely (if ever) see a Native person on a jury.[42]

More concerning, however, is Grassley's assertion that "the non-Indian doesn't get a fair trial." This type of statement reveals much about what the speaker believes about Native people—that Native people are morally deficient or somehow incapable of dispensing justice fairly. Empirical reviews of tribal court decisions by legal scholars have concluded otherwise—namely, that tribal courts protect due process rights—and that nonmembers are victors in tribal courts at the same rate as tribal members.[43]

Racism and Eurocentrism emboldens people to disparage the way that Native people have governed themselves. For example, in a 2012 law review article written in anticipation of the VAWA debates in Congress, Paul J. Larkin claimed that "for most of [American] history tribes had no formal judicial system."[44] Like Rehnquist in *Oliphant*, Larkin states this as though it were an unquestionable fact. In fact, the language about "formality" harkens back to the colonial-era rhetoric of tribal governments as "savage" and Anglo-American governments as "civilized." The term "formal" is loaded, as it suggests tribal governments had no systems that followed protocol or norms, which is a decidedly Eurocentric perspective. In fact, most tribal judicial traditions operated in a very formal way; while there were no courtrooms, black robes, or powdered wigs, tribal judicial traditions included formal protocol (sometimes emerging from ceremonial practices), specific obligations for clan relatives, and legal protections for the defendant as well as the victim. Again, the Larkin critiques harken back to a time of more overt racism, when tribal people were considered uncivilized (at best) or savage (at worst).

Category 2 — Ignorance of Sovereignty

Several senators and representatives appeared to be making their VAWA vote decision based on fundamental ignorance (or feigned ignorance) about the legal foundations for tribal authority. These statements also depend on many of the racist assumptions discussed earlier—because antisovereignty statements are implicitly related to the perception of how Native people govern.

Senator Grassley's rhetoric opposing VAWA 2013 operated from a place of ignorance about the inherent sovereignty of Native nations. On the floor of the Senate, he remarked, "*Unlike a State, a tribe is not a sovereign entity.*"[45] While it is true that some aspects of tribal sovereignty are currently curtailed or limited (*Oliphant* being the quintessential example)—the essence of tribal sovereignty has never been relinquished by tribal nations. Grassley's statement is incorrect as a matter of law. In fact, while the Supreme Court has curtailed tribal authority in certain contexts, it has also ruled that tribal nations are equal to or equivalent to states for particular purposes. In addition, as signatories to treaties, tribal nations are sometimes characterized as being elevated above states in terms of stature as the federal government maintains a government-to-government relationship with tribal nations.

Representative Doc Hastings from Washington State made similarly questionable legal statements on the floor of the House when arguing against VAWA 2013. His first flawed reading of the law stems from his mischaracterization of an important 1886 Supreme Court case: "In the nineteenth century, the Supreme Court in *United States v. Kagama* declared there are only two sovereigns in the geographical limits of the United States, and tribes are not one of them."[46]

In reality, *Kagama* (an important benchmark case in federal Indian law) says nothing of the kind. The opinion was not focused on the power of tribal governments but rather of the federal government. And while *Kagama* is a problematic Indian case in terms of language and outcome, the conception of tribal sovereignty was never explicitly dissolved. In *Kagama*, the court described tribal nations as having fewer attributes of sovereignty and being subject to the laws of the federal government. But both the court and Congress have reaffirmed the independent sovereignty of tribal nations on numerous occasions since *Kagama*. By reading such a message into the text of *Kagama*, Hastings attempts to revive nineteenth-century efforts to annihilate the existence of tribal nations, asking his colleagues and constituents: If tribes are not sovereign, what are they? Hastings leaves this provocative riddle for the listener to guess, but to him, tribal governments are not true sovereigns.

Later in the same floor statement, Hastings remarked, "Tribal self-government is therefore not a general government power equivalent to that of a state, but a federal policy governed by Congress for the promotion of Indian self-determination and to preserve and advance their way of life."[47]

The conflation of tribal self-governance with a mere "federal policy" is yet another example of treating tribal governments as subservient to state and federal governments. And even if Hastings were correct—that is, if tribes are not governments but rather beneficiaries of federal "policy," then the federal government certainly has been derelict in duty for centuries for never funding any federal programs at an adequate level.[48] And if the real goal is to "preserve and advance their way of life," then why not address the high rates of victimization that threaten the very essence of Native people's lives?

CATEGORY 3 — CONSTITUTIONAL OBJECTIONS

Several lawmakers in Congress repeatedly argued that non-Indians could not be treated fairly by tribal courts, yet no concrete evidence of such a risk was ever offered. Most of the concern about whether defendants receive a fair trial in tribal courts stems, in part, from the 1896 Supreme Court case of *Talton v. Mayes,* which ruled that the US Constitution and its amendments do not apply to Indian tribes since they were not constituencies to the drafting and ratification.[49] Because certain important rights for criminal defendants in the American justice system are codified in the Bill of Rights, many people mistakenly assume that tribal courts do not protect the same or similar rights in criminal cases. The supposition stems in part from the arrogant assumption that the Constitution is the only governing document in the world that protects civil liberties and individual rights. In truth, many tribal constitutions contain language very similar to the Bill of Rights and there is little evidence that tribal courts are in the habit of violating civil rights as enshrined in the American Constitution.[50] Nonetheless, many of those opposed to VAWA 2013 homed in on the fact that the US Constitution does not apply to tribal courts and would put non-Indians at risk of being tried in a court without protection for individual liberties.

Most of these statements ignored the fact that yet another congressional act statutorily mandates tribal nations to protect the very civil liberties that are enshrined in the Bill of Rights. Tribal courts must abide by the Indian Civil Rights Act of 1968 (ICRA), a federal law that mandates the application of the language of most of the Bill of Rights. This means that tribal courts must enforce American-style civil liberties, including freedom of speech and religion. Most of the language from the Fourth, Fifth, and Sixth Amendments is reflected in ICRA, nearly mirroring word-for-word the rights of criminal defendants, including the key language of due process and equal protection.[51] Moreover, many tribal constitutions and statutes provide for additional or expanded civil rights in certain circumstances. Despite this, opponents of VAWA 2013 repeatedly claimed that constitutional rights of non-Indians *would be* violated if they were to be prosecuted by a tribe.

Senator Grassley's prepared statement on the question of the constitutionality of VAWA 2013 asserted that it "might actually not accomplish anything at all for Native American women, while failing to protect the constitutional rights of other American citizens."[52] Oklahoma senator Coburn became more animated. One week after Grassley released his statement,

Coburn railed, "What we have done with this solution is to trample on the Bill of Rights of every American who is not a Native American. I have no doubt—I am 100 percent certain—that this portion of the bill is going to be thrown out by the first federal judge that hears it."[53]

Grassley and the others never provided specific examples of tribal courts that violated constitutional rights. Even were there evidence of constitutional rights being violated in tribal courts, we ought to note that state and federal courts sometimes violate constitutional rights, and such matters are expected to be resolved in the appellate courts. The solution to constitutional rights violations in contemporary Anglo-American courts is why appellate courts exist. Eliminating the courts altogether is not the solution. But rarely do these lawmakers acknowledge the existence of constitutional rights within tribal legal systems. No system of justice is perfect, but we don't strip state and the federal government of jurisdiction when they make a mistake. Tribal nations should receive the same courtesy.

Another important critique of this rhetoric should consider the rights of Indian defendants. If tribal courts truly present a constitutional crisis for non-Native defendants, why is it not also a constitutional crisis for Native defendants (who are also American citizens under federal law)? If these lawmakers were so concerned about civil rights in tribal courts, do they not also find it problematic that Native people are unquestionably covered by tribal jurisdiction too? None of these men have ever championed the plight of Native defendants in any context. It is only when the tribal court would preside over a non-Indian defendant that they suddenly care about civil rights. In fact, Senators Grassley, Coburn, and Cornyn as well as Representatives Hastings and Cantor all received an "F" grade from the National Association for the Advancement of Colored People (NAACP) civil rights report card for calendar year 2013.[54] The selective interest in civil rights is quite revealing, as the rhetoric elevates the rights of white defendants over the rights of Native defendants.

Linking implicit racism against Indians with concerns about tribal courts' constitutional violations, Hastings's rhetoric raised the stakes considerably by invoking unsubstantiated allegations that tribal courts were somehow discriminatory. His precise words were that the bill "openly allows discrimination against an individual based on race, sex, age, or if he's an Indian, who he's related to. Where the person's an American citizen, [he or she] can be expelled from their home and may not have any right to appeal a claim in an impartial federal court."[55] It is not clear how exercising jurisdiction over non-Indians has anything to do with discrimination. VAWA 2013 said nothing of discriminating against people based on sex or age. At most, the *Oliphant*-fix language could be considered a race-*conscious* statute—that is, restoring authority over all races of people, but again, the issue is not discrimination. In fact, it is trying to correct discrimination—namely, white people being above the law.

Senator Cornyn shared his colleague's concern about the vulnerability of non-Indian defendants in tribal courts with little regard to the vulnerability of Indian victims not adequately protected by federal courts: "This is a very dangerous, slippery slope because if non-tribe members are tried in tribal courts, they are not protected by the United States Constitution and they have no right of appeal to the federal courts."[56] In fact, ICRA has provided for a habeas corpus appeal from tribal courts to federal courts since it was passed in 1968. Moreover, the final VAWA 2013 provisions require that defendants receive notice about their right to a habeas petition in federal courts.

In addition to problematically presuming Anglo-American courts have exclusive claims to impartiality, Hastings's scope of VAWA's potential "victims" was expansive: "[VAWA 2013] affects non-Indians who live, work, or travel on 56 million acres of U.S. soil that happen to be called Indian Country. In other words, the bill makes 56 million acres of land in our nation 'Constitution-Free Zones' where Due Process and Equal Protection rights—as interpreted and enforced in U.S. courts—do not exist."[57]

The irony of this declaration cannot be overstated. Tribal nations are not constitution-free zones. Most tribal nations are governed by constitutions that are largely based on the American Constitution. Moreover, tribal nations have argued for years that their own constitutional rights of due process and equal protection have been denied for centuries. For example, Native people have had to fight for religious freedom for decades.[58] To say that reservations are "constitution-free" is to say much more about Anglo-American governance and very little about tribal governance.

The rhetoric regarding the constitutionality of VAWA 2013 demonstrates an implicit (although palpable) fear or prejudice of tribal nations exerting authorities over outsiders. These oppositionists never brought forth a defendant from a tribal court who had been treated unfairly or unconstitutionally, while advocates for VAWA had a plethora of witnesses whose lives—and deaths—made clear the failures of *Oliphant*.

CATEGORY 4—PATRIARCHAL PATERNALISM

Very few of the anti-VAWA statements even came close to acknowledging the plight of Native women—and those that did so seemed to be an afterthought. A few lawmakers crafted their objections to VAWA 2013 in terms that suggested they were truly concerned about the lives of Native women. Paternalism is nothing new to male politicians in the United States, but rarely is that paternalism geared to women of color. In the VAWA context, these politicians' claims to concerns about Native women were little more than window dressing for their opposition to the VAWA provisions. These statements included simplistic or condescending references to protecting Native women. Note that these lawmakers did not offer any true alternative that would allow a Native woman who is battered by a non-Indian to achieve redress or secure protection within tribal justice systems.

Showing a remarkable inability to grasp the very real vulnerability of Native women to violence at the hands of non-Indians, Grassley called VAWA 2013 "cruel": "What is very cruel is to provide tribal women the illusion of a solution that courts may well strike down on constitutional grounds in the future."[59] The invocation of the term "cruel" is curious here; is the concern about white defendants or is the concern about Native women?

House Majority Leader Eric Cantor, who stalled the vote on the VAWA 2013 bill in response to concerns about unconstitutionality, suggested that he had Native women's best interests in mind: "We want to protect the women who are subject to abuse on tribal lands, and unfortunately there are issues that don't directly bear on that that have come up, that have complicated it."[60]

These statements, unsurprisingly, were camouflage for the real concern—the non-Native men who might be arrested and charged for domestic violence. These statements had little to nothing to do with the real needs and lives of Native women.

VAWA 2013 Becomes Law

Despite the outspoken opposition, VAWA 2013 did become law, passing both the Senate and the House. The Senate vote was held first with a vote of 78–22 on February 13, 2013. The only senators voting "no" were white Republican men, including Senator Orrin Hatch, who was a coauthor of the original 1994 VAWA. Then the bill moved back to the House of

Representatives, where it stalled for two weeks. House Majority Leader Eric Cantor threatened not to bring it to a vote at all. A Republican representative from Oklahoma managed to break the stalemate and secure enough House votes for the tribal provisions to allow it to pass. Tom Cole, a Republican, is also a citizen of the Chickasaw Nation. Once he convinced some of his colleagues of the dire nature of crime in Indian country, several folded and agreed to support the provisions. In an interview with the *New York Times* prior to passage of the bill, he asked, "We're holding up a domestic violence bill that should be routine because you don't want to help Native women who are the most vulnerable over a philosophical point?"[61] The final House vote, held on February 28, was 286–138. As expected, the vote was partisan. No Democrats voted against the bill. The majority of the 138 "no" votes came from white men—but ten Republican women also voted against the bill. VAWA 2013 was signed into law by President Barack Obama on March 7 in a celebratory ceremony at the Department of the Interior.

The Aftermath and Future of VAWA 2013

The very day after the House Republicans relented and allowed the vote on VAWA, Paul Larkin of the Heritage Foundation posted a blog entry titled "Send in the Lawyers"—a clear suggestion that he (and others) intend to fight the constitutionality of the *Oliphant*-fix in the courts.[62] Larkin claimed that VAWA 2013 "became freighted with a needless federal constitutional controversy over tribal jurisdiction" and predicted that the Supreme Court would strike down the law as unconstitutional.

The anxiety expressed by Larkin and the Republican opposition seems out of proportion to the real impact of VAWA. The "fix" that generated such racist and misogynistic debate among legislators ended up being extremely narrow—some might say laughably narrow. Tribal governments can now exercise criminal jurisdiction over non-Indians in a very limited set of circumstances. The non-Indian defendant must have committed an act of intimate partner violence *and* must either live or work on the reservation.[63] This tightly bound exception was a result of months of compromise, as the original bill sought jurisdiction over all crime committed by non-Indians. But the final bill only extends to crimes of domestic violence. All other crimes are still off-limits to tribal courts. Should a non-Indian commit murder, sexual assault, child sexual abuse, kidnapping, or any crime, for that matter, the tribal government still cannot prosecute him. This means that activists will be returning to Washington in the coming years to expand this *Oliphant*-fix until tribes are no longer restricted by federal law in terms of the race of the person they can prosecute within their territorial boundaries. These activists will no doubt encounter the same types of rhetoric deployed in 2013.

Moreover, the *Oliphant*-fix provisions require that tribal courts comply with a series of statutory requirements that impose a burden on some tribal courts. Not every tribal nation is able to take on the burdensome task of complying with the mandates of VAWA 2013. (Nothing in federal law *requires* tribal nations to prosecute non-Indians.) As of 2018, only a handful of tribal nations have put the 2013 provisions into action. It is likely that lawmakers will point to these delays as proof that the law was unnecessary or as evidence that tribal nations don't wish to have jurisdiction restored. In truth, criminal jurisdiction in Indian country has been fraught with difficulties for well over a century. It is unreasonable to expect one piece of legislation to be a quick fix to the myriad problems associated with non-Indian crime.

Indeed, it has taken several years for the legislation to see fruition. The first tribal conviction of a non-Indian did not happen until May 2017—over four years after VAWA 2013 was signed.[64] The conviction was secured by the Pascua Yaqui Tribe, which began exercising the authority in 2013, but prior efforts to prosecute non-Indians ended in plea agreements, transfers to other jurisdictions, and jury acquittals. These acquittals serve to debunk the fears of lawmakers that tribal courts would be biased or unfair to non-Indian defendants.

While the opposition to VAWA ultimately "lost" when the bill became law, understanding how to respond to the rhetoric will be a crucial part of defending the law in federal courts. Within the next few years, it is expected that non-Indians convicted by tribes under VAWA 2013 will appeal to the federal court system (as is their right under the law). In fact, as tribal nations seek restoration over a broader set of crimes, the likelihood of anxiety and fear-based rhetoric will only increase.

Tribal Jurisdiction and the Courts

Since VAWA 2013 became law, there has been a significant Supreme Court case that also implicates the power of tribal courts to respond to violence within the boundaries of tribal nations. *Dollar General v. Mississippi Band of Choctaw*, decided in 2016, gives us a potential clue to how the Supreme Court will decide a constitutional challenge to VAWA 2013. *Dollar General v. Mississippi Band of Choctaw* was a case about tribal *civil* jurisdiction over a personal injury case.[65] The timing of the case is interesting because it was decided after VAWA 2013 was passed, and the underlying personal injury was the sexual assault of a young Choctaw boy by a non-Indian. The facts date to 2003, when the Dollar General retail store on the Mississippi Choctaw reservation partnered with the tribe to start a youth opportunity program that placed Choctaw youth in local businesses for the purposes of job training.

The white general manager of the Dollar General store allegedly molested a Choctaw boy, who reported the abuse. While the tribe was able to secure the manager's banishment from the reservation, it was, of course, unable to prosecute him pursuant to *Oliphant*. For reasons that are not entirely clear, the federal government also did not prosecute the crime. Seeking some form of justice, in 2005 the parents of the victim filed a civil lawsuit in tribal court seeking damages from the Dollar General corporation for the harm done to their son. Dollar General immediately objected to tribal jurisdiction. The main thrust of Dollar General's argument was that the principles in *Oliphant* should apply to civil adjudication in addition to criminal adjudication. Dollar General fought jurisdiction starting with the tribal trial court and ultimately appealing all the way to the US Supreme Court. Dollar General's argument was simple: as a non-Indian entity, Dollar General should not be subject to tribal authority. And its decision could have been devastating— the court could have taken the opportunity to completely eliminate tribal civil jurisdiction over non-Indians—bolstering and strengthening the racist *Oliphant* principles about tribal authority (and leaving victims without a criminal *or* civil remedy when attacked by a non-Indian).

Dollar General was argued in December 2015, when nine justices were on the Supreme Court; during the intervening months, Justice Antonin Scalia passed away—leaving eight justices for the remainder of the Obama administration. The court was not able to come to a majority decision in *Dollar General*. On the last day of the court's business in June 2016, the court released its per curium "tie vote"—meaning that neither party could claim victory. Since Mississippi Choctaw had won at the Fifth Circuit level, tribal nations retained civil authority over non-Indians by a single justice's vote. No doubt the Supreme Court will have an opportunity to revisit this issue in the future.

Without a written opinion in *Dollar General*, it is difficult to predict how the justices will rule on a VAWA 2013 challenge. Instead, we are limited to examining the oral arguments for possible clues as to the position of various justices.[66] Both Dollar General's counsel and several justices used language that is consistent with those opposing VAWA 2013, with a concerted focus on claims that tribal courts are simply not sophisticated enough to be trusted with authority over non-Indians.

Within the next decade, the court will almost certainly rule on the legality of the *Oliphant*-fix from VAWA 2013. The challenge will undoubtedly come from a non-Indian who is convicted of domestic violence in tribal court. It is always difficult to predict how the Supreme Court will decide a case, but to suggest that politics will not play a role in the VAWA 2013 challenge would be disingenuous. It is likely that the court will closely consider the legislative history of the law, once again engaging with the antitribal rhetoric of the lawmaker who opposed its passage. In that sense, the Supreme Court will further explicate the boundaries of tribal power.

Epilogue

This chapter has focused on the fight to hold non-Indians accountable for violence committed within tribal boundaries; a problem that dates back centuries. It is unlikely that the debate over this matter will subside in the coming years. Indeed, it would be shortsighted to say that this debate is solely about racial stereotypes of Native people as lawless and vengeful. It is true that lawmakers discussed in this chapter have characterized the legislation as some sort of power grab on the part of tribal nations. But it is necessary to consider what possible underlying financial interests are implicated by this rhetoric. These lawmakers are clearly distressed about the notion of a non-Native man being prosecuted in tribal court, but most tribal nations are so far removed and isolated from mainstream America that they rarely come to the attention of powerful lawmakers. And certainly there is no organized lobbyist group representing the rights of non-Native men who batter Native women.

As with many things, the true objection to tribal authority may lie within the jealous guarding of power possessed by oligarchs in the United States. Powerful private funders support the Heritage Foundation and the

Republican Party. These same funders often also have tremendous interest in the undeveloped energy potential that lies under many tribal lands, given that extraction of oil and other natural resources is a multibillion-dollar-a-year industry. In order to expand their extractive industries, non-Indian companies have always set their sights on tribal lands. In *Decolonization Is Not a Metaphor*, Native feminist scholars Maile Arvin, Eve Tuck, and Angie Morrill remind us that "within settler colonialism, it is exploitation of land that yields supreme value."[67] And that exploitation of land may actually be the true motivation for these objections to tribal self-government. Perhaps the true threat posed by tribal criminal authority is not to civil liberties but pocketbooks. It is important to consider how tribal authority could serve as a threat to revenue.

For the past several years, increased attention has exposed the relationship between exploitation of the earth and exploitation of Native women's bodies on Indian reservations. While sex trafficking of Native bodies has taken place for generations, the twenty-first-century understanding often ties the extractive industries to the exploitation of Native women.[68] Stories have come forward about transient non-Indian workers who abuse, rape, kidnap, drug, buy, sell, and kill Native women on or near reservations. Workers for the oil industry often live in what are called "man camps"—shanty towns of temporary housing with little to no oversight or deterrence to exploiting Native people.[69] Were the tribal nation able to intervene and prosecute non-Native offenders, it might threaten revenue.

For example, pipeline companies might find themselves needing to do more extensive (and expensive) background checks on the men they hire, to avoid wasting valuable human capital. If their workers were to be prosecuted, the companies may face further costs, such as defending their workers in tribal court—or replacing workers who are convicted for violence or banished from tribal lands. But the scope of tribal jurisdiction could present even more existential threats to energy revenue—if tribal courts were to regain jurisdiction over companies and individuals who exploit entire tribal nations.

While non-Indian batterers may not have a lobbying arm, we know that these companies do—and that they pour millions of dollars into their efforts to maintain and expand their dominion over tribal lands. Perhaps the reason why the Heritage Foundation is interested at all in far-off crimes on Indian reservations has to do with the fact that the Koch brothers (among others) are major contributors to the conservative think tank. Perhaps the reason why some Republican senators and representatives were so animated in their opposition to VAWA 2013 is that they receive significant campaign contributions from corporations interested in maximizing profits through the exploitation of land. And tribal authority simply can't stand in the way.

The Koch brothers are wealthy, in part, because of cheating tribal nations out of oil royalties in the 1980s. In 1989, the Senate Committee on Indian Affairs released a report that concluded, "Koch Oil, the largest purchaser of Indian oil in the country, was engaged in a widespread and sophisticated scheme to steal crude oil from Indians and others through fraudulent mismeasuring and misreporting."[70] A federal grand jury was convened to consider whether criminal charges should be brought against the Koch brothers, but no charges were ultimately filed. If tribal nations could prosecute non-Indians, it is conceivable that they could consider similar charges against non-Indians who enter reservations to lie and steal. Fortunately for wealthy businessmen, the current iteration of VAWA 2013 would never touch them as they are not in intimate relationships with Native women. Perhaps that is why the compromise was so successful at breaking the stalemate—tribes still can't prosecute businessmen who exploit reservation resources.

The borders of contemporary reservations, then, are completely malleable from the perspective of the powerful players of the settler state. Reservation borders only need to be respected when it is convenient. Big oil (and big energy) are interested in tribal lands but do not wish to be held accountable by tribes while in their territory. Thus, when Kevin Cramer expressed fear for his security on reservations after VAWA 2013 became law, we must consider his statement in a larger context—one that acknowledges the money to be made by destroying tribal land bases and exploiting the lives of Native people. Perhaps Representative Cramer was not so much concerned about his personal security as the security to further a never-ending colonial project of violence.

Notes

1. The full story of Representative Cramer's comments about tribal governments is available on the Last Real Indians blog: lastrealindians.com/north-dakota-con gressman-kevin-cramer-verbally-attacks-native-victims-assistance-program -director-at-state-meeting-threatens-to-ring-spirit-lake-tribal-councils-necks -by-melissa-me.

2. Several tribal nations issued sharply worded press releases about Cramer's statements. See, e.g., the Spirit Lake Nation response: lastrealindians.com/spirit-lake -nation-official-response-to-kevin-cramer-nd-congressman.

3. Robert A. Williams Jr. has explored the racist origins of federal Indian law in several book-length projects, including *The American Indian in Western Legal Thought: The Discourses of Conquest* (New York: Oxford University Press, 1990); *Like a Loaded Weapon: The Rehnquist Court, Indian Rights, and the Legal History of Racism in America* (Minneapolis: University of Minnesota Press, 2005); and *Savage Anxieties: The Invention of Western Civilization* (New York: St. Martin's, 2012).

4. Patrick Wolfe, "Settler Colonialism and the Elimination of the Native," *Journal of Genocide Research* 8, no. 1 (December 2006): 388.

5. Mishauna Goeman, "Ongoing Storms and Struggles: Gendered Violence and Resource Exploitation," in *Critically Sovereign: Indigenous Gender, Sexuality, and Feminist Studies,* ed. Joanne Barker (Durham, NC: Duke University Press, 2017), 99–126.

6. See Jacqueline Agtuca, *Safety for Native Women: VAWA and American Indian Tribes*, ed. Dorma Sahneyah (Lame Deer, MT: National Indigenous Women's Resource Center, 2014).

7. Sarah Deer, "Relocation Revisited: Sex Trafficking of Native Women in the United States," *William Mitchell Law Review* 36, no. 2 (Winter 2010): 621–683.

8. Sarah Deer, "Toward an Indigenous Jurisprudence of Rape," *Kansas Journal of Law and Public Policy* 14, no. 1 (Fall 2004): 121.

9. See generally Olwen Hufton, *The Prospect Before Her: A History of Women in Western Europe* (London: HarperCollins, 1995).

10. While sexual violence and domestic violence exist in every culture, the rates of Native men abusing Native women were significantly less than European rates. Sharon Block remarks that "very few reports document Native American men's rape of Native American women." Sharon Block, *Rape and Sexual Power in Early America* (Chapel Hill: University of North Carolina Press, 2006), 225. Native men do rape Native women on reservations today, and there is a tremendous need to confront this problem and explore the implications of introduced heteropatriarchy into the lives of Native people. I will leave that for another article, as the contours of jurisdiction over non-Indians necessitates its own exploration here.

11. See generally Andrés Reséndez, *The Other Slavery: The Uncovered Story of Indian Enslavement in America* (New York: Houghton Mifflin Harcourt, 2016) and Carl J. Ekberg, *Stealing Indian Women: Native Slavery in the Illinois Country* (Urbana: University of Illinois Press, 2007).

12. Karl Jacoby, *Shadows at Dawn: An Apache Massacre and the Violence of History* (New York: Penguin, 2008), 2.

13. David Peterson del Mar, *What Trouble I Have Seen: A History of Violence Against Wives* (Cambridge: Harvard University Press, 1996), 27.

14. A compilation of primary documents describing the brutal treatment of Native women and children in California can be found in *The Destruction of California Indians*, edited by Robert F. Heizer (Santa Barbara: Peregrine Smith, 1974; reprinted in 1993 by University of Nebraska Press).

15. Jack Norton, *When Our Worlds Cried: Genocide in Northwestern California* (San Francisco: Indian Historian Press, 1997 [1979]), 70.

16. Susan Lobo explains, "Relocation, initiated in the 1950s [was] based on government assumptions that Indian people, once removed or relocated from tribal homelands, would become urban . . . definitively." Susan Lobo, introduction, *American Indians and the Urban Experience*, ed. Susan Lobo and Kurt Peters (Lanham, MD: AltaMira, 2001), 76.

17. See generally Deer, "Relocation Revisited," 621.

18. Lawrence A. Greenfield and Steven K. Smith, "American Indians and Crime," Bureau of Justice Statistics (February 1999), www.bjs.gov/content/pub/pdf/aic.pdf.

19. Steven W. Perry, "American Indians and Crime: A BJS Statistical Profile, 1992–2002," Bureau of Justice Statistics (December 2004), https://www.bjs.gov/content/pub/pdf/aic02.pdf.

20. Patricia Tjaden and Nancy Thoennes, "Full Report of the Prevalence, Incidence, and Consequences of Violence Against Women: Findings from the National Violence Against Women Survey," National Institute of Justice (November 2000), https://www.ncjrs.gov/pdffiles1/nij/183781.pdf.

21. See US Census Bureau, Census 2010, special tabulation, Census 2010 PHC-T-19, Hispanic Origin and Race of Coupled Households: 2010, Table 1, Hispanic Origin and Race of Wife and Husband in Married-Couple Households for the United States: 2010 (April 25, 2012) (showing that more than 54 percent of Indian wives have non-Indian husbands).

22. Andre B. Rosay, "Violence against American Indian and Alaska Native Women and Men: 2010 Findings from the National Intimate Partner and Sexual Violence Survey," National Institute of Justice (May 2016), https://www.ncjrs.gov/pdffiles1/nij/249736.pdf.

23. It should be noted that the very notion of federal recognition itself is fraught with anti-Indian implications. Audra Simpson in *Mohawk Interruptus: Political Life Across the Borders of Settler* States (Durham, NC: Duke University Press, 2014) and Glen Coulthard in *Red Skin, White Masks: Rejecting the Colonial Politics of Recognition* (Minneapolis: University of Minnesota Press, 2014), as well as other scholars, have offered robust critiques of the very concept of colonial "recognition" of tribal nations.

24. Amy L. Casselman goes a step further, arguing that "jurisdictional conflicts in Indian country are also extremely gendered" because they allow non-Native men to prey on Native women with impunity. Amy L. Casselman, *Injustice in Indian Country: Jurisdiction, American Law, and Sexual Violence Against Native Women* (New York: Peter Lang, 2016), 131.

25. Interested readers are encouraged to consult David Wilkins and K. Tsianina Lomawaima, *Uneven Ground: American Indian Sovereignty and Federal Law* (Norman: University of Oklahoma Press, 2001) for a detailed account of how federal law has been used to oppress tribal nations.

26. *Oliphant* is but one example of how the US Supreme Court has constrained tribal authority. Interested readers are encouraged to consult David E. Wilkins, *American Indian Sovereignty and the U.S. Supreme Court* (Austin: University of Texas Press, 1997) and Dewi Ioan Ball, *The Erosion of Tribal Power: The Supreme Court's Silent Revolution* (Norman: University of Oklahoma Press, 2016) for other Supreme Court cases that restrict tribal autonomy and self-determination.

27. The *Oliphant* decision was applied to nonmember Indians until the "Duro fix" was passed by Congress in 1991.

28. Mark Rifkin, "Around 1978: Family, Culture, and Race in the Federal Production of Indianness," in Barker, *Critically Sovereign*, 169–206.

29. Statement of Diane Millich at the signing of the Violence Against Women Act, March 2013. Audio available at https://www.youtube.com/watch?v=ahE6D4Mj X1g. Transcript available at https://www.democracynow.org/2013/3/8/new_vi olence_against_women_act_includes.

30. Kevin Washburn, "Federal Criminal Law and Tribal Self-Determination," *North Carolina Law Review* 779, no. 3 (March 2006): 84.

31. For a full history of the Crow Dog case and the MCA, consult Sidney Harring, *Crow Dog's Case: American Indian Sovereignty, Tribal Law, and United States Law in the Nineteenth Century* (New York: Cambridge University Press, 1994).

32. Harring points out that "BIA officials had been attempting to acquire such jurisdiction since at least 1874, because they needed the coercive power of the criminal law as one means to force the assimilation of the Indians." *Crow Dog's Case*, 102.

33. Laura Sullivan, "Rape Cases on Indian Lands Go Uninvestigated," *All Things Considered*, July 25, 2007, https://www.npr.org/templates/story/story.php? storyId=12203114.

34. Alaska was added to PL280 upon statehood.

35. Carole Goldberg's groundbreaking work on Public Law 280 must be credited with documenting these problems. Her first book, *Planting Tail Feathers: Tribal Survival and Public Law 280* (Los Angeles: UCLA American Indian Studies Center, 1997), provides a comprehensive history of Public Law 280 and its aftermath.

36. In 1886, the US Supreme Court had characterized the relationship between tribal governments and state governments as "deadliest enemies." United States v. Kagama, 118 U.S. 375, 384 (1886). Thomas Biolsi explores this historical mistrust in *Deadliest Enemies: Law and Race Relations on and off the Rosebud Reservation* (Berkeley: University of California Press, 2001).

37. The tribal provisions primarily apply to women who live on Indian reservations,

trust land, or land that in some other way falls under the auspices of tribal jurisdiction. Native women living off reservation in rural or urban areas are not covered by the tribal provisions, although other general aspects of VAWA are applicable. For a comprehensive history of the role of Native women in lobbying for VAWA, see Agtuca, *Safety for Native Women.*

38. "*Special* domestic violence criminal jurisdiction" is a problematic term since the point of the legislation was to restore inherent criminal jurisdiction that was stripped away by *Oliphant.* The word "special" suggests that the federal government was bestowing or gifting the tribes with brand-new jurisdiction that they had never exercised in the past.

39. For more details on the Republican bill, see Rifkin, "Around 1978."

40. There were at least two additional provisions in VAWA 2013 that troubled Republican lawmakers. One provision mandated that LGBT populations receive nondiscriminatory services. The other provision provided more options for immigrant victims of intimate partner violence. For a complete overview of these efforts, see Nancy Whittier, "Carceral and Intersectional Feminism in Congress," *Gender and Society* 30, no. 5 (October 2016): 791–818.

41. Scott Keyes, "Top GOP Senator: Native American Juries Are Incapable of Trying White People Fairly," *ThinkProgress*, February 21, 2013, https://think progress.org/top-gop-senator-native-american-juries-are-incapable-of-trying -white-people-fairly-c399c20454cd. Emphasis added.

42. Washburn, "Federal Criminal Law and Tribal Self-Determination."

43. See, e.g., Christian M. Freitag, "Putting Martinez to the Test: Tribal Court Disposition of Due Process," *Indiana Law Journal* 72, no. 3 (July 1997): 831–867, and Bethany R. Berger, "Justice and the Outsider: Jurisdiction over Nonmembers in Tribal Legal Systems," *Arizona State Law Journal* 37, no. 4 (Winter 2005): 1047–1125.

44. Paul J. Larkin Jr. and Joseph Luppino-Esposito, "The Violence Against Women Act, Federal Criminal Jurisdiction, and Indian Tribal Courts," *BYU Journal of Public Law* 27, no. 1 (Fall 2012): 1–40. Both Larkin and Luppino-Esposito are affiliated with the Heritage Foundation.

45. 159 Cong. Rec. S582 (February 11, 2013) (statement of Sen. Grassley).

46. 159 Cong. Rec. H795 (February 28, 2013) (statement of Rep. Hastings).

47. 159 Cong. Rec. H795 (February 28, 2013) (statement of Rep. Hastings).

48. United States Commission on Civil Rights, "A Quiet Crisis: Federal Funding and Unmet Needs in Indian Country" (July 2003), http://www.usccr.gov/pubs /nao703/nao204.pdf.

49. Talton v. Mayes, 163 U.S. 376 (1898).

50. See Robert J. McCarthy, "Civil Rights in Tribal Courts: The Indian Bill of Rights at Thirty Years," *Idaho Law Review* 34, no. 3 (Summer 1998): 465.

51. These include the rights against unreasonable search and seizure, the right against self-incrimination, the right to counsel, and the right to a jury trial.

52. Prepared Statement of Senator Chuck Grassley of Iowa, Consideration of the

Violence Against Women Act (February 4, 2013), http://www.grassley.senate
.gov/news/Article.cfm?customel_dataPa geID_1502=44478.

53. 159 Cong. Rec. S576 (February 11, 2013) (statement of Sen. Coburn).

54. NAACP, "Federal Legislative Civil Rights Report Card—National Edition"
(2013), http://www.naacp.org/wp-content/uploads/2016/04/113th National
Report Card.1.PDF.

55. 159 Cong. Rec. H795 (February 28, 2013) (statement of Rep. Hastings).

56. John Cornyn, quoted in Alexandria Baca, "Sen. John Cornyn Cites Tribal
Provision in Vote against Anti-violence Bill," *Dallas News*, February 13, 2013,
http://trailblazersblog.dallasnews.com/2013/02/sen-cornyn-votes-against
-anti-violence-bill-cites-unconstitutional-amendment.html.

57. 159 Cong. Rec. H795 (February 28, 2013) (statement of Rep. Hastings).

58. John Roades, "An American Tradition: The Religious Persecution of Native
Americans," *Montana Law Review* 52, no. 1 (Winter 1991): 13.

59. 159 Cong. Rec. S. 510 (February 11, 2013) (statement of Sen. Grassley).

60. Eric Cantor, quoted in Seung Min Kim, "Senate Renews Anti-violence Law,"
Politico, February 12, 2013, https://www.politico.com/story/2013/02/senate
-passes-violence-against-women-act-087518.

61. Jonathon Weisman, "Measure to Protect Women Stuck on Tribal Land Issue,"
New York Times, February 10, 2013, http://www.nytimes.com/2013/02/11/us
/politics/violence-against-women-act-held-up-by-tribal-land-issue.html.

62. Paul J. Larkin, "Send in the Lawyers: The House Passes the Senate's Violence
Against Women Act," *The Daily Signal*, March 1, 2013, http://dailysignal.com
/2013/03/01/send-in-the-lawyers-the-house-passes-the-senates-violence
-against-women-act.

63. This requires a spouse or dating relationship. The two parties (defendant and
victim) must be spouses, former spouses, dating partners, former dating partners, or share a child in common.

64. Debra Utacia Krol, "Pascua Yaqui Tribe First to Use VAWA to Prosecute Non-
Indian," *Indian Country Today*, June 9, 2017, https://indiancountrymedianet
work.com/news/politics/pascua-yaqui-tribe-first-use-vawa-prosecute-non
-indian.

65. Dollar General Corp. v. Mississippi Band of Choctaw Indians, 136 S. Ct. 2159
(2016).

66. Theresa Rocha Beardall and Raquel Escobar, "What Then Remains of the Sovereignty of the Indians? The Significance of Social Closure and Ambivalence
in *Dollar General v. Mississippi Choctaw*," *The Indigenous Peoples' Journal of
Law, Culture and Resistance* 3, no. 1 (January 2016): 3–38.

67. Maile Arvin, Eve Tuck, and Angie Morrill, "Decolonizing Feminism: Challenging Connections between Settler Colonialism and Heteropatriarchy," *Feminist
Formations* 25, no. 1 (Spring 2013): 8–34, http://muse.jhu.edu/content/crossref
/journals/feminist_formations/v025/25.1.arvin.html.

68. Deer, "Relocation Revisited."

69. Kathleen Finn et al., "Responsible Resource Development and Prevention of Sex Trafficking: Safeguarding Native Women and Children on the Fort Berthold Reservation," *Harvard Journal of Law and Gender* 40, no. 1 (Winter 2017): 1–51.

70. Senate Report 101–216 (1989). According to *Indian Country Today*, "The committee sent the report to the Justice Department and DOJ convened a grand jury to examine possible criminal charges, but no indictments had been returned before the group was disbanded in 1992. In 1999, a federal court found Koch Industries guilty in a whistleblower case brought by estranged Koch brothers Bill and Frederick, who got a share of the fines imposed by the government. The tribes got nothing." Tanya H. Lee, "Money Koch Bros. Stole from Tribes Could Swing Mid-Term Elections," *Indian Country Today*, October 28, 2014, https://indiancountrymedianetwork.com/news/politics/money-koch-bros -stole-from-tribes-could-swing-mid-term-elections.

2

Race, Blood, and Belonging

Transnational Blackfoot Bands and Families along
the US-Canada Border, 1855–1915

Jeffrey P. Shepherd

The Blackfoot Confederacy spanned much of the present-day Montana-
Alberta borderlands through the late nineteenth century, but by the beginning of the twentieth century, the Niitsitapi faced the rapid colonization
of their lands in the form of Anglo settlement, transcontinental railways,
the US-Canada Boundary Commission, the military, and other agents of the
state—the legacy of broken treaties and the settler-colonial histories of the
United States and Canada. The hardening of the border that accompanied
these developments did not, however, terminate the cross-border movement
of Blackfoot bands. As the multiple examples in this chapter demonstrate—
particularly the transnational adoption dispute over Blackfoot youth Albert
Spearson—families visited each other across the line and band members registered on tribal rolls in the United States and Canada, developing fluid yet
contradictory notions of status, blood, and citizenship. In a very different
example of Blackfoot manipulation of the legal jurisdictions marked by the
international boundary highlighted in this chapter, the murder conviction
of a Blackfoot man named Spopee illuminates the intersection of Indigenous
notions of justice, racism, violence, and the carceral power of the US colonial state.

Looking at the Blackfoot Confederacy's border crossings contributes to
scholarship investigating Indigenous peoples' negotiation of international
boundaries that bisect aboriginal homelands. This growing body of work
has emphasized the social and cultural dimensions of these histories, but
there remains room to explore the legal implications of overlapping state,

territorial, and national jurisdictions and the confusion resulting from Canadian and American treaties made with Native people throughout the borderlands.[1] Indigenous peoples bisected by borders have contended with racial regimes rooted in different histories; they endured nation-states and the confusing discourse over citizenship, status, recognition, and multiple sets of immigration policies that have labeled them as aliens, foreigners, wards of the state, and refugees. For all of its compelling contributions, borderlands scholarship has not directed enough attention to issues of Indigenous sovereignty and law within borderlands spaces and it tacitly promotes the notion that Native people were separated after the borderlands became a "bordered land." Conversely, "American Indian history" has largely remained locked into nation-based frameworks. A critical legal perspective is especially important for Native peoples straddling international boundaries and confronting reservation borders. As observed by Dudziak and Volpp, "Law is an important technology in the drawing of dividing lines between American identities and the boundaries (or lack of boundaries) around American global power. Borders are constructed in law, not only through formal legal controls on entry and exit but also through the construction of rights of citizenship and noncitizenship, and the regulation or legitimation of American power in other parts of the world."[2] Because these boundaries are constructs of law, they are crucial sites of deconstruction.

Building on such insights, I argue that Blackfoot bands and families negotiated the legal contradictions and jurisdictional complexities of life as transnational actors in the US-Canada borderlands and sought to reconfigure them to their customary patterns of movement and interaction with their aboriginal homelands. Between 1855, with the signing of the Lame Bull Treaty (Blackfoot Treaty) in the United States, the signing of Treaty 7 in Canada in 1877, and the onset of World War I, Blackfoot bands undermined numerous international, national, territorial, provincial, and tribal legal regimes. At the borderlands of two imperial nation-states, Blackfoot bands manipulated the "legal voids" between competing notions of Indigenous sovereignty, wardship, and national citizenship. These voids and contradictions stem largely from the colonial nature of "Indian Law" as a combination of erasure and extermination, on the one hand, and racial assimilation and transformation, on the other.[3] South of the "Medicine Line," Blackfoot people saw their status deteriorate as judges and legislators redefined them as wards of the state who lacked legal personhood and the protections of the Constitution. North of the line, the Blackfoot faced Canadian assimilation and extinguishment of Native land title. These related Indian policies signaled the settler-colonial mindset of Canadian and American officials, but implementation at the edge of the United States and Canadian Dominion exposed legal fractures the Niitsitapi navigated to survive a changing world.[4]

As many scholars have noted, Native people demonstrated great agility when playing two imperial powers against each other or when they maximized the uncertainties of legal regimes in frontier spaces. Native people maintained ties to indigenous landscapes well beyond their bifurcation by international boundaries and reservation borders. This is true in the case of Albert Spearson, which entailed a transnational debate over adoption that revealed the permeability of these borders and the limits of the state to dictate familial norms to the Blackfoot. Just as law created and codified borders, Volpp and Dudziak alert us to the limitations of law to transcend particular borders of cultural practice—another form of authority beyond the realm of jurists. This chapter analyzes the occasional power of nation-states to police those same boundaries in moments of "crisis." As discussed in the case of Spopee, a "Canadian Indian" who allegedly murdered a white man in Canada and buried the body in the United States, officials invoked the American legal system's extensive carceral technologies in complete disregard for due process and Native rights. The trial and imprisonment of Spopee epitomized the reach of the American legal apparatus to penetrate the legal voids of the northern borderlands. In this demonstration of power, we see that the settler state can and will integrate peripheral spaces into sites of violent subjugation. To anchor these episodes in the Blackfoot borderlands world of the turn of the twentieth century, this essay discusses numerous examples of Indigenous movement across the international boundary, and questions of surveillance, power, and policing, and then turns its attention squarely to the legal borderlands Albert Spearson, Spopee, and their Blackfoot kin encountered on both sides of the US-Canadian border.

The Blackfoot Confederacy originated in the Algonquian-speaking cultures of the eastern woodlands before moving westward to the northern Plains of Alberta and Saskatchewan. By the nineteenth century, the Blackfoot Confederacy consisted primarily of the Siksika, Kainah, and Peigan-Pikuni (or Piegan).[5] As the Blackfoot mastered the horse, they experienced population growth, increased military power, and an expanded economic presence that enabled them to move southward into present-day Montana. Before the geopolitical map changed as a result of accelerated Anglo westward expansion in the 1840s, Blackfoot bands extended from present-day Edmonton to south of present-day Billings and from the Rocky Mountains to central Saskatchewan.[6]

Transcontinental migrations were part and parcel of the tectonic shifts of the 1840s following the transfer of Oregon Country to the United States from Britain, war with Mexico, and the discovery of gold in California.[7] In response to this population boom, the United States orchestrated the 1855 Lame Bull Treaty under the leadership of Washington governor Isaac Stevens with numerous northern Plains tribes, including the Blackfoot Confederacy. The treaty outlined Blackfoot lands across most of northern Montana. Emerging from the shadow of Manifest Destiny, Indian policy in this era stalled at a crossroads between removal and an awkward system of treaty making and reservations. The result was a unique set of stipulations. The 1855 treaty left aboriginal land title intact, it did not mandate concentration onto reservations, and it lacked a system of education or agricultural instruction. As William E. Farr notes, "It was not a so-called land treaty at all; it was a peace treaty" more characteristic of an earlier era in federal Indian policy.[8]

The treaty of "peace and friendship" caused immediate confusion. It facilitated westward migration and the construction of a transcontinental railroad by placing the Blackfeet on a reservation to be shared with Gros Ventre and Assiniboine. The federal government sent a few agents to the "reservation," but the remoteness, weather, financial difficulties, and other pressures limited their influence over the Blackfeet. The reservation boundaries remained unmapped; the northern border of the reservation was the international boundary as well. Non-Indians crossed into the reservation and poached game, cut timber, grazed cattle, and diverted rivers crossing the reservation. Most importantly, Blackfoot people paid little attention to the lines intended to limit their movement and separate them from their kin to the north. In short, the reservation was a fiction that epitomized the unpredictability of the legal regimes and the power of the state in the Canadian-US borderlands.[9]

Blackfoot worries increased as events on both sides of the international border signaled a new era for the Confederacy. On the US side, the completion of the transcontinental railroad in 1867 accelerated non-Indian settlement and commerce in Montana. In reaction to public outcries about massacres at Sand Creek in 1864 and Washita in 1868 and to the growing demands from "Friends of the Indian" to transfer control over Indian affairs to civilian hands, President Grant promoted the "Peace Policy" as an enlightened response to military violence. The Peace Policy, which promoted concentration of Indians onto reservations, merged with infighting between the House and the Senate that led to the end of treaty making in 1871, leaving Native Americans in a particularly ambiguous position as noncitizens barred from the privileges of the Fourteenth Amendment, but with a legacy of rights reserved over nearly a century of federal treaty making and litigation.

As US federal Indian policy shifted gears, Canadian confederation signaled a new era for the Blackfoot and other First Nations. Confederation released Canada from direct British rule to Dominion status, which was a form of quasi-national independence.[10] The 1867 British North America Act created Canada as a self-governing federation and in 1868 it established the short-lived Department of Secretary of State to oversee Natives. Oversight included codifying Indigenous identity in the 1869 passage of the Enfranchisement Act, which defined an "Indian" as a person with at least one-quarter Indian blood. This act also categorized Indians as wards, although if they chose detribalization they could become Canadian citizens. In addition, the act was gendered: it stated that non-Indian women marrying Indian men took Indian status, while Indian women marrying non-Indian men lost their status and tribal affiliation.[11]

These broad shifts in policy failed to curtail Blackfoot transnationalism. In 1870, Montana superintendent of Indian Affairs Lieutenant Colonel Alfred Sully wrote that the Blackfeet were "one of the largest nations of Indians at present in our country," but "they do not all properly belong to the United States." Overlooking the terms of Canadian confederation, he observed that "they claim in common a section of the country from the British line south some miles to the city of Helena, and north of the line to the Saskatchewan River." Sully added that "they of course do not take into consideration any treaties we have with Great Britain in regard to our boundary line, but look upon the whole of the country both north and south of the line as theirs."[12] Sully's successor, J. Armitage, noted in 1871 that the Blackfeet were "governed by imaginary boundary-lines and express themselves perfectly willing to remain in what they consider their own country." Agent William T. Ensign, who replaced Armitage, observed that the northern Piegan came to the agency more frequently than the Blood or Blackfoot bands, which "range north of the British line, from two hundred and fifty to four hundred miles from the agency."[13]

Blackfoot movement across their homelands sparked renewed efforts to map and reinforce borders and boundaries. Following the Treaty of Ghent in 1814, the Convention of 1818 established the boundary between the United States and British possessions in present-day Canada. Surveyors set the border at the 49th parallel, which ran between the western Great Lakes at the Lake of the Woods to the Rocky Mountains. Echoing the peaceful resolution of the dispute over the Oregon Territory in the 1840s, neither power paid much attention to the border until Native movement made its precise location a matter of international significance. In 1870, President Grant proposed a joint commission to map the border between the Lake of the Woods and the Rocky Mountains, and by 1874—nearly twenty years after the US-Mexico Boundary Commission completed its work along the southern border—the British, Canadian Dominion, and United States governments successfully surveyed and marked the boundary.[14]

Between the trial of Spopee in the 1870s and the transnational custody battle over Albert Spearson in the early twentieth century, the settler-colonial nation-states drastically diminished Blackfoot lands through the renegotiation of treaties and executive orders. American officials' redrawing of the lines of the Blackfeet reservation left tribal members with only a fraction of the land base established in the 1855 Lame Bull Treaty.[15] President Grant issued an executive order in 1873 to reduce the reservation by carving off the lands between the Missouri River and the Musselshell River south to the old Common Hunting Grounds and west to the Rocky Mountains. Another executive order in 1874 reduced access to the Teton and Sun Rivers. To make matters worse, there were several thousand Gros Ventres, Assiniboine, and River Crows crowded onto the shrinking reservation.[16] Agent John S. Wood wrote that the new boundaries were a "continual source of complaint" and he added that White Calf, a signatory of the Lame Bull Treaty, vehemently protested the elimination of hunting grounds on the reservation.[17]

The same year that the Boundary Commission completed its work and President Grant signed a second executive order again shrinking the Montana reservation, Indian agent R. F. May reported that the Blackfeet and Bloods repeatedly crossed the international boundary and preferred to stay in the north. May agreed that the 1874 executive order reservation was a failure because it lacked important hunting grounds.[18] In addition, the movement of the Flathead, Blackfeet, Cree, and Assiniboine between reservations was a source of great frustration for agents across the Plains. In correspondence between Charles Medary, the agent for Flathead, and agent Wood at the Blackfeet Agency, Wood said that he was "quite powerless to keep them [the Blackfeet] at home, without any military assistance which is not available here at present." Medary encouraged Wood to "keep the Indians within the liberal limits set apart for them by treaty," as inadequate as those limits may have been.[19]

Canada similarly began asserting its control over First Nations bands in the western Plains during the 1870s. Without prior consultation, Canada assumed control over lands previously controlled by the Hudson's Bay Company, but Canada lacked the personnel to effectively administer Dominion law. It further sought to restrict Blackfoot movement to territory north of the line with the creation of the North-West Mounted Police (NWMP), to prohibit Blackfeet from crossing the international boundary, and through policies that tied their status to the Canadian nation-state. Established in 1873, the NWMP were modeled after the Royal Irish Constabulatory (1820), an imperial paramilitary force developed in India. Headquartered in Fort Walsh and Fort McCleod, the Mounties functioned as police, judge, jury, and executioner of Dominion law in the Canadian West.[20]

As the Mounties oversaw Native communities and policed the border, the Dominion placed Indian Affairs under the jurisdiction of the Department of the Interior. Shifting control of Indians to the Department of the Interior signaled the Canadian government's effort to further scrutinize Native status and restrict tribal independence at the same time that Blackfeet and other First Nations accelerated their cross-border movements. The declining numbers of buffalo and dwindling of their aboriginal territory had created a crisis for the Blackfeet, who moved across the Montana-Alberta borderlands along with the Metis, Assiniboine, Cree, and Sioux, who similarly exposed the permeability of national boundaries through their transnational migrations. Assuming that the narrowing of racial and citizenship boundaries would help to control the Native population, in 1876 the Dominion passed the Indian Act, which consolidated "and revamped preconfederation legislation of the Canadas into a nation-wide framework."[21] The act promised to protect, civilize, and assimilate First Nations peoples pursuant to its broad program of paternalism. It retained preconfederation policies of quieting aboriginal land tenure, and it revised the definition of "Indian," according to Olive Dickason, "as any person registered as an Indian, or entitled to be registered; as well as any person of Indian blood belonging to a band and entitled to use its land." The act repeated stipulations based on gender and added that children born to white men and Native women would not be considered Indians.[22]

Rather than the hegemonic codification of a singular status for Indians in Canada, the United States allowed a patchwork of categories rooted in racial supremacy and settler-colonial law. Based on the Doctrine of Discovery—which also structured British colonial policy—the United States launched the treaty system after the ratification of the Constitution, which, importantly, noted Indians in two relatively minor ways. The "silence" of the Constitution grounded the view that Native nations were outside the governing document of the new United States. These silences had transformed into a booming chorus of anti-Indianism and Indian erasure by the 1830s epitomized by the Indian Removal Act and the rulings of the Marshall Court. The key component of the "Marshall Trilogy" was the ambiguous view that Indian polities were "domestic-dependent nations" that sat inside the territorial boundaries of the United States and somewhat beyond the Constitution.[23]

Although the original inhabitants of the continent were both inside and outside of American law—at the unstable edge of settler-colonial assimilation, racist removal from the national body politic, and self-governance—the post–Civil War legal regime sought clarification of the status of Indians. Between 1868 and the passage of the Fourteenth Amendment and the 1903 Supreme Court ruling in *Lonewolf v. Hitchcock*, Native peoples saw their status as independent nations recognized through treaties radically transformed. Rulings such as *Ex Parte Crow Dog* (1883), *Elk v. Wilkins* (1884), the Major Crimes Act (1885), and *United States v. Kagama* (1886) plunged Native people into a legal borderland as subaltern wards of the state.[24]

North of the Medicine Line, the conditions of Native peoples were similarly dire. Following the passage of the Indian Act, Canada negotiated Treaty 7 with the Blackfoot Confederacy in 1877 at Blackfoot Crossing in Alberta. With support from the prestigious head chief, Crowfoot, the Confederacy signed Treaty 7, which set aside one reserve on the Bow River for the Blackfoot, Blood, and Sarcee and another reserve west of Fort Macleod for the northern Piegans. Within a few months, the Bloods asked for a separate reserve on the Belly River. These three reserves constituted the remnant of Niitsitapi lands after the treaty, which, unbeknownst to the Confederacy, quieted title to the remainder of their territory. Treaty 7 sought to fix bands onto specific reserves with codified racial identities tying them to the Dominion of Canada, yet the language about "citizenship" *confirmed and confused* their status as Canadian citizens or Indians vis-à-vis the state.[25]

Treaty 7 reflected the perceptual chasm between First Nations bands and the Dominion over foundational issues such as land tenure, rights, status, and self-determination. Leaders such as White Calf had witnessed the failures of the United States to abide by the terms of the Lame Bull Treaty. Other signatories of Treaty 7 either were in attendance in 1855 or had knowledge of American policy thereafter and expressed concern about the Canadian promises of protection, education, and material advancement. Language differences prohibited the bands from fully understanding the scope and intent of the treaty. Translators had limited knowledge of both English and Native tongues. The most significant outcome of this confusion was the failure of Canadian policymakers to explain, and of Blackfoot leaders to comprehend, that by signing the treaty, band representatives agreed to the quieting of title to their land. As First Nations descendants of treaty signatories have noted, their language contained no equivalent of the words secede or surrender in reference to land.[26]

These changes in policy, including an 1879 reduction of the Montana reservation, ignored the conditions fueling cross-border movement. The destruction of the bison caused northern Piegans to migrate into the United States, and a brutally cold winter combined with Anglo hunting of Piegan game narrowed their options for survival. The growing pressure of American troops following Sitting Bull pushed some Natives northward, and Canadian policymakers became increasingly nervous that American filibusters threatened national sovereignty. Despite the uncertain situation facing the Confederacy, they persevered as a unified people. Agent John Young noted in 1879 that he believed that the Blackfoot, Bloods, and Piegan on either side of the line were "really one people . . . known by the general name of Piegan."[27] Emerging from the records by many names, members of the Blackfoot Confederacy shared vulnerability in addition to identity, a fact Spopee and Albert Spearson's families came to know very keenly.

Just as devastating as the material conditions facing Native communities were the legal regimes that sought to erase the sovereignty of the Niitsitapi peoples north and south of the line. In the Montana-Alberta borderlands—best characterized by legal voids, jurisdictional competition, and border uncertainties that challenged the technologies of surveillance—one case reflected the power of the American carceral state to penetrate those legal borderlands and punish one man: Spopee (Turtle), a Blood Indian born north of the line and convicted of murdering an American man in Canada.

During the winter of 1879 and 1880, Blood Indians like Spopee headed south, following a migration of buffalo during one of the coldest years on record. According to William Farr, "Some of the Indians went to their newly created reserves, expecting the Canadian government to feed them. Those expectations were out of the question. Canadian authorities at the time of Treaty 7 had disastrously miscalculated the disappearance of the buffalo north of the American border." Over three thousand northern Piegan, Blood, and Sarcee camped around Fort Macleod in September 1879, waiting for annuities and relief. Edgar B. Dewdney, commissioner of Indian Affairs for the North-West Territories, told those who were starving to follow the buffalo south into the United States.[28] Spopee and his wife had done so before, going to the Blackfeet Agency to receive rations like other "Canadian Indians."[29]

Other than a few sparse government reports, little is known of Spopee before he entered the legal borderlands of transnational criminal law. Spopee, born in Canada around 1850, was a member of the Fisheater band of Bloods, led by Meskato (Red Crow). His mother was Awakasiaki, or Antelope Woman; the Catholic census files for 1874 list her husband as Siapiatow (Comes in the Night). According to Farr, Spopee was related to Red Crow, probably as a cousin, and Spopee's aunt Natawista (Holy Snake Woman) was the sister of Seen from Afar. Holy Snake Woman was married to Alexander Culbertson, the fur trader from the American Fur Company and founder of Fort Benton. After the signing of Treaty 7 in 1877 at Blackfoot Crossing, Blood annuity books note that Spopee appeared for a payment in 1878. Band rolls state that he was twenty-nine years old and had a wife and a daughter.[30]

In 1879, during the migration south, events took a turn for the worse when Spopee and his traveling companion Good Runner allegedly killed a white man named Walmesley in Canada. For reasons that were hotly debated in court, Spopee and Good Runner brought their victim across the international boundary. A Blackfoot woman found Walmesley's body that November along Cut Bank Creek, north of the Montana Agency, and reported her discovery to Agent Young.[31] Agent Young informed Montana governor Potts, local sheriffs, and Major William Winder at Fort Macleod in Alberta.[32]

Contradicting reports and jurisdictional uncertainties associated with the location of the crime and Spopee's status as American, Blood, or Canadian quickly muddied the case. Newspaper coverage added to the confusion. The December 1 edition of the *Saskatchewan Herald* reported that "about two weeks ago the authorities here [Fort Macleod] received a letter from the Blackfoot Agency, to the effect that a white man supposed to hail from this country had been found near that place, with a bullet through his chest and a crushed head."[33] Agent Young, who initially took charge of the case, eliminated several suspects when Good Runner admitted that he and Spopee had followed the buffalo south and joined up with Walmesley, who was hunting the wolves that preyed on the bison, before he crossed into the United States. According to Good Runner, Spopee told him that Walmesley had hit and insulted him, and Spopee promised to kill Walmesley for the insult. Good Runner claimed that Spopee shot Walmesley and crushed his head and they then carried the body south of the boundary and buried it along Cut Bank Creek.[34]

Considering the transnational character of the crime, the legal jurisdiction for arresting Spopee was dubious. It was not clear that Governor Potts had the authority to dispatch Chouteau County sheriff John Healy and deputy sheriff Jefferson Talbert to capture a Blood Indian born and registered in Canada for an alleged crime committed in Canada. Acting on assumed federal jurisdiction, deputy US marshal Basil M. Boyle, who had only recently arrived to Fort Benton, set out in search of Spopee himself. Alexander M. Botkin, a veteran US marshall for Montana, wrote to the office of the US attorney general suggesting that this matter went beyond the jurisdiction of the governor's office and the sheriff's, advocating instead that the US military or the Indian Bureau take control of the case. He also noted that US officials should obtain the cooperation of the NWMP.[35]

Under orders from Governor Potts, Sheriff Healy ignored Botkin and went in search of Spopee among the thousands of Indians camped in the Judith Basin. Convinced of the legal basis for pursuing the suspect in Blackfoot territory, Healy reached the camp of Running Rabbit, the Blood chief overseeing the lodge in which Spopee sought refuge. Healy spoke to Running Rabbit in Blackfoot as he stared down the Blood band members, most of whom knew Healy because of his previous marriage to a daughter of Many Spotted Horses, leader of the Many Fat Horses band of the Bloods. Apparently the Blackfeet had adopted Healy after a tense encounter with The Weasel Head, another band leader, years before. The Weasel Head sought revenge against Healy for a previous insult, but Healy defended himself and spared the life of The Weasel Head in public. The Weasel Head became friends with Healy and adopted him into the band. Healy was thus acting on the fringes and borderlands of American law as well as the law of the Blackfoot, both of which he claimed familiarity with. Perhaps recognizing Healy's unique relationship to his tribe, Running Rabbit called Spopee to meet Healy, and before Spopee could escape, Healy had him in handcuffs.[36]

The trial lurched forward in unusual ways. Healy brought Spopee to Fort Benton, where probate judge John J. Donnelly conducted an examination and extracted a "confession" from Spopee. Spopee contradicted Good Runner's statement, claiming that he had actually urged Spopee to kill Walmesley. Regardless, Healy took them to prison in Helena, but the case did not go to trial for nearly a year due to lack of appropriations from Congress.[37] Despite the dubious jurisdiction of an American court's authority to convict a Native man from Canada for a crime committed in Canada, it was unclear whether Indians in Montana Territory were legally persons accountable under the law, despite the affirmative ruling of Indian humanity in *Standing Bear v. Crook*. Spopee was also "indigent" in the eyes of Canadian law and this underscored his liminal status. Natives could not vote or serve on a jury in the United States, but Indians in Montana and Dakota Territories could in some instances serve as witnesses and give testimony in court. Although unusual it was nonetheless irrelevant because Spopee was from Canada and the 1876 Indian Act categorized Indians of the Plains as "wards of the state" lacking standing in court. According to William Farr, "there was no definition of his rights as an Indian alien by the Americans, who were concerned only with the location of the murder, and neither the NWMP nor Canadian authorities demanded, or perhaps wanted, legal extradition."[38] Representatives from Canada made no request. Thus, Spopee was in a triple legal bind: he was a ward of the state as a Blackfoot south of the line and as an alien non-American and noncitizen of Canada who allegedly killed an Anglo north of the line, and he was a person of color in a US court.

His counsel sought humane representation of Spopee, but racial prejudice and the colonial nature of the legal system compromised the procedures. His court case began on November 29, 1880, in the federal grand jury of the Third Judicial District of Montana Territory, which charged that Spopee "feloniously, unlawfully, and of his malice aforethought, did make an assault . . . in and upon the body of one Charles Walmesley in the peace of god and of the United States." Associate judge Everton J. Conger presided over the case. Good Runner was a witness against Spopee *and* he was on trial with Spopee until the judge dropped the charges against Good Runner but kept him as a witness against Spopee.[39] During the brief testimony by Spopee, he said that he killed Walmesley in self-defense, after Walmesley threatened to kill him. Spopee admitted that the murder occurred north of the boundary and he confessed that he and Good Runner dragged the body south of the line to avoid capture by the NWMP. In contrast to the willingness of American jurists to seemingly violate Canadian sovereignty and legal jurisdiction by ruling on a crime committed outside of the country, Spopee was cognizant of those legal boundaries. Addressing the judge, Spopee asked, "If it is good to hang me, why don't you let Macleod do it? I killed the man in his country."[40] Spopee asked for witnesses, including White Calf, but the judge denied his requests on the basis that a "citizen" of another country lacked standing in American courts—overlooking the fact that Spopee likewise shared this lack of standing. Upon sentencing, Spopee said, "When I saw the Sioux I killed them; I stole their horses; my heart is brave. You are a great chief and can hang me, but you have no right to do so. I have spoken straight, and am done." Unmoved, the judge ordered Spopee's execution.[41]

These peculiarities continued after conviction and sentencing. The judge rejected the defense team's request for an appeal, but both Judge Conger and Governor Potts agreed to the commutation of the death penalty. President Hayes also approved the postponement of the execution and Spopee was instead imprisoned for life.[42] Spopee first served his sentence in Detroit until officials transferred him to Washington, DC, where he spent nearly thirty years. For reasons that remain unclear, President Woodrow Wilson issued a pardon in 1914 and ordered Spopee's immediate release and return to Montana. He briefly gained notoriety for his travails, but he died of old age within a few years.[43]

Spopee's story reveals the common practice of Niitsitapi people of crossing the international boundary, and it exemplifies how the US legal system violated Canadian sovereignty by extending US jurisdiction to a crime committed beyond its own territorial space. The United States has claimed extraterritorial jurisdiction when it believed that American law served the interests of civilization, which frequently manifested itself in the designs of US imperialism itself. In this case, the demand for justice in the killing of a white man by a person of color overrode the formal legal boundaries of any one state. The use of the legal apparatus to exact revenge for a white male American killed in another country, through the punishment of a Native person not enrolled in the United States, demonstrated the power of US imperialism to erase international boundaries and violate the rights of citizens and noncitizens at will. Thus, extraterritorial jurisdiction followed the dictates of American empire and the prerogatives of white settler colonialism.

The historical record leaves us with very little documentation with which we can draw conclusions about the thoughts of Spopee and the more general reactions of the Blackfeet and Blood bands that might have been familiar with the trial. Placed within the context of relations between Indigenous peoples and the US state, particularly the agents and institutions of the state charged with meting out corporal punishment and imprisonment, this act echoes others throughout the American West in the late nineteenth century. But unlike the historical memories of the Dakota associated with President Lincoln's execution of several dozen of its people in the 1860s, Spopee's trial and imprisonment seem to have fallen into obscurity. The removal from his band in Canada and entrapment in the US legal system not only alienated him from his culture but also very specifically barred him from the systems of conflict resolution, restorative justice, and ethically appropriate punishments that were the customs of his people. Had he faced his Blood peers and the band elders that held oversight of such complex issues, Spopee could have potentially atoned for his crimes in a more reasonable manner. Instead, he was tried in the colonial courts of a foreign nation-state and although spared the death penalty, his near-lifetime imprisonment resulted in what some scholars term a "social death." Disappeared from his people, extracted from his culture, and encased in brick and steel thousands of miles from his birthplace, Spopee suffered a kind of death that violated the legal norms of his own culture and cast doubt on the moral and ethical substance of US law itself.

Although the case against Spopee seems to indicate the closure of legal voids in the US-Canada borderlands, there were other troubling trends facing Blackfeet that revealed their unlikely evasion of nation-state boundaries. As part of the effort to confine Blackfeet to the reservation and police their movement, in 1880 the US military rounded up southern Piegan and "US Blackfeet" and forced them onto the reservation in Montana. The Indian Bureau, bolstered by the remaining US military forces, required Blackfeet to request permission to leave the reservation. In effect, the superintendents overseeing the reservation ignored the sovereignty of the southern Piegan as noted in the Lame Bull Treaty of 1855. These actions mirrored the denial of agency and self-determination to Native people that characterized court decisions such as *Kagama* during the 1880s, which signaled the pivotal and painful shift from the outright military conquest of Native peoples, to the rise of the US legal system and the concomitant extinguishment of Indigenous sovereignty.[44]

In the face of escalating enforcement, Blackfoot bands crossed the international boundary and reservation borders as they tried to cope with the decline in buffalo, the dangers of whiskey traffickers, and Canadian and US assimilation policies. The Indian agent at Fort Macleod, Alberta, wrote to Agent John Young at the Blackfeet Agency in Montana about several Nez Perce who had accompanied Blackfoot bands across the border and were living on the Blood reserve. Young replied to the agent at Fort Macleod and told him that six horses were stolen from the Flathead reservation and that they had reliable information from Crane Bull, a "Piegan from Canada," that those horses were taken to the Blackfeet reservation in Montana.[45] An 1881 series of letters between US commissioner of Indian Affairs Hiram Price to the Indian agent in Browning acknowledged complaints from Montana residents that Blackfoot bands crossed the border with impunity. Young was especially cowed by territorial representative Martin Maginnis, who observed that "Indians from the British Possessions and from our own reservations are roaming over the country hunting and . . . depredating upon the cattle of the stockmen."[46] Tensions were similarly brewing north of the international boundary. Head chief Crowfoot told Methodist missionary John McDougal, "If left to ourselves, we are gone. The whiskey brought among us by the traders is fast killing us all off and we are powerless before the evil. We are unable to pitch (camps and lodges) anywhere that the trader cannot follow us. Our horses, buffalo robes, and other articles of trade go for whiskey, a large number of our people have killed one another and perished in various ways under the influence."[47]

Such comments highlighted the changing nature of Blackfoot life in the Montana-Alberta borderlands, where regimes of boundary maintenance had replaced the open grasslands. Rather than free movement across their homelands, Niitsitapi encountered myriad systems regulating where they lived and with whom they associated on both sides of the international border and throughout their reservations and reserves. Agent Keller from the Crow reservation told the commissioner of Indian Affairs that he wanted members of the fourteen lodges of Piegans, some of whom hailed from Canada, to leave the Crow reservation in southeastern Montana and relocate to the Blackfeet reservation in northwestern Montana. In response, the commissioner chastised Agent Young on the Blackfeet reservation to keep the Indians on their "proper" reservation and to stop them from trafficking horses across the reservation and international borders.[48]

Concerns about cross-boundary movement dominated correspondence between officials in both nation-states. Colonel Ruger, from the 18th Infantry out of Helena, contacted Agent Young about Blackfeet from the Judith Basin crossing the international boundary with stolen cattle and horses. Ruger wanted to know how Young planned keep the Piegans on the reservation, how much rations they received, and whether there was game to hunt.[49] He added,

> Will you please give me any information you have or obtainable at the agency, as to the present whereabouts of the Blood Indians, Canadian, who were last winter in the same vicinity in the Musselshell Country with Indians belonging to your agency, particularly the Bloods of Running Rabbit's band and those with him. I would also like to have any information you can give of bands, with names of chiefs, and numbers of lodges of all Canadian Bloods and Blackfeet that were this side of the boundary line last winter, where and when they crossed the line to this side, their routes and movements thereafter. I would be glad, also, for any information bearing on the general question of the presence this side of the line of the Canadian Indians, their numbers, conduct, etc.[50]

Numerous incidents highlighted the permeability of the border throughout the 1880s. During the spring of 1881, a party of Kainah left Montana for Alberta after a winter of hunting buffalo. American troops encountered the group and told them that they could not offer rations because they were Canadian Indians. One of the soldiers noticed that Medicine Calf, who lived mainly in Canada, was wearing a medal from the United States, which he received for signing the Lame Bull Treaty of 1855. Admitting that they were "American Indians" based on the medal worn by Medicine Calf, the soldiers gave them food, but they must have been surprised as the group immediately returned to Canada. In short, Medicine Calf crossed the border in an apparent rejection of the settler-colonial divisions across his homelands.[51] Like Medicine Calf, young Blackfoot men similarly crossed the line. One Kainah man named Killed Both Sides recalled that he and other men "went [south] across the line to raid the Gros Ventres" during the 1880s. "It took us four days on horseback to reach their camps. During the night we went through the brush in the valley and stole the horses from the camp. After each of us had taken two horses, we rode northeast, and it took two days and nights of steady travelling before we reached home." In 1886 and 1887, the deaths of members of the Blood band from Alberta brought extended relatives to the north, in disregard for the prohibitions against crossing the reservation boundaries and the international border. In 1889, "the Last War Party" of Kainah men from Canada went south against the Crows in Montana. Prairie Chicken Old Man, a leader of the incursion, recalled that they "crossed the invisible line into Montana Territory" and took revenge upon the Crow.[52]

Considering this cross-border movement, officials in Canada and the United States accelerated their surveillance of reservation and international borders. American agents worked with the North-West Mounted Police, churches, and boarding/residential schools to monitor Native people crossing the border. As Michel Hogue notes in Metis and the Medicine Line, US military efforts to remove "foreign" and off-reservation Lakota and Metis from the Milk River Valley sparked Canadian interest in heightened co-operation to surveil and militarize the international border.[53] In 1894, the agent in Browning wrote confidently to the commissioner of Indian Affairs: "By an arrangement entered into between myself and those in charge of the Indians north of the 49th parallel the visiting of Indians of both countries is under complete control and the names of all those who were on the Agency and Canada rolls too and drawing rations at both places have been adjusted." The agent claimed that "any Indians coming from the north without passes are arrested and returned; if the offence is repeated they are put to hard labor and then under police escort and made to return home."[54] In 1895, an agent at Macleod wrote to George Steel at the Blackfeet Agency about "a number of Blood Indians . . . making a practice of running over to your reserve without passes and coming back with presents of blankets and clothing." Agent Charles Wilson said he was most "anxious to keep these Indians as much as possible upon the Reserve," and he thanked the American officials for capturing "all Bloods on the Piegan Reserve without passes," telling them to "act strictly by them."[55]

Correspondence between agents about the cross-border movement of the Confederacy revealed a quandary facing officials on either side of the line. At best, agents coordinated their efforts as a unified field of power that stopped cross-border movement of Native people. The sharing of intelligence and the common belief in the importance of maintaining borders for national identity provided the glue that bonded the policy and practice of each state. The ability of Indigenous people to continue crossing the Medicine Line frustrated officials and revealed the permeability of the border and thus the fluid nature of life in the borderlands. Each state reacted differently to these conditions, with the extreme response being epitomized by the US incarceration of the "Canadian Indian" Spopee. On the other end of the spectrum would be the transborder custody case of Albert Spearson, which clearly reflected the persistence of a vibrant Indigenous borderlands culture along the 49th parallel.

The collision of borderlands fluidity and the acceleration of settler-colonial policing of the international boundary emerges in the continued correspondence between US and Canadian officials at the turn of the century. For example, Agent Wilson on the Canadian Blood reserve responded to a May 1895 letter from Agent Steel in Montana stating, "I shall be pleased to cooperate with you in keeping the Indians on their respective reserves, and shall give instructions to the Scouts to keep a good look out for strange Indians." The concerns about keeping Indians on their reserves and watching out for "strange Indians" was indicative of the alarm over Natives' refusal to remain fixed in one location. Wilson continued, "I am informed that one of *my Indians* [emphasis added] and his wife are at present on your reserve, and have been for a few weeks. The Indian is said to be building some houses and stables for *your Indians* [emphasis added], but as he is away without a pass I would be obliged if you could order him to return. His name is 'Died Before' or 'Snake Eater' and rumor says he is trying to get cattle from you as a South Piegan." The use of the language such as "my Indians" and "your Indians" illustrates the power of the nation-state and its colonial functionaries to take literal and figurative possession of Native peoples without rights beyond those conferred upon them by the settler-colonial legal system and its matrix of categories and constructs.

Traditional movement undermined the international political borders as well as the integrity of reservation boundaries, but it also revealed the power of Native kinship relationships and ties to aboriginal homelands. Agent Wilson thought that the individual's father and mother were also Blood Indians and he did not see how such a person could be counted on the Montana reservation, because "he is registered with me and is in receipt of treaty."[56] Wilson wanted Steel to return Blood members to Canada because they were "drawing treaty presents from the United States Government" when they were simultaneously on the Blood rolls.[57] Exemplifying the mobility that agitated Wilson so much, in June of 1895 the North-West Mounted Police captured a Blood man crossing the boundary. Writing to Agent Steel, the Mounted Police said of Walks Long Time Rattling, "I have the honor to acknowledge the receipt of your favour of the 11th instant, on this subject. The Indian in question . . . was arrested by our patrol, at the boundary line, as soon as he entered Canadian territory, and brought to this fort, where he remains in the guard room, pending being handed over to his agent."[58] Foreshadowing twentieth-century legislation categorizing "unlawful entry" into the United States as a misdemeanor, as discussed by Kelly Lytle Hernández in this volume, traversing the international boundary that bisected the homelands of the Blackfoot Confederacy now constituted a criminal act that threatened the legitimacy of the nation-state.

Office of Indian Affairs agents requested a continued military presence in Montana in response to Native border crossing and defense of tribal sovereignty, although the Blackfeet posed no physical threat to the territory. Agent Thomas P. Fuller wanted the troops stationed at Fort Assiniboine to simultaneously guard the reservation and international borders. Writing to the commissioner in 1895, Fuller cautioned, "I think it is unwise to withdraw every soldier from this entire section of the country." He pointed to eight thousand "Blood, Blackfeet, North Piegan, all British Indians, who are constantly passing on and off" the reservation in Montana, when there were only a few thousand registered there. Echoing statements made previously, Fuller claimed that the band members were all "related with the Piegan Blackfeet, and are of one Nation." Thus, the military apparatus was now aimed at the incarceration of Blackfeet on the reservation and the enforcement of strict controls over transborder movement.[59]

Agent Fuller's observation that the Piegan were "all of one Nation" was fairly accurate. Several decades of boundary maintenance and border enforcement as expressed through military force and judicial rulings failed to sever ties between bands and families moving across the Medicine Line. This transnational mobility saw an occasional display of state power, such as the Spopee case, in which the Montana legal system exercised its surprising reach in the arrest, trial, and conviction of a Blood man born in Canada for a crime committed in Canada against a white male American citizen. Beyond such flashes of state power, Blackfoot peoples navigated a borderlands marked by legal voids and the jurisdictional cracks and fissures of a region that was not fully incorporated into the settler-colonial juridical regime.

In matters of kinship and custody, Niitsitapi families retained a degree of agency across reservation and international boundaries. The custody case of a Blood boy named Albert Spearson highlights this successful evasion of state interference in family matters. The first mention of Albert Spearson appears in October 1906, in a letter from a "Canadian Blood" man named Bobtail, who wrote to the agency in Browning about Albert Spearson, his nephew. Bobtail explained that his brother, Albert's father, Frank, died on the Blood reserve in Alberta when he took Albert to see his family north of the line. Frank was enrolled on the Blackfeet reservation in Montana, but his birthplace was unclear. In his letter to the agent in Browning, Bobtail wrote, "Sir—I am very sorry to tell you that my brother Frank Spearson died a few weeks ago in this Reserve. His son, Albert, is staying here with me." Bobtail told the agent he was not sure when he could go to Browning since he was "very busy at this time of the year," but he hoped that the nephew could remain on the Blood reserve.[60] The agent from Browning wrote back to Agent J. L. Levern, who oversaw the Blood reserve, and asked him to tell Bobtail that the commissioner of Indian Affairs was looking into the request.[61]

Writing again to Agent Levern at the Blood reserve in February 1907, the Browning agent relayed the commissioner's instructions. "Sir—Bobtail, a half-blood [Blood] Indian belonging to your reservation, claiming to be the uncle of a boy named Albert Spearson, whose father, Frank Spearson, a half-blood Blackfeet Indian enrolled on this reservation, died during September last at Stand Off, Alta., desires that the boy, Albert Spearson, be transferred to the Blood Agency [Alberta]." At first blush, such correspondence may have seemed confusing, but Frank Spearson was "from Canada" and had status on the Blood reserve and, like many Native people in the region, had crossed the border and sought enrollment on the Blackfeet reservation in Montana. Bobtail was essentially requesting that Albert Spearson be "returned" to his father's birthplace north of the line, even though Frank was enrolled on the reservation south of the line. In short, individuals such as Spearson were "transnational" when viewed from the perspective of Canada and the United States, but from their perspective as Native peoples, they were simply moving inside their traditional homelands. The challenge for the Blackfeet, as seen in this and other instances, was that the nation-states monitored their movement and demanded that they "be seen" by the states, register on one side of the line or the other, and remain fixed within the spatial and status categories established by the settler-colonial bureaucracies.

On the secretary of the interior's behalf, the Montana Indian agent explained to the agent in Canada what he thought about the situation. In a pithy sentence that revealed the interconnections between band members living on different sides of the border, the agent offered, "The boy's mother was, it is understood, a half-blood Blood Indian [from Canada], but at the time of her death she was not a member of the Canadian Tribe of Indians, but was enrolled as a member of the Blackfeet tribe and was recognized as such." Mrs. Spearson, also deceased, was a mixed-race Blood Indian born in Canada and lacked "status"—probably because her Blood mother married a white man—but was registered on the rolls as a Blackfoot in Montana. The agent continued, "The boy has a half-sister married to Henry Potts, who lives on the North Piegan Reserve about fifteen miles west of MacLeod on the Old Man's River. This sister was a child of [Frank] Spearson's first wife and belonged to and was enrolled on this reservation [Montana]." The agent in Browning concluded, "I would thank you to inform me of the character and habits of Bobtail Chief, and to know if in your opinion he is a proper person to have charge of the boy."[62]

There is no documented response from the agent on the Blood reserve, but the agent from Browning again broached the subject that summer. Writing to Principal J. L. Levern, who had only recently moved from serving as an Indian agent to the Catholic boarding school in Stand Off, Alberta, the US agent initiated a detailed investigation of the boy's lineage and enrollment of his family on various reservations and reserves. In a long and convoluted sentence, the agent posed a series of questions. "It is desired to ascertain whether the boy's father originally came from Canada, and when he was enrolled at this Agency, whether Frank Spearson's parents were enrolled and recognized members of the Blackfeet tribe in Montana; what relatives he has in Canada, and if he was ever enrolled there; when he left the Blackfeet reservation and went to Canada, and if he intended to remain there and relinquish his rights as an Indian of this Country; when his wife died; and if the relatives, other than the boy's uncle, wish to have the requested changes made." As if to answer his own questions, the agent concluded: "It would appear, therefore that until a report can be had from the Agent at the Blood Agency, that the matter will remain at a standstill."[63]

After hearing nothing from the Blood reserve, the agent from Browning sent a letter to Bobtail, who of course had initially alerted the Browning agent to Frank's situation and likely knew more about the Spearson family tree than any of the Canadian officials. "Referring to your letter of December 20 1906, relating to the transfer of your nephew, Frank Spearson's son, 11 years old, to the Blood Reservation, and stating that Frank Spearson in his last will . . . offered a strong wish that his son will stay among his relatives belonging to the Blood Reservation, it is requested that you send a copy of the will or such other testimony as you may have to prove the statements made by you." The Montana agent was willing to approve the adoption and the move north of the border, but the appearance of a close relative in Browning transformed the situation into a transborder custody battle. Writing to Bobtail, the agent expressed concern about an aunt of the boy who "came in to the Agency today and states that the father of the boy, before leaving to Canada, stated to her in the presence of witnesses that he felt he would never get well and that in the event of his death gave the boy to her and her husband and directed the disposition to be made of the property for the care and education of the boy." The agent referred back to his previous request for documentation of Frank Spearson's wishes to leave the boy in Canada, "You are requested to furnish the information desired above, as early as practicable."[64]

Correspondence about the matter fell silent until January 1908, when Bobtail went to Browning. Bobtail crossed the border in the dead of winter because the aunt in the aforementioned letters secretly traveled to the Blood reserve and, according to Bobtail, "stole" Albert and brought him to the Blackfeet reservation during the autumn of 1907. In addition to discussing his adoption of Albert, Bobtail spoke with Montana agent Jeremiah Z. Dare about allotment proceedings on the Blackfeet reservation and expressed his concern that Albert, who was due to receive 320 acres of land from Frank Spearson's allotment, would lose his share. Writing to the agent on the Blood reserve, Agent Dare said that Bobtail was "still anxious when he left here to have the boy transferred to your agency." The Browning agent added that it would be best for the boy to stay on Blackfeet, although he did not mention that to Bobtail, who left the reservation believing that he could return and take Albert to Canada.[65] Moreover, the commissioner of Indian Affairs advised that the boy should remain in Montana.

Very little documentation extends into 1909, but the scant letters between the agents reveal that, in the late winter of that year or early spring of 1909 or 1910, Bobtail returned to Browning and took the boy to Alberta.

Correspondence between the Browning agency, the commissioner of Indian Affairs, and the office of the secretary of the interior indicate that Bobtail's actions contradicted their wishes to keep the boy in Montana. More impressively, the fact that the US secretary of the interior—or at least his office—weighed in on the fate of a young boy reveals the concern of federal officials about the surveillance of people moving across the international border. Although the boy posed no threat to either nation, this level of interest revealed an uneasiness about the ability of the state to fix individuals to specific sides of the boundary. And contrary to the twentieth-century trend toward the calcification of the border and the strengthening of the legal regimes on both sides of the line, Blackfoot won the day and Spearson found a home in Canada. In effect, Blackfoot wishes regarding who would adopt the child trumped US colonial efforts to keep the boy south of the line. This was an important assertion of Indigenous sovereignty and the fulfillment of a long struggle over the future of a child who had become the subject of a complex transnational adoption debate. Although Spearson returned to his northern homelands with his uncle, there are no doubt countless stories that did not end so fortunately: children were "adopted" by non-Indian families or they suffered painful consequences as wards in boarding or residential schools. Although the lack of documentation prohibits continued analysis, this historical trail seems to end on a positive note, with an Indigenous boy returning home with his family, clearly within the boundaries of his transnational homelands.

Between 1855 and 1915, the Blackfoot peoples saw their world turned upside down. The succession of broken treaties, military power, decline of the bison, concentration on reservations and reserves, the flood of non-Indians onto their homelands, and the debilitating impact of land allotment wrought undeniable changes to one of the most powerful nations of North America. Canadian and American legal regimes—drawing upon a common well of settler-colonial racial and cultural sentiments—categorized the Niitsitapi as wards of the state incapable of self-governance and denied equal status as citizens of the nation-state. Surrounded by a dizzying array of spatial and conceptual boundaries that proposed the simultaneous extraction of the Blackfeet from the national body politic and their assimilation into white society, members of the Confederacy undermined the power of the state in surprising ways. They refused to remain fixed to one reservation or reserve, they tried to maintain kinship networks across the Medicine Line, and they sought whatever advantages they could in a homeland that had been re-arranged with colonial maps, a capitalist economy, and a prejudicial legal system.

As the cases of Albert Spearson and Spopee illustrate, the US-Canada borderlands mark the carceral power of the state, legal voids and jurisdictional uncertainty, and the power of the Blackfoot Confederacy to maintain mobility and self-determination. Although these cases span a thirty-year period, they reveal the contradictory nature of Indigenous status vis-à-vis the Canadian and American nation-states: neither full citizens nor foreign nationals, Indigenous people like Spopee and Spearson sat in the liminal space of colonial law. Lacking standing in either court system as a full legal person, Spearson had the unlucky burden of being a double ward of the state as a child and as a Native person. Spopee was similarly hamstrung as a murder suspect, a noncitizen of Canada, a First Nations man trapped in United States courts, and a person of color in the racially charged Montana-Alberta borderlands.

Surprisingly, through the early twentieth century, the nation-states had not fully incorporated the borderlands into legal, economic, or material territoriality. As Indigenous peoples continued to undermine the spatial and symbolic limits of US and Canadian citizenship, national status, and territorial integrity, they spoke to the depths of the relationship with their aboriginal homelands. The clean and clear boundaries demanded by Ottawa and Washington could not encapsulate the long-standing geographies of the Niitsitapi. The nationalization of the borderlands that was symbolized by the US-Canada Boundary Commission, customs houses, and the establishment of the North-West Mounted Police revealed the limits of state building at the fringes of the nation. The boundaries of the reservations and reserves that should have contained the Blackfoot peoples and facilitated their cultural transformation into yeoman farmers were as permeable as the international boundaries that sought the segregation of "Canadian" and "American" Indians. If, as some scholars have suggested, nations are made at their borders, Indigenous peoples such as the Blackfeet retained their own homelands, and in the process, unmade the borders that sought to separate and divide them.

Notes

1. See, among others, Cynthia Radding, *Colonialism, Ethnic Spaces, and Ecological Frontiers in Northwestern Mexico, 1700–1850* (Durham, NC: Duke University

Press, 1997); Ramón A. Gutiérrez, *When Jesus Came, the Corn Mothers Went Away: Marriage, Sexuality, and Power in New Mexico, 1500–1846* (Redwood City: Stanford University Press, 1991); Juliana Barr, *Peace Came in the Form of a Woman: Indians and Spaniards in the Texas Borderlands* (Chapel Hill: University of North Carolina Press, 2007); James Brooks, *Captives and Cousins: Slavery, Kinship, and Community in the Southwest Borderlands* (Chapel Hill: University of North Carolina Press, 2002); Ned Blackhawk, *Violence over the Land: Indians and Empires in the Early American West* (Cambridge: Harvard University Press, 2008); Pekka Hämäläinen, *The Comanche Empire* (New Haven: Yale University Press, 2009); Brian DeLay, *War of a Thousand Deserts: Indian Raids and the U.S.-Mexican War* (New Haven: Yale University Press, 2009). For work on the US-Canada border, see, among others, Sheila McManus, *The Line Which Separates: Race, Gender, and the Making of the Montana-Alberta Borderlands* (Lincoln: University of Nebraska Press, 2005); David McCready, *Living with Strangers: The Nineteenth-Century Sioux and the Canadian-American Borderlands* (Lincoln: University of Nebraska Press, 2006); Beth LaDow, *The Medicine Line: Life and Death on a North American Borderland* (New York: Routledge, 2001); Hana Samek, *The Blackfoot Confederacy, 1880–1920: A Comparative Study of U.S. and Canadian Indian Policy* (Lincoln: University of Nebraska Press, 2010); Michel Hogue, *Metis and the Medicine Line: Creating a Border and Dividing a People* (Chapel Hill: University of North Carolina Press, 2015); Andrew Graybill, *The Red and the White: A Family Saga of the American West* (New York: W. W. Norton, 2014); Katrina Jagodinsky, *Legal Codes and Talking Trees: Indigenous Women's Sovereignty in the Sonoran and Puget Sound Borderlands, 1854–1946* (New Haven: Yale University Press, 2016). See also collections such as Sterling Evans, ed., *The Borderlands of the American and Canadian Wests: Essays on Regional History of the Forty-ninth Parallel* (Lincoln: University of Nebraska Press, 2006); Benjamin Johnson and Andrew Graybill, *Bridging National Borders in North America: Transnational and Comparative Histories* (Durham, NC: Duke University Press, 2010); Clarissa Confer, Andrae Marak, and Laura Tuennerman, eds., *Transnational Indians in the North American West* (College Station: Texas A&M University Press, 2015).

2. Mary L. Dudziak and Leti Volpp, introduction, "Legal Borderlands: Law and the Construction of American Borders," *American Quarterly* 57, no. 3 (September 2005): 593–610.

3. Deborah A. Rosen, *American Indians and State Law: Sovereignty, Race, and Citizenship, 1790–1880* (Lincoln: University of Nebraska Press, 2007), 204; Patrick Wolf, "Settler Colonialism and the Elimination of the Native," *Journal of Genocide Research* 8, no. 4 (2006): 388.

4. For comparisons of US-Indian history with Canadian Indigenous history, see, for instance, Roger Nichols, *Indians in the United States and Canada: A Comparative History* (Lincoln: University of Nebraska Press, 1998).

5. Malcolm McFee, *Modern Blackfeet: Montanans on a Reservation* (Lincoln:

University of Nebraska Press, 2013); Blackfoot Gallery Committee, Blackfoot Gallery Committee, *Niitsitapiisinni: The Story of the Blackfoot People* (Calgary: Glenbow Museum, Firefly, 2001); Olive Patricia Dickason, *Canada's First Nations: A History of the Founding Peoples from Earliest Times* (New York: Oxford University Press, 2001), 194. The Siksika are commonly referred to as the Blackfoot in Canada, the Kaina are known as the Blood, and Peigan-Pikuni (Piegan) in the United States. Blackfeet are the most western and southerly group.

6. McManus, *The Line Which Separates*, 58.

7. Samek, *Blackfoot Confederacy*, 17.

8. Treaty with the Blackfoot Indians, October 17, 1855; William E. Farr, "When We Were First Paid: The Blackfoot Treaty, the Western Tribes, and the Creation of the Common Hunting Ground, 1855," *Great Plains Quarterly* 21 (2001): 132; Jill St. Germain, *Indian Treaty Making Policy in the United States and Canada, 1867–1876* (Lincoln: University of Nebraska Press, 2004), 23.

9. John G. Jackson, *The Piikani Blackfeet: A Culture Under Siege* (Sevierville, TN: Mountain Press, 2000), 171; Dickason, *Canada's First Nations*, 282.

10. Dickason, *Canada's First Nations*, 283.

11. Dickason, *Canada's First Nations*, 258–259.

12. Montana Superintendency, no. 61, Helena, MT, September 20, 1870, Report to the Secretary of the Interior, 41st Cong., 3rd Sess., 656; McManus, *The Line Which Separates*, 66.

13. McManus, *The Line Which Separates*, 68.

14. McManus, *The Line Which Separates*, 8.

15. St. Germain, *Indian Treaty-Making Policy*, 23.

16. Samek, *Blackfoot Confederacy*, 13; William E. Farr, *Blackfoot Redemption: A Blood Indian's Story of Murder, Confinement, and Imperfect Justice* (Norman: University of Oklahoma Press, 2012), 114.

17. Farr, *Blackfoot Redemption*, 119.

18. Montana Superintendency, Blackfeet Agency, MT, September 25, 1875, Report to the Secretary of the Interior for 1875, 802; McManus, *The Line Which Separates*, 69; Farr, *Blackfoot Redemption*, 113.

19. Correspondence between Charles Medary, Indian agent, Flathead Agency, MT, October 25, 1875, and John S. Wood, Indian agent, Blackfeet Agency, folder 6, box 1, entry 2, Blackfeet Agency, Letters Received 1873–1909, Record Group 75, National Archives and Records Administration–Denver (hereafter cited as NARA–Denver).

20. Andrew R. Graybill, *Policing the Great Plains: Rangers, Mounties, and the North American Frontier, 1875–1910* (Lincoln: University of Nebraska Press, 2007); Dickason, *Canada's First Nations*, 280–281; Samek, *Blackfoot Confederacy*, 19.

21. Dickason, *Canada's First Nations*, 283.

22. Dickason, *Canada's First Nations*, 285.

23. David E. Wilkins, *American Indian Sovereignty and the U.S. Supreme Court: The Masking of Justice* (Austin: University of Texas Press, 1997).

24. Wilkins, *American Indian Sovereignty and the U.S. Supreme Court*, 60.
25. Jackson, *The Piikani Blackfeet*, 180; Blackfoot Gallery Committee, *Niitsitapi-isinni*, 66; Dickason, *Canada's First Nations*, 283; Samek, *Blackfoot Confederacy*, 15; Hugh Dempsey, *Crowfoot: Chief of the Blackfeet* (Norman: University of Oklahoma Press, 1978).
26. Treaty 7 Elders and Tribal Council, with Walter Hildebrant, Sarah Carter, and Dorothy First Rider, *The True Spirit and Original Intent of Treaty 7* (McGill–Queen's University Press, 1996), 124.
27. McManus, *The Line Which Separates*, 69.
28. Farr, *Blackfoot Redemption*, 17; David McCready, *Living with Strangers*, 90.
29. Farr, *Blackfoot Redemption*, 18.
30. Farr, *Blackfoot Redemption*, 14–16.
31. Farr, *Blackfoot Redemption*, 26; Blackfoot Agency Monthly Reports, December 1, 1879, Letters Sent, entry 3, vol. 4b, RBA, RG 75, NARA–Denver.
32. Farr, *Blackfoot Redemption*, 29.
33. Farr, *Blackfoot Redemption*, 30.
34. Agent John Young, Blackfoot Agency Monthly Reports, January 2, 1880, Letters Sent, RBA, RG 75, NARA–Denver; Farr, *Blackfoot Redemption*, 38.
35. A. C. Botkin, Marshall, to Devens, Att. General, November 23, 1879, Montana Historical Society, vertical files, copies from the US Department of Justice.
36. Farr, *Blackfoot Redemption*, 58.
37. Farr, *Blackfoot Redemption*, 67.
38. Farr, *Blackfoot Redemption*, 71.
39. *Helena Daily Herald*, December 27, 1880, 3.
40. Hugh A. Dempsey, ed., *A Blackfoot Winter Count* (Calgary: Glenbow Museum, 1965), 16.
41. *Helena Daily Herald*, December 27, 1880, 3.
42. *Benton Weekly Herald*, June 16, 1881, 5.
43. Farr, *Blackfoot Redemption*, 170.
44. Farr, *Blackfoot Redemption*, 7.
45. Letter from Macleod, Indian Agency Treaty No. 7, Fort Macleod, N.W. Territories, July 3, 1880 to Agent John Young, Blackfeet Agency, folder 36, box 5, entry 5, Blackfeet Agency, Letters Received 1873–1909, RG 75, NARA–Denver.
46. Letter from Commissioner of Indian Affairs Hiram Price to Agent Young, September 19, 1881, box 6, entry 5, Blackfeet Agency, Letters Received 1873–1909, RG 75, NARA–Denver.
47. Farr, *Blackfoot Redemption*, 23.
48. Acting Commissioner of Indian Affairs to Agent Young, April 4, 1881, box 6; entry 5, Blackfeet Agency, Letters Received 1873–1909, RG 75, NARA–Denver.
49. Letter from Ruger to Young, May 26, 1881, folder 39, box 6; entry 5, Blackfeet Agency, Letters Received 1873–1909, RG, 75, NARA–Denver.
50. Ruger to Young, May 27, 1881; folder 39, box 6, entry 5, Blackfeet Agency, Letters Received 1873–1909, NARA–Denver.
51. McManus, *The Line Which Separates*, 67.

52. McManus, *The Line Which Separates*, 68.

53. Hogue, *Metis and the Medicine Line*, 74.

54. Letter from agent at Montana, Blackfeet Reservation, August 15, 1894, to Commissioner of Indian Affairs, box 7, entry 5, Blackfeet Agency, Letters Received 1873–1909, NARA–Denver.

55. Letter from the Blood Reserve agent at Macleod, Alta., Canada, April 5, 1895 to Agent George Steel, Blackfeet Agency, folder 115, box 7; entry 5, Blackfeet Agency, Letters Received 1873–1909, NARA–Denver.

56. Wilson, Blood Reserve agent, Macleod, May 3, 1895, to Agent George Steel, Blackfeet Agency, folder 116, box 7, entry 5, Blackfeet Agency, Letters Received 1873–1909, NARA–Denver.

57. Letter from Wilson to Steel, May 20, 1895, folder 116; box 7, entry 5, Blackfeet Agency, Letters Received 1873–1909, NARA–Denver.

58. Letter from District Office North-West Mounted Police, Fort Macleod, NWT, June 14, 1895, to Agent George Steel, folder 117, box 8, entry 5, Blackfeet Agency, Letters Received 1873–1909, NARA–Denver.

59. Indian agent Thomas P. Fuller to Commissioner of Indian Affairs, May 10, 1898, vol. 4b, box 3, entry 3, Blackfeet Agency, General Letters Sent, 1875–1915, NARA–Denver.

60. Letter from Bobtail Chief, Blood Reserve, Stand Off, Alta., Canada, to Blackfeet agent, October 7, 1906, 53, volume/book 34, October 31, 1906, to January 28, 1907, box 18, entry 3, Blackfeet Agency, General Letters Sent, 1875–1915, NARA–Denver.

61. Letter from Blackfeet agent to Agent J. L. Levern, Stand Off, Alta., Canada, December 12, 1906, 288, volume/book 34, October 31, 1906, to January 28, 1907, box 18, entry 3, Blackfeet Agency, General Letters Sent, 1875–1915, NARA–Denver.

62. Letter from agent, Browning to Indian agent, Blood Reserve, Stand Off, Alta., Canada, February 7, 1907, volume/book 34, October 31, 1906, to January 28, 1907; box 18, entry 3, Blackfeet Agency, General Letters Sent, 1875–1915, NARA–Denver. For a recent analysis of the gendered dimensions of the Indian Act, see, for instance, Jagodinsky, *Legal Codes and Talking Trees*, and Jagodinsky, "A Tale of Two Sisters: Family Histories from the Strait Salish Borderlands," *Western Historical Quarterly* (Summer 2016): 10.

63. Letter from Blackfeet agent to J. L. Levern, Omni. Principal, Catholic Boarding School, Stand Off, Alta., Canada, August 5, 1907, 12, volume/book 36, May 14, 1907, to August 3, 1907, box 19, entry 3, Blackfeet Agency, General Letters Sent, 1875–1915, NARA–Denver.

64. Blackfeet agent to Bobtail Chief, Blood Reserve, Stand Off, Alta., Canada August 19, 1907, 146, volume/book 36, May 14, 1907, to August 3, 1907, box 19, entry 3, Blackfeet Agency, General Letters Sent, 1875–1915, NARA–Denver.

65. Agent Dare to Indian agent, Blood Reserve, Stand Off, Alta., Canada, February 18, 1908, box 19, entry 3, Blackfeet Agency, General Letters Sent, 1875–1915, NARA–Denver.

3

Abortion and Intimate Borderlands

ALICIA GUTIERREZ-ROMINE

From 1850 through 1969, physician-provided abortions were legal in the state of California.[1] Although the basic tenets of California's abortion statute allowed abortions in cases when the woman's life was at risk, these were not the only instances when California women sought them. For nearly 120 years, the law circumscribed women's reproductive options, granting access to abortions only with a physician's approval. However, women in California continued to acquire abortions, and providers of illegal abortions—both local and abroad—served countless women with the relief they desired.

Few legislators or members of the professional medical community possess strong feelings against tonsillectomies, pap smears, or prostate exams, yet from the late nineteenth century—even through the present—abortion divided the medical community. Abortion did not just create unbridgeable barriers between colleagues; it also created legal and metaphorical binaries and borderlands in the public discourse on abortion: legal versus illegal abortions, respectable versus disreputable women, and licensed versus unlicensed practitioners. While the "law [is] not an inescapable hegemony," it still, however, possesses real power.[2] Ultimately, outlawing abortions— except for those when a woman's life was at risk—had the immediate effect of criminalizing women's exercise of personal choice, as well as jeopardizing their health and welfare.

Historians have often discussed the expansion of women's reproductive rights within the context of the civil rights movement. As minorities pressed for civil rights, women's rights advocates recognized that access to birth control represented female emancipation. In being able to control their own bodies, women were able to control their "only significant biological disadvantage," as Linda Gordon described.[3] It would however, be imprecise to ascribe all expansions of reproductive rights to the civil rights movement.[4] Historically, abortion has been an integral part of women's lives. Although it has been subject to atypical legislation, most women have simply viewed abortion as another form of birth control. Since the law prohibited abortions on demand, California women, from the 1930s to 1969, often turned to the US-Mexico border to terminate an unwanted pregnancy.

Abortions occupied an ambiguous place in California's legal terrain. The procedure itself was not banned outright—rather the circumstances surrounding the woman and the provider either lent legitimacy to a specific abortion or stigmatized it. The very same procedure could be legal for one woman and illegal for another woman, or even legal for one pregnancy and illegal for another pregnancy for the same woman. It all depended on a number of factors: whether a physician performed the procedure, whether the patient had a condition that justified an abortion (this was also debatable), and even where the procedure took place—in a hospital or back alley, or in the United States or Mexico. The law created very specific criteria for what constituted legal abortion. All abortions outside of those parameters were illegal.

In the years before legalization, scores of American women crossed the border to procure illegal abortions.[5] These women's individual stories and motivations for obtaining abortions in Mexico were unique, and most of them elude us. What these women had in common, however, was a desire to exercise reproductive freedom in spite of the law and without regard for national boundaries—even though they were obviously aware of them. Legal ambiguity and geographic borderlands were significant to abortion decriminalization in California, and the emergence of a large-scale abortion travel industry on the border provided important context for efforts to liberalize abortion laws within the state. While borderlands, both legal and geographic, aren't typically a part of the conversation when discussing the expansion of women's reproductive rights in the 1960s and 1970s, the border—between legal and illegal, acceptable and illicit, and the United States and Mexico—was an important feature in a series of California abortion cases and, ultimately, in the decriminalization of abortion in the state.

In 1859, a Nevada County, California, grand jury found Julia Moore guilty of performing an illegal abortion on Ms. Lucy Nutall. According to the indictment, Moore fashioned a hooklike device out of a piece of metal, and on August 19, she did "feloniously, unlawfully and of her malice aforethought make a violent assault" upon Lucy Nutall.[6] Ms. Nutall died on September 2, probably from septic infection, a common cause of death from illegal abortions before the 1930s. The abortion, which the grand jury claimed Ms. Moore performed "violently, wickedly, and inhumanly," was a violation of California's Crimes and Punishment Act.[7]

The Crimes and Punishment Act—California's first legislative code— criminalized abortions when performed by nonmembers of the medical community. As written, the law sought to protect women like Lucy Nutall from the likes of Julia Moore.[8] On the American frontier, this represented a conservative effort to protect women from uneducated, unskilled, and unlicensed quacks. By 1935, however, the clause protecting physicians was conspicuously absent and the prerequisite that abortions be medically necessary took priority over physicians' authority.[9] While the 1850 statute may have implied that physicians could do no wrong, by the 1930s, lawmakers had grown increasingly suspicious of the medical community.[10] As the number of abortions increased in the state, so too did the number of physicians performing them.

Between 1872 and 1935, the California population grew significantly. As more people poured into the state, the number of women seeking abortions grew as well. The provisions of California's abortion law through 1935 allowed physicians to perform abortions when they concluded that carrying a pregnancy to term would result in irrevocable harm to the life or health of the mother. Since physicians practiced medicine independently, any doctor who believed pregnancy threatened his patient could legally perform an abortion. With little oversight, physicians performed these legal abortions with impunity as independent practitioners in their own offices or in patients' homes—rarely dealing with the bureaucratic mechanisms of the law. In fact, law enforcement only got involved when a patient became gravely ill or died. Given such freedom, most physicians were able to find a justification for a legal abortion for their private patients for the right price.

Beginning in the 1930s, hospitals began to play a more prominent role in maternal and gynecological care. As modern labor and delivery moved to the hospital, legal abortions did as well. The early 1930s represent a gray period in the history of abortion. While there were instances when it was acceptable for a physician to perform an abortion in his or her own office, increasingly, physicians needed to perform abortions in hospitals in order for them to be considered reputable or legal. The need for a hospital visit and stay increased the price of legal, or therapeutic, abortions—meaning that women of means were their typical recipients.[11]

Therapeutic abortion exceptions existed to protect the lives of pregnant women in the event of serious medical conditions that pregnancy could exacerbate. However, the law creating these exceptions did not specify *what* these medical conditions were—again, leaving this to physicians' discretion. Therapeutic abortion exceptions—or loopholes—allowed abortions when a woman's life was seriously in danger. However, advances in medical technology had made it "extremely rare to find an illness in a pregnant woman" that would prevent her from bringing her pregnancy to term.[12] Nevertheless, therapeutic exceptions continued to provide a space for physicians and patients to *negotiate* the terms of a "legal" abortion.[13] Consequently, the therapeutic designation became decidedly amorphous.

Moving abortions to hospitals also created opportunities for oversight—particularly in response to questionable abortion justifications—and resulted in the creation of hospital-based therapeutic-abortion committees. These committees would become increasingly significant, and they would eventually supplant individual physicians' judgment when it came to justifying abortions in the 1940s and 1950s. Because of this constellation of factors, more women began to turn to providers of illegal abortions.

In the wake of the Great Depression, abortion specialists thrived. Because of the procedure's relative ease, many individuals believed that they could perform it without medical experience. Additionally, since abortions had the potential to generate large profits, the lure was too great for some to avoid. In response to the proliferation of questionable abortions in the state, and concomitant with the crackdown on a particularly large, notorious, and *safe* abortion racket in California in 1937, the social landscape of abortion took a startlingly repressive turn.

In 1937, the California Supreme Court tried and convicted Reginald L. Rankin and a coterie of physicians, surgeons, and abortion specialists in the sensational Pacific Coast Abortion Ring trial.[14] In a departure from the abortion cases of the 1850s through the early 1930s, this case did not involve a patient fatality.[15] Because of their success in bringing down the Pacific Coast Abortion Ring, law enforcement officials and district attorneys had greater latitude when arresting and convicting providers of illegal abortions. Now, they no longer needed a patient fatality in order to prosecute and convict illegal abortionists. Specialization, sterilization of instruments, and antibiotics all contributed to decreased patient mortality. At the same time, decreased mortality meant that prosecutors were able to coerce patients to testify against their abortionists. After the demise of the Pacific Coast

Abortion Ring, crackdowns on illegal abortionists became much more productive in California. Fewer individuals risked performing illegal abortions, and it became much harder for women to acquire them.

Any evidence police collected from raids—speculums, patient cards with women's names on them, an operating table, a curette—was sufficient to convict providers of illegal abortions. District attorneys issued arrest warrants after law enforcement officers performed hours of surveillance on presumed clinics and stakeouts at the houses of presumed abortionists. Investigators' notes detailed when women entered and exited the clinics or homes, the license plates and descriptions of the cars involved, what the women looked like, and their apparent conditions when they left.[16] While the court could technically charge the patients as well, this rarely happened. Prosecutors frequently convinced women that they would be indicted if they did not testify against their abortionist. Pressure from police officers, investigators, prosecutors, or personal naiveté compelled these women to take the stand and describe their abortion experiences in detail.[17] Patients endured law enforcement's encroachment into the very intimate details of their personal lives. Rather than experience an invasive interrogation after an invasive abortion, many women chose an alternate route to escape the torment and public shame brought on by a public trial.

In 1939, an undercover investigator for the *San Diego Sun* visited local abortionists and described to readers what it was like getting an illegal abortion in the city.[18] According to the investigator, prices for the procedure varied from fifty to one hundred dollars.[19] A letter from a physician supporting abortion resulted in minimal obstacles. Providing the name of a friend that had an abortion by the same provider usually worked just as well. The investigator found that lacking a physician note or reference often resulted in skepticism, hostile interrogation, or flat-out refusal. By the 1950s and 1960s, this kind of negativity and enmity had come to characterize the illegal abortion experience—from providers of illegal abortions as well as from law enforcement officials.

The *Sun*'s investigator gathered the names and addresses of presumed abortionists from police, court, and local medical association records. The investigator found that some offices were not clean or hygienic. Many women probably felt they could not demand a sanitary environment, and many providers may have felt they did not need to provide them. It is possible that many women, in their desperation, chose to overlook these potentially hazardous conditions. The fact that these abortions took place *outside* of hospitals perpetuated their illegitimacy in the eyes of law enforcement and the medical field. For women who could acquire legal abortions and for the physicians who provided them, the therapeutic abortion exception continued to shield their actions.

By the 1950s and 1960s, exploitation of therapeutic abortion exceptions led to their control by hospital committees of three to five physicians. Rather than allow physicians to decide the fate of their own patients, the committee determined whether an abortion was therapeutically necessary. If a woman wanted a therapeutic abortion, she would speak to her physician, and then her physician would present her case before the committee. The committee would deliberate and return a decision, without ever meeting the woman. Under this new regime, "the rate of therapeutic abortions performed in hospitals declined dramatically."[20]

County and state officials recorded the numbers of therapeutic abortions that came before the committee for approval and the numbers that were authorized. This led some hospitals to employ deliberate quotas in order to stay under the radar and prevent further investigation. Citing concerns over the "critical gaze" of the Joint Commission on the Accreditation of Hospitals, Dr. Edmund Overstreet, an obstetrics and gynecology professor at the University of California, San Francisco, stated "individual hospitals . . . have been very fearful of subjecting [sic] suddenly increased abortion rates."[21] Although the number of applications for therapeutic abortions had "risen tenfold," the UCSF medical center limited the number of abortions to "five per week."[22] Committee members, aware that they were being monitored, were particularly strict in their interpretations of what they considered acceptable reasons for therapeutic abortions for other physicians' patients since "clinic patients were competing for precious slots with the private patients" of the committee members or hospital supervisors.[23] Rather than leave the decision for abortion to others and face delays, many women began to prefer the certainty found in a trip to the border.

Through the 1940s and 1950s, Los Angeles saw a decrease in abortion-related deaths. Most likely, this decrease was a result of fewer women attempting to procure abortions in the stricter environment—and not because abortions were necessarily any safer than they already were in the 1930s. According to data from the Los Angeles county coroner's office, there were 224 abortion deaths in Los Angeles County from July 1, 1938, through June 30, 1954. This number, 224 over sixteen fiscal years, is less than the

278 abortion deaths the coroner's office handled in the eleven fiscal years prior. The 224 abortion deaths performed between 1938 and 1954 also represented an insignificant percentage of the growing number of total cases that the coroner's office handled in that time—which was more than double the number of cases from the ten years prior.[24] Abortions represented 0.189 percent of the total coroner's 1938–1954 caseload. The 1938–1954 statistics also represent a shift in the providers of fatal abortions.

The percentage of physician- or medical professional–induced abortion deaths from this period actually increased, possibly a result of more women seeking therapeutic abortions from physicians. The percentage of abortion deaths from "other" causes increased as well. Significantly, while self-induced abortions represented a majority of causes of death between 1927 and 1938 (52.52 percent), that percentage dropped between 1938 and 1954 (40.6 percent). Possible explanations could include that women were taking advantage of therapeutic designations, seeking specialized, illegal abortionists, did not wait as long to go to the hospital if they experienced complications, or decided to resign themselves to an unwanted pregnancy. Although married women continued to remain the group with the highest abortion rates (or deaths, in these cases), the number of single women seeking abortions rose from 13.9 to just under 20 percent in the 1938–1954 data. The decline in the percentage of married women could be attributed to the increasing percentage of divorced women who died from abortions. It could also be linked to postwar economic success and the baby-boom era, which glorified families and motherhood. Likewise, the increase in single women who died from abortion could be related to changing social behaviors, boyfriends leaving to fight in World War II, or temporary relationships resulting from migration for wartime jobs.[25]

Migration and mobility became central to California's history, and you never had to look very far to find echoes of Mexico—whether metaphorically in the Spanish fantasy past or literally in the US-Mexico border.[26] Mexico represented a sense of freedom to some, an exotic, untamed land, or an easy, last resort for escape in the event that criminal activity went sour. In the late nineteenth century, newspaper articles about escaped murderers and criminals crossing back and forth across the border were common.[27] Early film producers held escape to Mexico as a safety net in the event that they were caught for trademark violations. In the 1910s, progressive reforms on law enforcement for "vice" in Los Angeles and San Diego accelerated the

Table 3.1.

Los Angeles County Coroner Annual Report Statistics for Abortion, 1927–1938. All fiscal years July 1–June 30.

Fiscal Year	Total # of Coroner Cases	# of Abortion Cases	Self-Induced	By Physician or Medical Professional	Other	Age: 10–20; 20–45	Marital Status
1927–1928	3,756	20 (0.532%)	5	3	2 undetermined; 4 spontaneous; 1 by fall to floor; 5 by instruments induced by unknown person	7:13	N/A
1928–1929	4,174	28 (0.671%)	19* (2 partial)	2	2 criminal by known person; 1 criminal by unknown person; 1 by fall to floor; 1 spontaneous; 2 undetermined	0:28	N/A
1929–1930	4,254	31 (0.729%)	13	5	4 criminal by unknown person; 2 spontaneous; 1 by fall to floor; 6 undetermined	1:30	N/A
1930–1931	4,603	33 (0.717%)	17	4	1 by fall; 3 criminal by unknown person; 4 undetermined; 4 spontaneous	6:27	N/A
1931–1932	4,604	28 (0.608%)	16	4	1 criminal by known person; 3 criminal by unknown person; 2 spontaneous; 2 undetermined	4:24	23 married; 4 single; 1 divorced
1932–1933	5,059	28 (0.553%)	13	4	1 criminal by known person; 2 by fall; 1 criminal by unknown person; 3 spontaneous; 4 undetermined (2 criminal or self-induced; 2 self-induced or spontaneous)	3:25	24 married; 4 single
1933–1934	5,083	21 (0.413%)	15	1	3 criminal by unknown person; 2 spontaneous	0:21	18 married; 3 single

1934–1935	5,315	25 (0.470%)	15	2	2 spontaneous; 3 criminal by known person; 3 undetermined (self-induced or criminal)	3:22	18 married; 2 single; 4 widowed; 1 divorced
1935–1936	5,377	29 (0.539%)	13	4	2 criminal by known person; 1 criminal by unknown person; 5 self-induced or criminal, undetermined; 4 spontaneous	6:23	23 married; 5 single; 1 divorced
1936–1937	6,070	15 (0.247%)	11	1	1 self-induced or criminal, undetermined; 2 criminal by unknown person	3:12	9 married; 4 single; 1 widowed; 1 divorced
1937–1938	5,783	20 (0.346%)	9	—	4 spontaneous; 2 septic; 5 criminal or self-induced, undetermined	0:20	17 married; 1 widowed; 1 divorced; 1 single

Table 3.2.

Los Angeles County Coroner Annual Report Statistics for Abortion, 1938–1954. All fiscal years July 1–June 30.

Fiscal Year	Total # of Coroner Cases	# of Abortion Cases	Self-Induced	By Physician or Medical Professional	Other	Age: 10–20; 20–45	Marital Status
1938–1939	6,190	19	10	2	1 criminal by unknown person; 2 spontaneous; 1 caused by fall; 3 criminal or self-induced, undetermined	1:18	15 married; 2 divorced; 2 single
1939–1940	6,282	22	6	5 (4 criminal, 1 therapeutic)	1 criminal by unknown person; 2 criminal by known person; 1 spontaneous; 3 self-induced or criminal, undetermined; 1 self-induced or spontaneous, undetermined; 1 attempted abortion; 1 self-induced or accidental; 1 incomplete abortion	3:19	15 married; 2 divorced; 4 single; 1 widowed
1940–1941	6,606	12	6	1	1 criminal by unknown person; 2 self-induced or criminal, undetermined; 1 incomplete abortion; 1 unknown cause	3:09	6 married; 1 divorced; 5 single
1941–1942	6,760	19	4	5	1 accidental, due to fall; 2 spontaneous; 1 therapeutic; 6 unknown cause, criminal or self-induced, undetermined	4:15	16 married; 1 divorced; 2 single
1942–1943	6,831	23	9	3	1 criminal by unknown person; 2 spontaneous; 4 undetermined whether criminal or self-induced; 4 unknown cause	3:19, 1 unknown	21 married; 1 single; 1 widowed
1943–1944	6,889	26	8	5 (4 criminal by physician; 1 justifiable by doctor)	2 criminal by unknown person; 6 undetermined whether criminal or self-induced; 3 unknown; 1 accidental due to fall; 1 induced by heavy lifting	1:25	22 married; 4 single

Year						
1944–1945	7,715	10	2	3	5 unknown	3:07	7 married; 3 single
1945–1946	7,862	12	4	1	3 criminal by unknown person; 3 spontaneous; 1 criminal or self-induced, undetermined	1:11	9 married; 3 single
1946–1947	7,469	11	6	N/A	1 criminal by known person; 1 criminal by unknown person; 3 unknown	5:06	7 married; 1 divorced; 2 single; 1 widowed
1947–1948	7,789	8	4	N/A	1 criminal by known person; 1 criminal by unknown person; 3 unknown	1:07	6 married; 2 single
1948–1949	7,539	11	5	N/A	2 criminal by known person; 1 spontaneous; 2 unknown	3:07	4 married; 1 divorced; 3 single; 1 widowed; 1 unknown
1949–1950	7,770	6	3	N/A	1 criminal by known person; 2 unknown	0:06	5 married; 1 single
1950–1951	7,774	6	1	1	1 criminal by known person; 1 undetermined, self-induced or criminal	0:04	4 married
1951–1952	8,134	15	7	1	3 criminal by known person; 1 criminal by unknown person; 2 criminal or self-induced; 1 spontaneous	0:15	7 married; 6 single; 2 divorced
1952–1953	8,534	13	8	1	4 criminal by known person	3:10	7 married; 3 single; 3 divorced
1953–1954	8,539	11	8	N/A	2 criminal by known person, 1 criminal or self-induced, undetermined	0:11	8 married, 3 single

existence of vice industries at the border. Tijuana represented a "den of vice" and a "shame and a disgrace" at America's southernmost gate.[28] Yet the gambling houses and pool halls at the border were all just a short trip from San Diego. They were even connected by rail.

In the 1920s, US law enforcement officials decried the bureaucratic process necessary to extradite American fugitives who had found refuge in Mexico. One of the most notorious examples of this was when Jack Johnson, an African American champion heavyweight boxer, fled to Tijuana to escape charges of violating the Mann Act. Some accounts claimed that hundreds of American offenders lived in Mexico without "molestation in that country" as efforts for their return "proved futile." The extradition process was drawn out and burdensome. When Dr. James Petrie, for example, fled to Mazatlan after he performed a fatal abortion, detectives in Los Angeles had to go to Sacramento for extradition papers. These papers had to be sent to Washington, DC, before they would be forwarded to the president of Mexico in Mexico City.[29]

Despite US attempts to intervene and suppress vice on the border, gambling halls, racetracks, and saloons thrived. American tourists, disgruntled drinkers under the yoke of Prohibition, gamblers, and families alike crossed the border in order to experience the novelty of an exotic country and culture or to enjoy illicit drinking and gambling away from authorities.[30] To Americans, the border towns of Mexico existed for their pleasure. In some respects, it is likely that even when reformers bemoaned the proliferation of vice on the border, they were relieved that the vice was at least happening elsewhere. For decades, the US-Mexico border was a place where American "tourists could fulfill their desire for exotic diversions."[31] Southern Californians characterized it as a place where they could engage in behaviors that were unsuitable in *American* civilization. As Mexican border towns became sites of American decadence, abortions made their way into this travel industry as well. Although American women had crossed the border for abortions for years, in the 1950s and 1960s California women increasingly sought abortions over the border in light of heightened therapeutic-abortion committee restrictions.

The Mexican government first addressed abortion in 1931. According to Mexican law, abortion was illegal except in cases of "negligence of the mother," if continuation of the pregnancy endangered the life of the mother, or if the pregnancy resulted from rape.[32] The law made abortion punishable with one to three years or three to six years of prison for the abortion provider—depending on whether the woman consented to the abortion. The "negligence" portion of the law, though vague, was designed to protect women who miscarried through no deliberate act of their own. Although abortion upon demand was illegal in Mexico,

> the U.S. demand for abortions produced a surreptitious market. Particularly in the 1960s, Tijuana and nearby Ensenada served as an "abortion emporium" for U.S. women who faced the alternative in the United States of back-alley abortions or safer but cost-prohibitive abortions by U.S. doctors acting illegally. Tijuana was a cheaper option. . . . It provided a whole coterie of movie stars with well-publicized "miscarriages." [And with that], Mexican abortions entered the [American] cultural mainstream.[33]

The border became more visible in American abortion legislation after the *Buffum* case in 1953, and this "surreptitious" market would not have flourished without it. *People v. Buffum* accelerated the abortion-tourism industry at the border and allowed providers of illegal abortions to profit immensely.

In 1953, Reginald Rankin and Dr. Roy L. Buffum were found guilty of conspiring to violate section 274—California's abortion statute.[34] Four women had separately approached Dr. Buffum in hopes of securing abortions. Buffum said he would not perform the procedure but took three of the women's telephone numbers and told them they would receive a call. Dr. Buffum gave the fourth woman his associate Reginald Rankin's telephone number. Rankin communicated with each of the women, indicated the price for the procedure, and made arrangements about where to meet in Long Beach. From that designated meeting point, Rankin transported them to the place where the procedure would be performed in Mexico.[35]

As mobility became integral to Southern California life and culture, abortionists in the region took advantage of the region's roads and freeways. Leaders in the Pacific Coast Abortion Ring, for example, regularly moved their physicians from clinic to clinic in order to fend off arrests or prevent feelings of ownership a physician might have had over the syndicate-run clinic. In 1948, five people in Oakland, California, were arrested for performing abortions in the back of a specially equipped trailer.[36] Later, in 1958 and 1959, a six-month investigation led to the arrest of a half-dozen men and women who operated a "floating" illegal surgery ring in which steerers took women to constantly changing clinic locations in Anaheim, Long Beach, or Los Angeles, where they would have their abortions. Rankin and Buffum's decision to use a vehicle in their abortion plan was not new. Rather, what was unique about the *Buffum* case was the fact that they successfully appealed their initial conviction. Specifically, the court reversed its decision because it recognized the limits of its power—the abortions took place across the border in Tijuana, Mexico, outside the reach of California law.[37]

Once Rankin drove women to Tijuana, they would pay him, and Rankin helped another man perform the operations. After the operation, Rankin drove the women back to Long Beach. From there, they went their separate ways. In the cases that brought about their arrests, three of the women required hospitalization after their abortions. Hospital physicians determined that the women had been operated upon illegally and called authorities.

Rankin and Buffum were initially convicted of the charges against them. Upon appeal, the decision was reversed. Although there was ample evidence to corroborate that Rankin and Buffum conspired in California, the fact that the crime was performed in Mexico led to disagreements over whether section 182 applied. Specifically, the court stated that although the statute made "no reference to the place of performance of an abortion," it "must assume that the Legislature did not intend to regulate conduct taking place outside the borders of the state."[38] During the trial, the prosecutors mentioned that the men violated Mexico's laws against abortion—which may have been prejudicial—since the California jurors potentially judged the men based on their culpability of violating Mexican law. California's conspiracy statute did not criminalize conspiracies to violate Mexican law. The judgment was reversed: the court recognized that the state's statutes did "not provide a punishment for such conduct."[39] In reversing their decision, the court effectively stated it had no jurisdiction in the matter.

Women had been traveling for abortions for years, and the *Buffum* case essentially condoned the proliferation of an illegal abortion industry just across the border. In 1962, Joel M. Taylor, special agent for the California Department of Justice, reported: "District Attorney's investigators of San Diego and Orange counties and other law enforcement officials have pointed out that the *Buffum* decision prohibits prosecution for an offense committed in Mexico even though the arrangements for the act were made in this country by citizens in California."[40] Efforts to close the *Buffum* loophole were fruitless. Despite Los Angeles Board of Medical Examiners undercover assignments and surveillance in Tijuana, authorities were unable to put a stop to the surge of American women procuring abortions along the border.

One estimate in 1967 claimed that there were about seventy-five abortionists "operating regularly in Tijuana and a few fly-by-nighters besides."[41] Border abortions were not limited to Tijuana alone, and this estimate does not include other border cities like Mexicali, Juarez, or Ensenada, which had their own abortion businesses as well. The *Buffum* decision allowed women and steerers to make arrangements in California for illegal abortions and carry those abortions out in Mexico. The alternatives to border abortions were often much more expensive. In the *Chicago Tribune*, one couple described their experience of flying to Mexico City for an abortion. Journalists wrote about the existence of clinics and lying-in homes like "la casa de las gringas," one of the busiest abortion mills in Mexico City that generated up to $1,300 per abortion.[42] The couple that spoke with the *Tribune* spent over $1,100 for their abortion: $500 for the procedure itself, $400 for airfare, and over $200 for lodging and transportation. After the *Buffum* case, women did not have to get plane tickets or prepare for an extended stay. Southern California's proximity to Mexico meant that a woman could acquire an over-the-border abortion in a day trip. Foreign abortions were no longer a hassle; rather, they were relatively simple considering Americans' ease of travel to Mexico.[43] The *Buffum* decision opened the floodgates of American abortion tourism in nearby border cities. Because Rankin and Buffum won their appeal, more precisely, since the California court recognized it could not act against abortions performed in Mexico, they had a significant impact on the development of California's 1950s–1960s Tijuana abortion phenomenon.

Women in colleges throughout the state would charter buses and cross the border for abortions. Some would meet steerers in parking lots in the United States who would transport them to clinics across the border.[44] Others would rent a car for a day. According to Gene Allen, chief investigator for the San Diego district attorney, the process through which women and abortionists made contact seldom varied. In most cases, once the woman had found an abortionist and made initial contact, she would be "instructed to get a motel room near the border or in Tijuana."[45] The woman would make another call to the abortionist once she got to the motel. She would be instructed to go to a bar, a restaurant, or even a shoe shop, where one of the abortionist's associates would pick her up. After the abortion, the woman was often in charge of her own transportation back to her motel.

The abortionists would frequently tell the women to look happy, to not arouse suspicion from border patrol agents. The preponderance of this practice, and the inability to successfully convict anyone for it, prompted the state to revise the abortion law. According to San Diego district attorney Don Keller, law enforcement officials, "including members of the Department of Professional and Vocational Standards, agreed that the *Buffum* case virtually prohibits prosecution for abortions even in cases where the abortionist meets the victim in California, accepts a fee, transports the victim to Tijuana, and performs an operation. It appears that as long as the *Buffum* case stands, the wholesale abortion mills will continue to operate in Mexico."[46] After the *Buffum* case, legislators in California were able to bring about legislation that made it illegal to conspire to commit an abortion outside of California—even if the abortion was legal in the jurisdiction in which it was performed. But these efforts did little to stymie the practice. In 1959, California's chief deputy attorney general expressed concern over the "international abortion ring operating in Mexico" and noted that local and federal agencies were preoccupied with developing "new legislation to combat the problem."[47] The California Department of Justice lamented the "considerable abortion activity in the Tijuana area" and pointed specifically to San Diego and Orange Counties as points of contact before transport.[48]

In San Diego in 1962, the state assembly's Committee on Criminal Procedure gathered for a hearing on AB 2614. The proposed bill attempted to standardize the justifications for therapeutic abortions in the wake of increasing US women's abortions in Mexico and frustration from physicians and patients over therapeutic abortion exceptions. The bill held that abortions could be performed in hospitals if their respective therapeutic committees determined "the continuance of pregnancy involves substantial risk that the mother of the child will suffer grave and irremediable impairment of physical or mental health or if the pregnancy resulted from rape or incest."[49] The bill attempted to depart from the ambiguous language embedded in the abortion statute, which stated that abortions were only legal to save the life of the mother.

At the time of the San Diego hearing, medical experts in the United States believed that the number of abortions performed in the country ranged between 375,000 and two million per year—with one million being a conservative figure.[50] Additionally, they estimated around five thousand deaths per year as a result of poorly performed abortions. In Los Angeles County, abortions continued to remain an insignificant portion of the

Table 3.3.
Los Angeles County Coroner Annual Report Statistics for Abortion,
1954–1970. All fiscal years July 1–June 30.

Fiscal Year	Total # of Coroner Cases	Number of Abortion Cases
1954–1955	8,634	14
1955–1956	9,450	11
1956–1957	9,584	18
1957–1958	9,959	8
1958–1959	9,950	11
1959–1960	10,786	10
1960–1961	10,825	17
1961–1962	12,073	13
1962–1963	12,516	15
1963–1964	12,642	7
1964–1965	12,670	7
1965–1966	13,128	5
1966–1967	12,387	3
1967–1968	13,781	1
1968–1969	*	*
1969–1970	14,035	4 mothers and 1 fetus

* Duplicate and/or inaccurate data in coroner's report.

coroner's caseload.[51] From 1954 to 1970, abortions represented an average of 0.09 percent of the total number of coroner cases. The percentage of abortion deaths represented in the Los Angeles county coroner's caseload had steadily declined since the 1920s and 1930s. Yet, abortion was of increasing concern in public debate and discourse. According to Kristin Luker, efforts to standardize the existing abortion law generated greater publicity for abortion and brought abortion into the public purview. As abortion became increasingly legislated and moved into the public arena, "widely varying interpretations of when an abortion is justified came into public view. The more public abortions became, the more opportunities for conflict arose."[52]

The border also became more visible to Americans in the 1950s and 1960s through increased regulation—specifically Operation Wetback in 1954 and the 1955 Senate committees on vice.[53] According to Holly Karibo, "drug smuggling and crime along the US-Canada and US-Mexico borders were hotly debated in the public arena."[54] Along the Mexican border, concerns about illegal immigration also contributed to the perception of the US-Mexico border as a lawless place. Karibo writes that the highly publicized

Operation Wetback "had the effect of bolstering perceptions that countless illegal immigrants were pouring across the border on a daily basis. Newspapers often explicitly linked the 'illegal Mexican aliens' with vice problems."[55] The border also played an important role in the context of heightened Cold War fears about national security. In public opinion, border cities and towns were "particularly susceptible to corruption and crime."[56] Concerns about borders emerged when unprecedented numbers of Americans were traveling across them and when fear "of subversion from the outside" was at its peak.[57]

As the abortion industry on the border grew, unskilled abortionists had greater opportunities to offer their services. Desperate women—many of whom simply crossed the border and asked around—did not often look for the most qualified abortionists and simply accepted the services of the first one they found. These unskilled abortionists' services did not necessarily result in death. Rather, women did not get hygienic treatment, pain relievers, or even complete abortions. Once women returned to the United States, they went to a county hospital if they were ill or to complete the abortion process.[58] At county hospitals, they were treated for infections or had dilation and curettements performed to complete the partial abortions begun in Mexico. Consequently, scores of unqualified abortionists were able to operate along the border.

Pat Maginnis often passed out leaflets with the names of physicians in Mexico and Japan who would perform safer abortions for American women.[59] While she attempted to maintain a reliable list of providers, some "butchers" preyed on the countless American women who went across the border in search of abortions.[60] Occasional crackdowns from American and Mexican officials complicated efforts to keep the list up to date. Maginnis's leaflets, however, provided tips to help identify reputable abortionists who would, for example, provide some type of pain reliever before the procedure and an antibiotic afterward—like Dr. Alfonso Paris, an abortionist in Tijuana under investigation by the California Department of Justice.[61] Maginnis encouraged women to look around once they reached Mexico—such as by asking taxi drivers for abortionists or regular gynecologists. She and her colleagues also cautioned, "if the price is lower than $300, you may not be too sure of getting a licensed physician. Ask to see a license if you are uncertain as to whether you are getting a bona fide physician."[62]

At the San Diego hearing for AB 2614, Mr. Zad Leavy, a Beverly Hills attorney who formerly worked with the Los Angeles district attorney, said women went "outside the medical profession for help" because of their

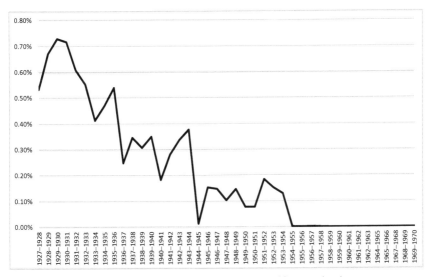

Figure 3.1. Percentage of abortion cases in coroner's office caseload.

utter "disregard of the law."[63] However, this didn't accurately reflect what compelled women to pursue illegal, potentially dangerous abortions. Some women used abortion as a means to navigate complex relationships in which they had limited agency. When Barbara Jackson discovered she was pregnant again, the college student was concerned. She already had a child from her ex-husband, from whom she received $150 per month in child support. She and her boyfriend discussed their options. At first, they considered getting married quickly, but "the possibility existed that if she had a child either out of wedlock or six months after the marriage, this would give the father of her three-year-old child some power to find her an unfit mother and take the child away from her."[64] Sometimes, women chose to have abortions because they were in unhappy marriages and did not want to add another child to the family. One nineteen-year-old woman sought an abortion because she and her husband had separated on many occasions, and they already had a fourteen-month-old child. In other cases, estranged husbands reported their wives' abortions, or intentions to abort, to authorities as a means of control, to shame them, or to exact revenge for leaving. Most women had complex issues to navigate, and their choice to have an abortion was not one they came to quickly. For many women, the decision to have an illegal abortion was not taken lightly since many knew it could be dangerous.[65] It was not simply "disregard of the law."

When the California Board of Medical Examiners interviewed Mrs. Raymond about her nineteen-year-old daughter, Mary, she explained why she helped her daughter secure a Mexican abortion.[66] According to Mrs. Raymond, Mary was engaged to a promising young man. While he was away in college, Mary went out and became pregnant by a "goon." After contacting friends, physicians, acquaintances, and the family doctor with no success, Mrs. Raymond drove Mary to Mexicali in hopes of finding an abortionist. Eventually, Mrs. Raymond found an abortionist in Ensenada. Mrs. Raymond "stated that she was not sorry that she had Mary aborted and would do it again if it became necessary. She felt that by having the abortion she *saved* Mary from becoming a social outcast, [and] preserved her engagement to a promising young man." In stark contrast to what Dr. Belous would later claim, Mrs. Raymond believed that the illegal abortion in Mexico "might possibly have saved Mary's life."[67]

In 1969, respected Los Angeles obstetrician Dr. Leon Belous appealed his 1966 conviction for referring Cheryl Bryant to an unlicensed physician for an illegal abortion. Dr. Belous defended his action. Rather than adhere to the strict constructionist view of the abortion statute, he argued that when he referred Ms. Bryant to Dr. Karl Lairtus, he did so because he feared she would resort to "butchery" in Tijuana.[68] Rather than see her mutilated in the hands of a greedy opportunist, he recognized her desperation and referred her to Dr. Lairtus for the procedure.[69]

On May 10, 1966, Karl Lairtus performed an abortion on Cheryl Bryant in an apartment office for $500. The police had received a tip from an unknown woman, and when they arrived, they found Cheryl recovering from her procedure. The police arrested Dr. Lairtus and while searching the office found notebooks indicating that Dr. Belous had referred thirteen other women to him. Dr. Belous was convicted of abortion and conspiring to commit abortion. The court of appeals affirmed the initial decision, so Dr. Belous took his case to the California Supreme Court. There he challenged the constitutionality of California's abortion statute.

The potential "butchery," Belous believed, was sufficient for him to state Ms. Bryant's life was in danger. Dr. Belous's fears were not solely based on a notion of nationalistic or ethnoracial inferiority. According to court records, Dr. Belous admonished the couple and warned them of the dangers of illegal abortions—especially those in Tijuana. Dr. Belous stated that "he was very familiar with the abortion business in Tijuana. He had visited the clinics there to learn about conditions and knew that women who went to

Tijuana were *taking their lives in their hands.*"[70] In fact, just weeks after Cheryl Bryant's abortion, the wife of a Woodland Hills dentist was found dead in a physician's office in Tijuana, Mexico, after an illegal abortion. Twenty-four-year-old Elyse Khedari had made arrangements for the abortion in Chula Vista, California. On Wednesday, June 8, 1966, a man picked Mrs. Khedari up from a motel at approximately seven-thirty in the morning. Her parents were told to meet her at a local bar three hours later to take her back home, but she never showed up. Her body was found the next morning. The physician who leased the office where her body was found—Dr. Miguel Sanchez Punzo—fled the city with his family.[71] That a physician performed this abortion meant little. What set these two abortions apart was geography—Cheryl's abortion in the United States and Elyse's in Mexico—and the fact that Elyse died and Cheryl didn't.

To some, Belous's argument worked to challenge the validity of the requisite "necessary to preserve life" clause in California's abortion statute. To what extent or degree must a woman's life be in danger? Was potential danger an acceptable justification for legal abortion? Or did the danger need to be imminent? The danger Dr. Belous imagined was premised in an assumption about what border abortions meant for American women. Specifically, Dr. Belous feared that Cheryl would "seek an illegal abortion in Tijuana under substandard medical conditions."[72] The basis of his concerns for Cheryl's life rested on several assertions: that illegal abortions were dangerous; that Mexican border towns offered American women an abortion emporium; and lastly, that illegal abortions in Mexico were inferior to illegal abortions in the United States.

The California Supreme Court debated tirelessly over this case. At the center of this case were the words "necessary" and "preserve." The court found no definition of either word that allowed them to sustain the existing law. Furthermore, courts had already rejected the interpretation of the existing statute that required certainty or immediacy of death. *People v. Abarbanel* (1965) and *People v. Ballard* (1959) had already established that requiring certainty of death would abridge a woman's constitutional rights—specifically her right to privacy and her right to life (since childbirth involved a risk of death, albeit small).[73] The court seemed to recognize that abortion laws did not reduce the number of abortions; rather, they simply reduced the number of *safe* abortions.

According to contemporary evidence, hygienic abortions performed early in pregnancy resulted in minimal risk to women, while illegal abortions were the greatest cause of maternal death in California. While not all abortions ended in death, the rate of infection from criminal abortions was also significantly greater. In an amicus brief for Dr. Belous, 178 deans of medical schools from California and the rest of the country stated that the unfortunate reality was that the "statute designed in 1850 to protect women from serious risks to life and health has in modern times become a scourge."[74]

After determining that the state's abortion law did not protect women, the court discussed whether the state had an interest in protecting the embryo or fetus. In examining legal precedents, the court found that there were differences in how the legal system punished the killing of a born child versus that of an embryo or fetus. Furthermore, the court recognized that the pregnant woman's rights took precedence over those of the unborn. In an amicus brief filed on behalf of Dr. Belous, a group of lawyers and law professors articulated that "unless an embryo develops to live birth as a child, it achieves no right to inherit, sue or even receive a birth certificate."[75] While the court debated whether the state's interest in the fetus could ever take precedence over the mother's, they decided that they could not forbid an abortion in any case where the result of childbirth could be death.

After Dr. Belous had referred Cheryl Bryant to Dr. Karl Lairtus, but before his trial had begun, Governor Ronald Reagan signed the Therapeutic Abortion Act (1967). The act was an attempt to liberalize the existing law and clarify the criteria for legal abortions. The law still prohibited abortions, but it provided exceptions within the first twenty weeks when necessary to preserve the life of the mother, when pregnancy would impair the physical or mental health of the mother, or when a girl under the age of fifteen had become pregnant through rape or incest. Although Belous was not convicted of violating the 1967 act, it did come into the California Supreme Court's discussion.

Ironically, in a case about women's legal access to abortions, the court devoted a significant amount of time discussing physicians' rights. The court recognized that physicians were the responsible parties who had to determine whether women had the right to an abortion. While physicians did not face criminal charges if they decided against an abortion and a woman died, they could face charges for performing an abortion when their criteria for doing so were challenged. If a physician decided a woman was entitled to an abortion, and a court decided he or she was wrong, the physician was punished. In having the punishments skewed to one direction, the physician's rights to due process and to practice medicine were deprived; furthermore, the structure of the law may compel physicians to deny abortions at all costs—much to the detriment of female patients. To some, the court's actions might suggest that physicians' rights eclipsed those of women.

Ultimately, Mexico became both a beacon and a specter—a possibility for women to find relief as well as a synonym for the potential dangers and perils of illegal operations in a purportedly vice-ridden and uncivilized country. The husband of the woman who told the *Chicago Tribune* her story of getting an illegal abortion in Mexico City expressed anger and frustration at their predicament. While his wife was satisfied with the care and treatment she received, he said he couldn't help but wonder what they were doing there. He said it made him "feel like a criminal . . . to have to go to a hot, dirty, foreign country." He continued, "I'm sure it was done as well as it could be done in Mexico. Still, why did it have to be done *there*?"[76] While this couple was fortunate to fly to Mexico City and pay for the services of a legitimate Mexican gynecologist, the $300 to ensure a "bona fide physician" at the border may have been too great a price for some women. Desperate or unsure, some women took their chances with self-inducing while others looked for cheaper abortionists at the border who were not necessarily as qualified.

Dr. Belous won his appeal at the California Supreme Court. The basis for his challenge was an assumption about the inferiority of Mexican abortions and the threat those abortions posed to American women. That the judges took on Dr. Belous's case—and California's antiquated law—suggests that the California Supreme Court accepted this fear of border abortions as a reasonable premise. While Mexico offered very real relief for countless women, the problem with Mexican abortions was the ambiguous and unrepresentative American law that drove women to them. While legislators in California grappled with their fears of Tijuana abortions, they failed to recognize that it was their California law that made women unsafe.

To American women in California, the law produced a certain kind of violence. It was a paternalistic, hegemonic system that favored physicians' ability to practice medicine free of legal constraints over women's autonomy. While the law itself could not stop women from exercising choice, it severely constrained their options and failed to protect them, demonstrating that even while the law attempted to regulate the most intimate aspects of women's lives, it did not necessarily see women as equal citizens. In their attempts to bypass the jurisdictional boundaries circumscribing their choices, women—standing on the borders of citizenship—exposed the limitations of state power in pursuit of personal autonomy.

Notes

1. California's abortion statute underwent a number of revisions (1861, 1872, 1935), but the basic tenets remained the same. According to the first abortion statute in 1850, "every person who shall administer or cause to be administered or taken, any medicinal substance, or shall use or cause to be used any instruments whatever, with the intention to procure the miscarriage of any woman then being with child, and shall be thereof duly convicted, shall be punished by imprisonment in the State Prison for a term not less than two years, nor more than five years: *Provided*, that no physician shall be affected by the last clause of this section, who, in the discharge of his professional duties, deems it necessary to produce the miscarriage of any woman in order to save her life." Crimes and Punishment Act § 45 (Stats 1850 ch 99 § 45).
2. Mary L. Dudziak and Leti Volpp, introduction, "Legal Borderlands: Law and the Construction of American Borders," *American Quarterly* 57, no. 3 (September 2005): 595.
3. Linda Gordon, *Woman's Body, Woman's Right: A Social History of Birth Control in America* (New York: Grossman, 1976), xxi.
4. The expansion of rights for some women often resulted from the exploitation of others. It would be imprecise to say there was a *total* expansion of reproductive liberties, as poor women and women of color continued to be targets for compulsory sterilization programs in the United States through the 1960s and 1970s. And finally, the history of abortion and sterilization does not begin in the 1960s. See Laura Briggs, *Reproducing Empire: Race, Sex, Science and U.S. Imperialism in Puerto Rico* (Berkeley: University of California Press, 2003); Leslie Reagan, *When Abortion Was a Crime* (Berkeley: University of California Press, 1998); Johanna Schoen, *Choice and Coercion: Birth Control, Sterilization in Public Health and Welfare* (Durham: University of North Carolina Press, 2005); and Alexandra Minna Stern, *Eugenic Nation: Faults and Frontiers of Better Breeding in America* (Berkeley: University of California Press, 2005).
5. It is impossible to quantify this given the secretive nature of abortions in this period. Some experts estimated that the number of illegal abortions in the United States ranged from two hundred thousand to two million per year. The figures for cross-border abortions, thus, are likely to be smaller since they were more accessible to women who lived closer to the border. Although the figures may be smaller, the issue was significant enough for the California Board of Medical Examiners and members of federal and local law enforcement to devote extensive worker hours to the issue and to create several hefty investigative files.
6. California Grand Jury, "Indictment of Julia Moore," September 19, 1859,

Nevada County, California, The Huntington Library, San Marino, California, HM 68279.

7. For an excellent analysis of abortion in mid-nineteenth-century California, see Albert L. Hurtado, *Intimate Frontiers: Sex, Gender, and Culture in Old California* (Albuquerque: University of New Mexico Press, 1999).

8. See footnote 1 for text of Crimes and Punishment Act § 45.

9. "Every person who provides, supplies, or administers to any woman, or procures any woman to take any medicine, drug, or substance, or uses or employs any instrument or other means whatever, with intent thereby to procure the miscarriage of such woman, unless the same is necessary to preserve her life, is punishable by imprisonment in the State prison not less than two nor more than five years." Laws of the State of California, *Statutes and Amendments to the Codes*, 1935, Section 274.

10. California's abortion statute was amended in 1861. The 1861 text read: "Every person who shall administer, or cause to be administered, or taken, or shall take, any medicinal substances, or shall use, or cause to be used, any instruments whatever, with the intention to procure abortion, or miscarriage, of any woman then being with child, and any woman who shall knowingly cause to be used upon herself, or consent to the use of such instruments upon herself with the intent to produce abortion, or miscarriage, when with child, and shall be thereof duly convicted, shall be punished by imprisonment in the State Prison, for a term not less than two years, nor more than five years; *provided*, that no Physician shall be affected by the last clause of this section, who, in the discharge of his professional duties, deems it necessary to produce abortion, or miscarriage, of any woman in order to save her life, nor shall any woman be affected by said last clause, when her Physician deems it necessary to have said abortion, or miscarriage, produced, in order to save her life, nor shall such Physician, or Surgeon, be arrested, indicted, or put on trial, or convicted by the testimony of such woman alone." Stats 1861 ch 521 § 1. The underlined portion was not in the 1872 revision. Although the statute still had a provision for physicians ("no Physician shall be affected by the last clause of this section"), the 1872 revision begins to chip away at some of the leeway that physicians had previously.

11. See Reagan, *When Abortion Was a Crime*; James C. Mohr, *Abortion in America: The Origins and Evolution of National Policy* (Oxford: Oxford University Press, 1979).

12. Loren G. Stern, "Abortion: Reform and the Law," *Journal of Criminal Law and Criminology*, 59, no. 1 (1968): 87.

13. For women who had private physicians at their beck and call, a therapeutic abortion was likely negotiable. In the event that a physician wanted to keep the business of a private patient, it would be in his or her interest to fabricate a justifiable reason for an abortion.

14. People v. Reginald L. Rankin, et al., 10 Cal.2d 198 (1937). Although most of the PCAR abortionists were physicians, many had previously lost their license or were sanctioned by the Board of Medical Examiners for performing abortions

without justification—that is, illegal abortions. Some of the abortionists, however, were not medical professionals. Rather, they were trained by obstetricians and gynecologists in the ring to perform the procedure. PCAR had very high standards, so even though these abortionists were not medical professionals per se, I would comfortably classify them as abortion specialists.

15. The Pacific Coast Abortion Ring did not lose a patient. Their abortionists exercised exceptional care, and in the few cases that required hospitalization, Reginald Rankin paid the women's hospital and medical fees (likely to keep them from speaking with the police).

16. "Monday October 25th, 1948—operative on location. . . . At 8:25 a.m. a gray two-door sedan Dodge California License No. 77-V-301, drove up to this location and parked at the curb. A woman driver about 40 yrs. of age, 5′ 7″, 120 lbs. buxom, brunette, wearing a green dress and tan coat, black leather gloves; got out and entered this residence. At 10:15 a.m. a two-tone (gray-black) 1948 Buick four-door sedan, California License No. 2-S-3653 drove up at this address headed the wrong way, parked and two women got out and entered this residence. No. 1 woman the driver, in her twenties, 5′ 7″, 110 lbs. wearing slacks; No. 2 woman, 45 yrs. 5′ 6″, 128 lbs. wearing light dress and coat, they remained therein until 10:40 a.m. when both came out entered car and drove north." From Confidential Report, Re: Miner Case, Operative J-9. Courtesy of Linda Heisig and Robin Beers.

17. For more on the interrogation and investigation procedures involving illegal abortions, see Reagan, *When Abortion Was a Crime.*

18. "$50 to $100—Most Places $50—Pays for Illegal Operations," *San Diego Sun,* June 27, 1939, 1.

19. In 1939, $50 would have the same buying power as approximately $880 in 2017.

20. John D'Emilio and Estelle B. Freedman, *Intimate Matters: A History of Sexuality in America* (New York: Harper & Row, 1988), 253.

21. "Abortion 'Quota' System Described," *AMA News,* May 2, 1969, newspaper clipping, California Committee on Therapeutic Abortion Records (Collection 1195). UCLA Library Special Collections, Charles E. Young Research Library.

22. "Abortion 'Quota' System Described," *AMA News.*

23. Carol Joffe, *Doctors of Conscience: The Struggle to Provide Abortion before and after* Roe v. Wade (Boston: Beacon, 1995), 64.

24. From July 1, 1927, to July 1, 1938, the Los Angeles County Coroner handled 54,078 cases. From July 1, 1938, to July 1, 1954, the Los Angeles County Coroner handled 110,114 cases.

25. Data for divorced women from 1927 to 1938 is 3 percent. The rate of divorced abortion fatalities from 1938 to 1954 was nearly double.

26. In short, the Spanish fantasy past is an artificial history that glorifies Spanish style and culture in Southern California while denigrating and erasing Mexican history, culture, and contributions. For a detailed analysis of the Spanish fantasy past, see William Deverell, *Whitewashed Adobe: The Rise of Los Angeles and*

the Remaking of Its Mexican Past (Berkeley: University of California Press, 2004), and Phoebe S. Kropp, *California Vieja: Culture and Memory in a Modern American Place* (Berkeley: University of California Press, 2006).

27. Some examples: "Chinese Coming by Way of Mexico," *San Francisco Chronicle*, April 7, 1890, 3; "To Clean Them Out: San Diego Aggressive over the Kidnapping," *San Francisco Chronicle*, May 24, 1892; "A Queer Case: Arrest of an American Citizen in Lower California," *Los Angeles Times*, September 20, 1893, 2; and "Murderer Morales near San Diego," *Los Angeles Times*, November 11, 1901, 11.

28. "Vice at Tia Juana," *Los Angeles Times*, January 21, 1916, section I, 14.

29. "Extradition Fight for Doctor Launched," *Los Angeles Times*, November 25, 1941, A2.

30. Rachel St. John, "Selling the Border: Trading Land, Attracting Tourists, and Marketing American Consumption on the Baja California Border, 1900–1934," in *Land of Necessity: Consumer Culture in the United States–Mexico Borderlands*, Alexis McCrossen, ed. (Durham, NC: Duke University Press, 2009), 114.

31. Marlene Medrano, "Sexuality, Migration, and Tourism in the 20th Century U.S.-Mexico Borderlands," *History Compass* 11, no. 3 (2013): 236; Eric Michael Schantz, "From the *Mexicali* Rose to the Tijuana Brass: Vice Tours of the United States-Mexico Border, 1910–1965" (PhD diss., University of California, Los Angeles, 2001).

32. Sarah Faithful, "Mexico's Choice: Abortion Laws and Their Effects throughout Latin America," Council on Hemispheric Affairs, September 28, 2016, www.coha.org. See also: Rudy J. Cardona, "Politics, Religion and Morality: An Obstacle to Women's Right to a Legal Abortion in Mexico," in *Verso Online Literary Journal*, California State University, Northridge, csun.edu; Ted G. Jelen and Jonathan Doc Bradley, "Abortion Opinion in Emerging Democracies: Latin America and Central Europe," Western Political Science Association Annual Meeting, Portland, Oregon, March 2012.

33. Steven W. Bender, *Run for the Border: Vice and Virtue in U.S.-Mexico Border Crossings* (New York: New York University Press, 2013), 81.

34. Section 182 of the California penal code states that "if two or more persons conspire: 1. To commit any crime. . . . They are punishable as follows: When they conspire to commit any felony, they shall be punishable in the same manner and to the same extent as if provided for the punishment of the said felony." Rankin and Buffum were found in violation of sections 182 and 274.

35. People of the State of California v. Buffum, 40 Ca1.2d 709 (1953).

36. "Illegal Operation: 'Travelling Abortion Mill' in California," *South China Morning Post & the Hong Kong Telegraph*, August 26, 1948, 7.

37. *People v. Buffum.*

38. *People v. Buffum.*

39. *People v. Buffum.*

40. Joel M. Taylor, "Alleged International Abortion Ring," March, 14, 1962,

California Department of Justice, Bureau of Criminal Identification and Investigation Report, Dept. of Consumer Affairs–Board of Medical Examiners Records, F3760:821, California State Archives, Office of the Secretary of State, Sacramento.

41. Gene Marine and Art Goldberg, "Abortion Reform: A Big Step Forward? No," *Ramparts*, July 1967, 46.

42. In 1969, $1,300 would have the same buying power as approximately $8,505 in 2017. Ruth Moss, "Not to the jurist, nor to the respectable surgeon," *Chicago Tribune*, October 19, 1969, J34; Jacquin Sanders, "The Shadow World of the Abortionist," *Austin Statesman*, June 7, 1970, B4.

43. Beginning in the July 1, 1954–June 30, 1955, coroner's reports, a new statistical category and annotation emerged: "found dead at scene" and "died under observation." Representative of the effects that mobility had on the abortion industry, these categories lasted only a couple of fiscal years, as by the July 1, 1956–June 30, 1957, report, the coroner's office and reports had been reorganized.

44. One group of six young women from Berkeley paid a contact $600 each to transport them to Juarez for illegal abortions. Instead of taking them to a clinic, their contact took them to the police, took their money, and fled to El Paso. The women were detained in Juarez and were unable to have the abortions. "Women Seeking Abortion Stranded in Juarez," *Sun Reporter* 26, no. 46 (December 7, 1958): 17.

45. Taylor, "Alleged International Abortion Ring," Dept. of Consumer Affairs–Board of Medical Examiners Records, California State Archives.

46. Taylor, "Alleged International Abortion Ring."

47. Letter from Archie D. Ross, assistant secretary to Richard R. Rogan, chief deputy attorney general, July 28, 1959, Dept. of Consumer Affairs—Board of Medical Examiners Records, F3760:818, California State Archives.

48. Taylor, "Alleged International Abortion Ring."

49. Assembly Interim Committee on Criminal Procedure, Abortion Hearing, AB 2614 (December 17–18, 1962).

50. Assembly Interim Committee on Criminal Procedure, Abortion Hearing, AB 2614.

51. In the July 1, 1956–June 30, 1957, fiscal year, the coroner's office reorganized and altered its reports. Instead of detailed accounts and numbers, the reports became biennial and provided only selected statistics. Although they continued to provide the number of abortions, they ceased to list abortionist categories, marital status, and age. They continued to use this limited approach to compiling data until the July 1, 1969–June 30, 1970, report, in which they, for the first time, specifically listed racial and ethnic data and a fetal death. In reference to the asterisk, there is an issue with dates in the July 1, 1967–June 30, 1969, coroner's biennial report, so I did not include the numbers because they appeared to be an accidental reprint.

52. Kristin Luker, *Abortion and the Politics of Motherhood* (Berkeley: University of California Press, 1984), 58.

53. See Kelly Lytle Hernández, *Migra! A History of the U.S. Border Patrol* (Berkeley: University of California Press, 2010); Eithne Luibhéid, *Entry Denied: Controlling Sexuality at the Border* (Minneapolis: University of Minnesota Press, 2002); Mae Ngai, *Impossible Subjects: Illegal Aliens and the Making of Modern America* (Princeton: Princeton University Press, 2004).
54. Holly M. Karibo, "Swashbuckling Criminals and Border Bandits: Fighting Vice in North America's Borderlands, 1945–1960," *Social History* 47, no. 95 (November 2014): 706.
55. Karibo, "Swashbuckling Criminals," 711.
56. Karibo, "Swashbuckling Criminals," 727.
57. Karibo, "Swashbuckling Criminals," 727.
58. In some instances, abortionists simply packed women with gauze in order to induce premature labor. The abortion, or miscarriage, would be complete once another physician removed the gauze.
59. Leslie J. Reagan, "Crossing the Border for Abortions: California Activists, Mexican Clinics, and the Creation of a Feminist Health Agency in the 1960s," *Feminist Studies* 26, no. 2 (Summer 2000): 323.
60. In the late 1950s, Patricia Maginnis would stand on street corners in the San Francisco Bay Area and pass out leaflets, cartoons, petitions, and surveys on or about abortion. By 1964, Lana Phelan and Rowena Gurner had joined her to create a small coalition—the Army of Three—to inform women about abortion options and to push legislation to repeal abortion laws.
61. "Dr. Paris and a male assistant appeared to be highly trained professional people. The office was well equipped, smelled of disinfectant, and all instruments appeared to be sterile. Dr. Paris performed the abortion in a highly efficient manner, [and] gave . . . a sedative prior to the operation and an antibiotic [after]." From Taylor, "Alleged International Abortion Ring," Dept. of Consumer Affairs–Board of Medical Examiners Records, California State Archives.
62. "Letters to the Army of Three," The Walker Art Center, http://www.walkerart.org/magazine/2012/andrea-bowers-patricia-maginnis-abortion#.
63. Assembly Interim Committee on Criminal Procedure, Abortion Hearing, AB 2614.
64. Names have been changed. County of Santa Clara District Attorney Investigator's Report, December 21, 1960, Dept. of Consumer Affairs–Board of Medical Examiners Records, BME, F3760:821, California State Archives.
65. Writing about illegal abortions creates a historiographical dilemma. For the most part, safe and successful abortions are invisible from the historical record. My ability to access sources on abortion is predicated on women dying or becoming injured from the procedure, since most women did not openly talk about their abortions. At first glance, it might appear that I am suggesting that abortions are dangerous; however, it is worth stating explicitly that there are countless successful illegal abortions that I am unable to write about because records do not exist. Women who had successful abortions rarely appear in the historical record.

66. Names have been changed. Taylor, "Alleged International Abortion Ring," Dept. of Consumer Affairs–Board of Medical Examiners Records, California State Archives.
67. Taylor, "Alleged International Abortion Ring." Names have been changed. Emphasis mine.
68. The statute permitted abortions only in cases when the life or health of the mother was in danger; when the fetus was likely to be born with a congenital deformity; or when the pregnancy was the result of a rape or incest.
69. Dr. Karl Lairtus was a licensed physician in Mexico but did not have the license to perform medicine in the United States—where Ms. Bryant's procedure took place.
70. People v. Belous, Crim. 71 Cal.2d 954 (1969), Crim. 12739. Emphasis mine.
71. "Authorities Free Parents of Dead Girl," *Los Angeles Times,* June 14, 1966.
72. Edward Husse, "Abortion Law—California Abortion Law Voided," *Dickinson Law Review,* 1969–1970, 772.
73. *Griswold v. Connecticut* (1967), *Loving v. Virginia* (1967), *Skinner v. Oklahoma* (1942), and *Perez v. Sharp* (1948).
74. Amici Curiae Brief on behalf of Medical School Deans and Others in Support of Appellant, 12, *People v. Belous,* (1969), California Committee on Therapeutic Abortion Records. UCLA Library Special Collections, Charles E. Young Research Library.
75. Application for Leave to File Brief of Amici Curiae in Support of the Position of Appellant, 16, *People v. Belous* (1969), California Committee on Therapeutic Abortion Records. UCLA Library Special Collections, Charles E. Young Research Library.
76. Moss, "Not to the jurist," 76. Emphasis mine.

Part II
Legal Borderlands of Property and Citizenship

4

Legal Ambiguities on the Ground

Black Californians' Land Claims, 1848–1870

Dana Elizabeth Weiner

In 1851 . . . other colored men with myself, drew up and published . . .
[a proclamation of] our determination to use all moral means to secure
legal claim to all the rights and privileges of American citizens.

Mifflin Gibbs, 1902

In the Methodist church at Sacramento in November 1855, Reverend Darius
P. Stokes of San Francisco addressed the inaugural meeting of the California Colored Convention.[1] He argued that African Americans underutilized
the public lands in their state. "There is plenty of land for us to cultivate,"
he proclaimed; indeed, he contended that they should take advantage of
this abundance. The meeting's committee on mining and agriculture said
African Americans needed to move onto public lands (which at that time
included lands eligible for homesteading), arguing that they saw no evident
legal impediments: "We can find no fact going to show that we may not
settle upon and lawfully possess portions of Government lands. We would
respectfully urge you to use all lawful means to secure for yourselves right
and just claims to the ownership of the soil, as a means to usefulness, re-
spectability, and wealth."[2] This rallying cry conveyed a vision of the West as
a vacant space, open for black settlement. This picture had two flaws, for the
West was never empty and opportunities for landownership in California
diminished after 1855 as legal strictures tightened around African American
land rights. In this context and in this ambiguous legal space, black Californians still claimed land.

From the beginning of the 1850s, a small but outspoken cohort of African American reformers like Mifflin Gibbs and Darius P. Stokes actively fought to protect their land and property claims. These black activists formed organizations including the Colored Executive Committee, which planned California Colored Conventions to fight for their rights.[3] They allied their efforts for equal citizenship with those of the larger struggle for equality across the nation, ongoing since the early national era. Black Californians joined in this national movement with that first statewide Colored Convention in 1855 and convened three more meetings up to 1865. Men (and occasionally women) from San Francisco, Sacramento, Marysville, and smaller communities participated in the conventions. African American reformers, in the Colored Executive Committee and beyond, also used the press, petitions, and the courts to publicize their sweeping equality agenda.[4]

Property formed a central component of the broader citizenship struggle for black California activists. Their demands for property rights were all the more important thanks to the economic reality of California. There, African Americans wanted to protect their property both because they believed they were entitled to equal rights and because in California—in contrast to most other areas of the United States and unusual for their time—they were able to buy land, acquire assets, and run businesses. Even before the end of the US war with Mexico and the beginning of American governance, African Americans claimed property rights. During the gold rush, they capitalized on the opportunities in the goldfields and the industries that served them. They thus created distinctive economic prosperity in California.[5]

Land rights formed an integral part of many nineteenth-century Americans' vision of self-sufficient citizenship; this was particularly true in relation to public land in the West. As they argued that they had the rights to own, protect, and work land as a citizenship privilege, black Californians shared in a long-term goal. As far back as the colonial era, as free blacks refused to be identified as human property, they had aimed to acquire land, in keeping with their view that self-proprietorship held the most secure route to their independence.[6] Their property rights were tenuous, but nevertheless black Californians saw landownership as their best strategy. In California, African Americans' access to land was closely tied to ideas about rights and citizenship; they saw owning property as the key to securing rights, even as they gained land through dispossessing others. In the early years of American governance, some black Californians seized moments of flexibility to claim citizenship rights, exploiting the contradictions between federal and state laws.

Both verbally and in print, African American leaders in California consistently lauded their property attainments and advocated land acquisition as the best route to self-sufficiency. Black Californians made reciprocal arguments; as they claimed they were entitled to the right to property, they also argued that their extant fiscal accomplishments and property entitled them to rights. They repeatedly noted in 1855, 1856, and 1857 that economic success and political rights were linked means of self-advancement. Black Californian activists emphasized their self-made success. When he addressed the 1855 convention, San Franciscan T. M. D. Ward argued that black Californians had demonstrated that they deserved equality since they benefited the community economically, morally, and mentally. His compatriots at that convention agreed, and passed a resolution that asserted that African Americans, as taxpayers, deserved rights. Both of these arguments tapped into the ideological strategy of claiming rights in consequence of having augmented the nation's coffers with tax money.[7]

These arguments were long-standing; in 1858 the state's Colored Executive Committee echoed such equal rights claims on the basis of black Californians' identities as taxpayers and property holders. They wrote to draw attention to "the millions of property owned in the State by colored men" and how "a moiety of their earnings has contributed to embellish every proud city of the land." They argued that they had performed "more than a proportionate share" of the work that went into building California and that this entitled them to "impartial justice." They seized an active role in the settler-colonialist project. This effort needed to continue, according to speakers at the California Colored Conventions who described acquiring land for agriculture, business, or mining as the most promising avenue of economic opportunity; they consistently recommended this course of action to their peers.[8] Even while property rights remained very important for African Americans, they faced mounting legal obstacles to them. At the state level, reform organizations became less active in the late 1850s, but black Californians remained aware of the need to safeguard their land rights.[9]

While California had a small African American population throughout this era, their land rights in the Golden State nonetheless merit scholarly attention from historians of black citizenship, for they offer lessons about little-known aspects of discrimination and battles against it.[10] Once the United States took over California in 1848, African Americans soon seized the unprecedented economic opportunities of the ensuing gold rush. Some capitalized on these favorable circumstances.[11] Simultaneously, slavery influenced their status, for even while efforts to legitimize the institution in California failed, it nonetheless illegally existed there. Slaveholding migrants still brought slaves to California, and many residents, even those who opposed slavery, held prejudices against African Americans. The legislature even tried to block African American migration to California five times between 1849 and 1858, but these measures did not pass.[12] Still, African Americans remained only a minimal portion of the overall population, as is evident in table 4.1.

Controversies over African American land rights arose in the context of long-standing, pervasive, multifaceted racial strife in California. Other historians have ably told stories of California's Indigenous, Californio, Hawaiian, and Chinese populations, but it is essential to note that the state had for centuries hosted encounters among different linguistic, national, and racial groups, as well as legal cultures.[13] This study assumes that race, property, and the law are contested social constructions, always political, produced in specific places and times.[14] While law can give only a partial picture of a society, it can be a significant one.[15] As people Americanized these lands, they brought with them the multifaceted racism that legal scholar Devon Carbado argues is intrinsic to that process and specific to the United States.[16] Americanization added a new layer that further complicated extant biases in California. For example, per the Treaty of Guadalupe Hidalgo that ended the US war with Mexico in 1848, Mexican citizens who remained in the areas that Mexico had ceded were entitled to US citizenship. Nevertheless, from the beginning white Californians limited this citizenship, as is evident from the 1849 California Constitutional Convention's debate over whether Californios qualified as "white male citizens."[17] Convention attendees also "deemed" Indigenous Californians "nonwhite and ineligible for citizenship."[18]

These examples, among many, prove that racial hierarchies lay bedrock-deep in the history of rights—including land rights—in California. Race's social meaning emerged in the Spanish conquest and violent divestment of Indigenous lands and the establishment and destruction of the missions. Later it pervaded the colonial and Mexican land grants, as well as the wholesale American invasion of the gold country and the state as a whole, both again at the expense of Indigenous lives and land rights. Immigrants from China and elsewhere, as well as those of African descent, presented further challenges to land grants and to Indigenous sovereignty. Race and denial of citizenship rights of people defined as nonwhite underlay all of these developments, and in overlapping ways.[19]

Table 4.1.
Estimated California Demographics, ca. 1846–1870.

	Pre-1846	1850	1852	1860	1870
Indigenous population	100,000–150,000	100,000–110,000	32,529–200,000	17,798–35,000	7,241–30,000
Black population[1]	—	962	2,206	4,086	4,272
Chinese population	—	—	11,794	34,935	50,000
Total non-Indigenous population	15,000; majority were Californios[2]	92,597	260,949	379,994	560,247

Sources: Tomás Almaguer, *Racial Fault Lines: The Historical Origins of White Supremacy in California* (Berkeley: University of California Press, 1994), 26, 27, 70, 176; Clayton E. Cramer, *Black Demographic Data, 1790–1860: A Sourcebook* (Westport, CT: Greenwood, 1997), 147; Benjamin Madley, *An American Genocide: The United States and the California Indian Catastrophe, 1846–1873* (New Haven: Yale University Press, 2016), 346–347; Philip M. Montesano, *Some Aspects of the Free Negro Question in San Francisco, 1849–1870* (San Francisco: R and E Research Associates, 1973), 12; Joshua Paddison, *American Heathens: Religion, Race, and Reconstruction in California* (Berkeley: University of California Press, 2012), 17; Quintard Taylor, *In Search of the Racial Frontier: African Americans in the American West, 1528–1990* (New York: Norton, 1998), 104.

1. Actual numbers of people of African descent were probably higher than recorded; over time, some individuals changed their racial identification in censuses, whether due to evading former slaveholders, changing definitions of "black," or seizing the social or economic capital of a different racial identity. Cramer, *Black Demographic Data*, 2–3; Jack D. Forbes, "The Early African Heritage of California," in *Seeking El Dorado: African Americans in California*, ed. Lawrence Brooks De Graaf, Kevin Mulroy, and Quintard Taylor (Los Angeles and Seattle: Autry Museum of Western Heritage and University of Seattle Press, 2001), 80–82.

2. Other issues with census data include that published census records did not then distinguish Californios, Mexicans, or other Latinos as a separate category; the census first did so in 1930. Albert L. Hurtado, *Intimate Frontiers: Sex, Gender, and Culture in Old California* (Albuquerque: University of New Mexico Press, 1999), 93; Natalia Molina, *How Race Is Made in America: Immigration, Citizenship, and the Historical Power of Racial Scripts* (Berkeley: University of California Press, 2013), 5.

The agents of the American settlement of California participated in extraordinary violence against the Indigenous population—distinct to California in its scale if not in character.[20] White Californians believed they were destined to exterminate local Indigenous people and simultaneously feared being overrun by the Chinese population.[21] White supremacy underlay settlers' violent displacement of Indigenous people from their California lands and their presumption of superior American land uses. This sense of entitlement followed from the Doctrine of Discovery as the US Supreme Court laid out in 1823 in *Johnson v. M'Intosh*.[22] In the early 1850s, agents of the Department of the Interior negotiated treaties with about 25,000 Indigenous Californians that would have created large reservations, but these laws stalled in the US Senate. White Californians who wanted unimpeded access to these lands imposed overwhelming pressure, and after the treaties failed, the federal government claimed much of this land as "part of the public domain" and thus open to homesteading.[23]

Laws and policies that denied the legitimacy of nonwhite land claims went beyond this wholesale eradication of Indigenous title; Anglos also found the differences between their landownership system and the Mexican one convenient for the displacement of many Californios from their land. After Mexican independence in 1821, the Mexican Congress distributed "large tracts of [ostensibly] unoccupied land to individuals" to facilitate expanded settlement of this region. The Mexican government granted over seven hundred such tracts from 1833 to 1846. After the US takeover, the Federal Land Law of 1851 established the Board of Land Commissioners as the adjudicator of these claims, and it failed to take into consideration traditional land boundaries and communal land practices. Many of the Anglo lawyers who shepherded cases through the courts from 1852 to 1855 took a share of the land in the process, too. While many Californios retained their claims for a time, by 1880 Americans had found ways to acquire many of their lands.[24]

The land-hungry migrating American population was eager to seize California lands immediately as they came under US control, but they had to wait. California had stricter land grant policies than did other new nineteenth-century states, and initially, authorities selectively recognized Indigenous populations and the Californios who already occupied these lands. Historian Paul Gates notes that federal practice in other lands that had "an alien population" was free distribution of land grants to landless Americans at the point of territorial transfer. Landless migrants to California had to exercise patience until 1853, when US law sanctioned their settlement "on unsurveyed land." Even then, it was unclear what yet fell into the public domain and thus upon which lands people could settle at discounted land prices. Disputes over the legitimacy and extent of Spanish and Mexican land grants, themselves laden with racialized concepts of citizenship, continued until

1856 and beyond. Many new Californians who tried to acquire a portion of the public lands faced difficulties, not the least from wealthy landowners who sought to monopolize the land and oust smallholders, but African Americans encountered specific challenges of legitimacy.[25]

At the same time that black Californians sought property rights, the state and the nation were undergoing turmoil; partisan politics, informed by escalating racism, operated to impede African Americans' citizenship rights. Even when the writers of the California Constitution were debating its content in 1849, many used partisan justifications to block African American rights. During the 1850s, California's new government imposed ever more rigid racial categories on the population, and soon, extensive antiblack legislation emerged in the Golden State. The state's "Black Laws" formalized devastating discrimination and racialized citizenship limitations. These laws disenfranchised African Americans and barred them from court testimony against white people, among other issues; they also interfered with black Californians' homestead rights.[26] The "Black Laws" were just one local manifestation of African Americans' subordinate citizenship, and this legislation was in keeping with widespread antebellum ideas that African Americans lacked state and federal citizenship rights.[27]

This pattern held and even increased over the years; as the United States became ever more divided along sectional lines, many white Californians held fast to racial stratification. Beginning in the latter half of the 1850s, black Californians met with ongoing resistance as they sought to remove prejudicial laws. The Southern-born, proslavery faction of the Democratic Party that dominated state politics for most of the 1850s aimed to quell African American advancement and political upheaval, even beyond the Civil War.[28] Black Californians took action to claim land rights in this legal background.

Sectionalism and racialized political tensions had concrete effects for black Californians, particularly after the US Supreme Court's 1857 decision in *Dred Scott v. Sandford* in March 1857. Chief Justice Roger Taney's decision in *Dred Scott* both grew out of and increased sectional tensions; by setting the notorious precedent that African American people were not citizens, it decimated their rights nationally and extended slavery's reach further into the free states.[29] Even as *Dred Scott*'s legal legacy has engendered hundreds of pages of analysis, a dearth remains in terms of historical understanding of that landmark case's effects for black Californians' property rights. Historians have noted that *Dred Scott*'s effects on California African

American rights led to their 1858 exodus to Victoria, British Columbia, but have neglected to examine how officials' interpretations of the decision affected the land and property of those who remained in California.[30] As *Dred Scott* legally solidified two-tiered citizenship, it, along with other legal precedents about citizenship, had substantial effects on land rights. This landmark decision was thus relevant to California African Americans both because of its implications for fugitive slaves there and because of its effects on western African Americans' rights since they, like other Americans in the region, prioritized access to land, especially public land.[31] In addition to weakening their legal position in California—as elsewhere in the nation—*Dred Scott* undermined blacks' already tenuous land rights there.

In September 1862, San Francisco entrepreneur and newspaper editor Peter Anderson wrote, "The idea of a homestead for every family has become almost universal among the American people."[32] In California in the 1850s, federal, state, and local land laws lacked clarity and were sometimes contradictory; this has led to scholars' misapprehension that people of African descent completely lacked land rights there. In fact, some black Californians exploited this legal ambiguity to fight for their land rights, at the very moment when racialized interpretations of laws, often influenced by *Dred Scott*, to some degree interfered with their ability to own public land. California historians including Robert Chandler overstate the case in claiming that from 1850 to 1860, "only white men could gain public land." As evidence of this policy, Chandler cites the 1858 decision of A. C. Bradford, the pro-Southern registrar at the US General Land Office in Stockton. Bradford was unequivocal: "By the laws of the United States, colored men are not entitled to the right of preemption."[33] As the local representative of the federal government, Bradford interpreted federal law in such a way that African Americans lacked land rights, but how widely people shared this interpretation is difficult to assess.

Chandler presents evidence from Stockton and the area around Marysville, but more data is needed to establish that this was actually statewide policy. He gives no examples to prove that this decision would have applied outside of that branch of the land office. He cites a May 21, 1863, article in the *Marysville Appeal* that indicates that some people in the region had, between 1857 and 1863, refused to allow African Americans to homestead. It states, "Heretofore colored men have been forcibly expelled from portions

Table 4.2.

Milestones in California African American Property Rights, 1841–1870.

Date	Federal or state	Law or decree	Effects on African American land rights
1841	Federal	Preemption Act, requires citizenship to preempt	Depended on interpretation
1843	Federal	Attorney General Hugh Legaré, free African Americans can preempt public land	Affirmed
1851	CA State	California statutes re homesteads had no racial qualifications for homesteads	Affirmed
1853	PA State	Supreme Court decision, *Foremanns v. Tamm*, free African Americans can preempt public land	Affirmed
1854	CA State	Supreme Court decision in *People v. Hall*, nonwhites were not citizens	Diminished
1857	Federal	Supreme Court, *Dred Scott v. Sanford*, African Americans were not citizens	Diminished
1857	Federal	US Land Office, following from *Dred Scott*	Diminished
1859	Federal	Joseph Wilson of US Land Office, following from *Dred Scott*	Diminished
1860	CA State	Assembly, homesteads only for "free white men"	Diminished
1861	CA State	Supreme Court decision, *Williams v. Young*, "mulattoes" could have homesteads	Affirmed
1862	Federal	Homestead Act	Depended on belief re black citizenship
1862	Federal	Attorney General Bates, African Americans are citizens with rights	Affirmed
1863	Federal	Joseph Wilson of US Land Office, following Bates	Affirmed
1866	Federal	Civil Rights Act, African Americans have right to property Fourteenth Amendment, defines national citizenship	Affirmed
1868	Federal		Affirmed

of the public domain which they had improved and paid taxes upon in this District," but it offers no specifics or documentation.[34] The antiblack limits on holding public land appear to have been short-lived developments of the late 1850s that resulted from *Dred Scott,* which indeed restricted California African Americans' access to the public domain. Since *Dred Scott* set the precedent that even free blacks lacked citizenship, the debates over homestead rights that followed that decision reveal much about the law, white Californians' biases, and African Americans' citizenship ideas.[35]

Dred Scott's land effects soon emerged, with a federal proclamation from the Secretary of the Interior in August 1857 that "free colored persons are not entitled to the benefits of [preemption, or squatter rights]."[36] American citizens had been able to preempt land as early as 1841 (and on an informal basis, even earlier).[37] Claims under the US Preemption Act of 1841 allowed certain people to claim up to 160 acres of land upon which they were already living and making improvements. To qualify, individuals had to fit the criteria of an independent citizen, defined somewhat broadly in this case as "being the head of a family, or widow, or single man, over the age of twenty-one years, and being a citizen of the United States," or having begun the naturalization process. They could pay for this land at $1.25 per acre and could do so before it went up for general sale. This initially applied only to surveyed public lands, but the US government extended the preemption right to some unsurveyed public lands in 1853.[38] The 1857 US Land Office decree entailed that *Dred Scott* meant that since African Americans, as noncitizens, lacked government protection for their rights, they could no longer use preemption to claim public lands. This was, where enforced, an immense blow.

Post–*Dred Scott,* the activists at the October 1857 California Colored Convention were undaunted; even as the speakers repeated their recommendation that African Americans own and work the land, they also protested the land office's decision to deny them preemption rights. Convention chair William H. Hall said that in the meantime, African Americans ought to continue purchasing land even if the government might refuse them preemption rights—and thus discounted prices. On principle, he claimed that their need for land and to prove themselves as citizens overruled the unjustly high price of these lands.[39] The denial of black Californians' preemption rights led to financial disadvantage.

At the national level, even by 1858 some people had pushed back against *Dred Scott* and the associated 1857 Land Office proclamation. Frederick C.

Brightly—the Philadelphia lawyer who compiled the revised text of the pre-emption law—opposed both rulings, for he argued that both the 1857 Land Office proclamation and *Dred Scott* contradicted legal precedents from 1843 and 1853 that had previously affirmed African Americans' preemption rights. In 1843, US attorney general Hugh Legaré had stated that free African Americans were citizens and that they were "eligible to purchase land under federal law." They thus could buy public land. Legaré's 1853 citation was to a Pennsylvania Supreme Court case that had explicitly affirmed free African Americans' preemption rights. Legaré would not, however, rule on whether African Americans were citizens; he thus established multiple categories of citizenship.[40] Despite Brightly's efforts and Legaré's middling stance, neither of these precedents proved definitive.

In March 1859 Joseph S. Wilson of the US Land Office continued to claim that African Americans, thanks to *Dred Scott,* lacked preemption rights. Wilson argued in a widely reprinted letter to the *Pittsburgh Gazette* that "colored persons are not citizens of the United States, as contemplated by the pre-emption law of . . . 1841, and are therefore, not legally entitled to pre-empt public lands."[41] From 1857 to 1862, black Californians lacked assistance from the federal government regarding land rights.[42]

Still, despite these setbacks and *Dred Scott*'s effects, California activists nevertheless tirelessly promoted land acquisition, deeming it the linchpin of their mechanism to improve their economic and citizenship status. In 1859, a group of "about forty" business-minded California African Americans, including many men from the convention movement, founded a savings and land association. Their first agenda was to raise $10,000 for land speculation, and if they attained that goal in one year, they aimed to expand their capital pool to $100,000. Newspaper editor Peter Anderson argued in a letter to the New York *Weekly Anglo-African* that this association might hold the key to combating *Dred Scott*'s intended agenda. Anderson claimed the Supreme Court decision aimed to diminish free African Americans' political and economic rights, rather than those of enslaved people. Anderson asserted, "[Chief Justice] Taney did not aim the fatal blow particularly at the slave but at the free colored people of the United States. While recovering from the infliction of that blow let us endeavor to get a better foundation to stand upon ourselves."[43]

Anderson's letter also reveals his ideas that black Californians were entitled to conquer and potentially forcibly acquire land. In calling for African Americans to rally behind the land speculation project, Anderson wrote that they ought to focus their "whole power and energies for the ostensible object of acquiring territory, either by conquest or purchase."[44] This willingness to consider "conquest" indicates that he, too, may have subscribed to the idea of western lands as open for the taking. While the savings and land association's efforts do not appear to have borne fruit, groups like theirs show California African Americans' sense of the legitimacy of their own claims in comparison with those of others, as well as how they creatively sought to improve their land rights despite legal challenges.

Anderson and his compatriots faced further challenges at the state level, as African Americans' rights to homestead on public land in California diminished even further in 1860. The State Assembly added a new racially restrictive provision that a homestead claimant must be "a free white person . . . and a citizen of the United States." The assembly appended the word "white" to the qualifications for certain homestead rights, and it also requested that the US government pass a homestead bill to facilitate qualified settlers'—meaning whites'—access to public lands. Earlier statutes had been race-blind in their language. The 1849 California Constitution had established the right for "all heads of families" to have "a certain portion of the homestead and other property" preserved from "forced sale." The former state homestead statute—in operation since 1851—had also lacked such racial qualifications.[45]

Black Californians persisted, and eventually they garnered some results from their long-standing efforts to acquire land and to use ambiguous laws to their advantage; the nation's changes after the Civil War began in 1861 facilitated these shifts. A combination of political transformation and the aid of the California Supreme Court and the US Land Office helped them. In the realm of politics, African Americans in California finally had some allies as local and national divisions weakened the formerly dominant local Democratic Party, making space for the Republican Party to come to power in 1861. Over the next few years the Union Party unified free soil Democrats and Republicans and proved somewhat receptive to black Californians' rights; they thus finally secured more access to public land.[46] In turn, most African Americans in California supported the Republican Party.[47] *Dred Scott* had lost much of its support across the nation, and this, too, had clear effects on land policy.[48]

In *Williams v. Young*, a January 1861 California Supreme Court decision, the court defined people of "mulatto" ancestry as eligible for homesteads. The Youngs, the mixed-race family in question, faced eviction from their Shasta home due to a dispute over who held the legitimate title to the homestead they had been occupying since 1855, and thus had claimed since before the ruling in *Dred Scott*.[49] They retained title to their land and won a legal victory just before the outbreak of the Civil War. In María Montoya's analysis of the Maxwell Land Grant in New Mexico, she demonstrates that US courts refused to recognize western land claims based on Indigenous and Mexican land use practices. In contrast to her findings there, while the Young family were also nonwhite, as were most of the Maxwell claimants, the formers' legal claim was firmly within the American legal system and property practices. In keeping with Montoya's argument that land disputes in the Southwest were "not simply about Whites removing people of color" (although they were often about that), but rather could often involve alliances of landowners across perceived racial boundaries, in this case the interests of the Young family overrode those of the Indigenous Shasta population.[50] Right from the beginning of the gold rush, miners and militias near the Northern Mines had responded to smaller skirmishes with Indigenous people with massacres that decimated the Shasta and neighboring groups. These settlers faced few consequences for what Benjamin Madley deems their "genocidal tendencies and tactics," and the Shasta area was at the center of vigilante activities well into the mid-1850s.[51] The Youngs fought their legal land battle on a place itself only recently and forcibly opened for settlement.

Given these ambiguities in the law and complicated racial dynamics, perhaps it is to be expected that on the ground people held widely varying ideas about African Americans' ability to own property. In this context, black Californians' fight to maintain property rights represents not only persistent pursuit of their goals but also a reasonable course of action in light of having a basis for hope for change. In September 1862, Peter Anderson remained at the forefront of promotion of public landholding, arguing that African Americans needed to be more attentive to "the homestead question," due to its importance for their rights. Indeed, he claimed they closely resembled their white counterparts and on that basis deserved rights. Anderson believed they must "prove nothing more nor less than that, as men and as Americans we are moved by the same impulses, guided by the same motives, and have the same Yankee-like go-a headativeness as the white American. We assume for ourselves . . . that we are just like other men, in inclination, instinct and capacity, and can do whatever it is right and proper that other men should do, similarly circumstanced." Anderson noted, despite these similarities, that few African Americans had attained homesteads, even as they embraced the opportunities he saw settlement as offering them, with all of its great promise and expanded access. He claimed that this was because, "by the force of circumstances and disabling laws," most blacks stayed in cities and worked for others. The editor contrasted this with the numerous immigrants who had already accessed nearby lands, the "thousands, nay, millions of Europeans [who] have, in the Western States, acquired homesteads and fortunes." Anderson reinforced arguments his compatriots in the California Colored Conventions had made about the link between African Americans' ambitions, economic success, and their need to establish their rights as citizens. He described it as a "duty" and immediate priority for African Americans to secure homesteads and to take advantage of the Homestead Act Congress had passed that May.[52]

Like the 1841 Preemption Act, the Homestead Act also allowed settlers, provided that they met household status and citizenship criteria, to claim and settle on 160 acres at advantageous prices. The language of this act differed slightly from the 1841 act; it was open to "any person," of the minimum age of twenty-one *or* who was the "head of a family," as long as they were a US citizen or in the process of naturalization, provided they had not "borne arms against the United States Government or given aid and comfort to its enemies." After six months they could pay $1.25 per acre and buy the land, or if they stayed for five or more years they could become the land's owners after paying ten dollars in fees.[53] Again, the question of eligibility hinged on whether officials recognized African American citizenship. Some were willing to do so, and the Civil War and Reconstruction brought further changes in this realm, too. The Homestead Act appears to have applied to former slaves and, after the Fourteenth Amendment, to African Americans in general.

African Americans who sought full citizenship rights appealed to both state and national land offices to protect their property. They eventually found a few allies on the federal government side, including US Attorney General Edward Bates, a conservative Republican from Missouri who had staunchly advocated "compulsory deportation" of freed slaves, clearly a position opposed to African American rights.[54] Still, the war had changed his views, much as it had that of Abraham Lincoln, the president who had appointed him; Bates asserted in November 1862 that native-born free men of African descent were US citizens and that states could not abridge federal citizenship rights.[55]

One individual who benefited from shifts in federal ideas about citizenship was Benjamin Berry. He was a formerly enslaved landholder who became an "actual and bona fide settler upon the Public Lands"; in 1863 he worked a plot of land near Marysville. Berry, then sixty-seven and recently married, had followed correct preemption practices, including selecting unsurveyed, "unoccupied, vacant public land," and making the requisite "improvements." Long after Berry settled on the land, some white settlers who knew he lacked equal legal rights sought to oust him; in fact, they "attempted to acquire title to the land claimed by him, through the State." The Republican newspaper the *Marysville Appeal* wrote up Berry's case at length. The editor noted that in previous years and under Democratic administrations, the US Land Office had followed "the spirit of the infamous Dred Scott decision" and refused African Americans the right of preemption, even as the federal government happily accepted revenue from African American taxpayers.[56]

Circumstances were different in 1863. Indeed, Marysville land registrar A. J. Snyder wrote to the US Land Office on Berry's behalf. With the aid of the previously mentioned acting commissioner Joseph S. Wilson of the US Land Office, Berry kept possession of his property despite challenges to his rights to ownership that were apparently based on his race.[57] This was an evident reversal in Wilson's former position; he argued that Bates's November 1862 precedent had established that Berry and other free blacks were US citizens and had the right to preempt land. Wilson deemed African Americans "entitled to the benefit of the pre-emption laws," and of the federal Homestead Act.[58] Black Californians like Berry then could use government offices to claim citizenship rights. The editor of the *Marysville Appeal* praised the US government as it, "even in the midst of a great civil war, finds time to do justice to the humblest individual," and claimed that other African Americans should "hasten to make themselves independent by entering on the unoccupied public lands."[59] They, too, depicted these lands as empty. Berry was still living in the area as of August 1868, proving that at least one local African American felt sufficiently secure in his rights in Marysville to stay there.[60]

Berry was not alone, and California activists cajoled their peers to increase the local African American population. Peter Anderson expanded his agenda in response to the recently issued Emancipation Proclamation to include calling for freed people to move west and "take up lands" that he regarded as open for the claiming, all to facilitate their own prosperity and the nation's advancement. He argued that they needed to put in the work to establish themselves in new homesteads in the West.[61] Building on the ongoing presence of a small number of African Americans since the gold rush, by the mid 1860s, in little towns in the gold country like Nevada City, Grass Valley, and Yuba City, in Sacramento, and even in El Monte in Southern California, some African Americans owned productive property and achieved middle-class status.[62] Nevertheless, for those who lacked independent means, there were substantial economic bars to landownership; financial constraints meant that even after they attained eligibility, homesteading was still out of reach for many.

What stories do we tell about rights, opportunity, and property in California? Which black histories can scholars uncover from the early American years there? Patricia Nelson Limerick has stated, "Of all the persistent qualities in American history, the values attached to property retain the most power."[63] Land is at the center of the histories of citizenship and rights, and conflict over access to it collided with the American colonial project in California. As Anglo Americans pursued gold and land after 1848, they also sought to exterminate Indigenous people and eliminate opportunities available to racialized others competing for the spoils of dispossession. Did African Americans join them? The perceived boundaries around the races affected conceptions of citizenship and became more important as the American population boomed in California and after the United States took over. By 1848, US racial thought had already well established the idea of blackness as a heritable trait that could obstruct people's rights. As California made the transition to American rule, how did the new regime treat land rights for its African-descended population? Were land rights among their citizenship privileges? In what ways did black Californians, too, engage in the colonial project?

This critical legal investigation into African American land rights in California from 1848 to 1870 highlights the ambiguity of black citizenship status. This moment unmasks the borders of race and citizenship in the West, as do the chapters by Tom Romero, Brian Frehner, and Danielle Olden in this collection.[64] Before 1868, citizenship was a vague, poorly understood concept, one often invoked but rarely defined. Even with black Americans' long-standing efforts in California and elsewhere, they did not earn a national guarantee of citizenship in the US Constitution until the Fourteenth Amendment, and even then, it proved a fragile one.[65] Black Californians' desire to access public land clashed with both escalating legal claims like *Dred Scott v. Sandford* that free blacks lacked citizenship and with Indigenous and Mexican Californians' prior land rights.[66] *Dred Scott*'s ramifications for land in the West are poorly understood, and this exemplifies the broader historical phenomenon in which jurists at the state and local levels applied Supreme Court decisions unevenly on the ground.[67] The eastern precedents that informed *Dred Scott* fit poorly with western experiences, and yet the case's fallout still harmed black Californians.

Efforts at exclusion and policing of borders including citizenship have been central to what Mary Dudziak and Leti Volpp deem the "American national mythology."[68] By the mid-nineteenth century, Americans had for decades been constructing US citizenship relationally. As Evelyn Nakano Glenn has proven, white male citizens understood themselves in opposition to "noncitizens," who encompassed women, aliens, enslaved people, and—according to many—all African Americans. In turn, blacks pushed back against these exclusion efforts, and argued—using in this case property claims—that they merited citizenship.[69]

California African Americans' arguments for legal rights played out not only in a virtual legal borderland that defined the racialized legal borders around citizenship but also in a literal borderland in that the US state of California came into existence through the establishment of a border between Alta and Baja California in the negotiations that followed the US war with Mexico. This was an effort to stabilize American power over a region that already had several populations, themselves not in agreement about sovereignty or racial supremacy.[70]

African Americans' position with respect to other Californians during the American push westward was complex, for their opportunities to gain land and status in California often occurred at the expense of other "racialized" people. They did this through violent seizure of Indigenous Californians' lands, as well as delegitimation of Californios' land titles.[71] They themselves were agents of the American takeover. At least to some degree, they bought into the idea of an empty West, theirs for the taking, as an untouched land of opportunity, and thus partook of the larger systemic erasure of Indigenous Californians' land rights, along with those of Californios.[72] This study thus raises intriguing questions about the roles of nonwhite people acting to invalidate land rights of others.[73] Cheryl Harris notes that the "settlement and seizure of Native American land supported white privilege through a system of property rights in land in which the 'race' of the Native

Americans rendered their first possession rights invisible and justified conquest." This holds true in California, but whiteness may not have been, as she asserts, the "prerequisite to the exercise of enforceable property rights." Yes, as she argues, *Johnson* set the precedent of prioritizing white property rights over those racialized as nonwhite, but further exploration is needed to see what happened when nonwhite people—such as free African Americans—obtained western property rights at the expense of other people of color.[74]

In the same years when rulings like *Dred Scott* undermined black citizenship rights, black Californians seized legal ambiguities and used claims to federal land offices to argue that they nevertheless had rights. African Americans in California not only fought for their rights against federal limitations like *Dred Scott* but also fought against many state and local restrictions on their citizenship, including assumptions that they did not deserve it.[75] Evelyn Nakano Glenn has argued in reference to a later era that citizenship needs to be considered "at the local level." Even as state and federal laws proclaimed formal definitions of citizenship, still people on the ground made decisions about whether to enforce citizenship restrictions.[76] Black Californians used the court system to try to retain the assets that propped up their citizenship claims, and cited legal precedents to catalyze debates about federal and state citizenship rights.

Like African Americans elsewhere, those in California faced state-level denials of vital citizenship rights that only federal protections could resolve. Some black Californians eventually succeeded at selectively using federal laws to compensate for state and local discrimination. Over time, federal protections took the form of Republican officeholders who were willing to push for and protect African American rights. With its exploration of African Americans' legal status, citizenship, and land rights, this chapter demonstrates the need to pay attention to both national and local contexts—in this case, western legal contexts—when tracing the evolution of race, rights, and the law.

As the boundaries of race and rights for African Americans became looser in some places and in others more restrictive, they fought on for their full citizenship. In the years after the Civil War, African American citizenship remained anathema to most white Californians, as seen in the state's resistance to the Reconstruction Amendments. California Democrats even made a concerted effort to obstruct the Thirteenth Amendment in 1865. Meanwhile, black activists retained their economic focus; the African American leaders at the 1865 Colored Convention reiterated their need to own and to work productive land, as "independent" producers.[77] The focus on land is evident, for even in their failed endeavors, black Californians' ongoing desire to secure and work land is visible; court proceedings from January 1866, as reported in the *Pacific Appeal,* show this. The Pacific Agricultural Association lost out on a plot of land that they had attempted to lease for an "agricultural enterprise." White squatters took possession of the land, and the association was unable to retain it.[78] In the aftermath of the recent legal changes, this 1866 instance demonstrates African Americans' sense that they were entitled to landed property, even if they were not successful in their goal.

During Reconstruction, state and national politics remained a minefield for California's African Americans. In addition, a racially divisive platform once more proved effective for the state Democratic Party, which returned to power over the next few years while vocally opposing the vote for African American and Chinese men. People still very much contested the parameters of citizenship for African Americans, and they only began to be more secure through legislation in the late 1860s. In 1866 and 1868, the Civil Rights Act—with its explicit guarantee of African Americans' property rights—and the Fourteenth Amendment more broadly attempted to define the fuzzy boundaries around citizenship. The California Democrats refused to expand citizenship's borders, further marginalizing Mexican Americans and Indigenous people, and even blocked the state's ratification of the Fourteenth and Fifteenth Amendments. The former created national citizenship rights and the latter enfranchised all white and black adult male citizens; both had important exclusions for Indigenous and Chinese men.[79] While the amendments still passed without California's endorsement, since there were sufficient affirmative votes from other states, this overt local rejection of African American citizenship exemplifies California's importance for understanding the relationship between partisan politics, race, and rights.[80]

From 1848 to 1870, black Californians created opportunities by exploiting ambiguities in the law; in the process, they engaged in an ongoing struggle over which Americans were entitled to call themselves citizens and what this meant. The stalwart efforts Californians of African descent made to claim land encourage historians to reconsider citizenship's boundaries and what stories we tell about different Americans' overlapping land rights claims. These activists resisted the effects of discriminatory laws, which in this era were themselves often founded in and exacerbated by partisan politics and sectionalism, at all levels of government. Black Californians' assertions that they had the right to public land were a major component of their equal rights struggle, and one that illustrates the inextricable nature of state and national politics on the western border of the nation.

Notes

The author wishes to thank Kim Hogeland, Katrina Jagodinsky, Pablo Mitchell, her fellow participants in the Laying Down the Law Workshop, the Clements Center for Southwest Studies, David Brodnax Sr., Paul Finkelman, Amy Milne-Smith, Silvana Siddali, and Leandra Zarnow for comments and suggestions. She also thanks Wilfrid Laurier University and the Huntington Library for research funding.

Epigraph: Mifflin Wistar Gibbs, *Shadow and Light: An Autobiography with Reminiscences of the Last and Present Century*, Blacks in the American West (Lincoln: University of Nebraska Press, 1995 [1902]), 47.

1. This chapter focuses on free people of African descent who came to California via the United States. They were not the first people with African ancestry there; indeed, black people had lived in California as far back as Spain's initial colonization of Los Angeles. Jack D. Forbes, "The Early African Heritage of California," in *Seeking El Dorado: African Americans in California*, ed. Lawrence Brooks De Graaf, Kevin Mulroy, and Quintard Taylor (Los Angeles; Seattle: Autry Museum of Western Heritage; University of Seattle Press, 2001). "African American" and "black" will be used interchangeably here to indicate people defined at this time to be of African descent. "White" will be used to designate people who the law acknowledged as having that identity. In this era, US definitions of "black" varied from the vague standard of "visible admixture" of blood to "somewhere between a quarter and an eighth Negro ancestry." Clayton E. Cramer, *Black Demographic Data, 1790–1860: A Sourcebook.* (Westport, CT: Greenwood Press, 1997), 2–3. California's 1850 testimony law, as it denied that right to "Negroes," "mulattoes," and "Indians," defined "mulatto" and Indian people, respectively, as "Every person who shall have one eighth part or more of Negro blood shall be deemed a mulatto, and every person who shall have one half Indian blood shall be deemed an Indian" Rudolph M. Lapp, *Blacks in Gold Rush California*, Yale Western Americana Series (New Haven: Yale University Press, 1977), 192.

2. "Proceedings of the First State Convention of the Colored Citizens of the State of California. Held at Sacramento Nov. 20th, 21st, and 22d, in the Colored Methodist Church, 1855," in *Proceedings of the Black State Conventions, 1840–1865*, ed. Philip Sheldon Foner and George E. Walker (Philadelphia: Temple University Press, 1986), 120, 130.

3. Mifflin W. Gibbs, Jonas Townsend, William Newby, et al., Petition to the California Legislature, 1852, Petition 44, California State Archives, Sacramento, quoted in Lapp, *Blacks in Gold Rush California*, 194–195.

4. These activists also set up local organizations and meetings, gave public lectures, and ran large-scale petition campaigns to change the testimony laws. Quintard Taylor, *In Search of the Racial Frontier: African Americans in the American West, 1528–1990* (New York: W. W. Norton, 1998), 78–79, 82, 83; James A. Fisher, "The Struggle for Negro Testimony in California, 1851–1863," *Southern California Quarterly* 54, no. 4 (December 1969): 315, 317; Lapp, *Blacks in Gold Rush California*, 200, 217; Willi Coleman, "African American Women and Community Development in California, 1848–1900," in *Seeking El Dorado*, 105; Richard Newman, Patrick Rael, and Phillip Lapsansky, *Pamphlets of Protest: An Anthology of Early African-American Protest Literature, 1790–1860* (New York: Routledge, 2001). For further discussion of black Californians' citizenship activism and their numerous legal obstacles, see Dana Elizabeth Weiner, "Debating African Americans' Place in California, 1850–1870," in *Africa and Its Diasporas: Rethinking Struggles for Recognition and Empowerment*, ed. Behnaz Mirzai and Bonny Ibhawoh (Trenton: Africa World Press, 2018).

5. Gibbs, *Shadow and Light;* Taylor, *In Search of the Racial Frontier*, 84, 86–87; Dolores Hayden, "Biddy Mason's Los Angeles, 1856–1891," *California History* 68, no. 3 (1989).

6. T. H. Breen and Stephen Innes, *"Myne Owne Ground": Race and Freedom on Virginia's Eastern Shore, 1640–1676* (New York: Oxford University Press, 2005), xviii, 6; Stephen A. Vincent, *Southern Seed, Northern Soil: African-American Farm Communities in the Midwest, 1765–1900*, Midwestern History and Culture (Bloomington: Indiana University Press, 1999), x; James Oliver Horton and Lois E. Horton, *In Hope of Liberty: Culture, Community, and Protest among Northern Free Blacks, 1700–1860* (New York: Oxford University Press, 1997); Dylan C. Penningroth, *The Claims of Kinfolk: African American Property and Community in the Nineteenth-Century South*, The John Hope Franklin Series in African American History and Culture (Chapel Hill: University of North Carolina Press, 2003). On citizenship and independent property, see Evelyn Nakano Glenn, *Unequal Freedom: How Race and Gender Shaped American Citizenship and Labor* (Cambridge, MA: Harvard University Press, 2002), 1–2.

7. F. G. Barbadoes, C. M. Willson, and Wm. H. Hall, *Address of the State Executive Committee to the Colored People of the State of California* (Sacramento: Printed for the Committee, 1859), 15; "Proceedings of the First State Convention of the Colored Citizens of the State of California . . . 1855," 119, 117.

8. Barbadoes et al., *Address of the State Executive Committee*, 14; "Proceedings of the First State Convention of the Colored Citizens of the State of California . . . 1855," 119. The minutes from later at the 1855 meeting stated that black Californians owned assets valued at "nearly $3,000,000." Barbadoes et al., *Address of the State Executive Committee*, 130; "Proceedings of the State Convention of the Colored People of California, San Francisco, October, 1857," in *Proceedings of the Black State Conventions, 1840–1865*, 166; "Proceedings of the Second Annual Convention of the Colored Citizens of the State of California,

Held in the City of Sacramento, Dec. 9th, 10th, 11th, and 12th, 1856," in *Proceedings of the Black State Conventions, 1840–1865*, 147, 152. For other examples of this, see Gibbs, *Shadow and Light*, 45, and Thos. Duff, *Mirror of the Times*, December 12, 1857.

9. California African Americans were hardly idle when it came to trying to improve their circumstances, even when their statewide meetings were on hiatus. While the convention movement was not active again until 1865, from the last years of the 1850s until then California African Americans labored in local networks. They had important allies in the courts and a few in other positions in government, such as Sacramento's district attorney Cornelius Cole, who took aim at the many legal disadvantages black Californians faced. See Lapp, *Blacks in Gold Rush California*, 207.

10. William Francis Deverell, *Whitewashed Adobe: The Rise of Los Angeles and the Remaking of Its Mexican Past* (Berkeley: University of California Press, 2004); María Raquél Casas, *Married to a Daughter of the Land: Spanish-Mexican Women and Interethnic Marriage in California, 1820–1880* (Reno: University of Nevada Press, 2007); Joshua Paddison, *American Heathens: Religion, Race, and Reconstruction in California*, Western Histories (Berkeley: Published for the Huntington-USC Institute on California and the West by University of California Press, 2012); D. Michael Bottoms, *An Aristocracy of Color: Race and Reconstruction in California and the West, 1850–1890*, Race and Culture in the American West (Norman: University of Oklahoma Press, 2013); Glenna Matthews, *The Golden State in the Civil War: Thomas Starr King, the Republican Party, and the Birth of Modern California* (New York: Cambridge University Press, 2012). While they provide important context for this study, previous works on California African Americans have underestimated the importance of property claims to their citizenship activism. William Loren Katz, *The Black West* (Seattle: Open Hand, 1987); Lapp, *Blacks in Gold Rush California;* William Sherman Savage, *Blacks in the West*, Contributions in Afro-American and African Studies, no. 23 (Westport, CT: Greenwood, 1976); Taylor, *In Search of the Racial Frontier.* This area of inquiry has been studied narrowly, with targeted studies of fights against the testimony laws and streetcar segregation. Robert J. Chandler, "Friends in Time of Need: Republicans and Black Civil Rights in California during the Civil War Era," *Arizona and the West* 24, no. 4 (Winter, 1982); Barbara Y. Welke, "Rights of Passage: Gendered-Rights Consciousness and the Quest for Freedom, San Francisco, California, 1850–1870" in *African American Women Confront the West: 1600–2000*, ed. Quintard Taylor and Shirley Ann Wilson Moore (Norman: University of Oklahoma Press, 2003).

11. Forbes, "The Early African Heritage of California."

12. While conditions for free and enslaved African Americans in California were linked, this study focuses on free individuals. For an excellent recent work on slavery in California, see Stacey L. Smith, *Freedom's Frontier: California and the Struggle over Unfree Labor, Emancipation, and Reconstruction* (Chapel Hill:

University of North Carolina Press, 2013), 61, 63; Lapp, *Blacks in Gold Rush California*, 239–240. See also Paul Finkelman, "The Law of Slavery and Freedom in California, 1848–1860," *California Western Law Review* 17, no. 3 (1981): 440; Taylor, *In Search of the Racial Frontier.* Biases among people opposed to slavery were also common in other regions, including the Old Northwest. Stephen Middleton, *The Black Laws in the Old Northwest: A Documentary History*, Contributions in Afro-American and African Studies (Westport, CT: Greenwood, 1993); Stephen Middleton, *The Black Laws: Race and the Legal Process in Early Ohio* (Athens: Ohio University Press, 2005); Dana Elizabeth Weiner, *Race and Rights: Fighting Slavery and Prejudice in the Old Northwest, 1830–1870*, Early American Places (DeKalb: Northern Illinois University, 2013). Oregon did pass similar exclusion measures. Cramer, *Black Demographic Data*, 33–34.

13. Albert L. Hurtado, *Intimate Frontiers: Sex, Gender, and Culture in Old California* (Albuquerque: University of New Mexico Press, 1999), xiii, xxi; Tomás Almaguer, *Racial Fault Lines: The Historical Origins of White Supremacy in California* (Berkeley: University of California Press, 1994); Paddison, *American Heathens.*

14. On race and the law, see Laura E. Gómez, "Looking for Race in All the Wrong Places," *Law & Society Review* 46, no. 2 (2012): 230–231, 239. On race, see Barbara Fields, "Slavery, Race, and Ideology in the United States of America," *New Left Review* 181 (1990); David R. Roediger, *The Wages of Whiteness: Race and the Making of the American Working Class*, revised ed. (New York: Verso, 1999 [1991]); Joanne Pope Melish, *Disowning Slavery: Gradual Emancipation and "Race" in New England, 1780–1860* (Ithaca: Cornell University Press, 1998); Almaguer, *Racial Fault Lines*; Natalia Molina, *How Race Is Made in America: Immigration, Citizenship, and the Historical Power of Racial Scripts* (Berkeley: University of California Press, 2013). On law, see Hendrick Hartog, "Introduction to Symposium on 'Critical Legal Histories': Robert W. Gordon, 1984," *Law & Social Inquiry* 37 (2012): 150; Robert W. Gordon, "Critical Legal Histories," *Stanford Law Review* 36 (1984): 109; Ian Haney-López, *White by Law: The Legal Construction of Race*, Critical America (New York: New York University Press, 1996), 10; Emily Snyder, "Indigenous Feminist Legal Theory," *Canadian Journal of Women and the Law* 26, no. 2 (2014): 370; Barbara Young Welke, *Law and the Borders of Belonging in the Long Nineteenth Century United States*, New Histories of American Law (New York: Cambridge University Press, 2010), 4. On property, see Cheryl I. Harris, "Whiteness as Property," *Harvard Law Review* 106, no. 8 (1993): 1728, 1729, 1730.

15. Laura F. Edwards, "The History in 'Critical Legal Histories,'" *Law & Social Inquiry* 37 (2012): 196–197.

16. Devon W. Carbado, "Racial Naturalization," *American Quarterly* 57, no. 3 (2005): 639.

17. Paddison, *American Heathens*, 2; Glenn, *Unequal Freedom*, 146.

18. Almaguer, *Racial Fault Lines*, 9.

19. Almaguer, *Racial Fault Lines*, ix, 4–5, 9, 19; Molina, *How Race Is Made in America*, 7–8; María E. Montoya, *Translating Property: The Maxwell Land Grant and the Conflict over Land in the American West, 1840–1900* (Berkeley: University of California Press, 2002), 5, 14, 81, 167. See also Steve Martinot, introduction, Albert Memmi, *Racism*, trans. Steve Martinot (Minneapolis: University of Minnesota Press, 2000), xvii–xviii.

20. Regarding genocide in California, see Benjamin Madley, *An American Genocide: The United States and the California Indian Catastrophe, 1846–1873* (New Haven: Yale University Press, 2016); Brendan C. Lindsay, *Murder State: California's Native American Genocide, 1846–1873* (Lincoln: University of Nebraska Press, 2012). California was not alone in its efforts to discourage African Americans from settling in the state; this was common in both the Old Northwest (Michigan, Ohio, Illinois, and Indiana) and much closer in Oregon. Middleton, *The Black Laws in the Old Northwest*; Middleton, *The Black Laws: Race and the Legal Process in Early Ohio*; Weiner, *Race and Rights*, 42–44; Cramer, *Black Demographic Data*, 32–34.

21. Paddison, *American Heathens*, 4.

22. *Johnson v. M'Intosh* provided the standard justification after 1823 for US confiscation of Indigenous lands. Johnson v. M'Intosh, 21 U.S. (8 Wheat) 543 (1823).

23. Almaguer, *Racial Fault Lines*, 108, 144–145; William J. Bauer, *California through Native Eyes: Reclaiming History*, Indigenous Confluences (Seattle: University of Washington Press, 2016), 26, 38.

24. Bauer, *California through Native Eyes*, 47, 66–67; Glenn, *Unequal Freedom*, 148.

25. Paul Wallace Gates, *The Farmer's Age: Agriculture, 1815–1860*, The Economic History of the United States (New York: Holt, Rinehart and Winston, 1960), 387–388; Paul W. Gates, "The Suscol Principle, Preemption and California Latifundia," *Pacific Historical Review* 39, no. 4 (1970): 461–462.

26. Gibbs, *Shadow and Light*, 46; Lapp, *Blacks in Gold Rush California*, 186; Taylor, *In Search of the Racial Frontier*, 82.

27. This has been the subject of much fruitful scholarship, including James H. Kettner, *The Development of American Citizenship, 1608–1870* (Chapel Hill: Published for the Institute of Early American History and Culture, Williamsburg, Va., by the University of North Carolina Press, 1978), 312, 314, 321. See also Ariela Gross, *What Blood Won't Tell: A History of Race on Trial in America* (Cambridge: Harvard University Press, 2008), 8; Mark A. Graber, *Dred Scott and the Problem of Constitutional Evil*, Cambridge Studies on the American Constitution (New York: Cambridge University Press, 2006), 28–29; Glenn, *Unequal Freedom*, 33.

28. Their long-standing Southern allegiances are evident in their joining the Southern Democratic faction in the election of 1860: Leonard L. Richards, *The California Gold Rush and the Coming of the Civil War*, 1st ed. (New York: Alfred A. Knopf, 2007), 226–228. Unlike in other areas of the country, the California

Whig Party was weak, so political contests there were often intraparty affairs within the Democratic Party. Smith, *Freedom's Frontier*, 8.

29. Dred Scott v. Sandford, 60 U.S. 393 (1857). Taney's decision in *Dred Scott* built on a long-standing effort by Southern jurists to deny African Americans citizenship rights. Kettner, *The Development of American Citizenship*, 312, 314, 321. While *Dred Scott* certainly reached beyond the issues Dred Scott himself intended to raise, it was no particular shock to see Roger Taney advocating this position. In 1832, Taney had argued, "free blacks were not and could not become citizens." Paul Finkelman, *Dred Scott v. Sandford: A Brief History with Documents*, The Bedford Series in History and Culture (Boston: Bedford, 1997), 30; Graber, *Dred Scott and the Problem of Constitutional Evil*, 31.

30. Lapp, *Blacks in Gold Rush California*, 239; Taylor, *In Search of the Racial Frontier*, 92. On *Dred Scott* more generally, see Graber, *Dred Scott and the Problem of Constitutional Evil*; Don Edward Fehrenbacher, *The Dred Scott Case, Its Significance in American Law and Politics* (New York: Oxford University Press, 1978).

31. *Dred Scott* has additional relevance for California history since the 1852 Perkins case made some of the same claims that free states lacked the right to deem slaves free upon entrance that Taney later did. In re Perkins, 2 Cal. 425 (1852); Finkelman, "The Law of Slavery and Freedom in California, 1848–1860," 455–456.

32. [Peter Anderson], "Homesteads," *Pacific Appeal*, September 20, 1862.

33. *Sacramento Daily Union*, October 1, 1858. Bradford was one of many of the "Chivalry" faction of pro-Southern Democrats in California whose actions were congruent with that party's general scorn for African Americans. "The New Land Districts—Location, Officers, Etc., Etc," *Alta*, May 16, 1858; Graber, *Dred Scott and the Problem of Constitutional Evil*, 31; Chandler, "Friends in Time of Need," 322, 329.

34. Robert Chandler, "An Uncertain Influence: The Role of the Federal Government in California, 1846–1880," *California History* 81, no. 3/4 (2003): 14; "An Interesting Land Case—the Colored Man Has Rights Which the Government Respects," *Marysville Appeal*, May 21, 1863. See also Shirley Ann Wilson Moore, *Sweet Freedom's Plains: African Americans on the Overland Trails, 1841–1869*, Race and Culture in the American West (Norman: University of Oklahoma Press, 2016), 44.

35. Dred Scott v. Sandford, 60 U.S. 393 (1857).

36. Frederick Charles Brightly, *An Analytical Digest of the Laws of the United States from the Adoption of the Constitution to the End of the Thirty-Fourth Congress, 1789–1857*, vol. 1 (Philadelphia: Kay and Brother, 1858), 472–473, note e.

37. W. W. Robinson, *Land in California: The Story of Mission Lands, Ranchos, Squatters, Mining Claims, Railroad Grants, Land Scrip, [and] Homesteads*, The Management of Public Lands in the United States (New York: Arno, 1979 [1948]), 167; Gates, *The Farmer's Age*, 387, 388.

38. The Preemption Act of 1841, 27th Congress, Ch. 16, 5 Stat. 453 (1841); Gates, "The Suscol Principle," 458.

39. Lapp, *Blacks in Gold Rush California*, 233, 234; The Preemption Act of 1841, 27th Congress, Ch. 16, 5 Stat. 453 (1841). Hall, a barber and businessman prominent in California activism, then lived in Oroville in the gold country. C., "Colored Men of California. No. Vii. William Henry Hall," *Pacific Appeal*, August 29, 1863. As at their other meetings, the 1857 convention put into the proceedings detailed data about black Californians' property holdings and their status as taxpayers. "Proceedings of the State Convention of the Colored People of California, San Francisco, October, 1857," 167.

40. Brightly, *Analytical Digest*, 1, 472–473, note e; Benjamin F. Hall and United States Attorney-General, *Official Opinions of the Attorneys General of the United States: Advising the President and Heads of Departments in Relation to Their Official Duties*, vol. 4 (Washington: Robert Farnham, 1852), 147–148; Benjamin Grant, *Reports of Cases Argued and Adjudged in the Supreme Court of Pennsylvania*, vol. 1 (Philadelphia: H. P. & R. H. Small, 1859), 23–25; Graber, 29, note 84.

41. "Negroes Excluded from the Public Lands," *Winchester Randolph County Journal*, March 31, 1859.

42. Wilson's determination was only one instance in which an official interpreted *Dred Scott* as diminishing the rights of free blacks, as seen in 1859 in the Mississippi High Court of Errors and Appeals. Justice William Harris asserted, following Taney's ruling in *Dred Scott*, that comity did not apply to a free black woman living in Ohio. This meant that Mississippi was not required to honor the property rights Ohio would have granted. Nancy Wells was seeking to recover property in Mississippi that she had inherited from her father; per Harris, in Mississippi Wells lacked the rights that she would have enjoyed had she been in Ohio. Based on *Dred Scott*, comity did not apply to her. Like black Californians seeking land rights, Wells directly felt the widespread effects of *Dred Scott*. Mitchell v. Wells, 37 Miss. at 239 (1859) in Paul Finkelman, "Book Review," *The Color of Law: The Color-Blind Constitution*. By Andrew Kull, *Northwestern University Law Review* 87, no. 937 (1992): 962. See also Finkelman, *An Imperfect Union: Slavery, Federalism, and Comity*, Studies in Legal History (Chapel Hill: University of North Carolina Press, 1981), 287–293.

43. Lapp, *Blacks in Gold Rush California*, 265; "Tall Son of Pennsylvania" [Peter Anderson], "Our San Francisco Letter, San Francisco, Oct 24, 1859," *Weekly Anglo-African*, November 26, 1859; "Tall Son of Pennsylvania" [Peter Anderson], "Our San Francisco Letter, San Francisco, Oct 20, 1859," *Weekly Anglo-African*, November 19, 1859; Anderson frequently corresponded under this pseudonym. C. Peter Ripley, ed. *The Black Abolitionist Papers: The United States, 1859–1865*, vol. 5 (Chapel Hill: University of North Carolina Press, 1985), 185, n. 1. Other activists like Frederick Douglass and James McCune Smith had also argued that *Dred Scott* targeted free African Americans as well as

slaves. Nicole Etcheson, "General Jackson Is Dead: James Buchanan, Stephen A. Douglas, and Kansas Policy," in *James Buchanan and the Coming of the Civil War*, ed. John W. Quist and Michael J. Birkner (Gainesville: University Press of Florida, 2013), 96.

44. [Anderson], "Our San Francisco Letter, San Francisco, Oct 24, 1859."
45. California Constitution (1849), art. XI, sec. 15. Delilah L. Beasley erroneously claims that the 1860 change outright barred African Americans from holding homesteads, but instead it racially limited their ability to protect their homestead claims. Delilah L. Beasley, *The Negro Trail Blazers of California; a Compilation of Records from the California Archives in the Bancroft Library at the University of California, in Berkeley; and from the Diaries, Old Papers, and Conversations of Old Pioneers in the State of California* (Los Angeles: Times Mirror Printing and Binding House, 1919), 60. *The Statutes of California, Passed at the Eleventh Session of the Legislature, 1860* (Sacramento: Charles T. Botts, State Printer, 1860), 87, 417; *The Statutes of California, Passed at the Second Session of the Legislature* (Sacramento: Eugene Casserly, State Printer, 1851), 296. California's land laws had been more permissive for African Americans than those of nearby Oregon; as noted above, before 1860, the California land laws had no mention of race. Oregon's Donation Land Act (1850) explicitly limited the right to homestead in Oregon Territory to whites. *The Donation Land Claim Act, 1850: An Act to Create the Office of Surveyor-General of the Public Lands in Oregon, and to Provide for the Survey, and to Make Donations to Settlers of the Said Public Lands*, Thirty-First Congress (September 27, 1850); Patricia Nelson Limerick, *The Legacy of Conquest: The Unbroken Past of the American West*, 1st ed. (New York: W. W. Norton, 1987), 45.
46. Smith, *Freedom's Frontier*, 12–13.
47. Jennie Carter and Eric Gardner, *Jennie Carter: A Black Journalist of the Early West*, Margaret Walker Alexander Series in African American Studies (Jackson: University Press of Mississippi, 2007), 51, n. 1.
48. Graber, *Dred Scott and the Problem of Constitutional Evil*, 22.
49. Williams v. Young, 17 Cal. 403, January (1861). Chandler briefly mentions this case: Robert J. Chandler, "The Press and Civil Liberties in California during the Civil War, 1861–1865" (PhD diss., University of California, Riverside, 1978), 208.
50. Montoya, *Translating Property*, 3–4, 14, 80–81, 118, 163.
51. Madley, *An American Genocide*, 182, 196–198, 220–222, 241–242.
52. [Peter Anderson], "Homesteads," *Pacific Appeal*, September 20, 1862.
53. The Homestead Act, 37th Congress, Ch. 75, 12 Stat. 392 (1862).
54. Foner, *Free Soil, Free Labor, Free Men*, 211, 270; Foner, *The Fiery Trial: Abraham Lincoln and American Slavery*, 1st ed. (New York: W. W. Norton, 2010), 224, 235.
55. James Oakes, *Freedom National: The Destruction of Slavery in the United States, 1861–1865*, 1st ed. (New York: W. W. Norton, 2013), 358; Adam Rothman,

Beyond Freedom's Reach: A Kidnapping in the Twilight of Slavery (Cambridge: Harvard University Press, 2015), 131.

56. "An Interesting Land Case—The Colored Man Has Rights Which the Government Respects," *Marysville Daily Appeal*, May 21, 1863.

57. Beasley, *The Negro Trail Blazers of California*, 62.

58. *Pacific Appeal*, May 30, 1863; "An Interesting Land Case," *Marysville Daily Appeal*, May 21, 1863; Chandler, "An Uncertain Influence," 14; Rothman, *Beyond Freedom's Reach*, 131.

59. "An Interesting Land Case," *Marysville Daily Appeal*, May 21, 1863.

60. The *Marysville Appeal* included him on a list of locals with unclaimed mail in the Marysville post office. "List of Letters," *Marysville Daily Appeal*, Number 33, August 8, 1868.

61. Peter Anderson, "The Freedmen," *Pacific Appeal*, February 14, 1863.

62. Carter and Gardner, *Jennie Carter*, xiv–xv, 57–58, 76 n. 7; Patty R. Colman, "John Ballard and the African American Community in Los Angeles, 1850–1905," *Southern California Quarterly* 94, no. 2 (2012): 209.

63. Limerick, *Legacy of Conquest*, 53.

64. See chapters 5–6, 10.

65. Gross, *What Blood Won't Tell*, 72; Haney López, *White by Law*, 50; Christian G. Samito, *Becoming American under Fire: Irish Americans, African Americans, and the Politics of Citizenship During the Civil War Era* (Ithaca: Cornell University Press, 2009), 1.

66. Dred Scott v. Sandford, 60 U.S. 393 (1857).

67. In chapter 10, Danielle Olden similarly highlights the unexpected consequences of the *Brown* decision for school segregation in Colorado.

68. Mary L. Dudziak and Leti Volpp, introduction, "Legal Borderlands: Law and the Construction of American Borders," *American Quarterly*, 57, no. 3 (September 2005): 596.

69. Glenn, *Unequal Freedom*, 10–11, 13, 20.

70. Dudziak and Volpp, introduction, "Legal Borderlands," 594, 596, 598. In chapters 5 and 6 of this book, Tom Romero and Brian Frehner also explore legal borders around rights.

71. Madley, *An American Genocide*; Lindsay, *Murder State*; Almaguer, *Racial Fault Lines*.

72. Jean M. O'Brien, "Indians and the California Gold Rush," in *Why You Can't Teach United States History without American Indians*, ed. Susan Sleeper-Smith et al. (Chapel Hill: University of North Carolina Press, 2015), 102–103, 106–107.

73. These developments occurred simultaneously with some Indigenous groups' embrace of slavery and its concomitant assertions of power over African Americans as property. See Tiya Miles, *Ties That Bind: The Story of an Afro-Cherokee Family in Slavery and Freedom* (Berkeley: University of California Press, 2005); Fay Yarbrough, *Race and the Cherokee Nation: Sovereignty in the Nineteenth Century* (Philadelphia: University of Pennsylvania Press, 2008).

74. Harris, "Whiteness as Property," 1716, 1721, 1724.

75. These beliefs are even evident in cases that ostensibly addressed the rights of other nonwhite groups. In *People v. George W. Hall* in 1854, the California Supreme Court argued that African Americans were not citizens and upheld the testimony ban of nonwhites in cases involving whites in California. That the court made this point in a case about a Chinese man's right to testify against a white man reveals that African Americans' status was indeed low in California law. The People of the State of California v. George W. Hall, 4 Cal 399 (October 1854), 332.

76. Glenn, *Unequal Freedom*, 2.

77. "Proceedings of the California State Convention of Colored Citizens, Held in Sacramento on the 25th, 26th, 27th, and 28th of October, 1865," in *Proceedings of the Black State Conventions, 1840–1865*, 176, 192.

78. "Failure of an Agricultural Enterprise," *Daily Alta California*, January 17, 1866, 1, col. 1; Chandler, "The Press and Civil Liberties," 219.

79. At issue for many westerners was their ongoing desire to exclude Indigenous and Chinese populations. Paddison, *American Heathens*, 23, 27–28.

80. Smith, *Freedom's Frontier*, 181, 182, 211; Bottoms, *An Aristocracy of Color, 1850–1890*; Gabriel Chin and Anjali Abraham, "Beyond the Super-Majority: Post-Adoption Ratification of the Equality Amendments," *Arizona Law Review* 50 (2009); Kenneth L. Karst, *Belonging to America: Equal Citizenship and the Constitution* (New Haven: Yale University Press, 1989), 51; Paddison, *American Heathens*, 96, 156; Molina, *How Race Is Made in America*, 72.

5

Ditches and Desirability

Regulating Race through the Flow and Quality
of Immigration and the Application of Western
Water Law in the Nineteenth and Early
Twentieth Centuries

Tom I. Romero II

In his opening statement to the 1,400 delegates of the thirteenth annual
meeting of the National Irrigation Congress in August 1905, in Portland,
Oregon, George C. Pardee, president of the association and governor of
California, ignited what seemed to be a firestorm.[1] Elected as governor of
California in the same year that the Newlands (Reclamation) Act was passed
by Congress, in 1902, Pardee had made a name for himself by supporting
and developing irrigation and waterworks projects to increase the state's agricultural output while providing safe drinking water to the state's population base.[2] A friend and confidant of President Theodore Roosevelt, Pardee
understood well that the fortunes of his state and that of the entire American
West seemingly rested in the successful application of the Reclamation Act
and concomitant revisions in state water laws to encourage settlement and
growth.[3]

As president of a national association known for its influence in shaping
what would become the Reclamation Act, Pardee boldly declared what he
hoped to be the most likely by-product of the federal irrigation law: "*Water
is the best immigration agent.* No one doubts that so rapidly as the Government reclamation works are completed, the land which lies under the
ditches will be sought by eager purchasers."[4]

The fitness of those immigrant purchasers, however, would soon come into question. Not long after Governor Pardee's address, Oregon delegate Charles Wood Eberlein spoke to the crowd, which had swelled to nearly double in size.[5] Declaring that three of the four "great principles" that animated the National Irrigation Congress had been achieved,[6] Eberlein declared that all were merely prologue and "preparation for the last, but greatest of all (principles). . . . To make homes on the land."[7] According to Eberlein, "the real problem of irrigation is for the first time before this Congress" and the "most vital issue before the arid states today is the *character of the populations* that shall follow the reclamation engineer, and take possession of the land."[8] Eberlein would accordingly use the remainder of his speech to detail the evils brought about by unfettered and unrestricted immigration. Railing against the over 48,000 immigrants "dump[ed]" into the nation's ports every month and to the resulting "subversion" of American civilization and its institutions by the unassimilable "aliens," Eberlein laid bare the following questions that would confront the arid West:

> Never until the day on which the waters of the Truckee were turned through the headgates on to the parched ground of Forty Mile Desert was the danger of foreign immigration localized. The populous East, with all its power to absorb population, will surely reach its limit, and where shall these colonies of Europeans go? Where can they go in masse but to the reclaimed lands of the West?[9]

Eberlein subsequently advocated that the congress "pool its brains and devise plans for the settlement of reclaimed lands by honest, industrious, intelligent settlers from the West and Middle West, having special reference to the character and fitness of the settler. Let his place back East be taken by the foreign immigrant and the dangerous swarming tendency of the foreigner will be prevented." In accomplishing this goal, Eberlein called for robust action on the part of states to "furnish reliable information" and direct assistance to "honest" and "deserving" "homeseekers" on claiming lands taken for cultivation. Eberlein ended his speech by arguing that Congress should be singularly invested in the reformation of existing federal immigration law to protect the West from the threatened evils of "unrestricted foreign immigration."[10]

This chapter explores the emerging connection between water and immigration law and policy in the American West in its formative years of development in the late nineteenth and early twentieth centuries. While historians of immigration and water law have documented this era in detail, none have examined their close connection.[11] Indeed, building upon my own work on the connection between water law and critical race theory and LatCrit theory, this chapter highlights the central role of water law and policy in creating color lines and subsequent racial hierarchy in the history of the American West.[12] More specifically, the chapter argues that water law provided a powerful means to distinguish between "desirable" and "undesirable" immigrants in racial terms. Access to water rights and citizenship for some and its denial to others reinforced a racialized land- and socialscape of white ethnics vis-à-vis Mexicans and Mexican Americans (regardless of citizenship) and other groups deemed nonwhite that would emerge.

The analysis begins by examining in greater detail the larger social, political, economic, and legal context preceding the 1905 meeting of the National Irrigation Congress (NIC) and the long-simmering issue of who would settle the American West. At issue at this meeting and in the larger struggle for irrigation was the cultural and racial ability of certain immigrant groups to reap the ostensible benefits of federal reclamation efforts to develop and grow bountiful and productive farms out of the Great American Desert. The focus then turns to immigration debates in the irrigation conference as representative of a flashpoint to a much larger struggle to exclude and control certain "nonwhite" immigrant groups in the late nineteenth- and early twentieth-century United States.

During this time, the development of water law in the American West, particularly the emergence of the Doctrine of Prior Appropriation, played a powerful if not more subtle and pernicious role in effectively regulating immigration by identifying who would and would not benefit from the acquisition of ditch and related property rights. Using Colorado as a case study (where a "pure" form of prior appropriation law emerged), the chapter turns to an exploration of how water law in the state worked hand in hand with the state's own Bureau of Immigration to create a racially "desirable" balance of irrigators and the laborers to work reclaimed arid lands into the late 1920s. Although this balance would be disrupted with the advent of the Great Depression and concomitant fears in Colorado and much of the American West regarding the "Mexican menace," the core principles in the hydrology of water and immigration law had already been formed in the early jurisprudence and application of the Colorado Doctrine. This hydraulic connection would thereby ensure water's centrality to the issue of migration and racial formation well into the twenty-first century.[13]

A Flood of People, a Dearth of Water

In 1902, Congress authorized "potentially the biggest public works program in American history" when it enacted the Newlands Reclamation Act, which authorized the federal government to commission water diversion, retention, and transmission projects in arid lands located mostly in the American West.[14] The Reclamation Act initially included sixteen western states, and later amendments in 1905 and 1906 extended the program to the entire state of Texas.[15] Its goal was to turn large portions of what had long been known as the Great American Desert and other parts of the United States into fertile farms and orchards.[16]

One of the primary catalysts behind the passage of the act was the National Irrigation Congress. Its first meeting convened in Salt Lake City in 1891 after Utah governor Arthur Thomas called for a convention "to consider matters pertaining to the reclamation of public lands of the West."[17] The NIC sought to create consensus among states and the federal government over the control and development of the nation's waters; ostensibly national in scope, the NIC was formed to unify the arid American West "behind one policy and to advertise irrigation to the 'nation'—that is, to help make irrigation 'respectable' to untutored eastern investors" who had long questioned the wisdom of development in the Great American Desert.[18]

From its inception, the NIC included some of the most notable figures in late nineteenth- and early twentieth-century water law and policy, including Francis E. Warren, Elwood Mead, William Ellsworth Smythe, William Morris Stewart, Joseph Carey, Francis G. Newlands, and George Maxwell.[19] Although the organization was beset by competing visions and unstable leadership, the NIC nevertheless represented the largest collection of water professionals and policymakers committed to irrigating the arid West. Collectively, the proponents of irrigation were fervent in their belief that reclamation would encourage Western settlement, thus spurring region-wide economic development and prosperity.

The question about how to balance the precarious relationship between water, migration, and development, however, had long vexed the inhabitants of what would become the American West. Ancestral Puebloans, for example, as early as five or six hundred years before the arrival of the Spanish in the American Southwest, had instituted an elaborate system of water control based on ditches and reservoirs.[20] Lured into what would become southern Colorado and northern New Mexico by an extended period of "reliable rainfall," Ancestral Puebloans engineered ingenious water infrastructure to establish an agricultural lifestyle based upon the cultivation of maize.[21] From roughly 550 of the Common Era to around 1300, Ancestral Puebloans migrated between Mesa Verde and Chaco Canyon in search of good soils, streams, and adequate rainfall before abandoning both as a result of drought that began around 1135.[22]

The deployment of large-scale irrigation and related settlement in the American West, however, would be amplified in 1846, when the US Army entered the territory of Mexico, occupying by force of arms the area that today comprises the states of New Mexico, California, Arizona, Nevada, Utah, and parts of Colorado. Within two years of US occupation, the Treaty of Guadalupe Hidalgo formally ended hostilities between the United States and Mexico and reshaped the political, social, and legal geography of the region that would be most impacted by reclamation.[23]

Of most immediate importance was the discovery of gold flakes in the American River (about forty-five miles east of what would become Sacramento) a week before Mexico officially signed the Treaty of Guadalupe Hidalgo. Suddenly, the dry and thirsty American West immediately was flooded by Americans, Europeans, Mexicans, Peruvians, Hawaiians, British Columbians, and Chinese seeking a better life through mining.[24] From individual pan and rocker mining, to more sophisticated long toms and sluices connected to dams and flumes, to large-scale hydraulic strip-mining operations, access to and exclusion of others from water was central to the extraction and exportation of the region's mineral wealth by its diverse migrants.

Complicating the situation were migrants to the region looking to settle and farm on these same lands, especially after passage of the Homestead Act in 1862.[25] In lands largely devoid of constantly flowing rivers and natural lakes, however, settlers encountered dramatic hardship never contemplated by the act's drafters. A telling example is found in the case of an abandoned ranch found by one homesteader in eastern Colorado in the 1860s: "Its owner left a crude sign that with minor rewording could have spoken for thousands of [migrants] knocked to their knees during hard times: 'Toughed it out here two years. Result: Stock on hand, five towhead and seven yaller dogs. Two hundred and fifty feet down to water. Fifty miles to wood and grass. Hell all around. God Bless Our Home.'"[26] Not surprisingly, legal as well as social and political conflict over water was inevitable, and migrants to the region innovated the nascent water law regimes in the region to account for these challenges.

In the early 1860s, for example, the Colorado territorial legislature enacted a series of statutes that appeared to adopt both the common-law riparian rights doctrine[27] and the emerging doctrine of prior appropriation.[28] Although the 1876 Colorado Constitution explicitly embraced prior appropriation as the controlling legal doctrine in the state, it left open the question of what legal regime existed prior to statehood.[29] In approaching the problem in 1882, Colorado courts simply asserted that the issue did not exist. As Justice Helm of the Colorado Supreme Court argued in 1882 in *Coffin v. Left Hand Ditch Co.*, "we think that the [prior appropriation] doctrine has existed from the date of the earliest appropriations of water within the boundaries of the state."[30] Notably, the Colorado Supreme Court understood that the unique ecological challenges facing the state's recent migrants who came to settle and not mine the land required a different conception about the legal rules governing access to water. According to Justice Helm,

> Water in the various streams . . . acquires a value unknown in moister climates. . . . Vast expenditures of time and money have been made in reclaiming and fertilizing by irrigation portions of our unproductive territory. Houses have been built, and permanent improvements made; the soil has been cultivated, and thousands of acres have been rendered immensely valuable, with the understanding that appropriations of water would be protected. Deny the doctrine of priority or superiority of right by priority of appropriation, and a great part of the value of all this property is at once destroyed.[31]

To be sure, as migrants flooded the American West in the years after the end of the Mexican American War, prior appropriation, as Donald Pisani has shown, suddenly emerged as the most important (if not poorly defined) legal doctrine governing water disputes in the arid West.[32]

In spite of its origins in the hard-scrabble mining camps of California, prior appropriation would become known as the Colorado Doctrine as its basic principles in the service of settlement and homesteading spread throughout the law and jurisprudence of much of the American West.[33] Most importantly, the doctrine of prior appropriation helped to fuel a fervor for agricultural settlement, almost religious in its faith, that "out of aridity would come a level of prosperity beyond anything Americans had seen before, making the West the home of the future."[34] By the end of the nineteenth century "irrigation had become a veritable crusade," spurring sharp increases in the amount of irrigation during this time.[35] Although proponents urged large-scale irrigation on moral, religious, and even scientific grounds, a connection to racialized notions of citizenship would come to animate most of the discussion.[36]

The question of who could become an American, and by implication, receive the protection of water and other laws, was one that had already begun to be defined in the West from the moment gold flakes were discovered in the American River in 1848. Nationally, the law was clear that only "white persons" were and could become citizens.[37] Not surprisingly, "the arrival of black slaves during the Gold Rush heightened anxiety among European Americans that slavery might compromise [the American West's] prospect of becoming a haven for free white labor."[38] These fears were only exacerbated by Chinese immigrants who began to pass through the Custom House of San Francisco in sizable numbers beginning in 1852. Pushed out of China by a particularly violent and tumultuous period in the country's history, Chinese immigrants to California's gold fields "gobbled up" the claims of white miners who "either sold or abandoned 'exhausted' claims and moved on to new diggings."[39] According to Liping Zhu, the Chinese miners' "cooperative strategies, extraordinary patience, low expenditure, and superb *water management* allowed them to thrive in the gold fields. In a few years, Chinese possessed most of the claims around the American River and its tributaries" and within a few short decades were often the largest national and most successful group in the mining West.[40]

The physical as well as economic visibility of the Chinese miners made them subject to immediate suspicion. Thus, "when Chinese immigrants followed blacks into the mining region, whites drew close analogies between black slaves and Chinese 'coolies.'"[41] Such fears were exacerbated by American companies who preferred to hire non-European and non-American labor and largely hired Chinese whenever possible. White workers, however, believed that such laborers "were mere pawns of capitalist interests and other monopolistic forces that relied upon unfree labor. Consequently, white male laborers believed that Chinese workers threatened both their precarious class position and the underlying racial entitlements that white supremacy held out to them and to the white immigrants who followed them into the new class structure."[42]

Chinese immigrants subsequently encountered economic and social barriers that pushed them to work not only as miners but as cooks, laundry-men, and perhaps most visibly, as railroad laborers in the completion and extension of the Transcontinental Railroad through the trans-Mississippi West. Largely because the region was heavily industrialized and was linked seamlessly with national and international labor and capital markets, the Chinese competed with a myriad of ethnic and racial groups for daily wages.

The "Chinese question" had suddenly become a national issue when, in 1876, both the Democratic and Republican Parties adopted anti-Chinese plans as part of their party platforms. Two years later, Californians amended their constitution to allow the state to regulate the immigration of aliens "who are or may become vagrants, paupers, mendicants, criminals, or in-valids afflicted with contagious or infectious diseases, and from aliens oth-erwise dangerous or detrimental to the well-being of peace of the State."[43] The constitution also forbade the employment of any Chinese by local government and private corporations while denying them the right to own and inherit real property.[44] Although the provisions of these constitutional amendments were soon declared in violation of the Burlingame Treaty and the US Constitution, they would anticipate the federal exclusion of all fu-ture Chinese immigrants in 1882.[45] By 1900, approximately 90,000 Chinese lived in the United States, and in tandem with state antimiscegenation laws, the federal antiexclusion law (which also included a provision making Chi-nese nationals ineligible for citizenship) ensured that the overwhelmingly male Chinese population would be unable to increase naturally.[46]

The regional and national success of the anti-Chinese movement and re-lated laws and legislation came at nearly the same moment that the first organized campaigns to expand irrigated agriculture in the United States exploded. While historians have attributed these efforts to a variety of envi-ronmental, economic, and political factors, less clear has been the role that immigration played in the irrigation crusades of the 1890s. Donald Pisani, in particular, has noted the ability of irrigation crusaders to link their move-ment to "those who feared the rising tide of 'new immigration' [and in turn] touted the West as a place to isolate the contagion of dangerous ideas as well as a classroom to teach the virtues of American institutions." The issue of immigration would play an increasingly central and contentious role in the water law and policy debates that would emerge around a national irriga-tion act.[47]

Irrigation crusaders recognized that, at its core, government-subsidized irrigation was not an engineering feat that merely captured and moved water to arid property. Rather, they believed it was the only means by which to reconstruct one of the quintessential building blocks of the American republic: the yeoman family farm.[48] Yet, in the American West, such family farms at the outset of the 1890s were likely to be occupied or owned by the foreign-born.[49] Thus, limiting immigration seemed counterproductive to the goals of the irrigation crusade. As one proponent of immigration wrote in 1892, the settlement of the "far West" could not "be done so readily if we shut out the foreigners who have been so useful" and successful in activities like irrigated agriculture.[50]

Irrigation crusaders, moreover, linked irrigated agriculture as perhaps the country's only outlet for the ills of density, crime, disease, and cultural "denigration" associated with unchecked immigration. According to Washington congressman Wesley L. Jones, the irrigated farm would "shrink" and ultimately kill "the seed of anarchy and lawlessness [of the nation's recent immigrants], thereby making love for family and country . . . well up in the heart and grow stronger and stronger from day to day."[51] Irrigation and the "rising tide of 'New Immigration'" therefore became a prevailing and common theme in the battle for a national irrigation law.[52]

As the battle over Chinese immigration anticipated, however, only certain kinds of immigrants and migrants would be welcome to be part of the crusade to irrigate the Great American Desert. In 1892, for example, the leading group of charitable organizations held its annual conference for the first time in Denver, Colorado.[53] Of critical concern at this meeting was the widespread belief that crime had been "rising like a flood in one of our Western rivers."[54] Although conference delegates identified a multitude of sources driving this trend, undeniable for the organization was the "human contagion and infirmity" that was the result of unrestricted immigration to the nation. Though its "ills" were seemingly confined to the country's ports of entry, the "closely allied subject of inter-state migration" meant that the "same evils may attend this transit of migrating persons within the country . . . many of whom are unable or unwilling to earn their own living in conformity with our laws and social requirements."[55]

As soon as President Theodore Roosevelt signed the Reclamation Act into law on June 17, 1902,[56] the issue of "desirability" would become central in determining which immigrants to the region would receive or be denied the benefits of the national law that would all of a sudden make 90 million acres of land open to settlement.[57] The battle accordingly turned to which settlers would be worthy to work this land. One editorial laid out the challenge:

The great West [with the extension of its irrigation system] can furnish homes for millions of people, and it is into the great trans-Mississippi country which is crying with open arms for the agriculturist and the artisan that the immigrant should be taken, there to work out his material redemption and become an honest, prosperous member of the body politic. . . . In our agricultural sections the Germans, Belgians, French, and Italians (by these latter I don't mean Sicilians) are fitted to make splendid agriculturalists, and the German and French particularly, are among the most prosperous class of farmers scattered through the great regions of the West—thrifty industrious and conserving the established institutions of this country—they are *desirable* immigrants and we can't have too many of this class.[58]

Critically, the Reclamation Act had its own statements about desirability built into the law. Section 4, for example, prohibited the employment of "Mongolian labor" on any irrigation project. Just as effective was the requirement that beneficiaries of reclamation projects comply with all homestead laws, excluding all "aliens ineligible for citizenship" from the law's benefits.

The primary sponsor and author of the Reclamation Act, Senator Francis G. Newlands (D-Nevada), had long connected the twin issues of immigration restriction according to social or cultural desirability and the growth of irrigated agriculture in the American West. Entering Congress as a representative in 1893, Newlands became one of the central figures not only in the growth and settlement of the American West but also in debates over the emergent overseas US empire in the Caribbean and the Pacific and the exclusion of nonwhite immigrants. In his career, "he articulated a populist anti-imperialist vision and condemned [nonwhite] immigrant workers and plantation agriculture in equal measure."[59] Irrigation, in turn, "offered white farmers a way to battle corporate dominance and the other forces corroding democracy."[60]

As irrigation crusaders worked to operationalize the new reclamation law, it is no surprise that the issues of irrigation and immigration would come to a head in the 1905 annual meeting of the National Irrigation Congress. As conference delegate J. M. Patterson declared, "the settlement [by immigrants] of these reclaimed lands is the greatest question that is facing the great West today."[61] The gauntlet over immigration that Charles Wood Eberlein threw down on the opening day of the 1905 annual meeting interrogated directly the discourse of immigrant desirability. Writing just a year later, Eberlein made the following observations: "Foreign immigration into the United States is over sixty percent greater than two years ago, and the immigration of *undesirable nationalities*, more than eighty percent greater than in 1904."[62] Eberlein accordingly railed against the "riff raff of Southern Europe" in contrast to the "best obtainable immigration from the British Isles and for the Mississippi Valley."[63]

Other conference delegates attenuated some of Eberlein's more controversial positions. Most notably, William Ellsworth Smythe, the founder of the National Irrigation Congress and an early leader of the irrigation crusade through his journal, the *Irrigation Age*, agreed with Eberlein regarding the connection between the nation's irrigation and immigration laws. Smythe accordingly argued that the real purpose of the crusade behind passage of the national irrigation law

> was not merely to listen to papers on the subject of irrigation; it was not even to pass laws, nor even to store the floods and distribute the water over the land; but the one great fundamental purpose of this constructive movement, the greatest of modern times, was to build homes, to make a door so wide that every man in the United States and *the good people in many foreign countries* should be able to pass readily and gladly from the place where they were not wanted to the place where they are wanted.[64]

Smythe viewed "the prompt and successful settlement of the arid lands to be reclaimed under the National Irrigation Act" as directly connected to "finding a wise solution of the kindred problem of foreign immigration."[65] Smythe subsequently proposed that a "Special Committee on Immigration and Settlement of Arid Lands" be established at the meeting.

Smythe's call for the congress to take up the issue of immigration created immediate confusion and backlash. Speaking the next day, Smythe himself directly addressed the controversy: "Some of the newspapers have said that in making my motion for a Special Committee of Fifteen on Arid Lands at the first general session on Monday morning, I was in favor of opening the gates to all sorts of foreign immigration without any distinction whatever; while other newspapers have stated that I evidently aimed at barring every foreigner from the irrigated soil of the West."[66] Consequently, Smythe had the following added to the official record of the congress's proceedings to "say precisely" his position:

The fate of the national irrigation policy rests, in the last analysis, upon the success of the settler on land to be reclaimed by the government; and the ability of the nation to meet the influx of foreign immigration, and to avoid the perils inherent in the congestion of masses of people in great cities, is also largely dependent upon the success of the national irrigation policy in providing an outlet for surplus population.[67]

Smythe subsequently proposed that the Congress, after consulting with the president of the United States, create an immigration commission to report back at the 1906 meeting the scope and content of irrigation and immigration law.[68] Smythe believed the already settled irrigators had the "sacred obligation" to solve the immigration question. Admonishing conference delegates who wished to eliminate altogether immigration to the soon-to-be-irrigated American West, Smythe argued that "we must remember that our priority of settlement gives us no pecuniary advantages over the millions to come later."[69]

Other conference delegates such as G. W. Burton of California, himself a "foreigner," seemed to take an even more radical position in favor of immigration. In endorsing Smythe's resolution, Burton argued:

> We need every man that we can get. I may be speaking rank heresy on the Pacific Coast, but I don't care whether a man is black, yellow, or white, if he is *industrious*. . . . Exclude the objectionable immigrant, the pauper in his own country, the man who brings contagious diseases into this country, and the man that is a criminal in his own country; but let this flag that has floated over an asylum for the oppressed of all nations for a hundred years float over us still.[70]

Fellow Californian John Fairweather wholeheartedly agreed: "My doctrine on the foreign immigration question is let all come that like, if they make good citizens, and declare their intentions after they get here; but if they shortly prove that they are not good citizens, bounce them out at once."[71] Despite ostensibly advocating for an open immigration policy, delegates such as Burton and Fairweather nevertheless indicated that there was a discernable line between "desirable" and "undesirable" immigrants, one, however, that had less to do with race or nationality and more to do with those who had the drive to take up the plow and irrigate the dry desert West.

The issue for many became the role of the state in controlling the flood of migrants (citizen and foreign alike) flowing into the North American West.

Having successfully lobbied the federal government for a national irrigation law, conference delegates, such as C. E. Wantland, recognized government's role in confronting "the immigration question."[72] The question consequently turned to which organ of government—state or federal—would be in the best position to promote settlement of desirable migrants to the arid West. On the side of the federal government stood conference delegates like J. A. Filcher from California. According to Filcher, "the immigration question, like that of irrigation is a national one" and therefore, the federal government should be "vitally interested in the kind of people that shall settle upon these [reclaimed] lands." Filcher suggested that the Department of the Interior should be charged "to colonize any reclamation district." In practice, it would look like this:

> For instance, take Nevada, where the water is ready to be turned on one great project. Have a bulletin issued from over the official stamp of the Interior Department, setting forth the work which has been accomplished, the quality and character of the land, terms and conditions on which it can be obtained. We have Consular reports from all over the world, as well as bulletins from the departments on other subjects, and it seems to me there could be nothing more pertinent than bulletins setting forth tersely the fact that the government has opened the way for a thousand or ten thousand homes for homeless people.[73]

Others saw the issue of foreign settlement of the reclaimed West as too important for federal control. Rather, it was a special "duty" of Western state legislatures "to adopt intelligent measures to protect their own people from an influx of *undesirable settlers.*"[74] Citing the work of state agencies in Colorado and California, conference delegates called for the organization of state immigration bureaus "in each of the arid states at the earliest possible moment."[75] Delegate Wantland consequently invited delegates to come to Denver in January 1906 for the "purpose of forming a Western Immigration Congress. . . . The agitation started here in favor of a better appreciation of the needs of the West concerning immigration and colonization matters will, we hope, pull us out of the woods and prove to be a starting point for a great new movement."[76]

The 1905 convention ended in much the same way it started, with great anxiety over how and in what ways the "foreign immigration question" would impact those states hoping to be most transformed and to most benefit from reclamation. Although the chairman of the meeting would declare that "no one in this Congress, so far as I know, wishes to abolish, abridge, or in any way interfere with those provisions of the present immigration laws allowing foreigners free access to this country," he nonetheless feared those immigrants, especially recent ones, who refused to assimilate:

> The poor man, whether Englishman or Italian, has a right here, if he comes honestly intending to be a citizen, and we want to do the most we can for him. . . . We must get away from this colonization idea, this thing of bringing in people in droves, and settling them together where they can reproduce a section of Italy or of Poland or of Russia. The West cannot stand that sort of thing. We want American citizens, wherever they come from.[77]

The distinction between the poor man from England, Italy, Poland, or Russia was in some sense a distinction without difference as each man under prevailing law was eligible to become an American citizen who could then come to own an irrigated farm. Those "nonwhites" ineligible for citizenship or those whose status would come increasingly into question based upon their suitability to reinforce the region's and nation's color lines could and often would be denied all the benefits of ownership of irrigated lands. Nevertheless, as the Reclamation Act quickly gave way to the interests of large-scale agribusiness in the early decades of the twentieth century, the question of water ditches and desirability would take on an altogether different tone.

Apples, Alfalfa, and Migration: The Western Garden of Eden

On November 19, 1909, former Colorado governor Alva Adams addressed the annual meeting of the National Farm Land Congress in Chicago. Lambasting both the density and idleness of the "eastern states," Adams pointed to the "bright and fair road that leads to Colorado" by which "every honest, industrious man can be gratified."[78] At the center of this opportunity was the revolutionary impact that irrigation was having on the state where "there is more land than people." According to Adams, "the best investment made by the United States since the Louisiana Purchase has been the forty-two millions spent in conserving the water . . . to make wet the dry lands" of a state like Colorado. There was no doubt, moreover, in Adams's mind about the Reclamation Act's significance: "In effecting the happiness of our people, the water reclamation and conservation policy will prove as beneficial as Lincoln's Emancipation Proclamation."[79]

THE GOSPEL OF IRRIGATION

Apples

and

Alfalfa

By
HON. ALVA ADAMS

DELIVERED AT
THE NATIONAL FARM LAND CONGRESS
CHICAGO, NOVEMBER, 1909

(Reprinted from The Chicago American)

Issued by
The Colorado State Board of Immigration
DENVER, COLORADO

Figure 5.1. Photograph of the title page of Alva Adams, "Apples and Alfalfa" (1909), courtesy of the Stephen H. Hart Library, Colorado History, Denver, Colorado. The publication of materials promoting Colorado's legal, political, and physical solutions to the problem of aridity and the state's subsequent readiness for newcomers to irrigate its lands occupied the work of the Colorado Bureau of Immigration for decades after it was established in 1871.

Waxing poetic about alfalfa that "grew so high that it blossomed above the clouds" and the "sweeter appeal" of "pink and red and white [apple buds] in their setting of fresh, soft green leaves," Adams insisted that Colorado and its bountiful fields of alfalfa and apples would be at the forefront of a "new empire[.] Not an empire of conquest, of battle fleets and armies but an empire of homes."[80] The occupiers of those homes would be immigrants to the state. Indeed, according to Adams, "apple orchards and alfalfa fields are better nurseries for citizenship than decks of ships or military camps."[81] Linking the solutions of immigration and irrigation together and Colorado as "the seat of the original garden of Eden," Adams's address, as republished and widely disseminated by the Colorado Bureau of Immigration, symbolizes the special role of state government advocated by the 1905 national conference delegates in the immigration debate.

Water law in the state worked with state and corporate interests to create a racially "desirable" balance of irrigators and the laborers needed to reclaim arid lands into the late 1920s. In the scope of this analysis, this section will explore the consequences of a massive transformation in the ideology of irrigation, one that moved from reclamation as homesteading and assimilation of the desirable immigrant to one that advocated reclamation as promoting international corporate profits dependent upon access to a cheap and docile labor supply.

Sparsely populated by Native Americans, Mexican Americans, and American and European traders, trappers, and miners when gold was first found at the confluence of the Cherry Creek and South Platte Rivers in 1859, Colorado's population had grown to nearly 800,000 people by the time of Adams's address. While the number of residents remained relatively low in its first several years of existence, first as a territory in 1863 and then as a state in 1876, Colorado's population boomed in the last two decades of the nineteenth century. Driving its growth was migration and immigration to the state. In 1870, Colorado had nearly seven thousand foreign-born people living within its borders. A decade later, one of every five persons living in the State was foreign-born, a trend that would only accelerate by the turn of the century.[82]

A quandary in Colorado and much of the arid North American West was a mismatch between where much of the available water was located and where the people lived. While most of Colorado's largest supplies of water rapidly flowed westward away from the Continental Divide, most of the

people were huddled on the eastern slope (known as the Front Range) of the
Rocky Mountains served largely by the Platte River system and watershed.
The discovery of gold in what would emerge as Denver, Colorado, "set in
motion a rush to settle stream valleys up and down the Front Range." Many
of these early migrants and immigrants to Colorado Territory, moreover,
were familiar with the irrigation practices of New Mexicans and quickly
adopted the *acequia* or ditch as the central organizing principle of Adams's
budding alfalfa and apple empire. One visitor to Colorado in 1867 remarked
on all of the ditches "being carried from Clear Creek over all parts of the un-
dulating slope stretching down from the mountain. . . . We found a number
of men at work constructing new ditches. . . . Our course was sometimes
impeded by the number of these ditches which are not yet bridged."[83]

Unlike the traditional acequias of the Southwest, however, Colorado's
newer ditches lacked the communal and cohesive concept of shared ownership and social obligation to keep the ditch running. Instead, migrants and
immigrants brought with them still inchoate notions of private property in
the backbreaking construction of building a system of water control, storage, and delivery.[84] Immigrants to the state soon realized, in the words of
one local booster:

> that the only way that he can render his land productive is to cause
> the waters of neighboring streams to forsake their channels and flow
> in new courses over field and farm. Great main water-ways must be
> constructed for many miles and expensive appliances and manage-
> ment must be devised and inaugurated, before the vision is realized.
> This the settler alone or in aggregation cannot usually accomplish.
> Capital, the hope and helper of labor must be induced to undertake
> the enterprise.[85]

Not surprisingly, state government worked to attract both capital and labor
in the guise of the Colorado Bureau of Immigration. Commissioned first by
the Territorial Legislature in 1871 and thereafter a permanent organ of state
government into the 1920s, the bureau was "organized to bring to Colorado
persons and their families who may BETTER THEIR CONDITION by setting
upon the irrigated lands of the finest state in the 'Arid Region.'" Most importantly, through detailed reports on irrigation, crops, and land available
in the state, the bureau hoped to help "those whom it brings West to find
homes where they may be assured of permanent prosperity."[86] Buttressing
the ideology of the irrigation crusaders, the yeoman family farm was the end
goal of the bureau's booster efforts.

Water and irrigation accordingly became the single most important variable for the bureau to highlight in its activities. Revealing are a series of rainfall maps produced by the bureau in the early twentieth century, which charted average rainfall in the state. Likely intentionally, the areas with the greatest rainfall coincided with some of the state's most developed water infrastructure and oldest and most secure water rights. An 1883 bureau publication opened with a description of the role of the growth of the immigrant Greeley colony in 1870 and the construction of their "main" ditch at the time. "When the Greeley colonists built their main ditch, a water right for eighty acres of land cost from seventy-five to one hundred dollars; now, twelve years later the same right would sell for more than one thousand dollars."

Such economic promise, accordingly, was the direct function of a legal system designed to control access, distribution, and use of water: "*By* the laws of the state the first ditch constructed has a priority right to the water appropriated . . . the laws provide for measurement, proof of quantity and date of appropriation so that there may be no controversy as to whom the water rightfully belongs. Every equitable safeguard which experience suggests is made to protect the rights of those who invest in these enterprises."[87] In short, water law and immigration were inexorably connected to Colorado's growth.

Immigrant and migrant "colonists" who established what became Greeley, Colorado, and irrigated agriculture in the northeastern section of the state provide an illustrative sampling of the intersection of water law and immigration policy. In the late nineteenth century, Northern European immigrants, especially Germans from Russia, comprised a majority of the immigrant population in this part of the state. Lured in no small measure by the screeds of the Colorado Bureau of Immigration and other boosters promoting vast economic possibilities, immigrants viewed Colorado's water law as central to their ability to Americanize in the arid land. According to one source from 1910, "few [Germans] have failed, and many by hard work and the practice of a thrift perhaps surpassing that of any other race" had succeeded in acquiring substantial rights in property. Indeed, one study found that within one generation, "a large percentage of the irrigated land in the Rocky Mountain Region is owned by descendants of the German Russian people"; these immigrants fulfilled the grandest visions of Colorado's own irrigation crusaders.[88]

The doctrine of prior appropriation extolled by Colorado's Bureau of Immigration gave desirable immigrants like Colorado's German-Russians

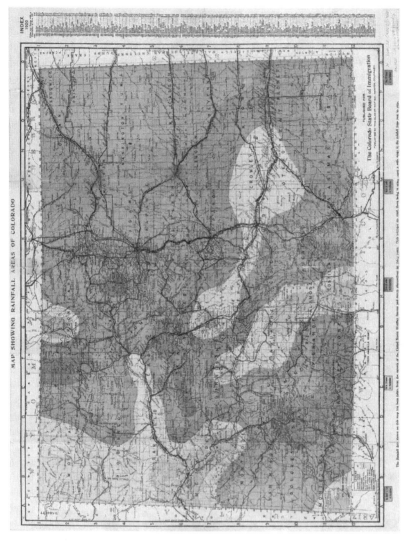

Figure 5.2. Rainfall maps produced by the Colorado Bureau of Immigration provided powerful visual evidence of the state's ripeness for irrigation. (Map reproduced by permission, Western History Collection, Denver Public Library, call number CG4311.C883 1920 .C6.)

the opportunity to purchase rights to water to have that same water delivered to their property from a natural stream using a system of ditches. The first of these ditches, Greeley No. 3 Ditch, was constructed in 1870 and watered the townsite that would become known as Greeley. Construction also began in 1870 for Greeley No. 2 Ditch, the largest of the Union Colony ditches, which would serve the surrounding agricultural lands. By the end of the century, an intricate system of ditches, canals, and reservoirs buttressed by an increasingly sophisticated jurisprudence of priority of right, made tens of thousands of acres of farmland productive.[89]

Despite its populist origins in the service of the yeoman immigrant farmer, Colorado water law quickly pivoted to reinforce commercial interests. Since the construction of miles-long canals and storage reservoirs required vast expenditures of capital, developments in Colorado water law enabled large-scale national and international investment and ownership in Colorado's irrigated lands.[90] Of importance were investments in sugar beets by international sugar conglomerates in northeastern Colorado in the first decades of the twentieth century. Sugar beets require late-season irrigation, made possible through the legal development of reservoirs and associated storage rights recognized by Colorado water law during the 1890s.[91] International sugar companies emerged to fundamentally alter the northern Colorado economic and social landscape.[92]

In 1899, the year the first sugar beet processing plant opened in the state, over 15,000 acres of Colorado land were devoted to the sugar beet.[93] By 1939, the Great Western Sugar Company, the largest and most influential of the sugar companies, had contracted for 238,509 acres to be devoted solely to the sugar beet crop.[94] Harvesting Colorado's largest and most profitable crop required a sizable labor force. Initially, sugar beet farmers turned to the German-Russians, whose desirable ethic of hard work and thrift made them successful. Their very success and emergence as landowning farmers created a vacuum that would come to be filled by other less desired groups.

As Colorado emerged as a focal point of a much larger international sugar industry seeking to cultivate irrigated lands, national and international companies like Great Western Sugar became the primary agent promoting and encouraging migration to places like northeastern Colorado in the first decades of the twentieth century. In so doing, their activities disrupted the precarious ethnic and racial balance of desirability forged by Colorado water law. Sugar companies like Great Western, for instance, heavily recruited Japanese laborers, many of whom previously worked in Wyoming coal mines and on railroad crews, until the "Gentleman's Agreement" stopped all immigration from Japan after 1907.[95] Other ethnic and racial groups were subsequently recruited to Colorado's beet fields; Great Western Sugar was accused of importing different ethnic groups in order to prevent the "economic solidarity" of any one group and of actively encouraging competition between ethnic groups in order to discourage cooperation and unionization.[96]

Of note to the issue of immigration was also the success of many British corporate entities involved in the acquisition of water rights in Colorado. According to David Schorr in his study of the doctrine of prior appropriation in nineteenth-century Colorado, the largest irrigation works in Colorado at the time were controlled by foreign capital, especially from Great Britain. In communities along the state's Front Range, the British-owned Northern Colorado Irrigation Company was responsible for many of the major canals providing water to the area. Schorr explains that these foreign corporations were also frequently victims to xenophobic treatment. Coloradans, themselves relatively recent migrants to the state, were fierce in their isolationism—especially with regard to the water resource and its challenge to their yeoman ideal—and thus became wary that European ownership of water would result in a feudal system, where farmers would come to occupy the position of a tenant or servant.[97]

Ironically, just as German-Russians both succeeded and assimilated as large landholders, a feudal system dependent upon the peonage of Mexican laborers did in fact emerge in northern Colorado. Prior to the twentieth century, ethnic Mexicans were not identified as an immigrant group in the state and most "Mexicans" had lived in the San Luis Valley and other reaches in the southern half of the state since the 1850s, when they brought their concepts of water law and water management to what would become Colorado.[98] Indeed, they were Colorado's first nonindigenous settlers. Not surprisingly, there were very few "Mexicans" who lived outside of southern Colorado during the last decades of the nineteenth century. In what would become the sugar beet capital of the world, only ten Mexican nationals lived in Weld County in 1900. By 1930, however, immigrants from Mexico and migrant Mexican American workers had emerged not only as the largest non-Euro-American group in Colorado but also as the single largest group harvesting the state's beet fields.[99]

The emergence of Mexican and Mexican American labor in Colorado's beet fields and beyond was wrapped up in a larger national discourse of

Table 5.1.
Weld County Immigration Data.[a]

	Total Population	Foreign-Born Population	Mexican Population	Russian Population	German Population	Irish Population
1870	1,316	320	4	N/A	76	84
1880	4,918	728	N/A	N/A	111	83
1890	11,736	1,873	6	72	274	167
1900	16,808	2,285	1	126	385	131
1910	39,177	6,018	92	1,937	663	150
1920	54,059	8,224	756	3,733	501	118

[a] US Bureau of the Census, *State Compendium(s) Colorado: Statistics of Population, Occupations, Agriculture, Irrigation, Drainage, Manufactures, and Mines and Quarries for the State, Counties, and Cities,* inclusive of those compiled for the 1870–1920 census years, https://www.census.gov/library/publications.html.

nativism, racism, and immigration restriction in the early decades of the twentieth century. Water, as Eric Boime has shown, was intricately tied to the conversation as reclamation proponents, such as former Colorado Agricultural College professor Elwood Mead, "conflated their populist disdain for land monopoly with their contempt for non-Anglo immigrants." In their eyes, irrigated "farm communities not only excluded Chinese, Japanese, and Mexican residents: They provided a bulwark against them."[100] Desirability accordingly took on a whole new meaning as the hopes and fears about the "alienizing of America" fell unevenly on paradoxical understandings of a Mexican labor force that would emerge to cultivate those millions of irrigated acres reclaimed by Western water law and policy.[101] Rather than fulfilling an initial promise to Americanize foreigners, water law and policy like the Reclamation Act were part of a complex interplay of water, immigration, and commercial law that inscribed racial hierarchy on the irrigated lands of the American West.

At the top were the white-owned sugar companies who purchased and refined the sugar beets, which were grown by local, almost exclusively white growers throughout the state.[102] The white farmer "to make a profit at the price he gets, must have low wage labor or else he won't grow beets; and without beets the sugar companies could not operate their factories and make a profit."[103] The harvest of sugar beets, however, was not easy; the beets required intensive cultivation during most of the seven-month growing season.[104]

Figure 5.3. Mexican and Mexican American families came to dominate the wage labor force of Colorado's agricultural economy in the 1920s. Very few of these families had rights to the water or the land on which they worked. (Photo reproduced by permission, Western History Collection, Denver Public Library, call number z-114.)

What marked this particular form of labor was that "it is dependent upon the labor of the family: the father, the mother, and little children."[105] As one sugar company circular noted, "an inexperienced man can work 9 acres, a woman 7 acres, and children in proportion to age."[106] Thinning the beets, in particular, was identified as work "better suited to boys [and girls] than men."[107] This was not work that "native-born Americans," either as individuals or families, were likely to seek or want.

Mexicans emerged as the largest single foreign-born group in northeastern Colorado's sugar beet fields because Mexicans and other Latin Americans were exempt from the wholesale exclusion imposed on the Chinese and other Asians and ultimately the large-scale restrictions on Southern and Eastern Europeans that culminated in the 1924 National Immigration Act.[108] Mexican immigrants as well as Mexican Americans filled the "vacuum" left by the embargo on cheap European and Asian labor.

Great Western in fact was one of the most vocal proponents and importers of Mexican labor to fill this labor shortage. In its own publication, the company extolled the virtues of Mexican beet workers "plowing, leveling, harrowing, hauling manure, *digging ditches, cleaning out ditches,* [and] repairing fences." An article, written by a "fieldman," conceded that Mexicans were generally "no good" working on a team but argued that "with a little time and patience on the part of the farmer, they develop into good farm hands." As one farmer went on to report, "I never saw two better men with a manure fork than my two *Mexican boys.*"[109] Proponents of Mexican immigration also "insisted that Mexicans were an inferior race . . . well suited for hard labor . . . [who would] return to Mexico when their labor was no longer needed."[110] Contrary to the sugar companies' propagation of the notion that sugar beet laborers were foreign "Mexicans," a vast majority of the families were in fact American citizens, born and reared largely in Colorado, New Mexico, and Texas.[111] Regardless of citizenship, it became gospel among the companies that Mexicans will do "the work no white man will do."[112]

Such attitudes helped push Mexican American and Mexican families into this narrow segment of the labor market—providing over two-thirds of the sugar beet laborers in Colorado.[113] Every winter and early spring, representatives of the sugar companies would travel throughout the American Southwest and northern Mexico to recruit Mexican American and Mexican families for the sugar beet harvest. Although Mexican immigrants and Mexican Americans were legally categorized as white, in social practice they were treated as nonwhite in most of their everyday actions and experiences.[114]

Nowhere was this dichotomy reflected more than in the standard beet labor contract that heads of Mexican and Mexican American households were compelled to sign because no other employment opportunities existed in the racially stratified labor market.[115] Indeed, Colorado served as a testing ground to formulate the parameters between water and immigration law as Great Western was one of the first sugar companies to introduce a written contract between itself, its growers (or farmers), and the migrant beet laborer. In this contractual relationship, Great Western acted as an agent for its growers, recruited and gathered up field labor, shipped the laborer into its beet-growing territory, and distributed the laborer to the growers. The sugar companies, however, were not themselves legally responsible for the wages paid to the laborers, as this was the responsibility of the growers, who most often paid by acreage cultivated (twenty dollars per acre).[116]

The father would sign the contract on behalf of the family; the size of the acreage assigned to the family would be based upon the proportional share to which every member of the family could be expected to work. Although beet labor contracts typically included clauses providing that children under eleven years of age would not be allowed to work in the fields, one critic cited a long list of "open" and "flagrant" violations of these provisions.[117] It was common for children as young as six years old to be working in the fields, not only preventing them from attending school but also posing a direct threat to their lives.[118]

Further exacerbating the tenuous existence of these families, sugar companies secured the next season's labor supply by giving credit for food and supplies to families during the winter. The problem was that the credit was to be paid out of the next season's work. In this "system of peonage" reminiscent of the racial apartheid of sharecropping in the American South, families would "start work in the spring handicapped by a debt to the sugar company which will reduce the amount coming to [them] in the fall."[119]

Ultimately, water law worked with immigration and labor law to create a racialized order in Colorado's irrigated sugar beet fields. The white-owned company unilaterally established the conditions under which the contract was to be performed. It left all disputes between the white grower and the Mexican laborer to the company's final judgment; it provided no guarantee that the laborer would receive pay when work was completed; nor did it stipulate when the work season ended. Regarding this final point, Mexican workers were "compelled to work in the field until late in the winter, under terrible weather conditions, without extra pay, and under penalty of losing the money they have already earned, if they stop work before 'all the crop is harvested.'"[120]

It is no surprise that Mexicans were treated harshly by their white immigrant employers.[121] German-Russians at first shunned Mexican beet laborers and refused to view them as equal in social status.[122] Despite the efforts of sugar beet companies who were recruiting Mexicans, Colorado's white farmers reflected national attitudes in viewing Mexicans as lacking in ambition, illiterate, nonpolitical, and unwilling to assimilate to prevailing cultural norms.[123] Mexicans, moreover, received lesser wages than their European counterparts for doing the same work.[124]

Difficulties also arose where Great Western Sugar tried to convince white farmers to provide housing and suitable living conditions to Mexicans in order to encourage a more productive workforce.[125] Arguing that farmers would not want undesirable "leftovers" who would willingly choose to live "in a corral where cattle are fed, and where manure is within a few feet of the door," or on a "ditch bank where little children are in constant danger of being drowned," Great Western tried to counter the belief that Mexican labor "will put up with conditions that the Russians will not."[126] Unfortunately, many of these efforts were in vain and farmers simply refused to provide adequate living facilities for Mexican workers due to deep-seated prejudices.[127]

Great Western found a partial solution to the so-called Mexican problem in its funding and construction of segregated worker colonies, which were kept separate from the white communities in northern Colorado. However, these colonies were hardly a suitable form of shelter despite company promotional materials detailing "satisfactory" two-room houses, large tracts of land, and tree-lined and orderly street-plans.[128] In general, the Mexican colonies were small, lacked running water and electricity, and represented no more than "poor dilapidated shanties."[129] In addition, rather than providing free housing to Mexican tenants, sugar companies provided another exploitable tool of the standard beet contract by requiring families to receive even lower wages in exchange for housing arrangements.[130] The systemic discrimination experienced by Mexicans and Mexican Americans was undeniable. One individual affiliated with Great Western Sugar even admitted, "in Colorado there is less race prejudice against an Indian than against a Mexican."[131]

Such attitudes accordingly reinforced an emerging discourse around the "illegality" of the Mexican. Mexican beet laborers and the conditions under which they labored seemed to serve as prima facie evidence of not only undesirability but also unfitness to ever be a citizen. Increasingly, "undesirable" became replaced with "illegal," especially when talking about Mexicans. One farmer in Colorado, reflecting the attitudes of many in the state and nation, declared that Mexicans were nothing more than "treacherous, shiftless thieves."[132] Collectively, the dramatically new edifice of immigration law and enforcement enacted by the federal government during the 1910s and 1920s, public sentiment against immigration, and radically different priorities for the national irrigation act and its operationalization by state water law ossified the state's and the nation's racial order at the dawn of the 1930s.

The Past, Present, and Uncertain Future of Water and Immigration Wars

In the early months of 1935, the governor of Colorado, "Big Ed" Johnson, initiated the first of several measures intended to deter undocumented immigrant labor from Mexico from entering the state. Animated by speculation that an "alien menace" from Mexico not only exacerbated the economic crisis gripping the nation but also directly contributed to the financial meltdown several years earlier, Governor Johnson, himself the son of immigrants, felt the need to act in the face of what he perceived as a federal inability to control the nation's borders.[133] First, Governor Johnson sent letters to the federal government demanding the deportation of "alien labor."

The governor then stated that if the federal authorities refused to enforce its immigration laws, he would deploy the Colorado National Guard to do the job.[134] In anticipation of such a call, Governor Johnson approved a plan to establish a "concentration camp" for the Mexican "aliens" at the National Guard's training facility on the western outskirts of the Denver metropolitan area.[135] Under the plan approved by Governor Johnson and opposed only by "a group of local communists," all aliens on relief were to be placed in the camp in preparation for their eventual deportation. A year later, Governor Johnson declared martial law and deployed the National Guard to Colorado's southern border to prevent Mexicans from entering the state, putting at serious risk the planting of the state's sugar beet crop for the year. Less than two decades after they had become the latest group of immigrants to be recruited to work the thousands of acres brought into cultivation because of Colorado's water law and national irrigation policy, Mexicans were met by force of arms and denied entry into the state.[136]

Mexican immigrants and Mexican Americans who migrated to Colorado as yeoman farmers hoping to assimilate on an irrigated farm did not encounter the Eden promised by the state's immigration bureau. Indeed, the benefits of the water law were never intended for Mexicans. As one Bureau of Reclamation circular unabashedly declared in 1919, "the primary Purpose of the Reclamation Law" was to create on these irrigated lands the "gradual welding of all Aryan races in a final race" that "will dominate the world." Mexican immigrants and Mexican Americans, therefore, were never intended to receive the "true birthright" provided by water and immigration law: "room to breathe, sunshine, a sure reward for intelligent labor, the individual home, and an opportunity to become independent."[137] Largely denied property and water rights, Mexicans and Mexican Americans instead entered agricultural labor markets with few enforceable protections. Their status as "immigrants," moreover, made Mexicans and Mexican Americans "fugitive" targets who came to be chased, harassed, and detained by agents of the local, state, and federal government as economic conditions and national priorities over immigration changed.[138]

The uneasy tension between desirable and undesirable immigration and its relation to irrigation fueled undeniable growth in Colorado and much of the American West. Examining northeastern Colorado alone, there is a clear connection between the surge in population in Weld County, both domestic and foreign, and a marked increase in irrigable acreage. In 1889, there were 112,060 acres irrigated in Weld County.[139] A decade later, in 1899, this number rose to 226,613 acres irrigated, a 102.2 percent increase.[140] According to census data taken in 1910, the amount of irrigable acreage had eclipsed 300,000 acres,[141] and by 1920, the amount of acreage irrigated in Weld County had increased to 382,701, with over 200 main ditches present in the county, 240 lateral ditches, and 238 independent enterprises engaged in irrigation works in the region, and more than 5,000 active farms in the county, many requiring vast amounts of Mexican labor.[142] To be sure, this was a trend seen throughout much of the American West as the employment of Mexican labor during the "high tide of immigration that brought 678,291 reported immigrants from Mexico" was proportional to the expansion of irrigable land by the 1930s.[143]

The notion of "desirability" fundamentally changed in the first decades of the twentieth century. The very success of the German-Russians as yeoman irrigators was short-lived as their achievements were dependent upon highly capitalized corporate ditches serving international sugar beet operations. The independence of these white yeoman farmers required them to seek a transient nonwhite workforce to work the vast sugar beet empire that had emerged as a result of irrigation. The white-dominated sugar industry sought Mexican laborers to work but not to own irrigated lands.[144]

By the beginning of the Great Depression in 1929, the arid American West had been transformed both by water and by immigration. But it was transformed in ways not envisioned by those late nineteenth-century irrigation crusaders who had so fervently hoped that the ditch and the corresponding water law of the American West would resolve the immigration debate. The irrigated lands of the American West would not serve to end the immigration debate by providing a pathway to assimilation for all immigrants to the United States. Instead, water and immigration law and policy, especially after 1905, buttressed the notion of *priority* of right and private enterprise over the labor of the "foreign" racialized field hand.

Donald Worster reminds us that the application of water law and policy to the American West created "a modern hydraulic society . . . a social order based on the intensive, large-scale manipulation of water and its products in an arid setting." In turn, it created a "coercive, monolithic, and hierarchical system" that is "reflected in every mile of the irrigation canal."[145] Eric Boime further explains that in a reclaimed North American West where "Anglos, Asians, Mexicans, and Native Americans commingled and contended," conceptions of race "dovetailed" the irrigation project to nation building and national security.[146] In the process of reclaiming arid land, water law would obscure under the mantra of "property rights," "illegal aliens," and seemingly unconnected water and immigration "wars" the creation and maintenance of a racialized order necessary for the rapid growth of the American West that would emerge during the twentieth century.

Notes

1. *Official Proceedings of the Thirteenth National Irrigation Congress* (August 21–24, 1905, Portland Oregon), 14–15.
2. *Reclamation Act/Newlands Act of 1902.* Public Law 57–161. *U.S. Statutes at Large* 32 (1902): 388.
3. *Official Proceedings of the Thirteenth National Irrigation Congress,* 15; see also George C. Pardee, "Colonization and Irrigation," *Official Proceedings of the Eleventh National Irrigation Congress* (January 6, 1903, Ogden, Utah), 90–95.
4. *Official Proceedings of the Thirteenth National Irrigation Congress,* 15 (emphasis added).
5. "Irrigation of the Lands," *San Francisco Chronicle,* August 22, 1905, 3.
6. These three were save the forests, store the floods, and reclaim the desert. Charles Wood Eberlein, "The Making of Homes," *Official Proceedings of the Thirteenth National Irrigation Congress,* 21.
7. Eberlein, "The Making of Homes," 21.
8. Eberlein, "The Making of Homes," 21–22 (emphasis added).
9. Eberlein, "The Making of Homes," 22.
10. Eberlein, "The Making of Homes," 22.
11. This is true if we also consider immigration as a racial project. As one historian notes, the "subjects of race and racial ideology" are "notably absent in the history of U.S. reclamation and, to some extent, the larger field of environmental history." Eric Boime, "'Beating Plowshares into Swords': The Colorado River Delta, the Yellow Peril, and the Movement for Federal Reclamation, 1901–1928," *Pacific Historical Review* 78, no. 1 (February 2009): 30.
12. Tom I. Romero II, "The Color of Water: Observations of a Brown Buffalo in Water Law and Policy in Ten Stanzas," *Denver Water Law Review* 15, no. 2 (2012): 329–367. As in this article, I use the terms "color" and "color lines" to describe legally enforced boundaries between whiteness and nonwhiteness. I

have explored in other places how race and color are used in contemporary no-menclature to distinguish between whites, Latinos (including differences in the use of the terms Spanish American, Mexican American, Chicano, and Hispano), Asians, American Indians, and blacks in legal discourse. Tom I. Romero II, "¿La Raza Latina?: Multiracial Ambivalence, Color Denial and the Emergence of a Tri-Ethnic Jurisprudence at the End of the Twentieth Century," *New Mexico Law Review* 37, no. 2 (2007): 249–255.

13. Tom I. Romero II, "Bridging the Confluence of Water and Immigration Law," *Texas Tech Law Review* 48, no. 4 (2016): 779–827.

14. Donald J. Pisani, "Federal Reclamation and the American West in the Twentieth Century," *Agricultural History* 77, no. 3 (2003): 393.

15. "Water in the West," *National Park Service*, accessed April 4, 2016, http://www.nps.gov/nr/travel/ReclamationDamsIrrigationProjectsAndPowerplants/water_in_the_west.html.

16. See generally Donald J. Pisani, *Water and American Government: The Reclamation Bureau, National Water Policy, and the West, 1902–1935* (Berkeley: University of California Press, 2002), 1–31; and William D. Rowley, *The Bureau of Reclamation: Origins and Growth to 1945*, vol. 1 (Bureau of Reclamation, Department of the Interior, 2006), 47–85.

17. "Memorial to the Congress of the United States," *National Irrigation Congress*, September 15–17, 1891, Salt Lake City, Utah, 4.

18. Donald J. Pisani, *To Reclaim a Divided West: Water, Law, and Public Policy 1848–1902* (Albuquerque: University of New Mexico Press, 1992).

19. Pisani, *To Reclaim a Divided West*, 239, 286.

20. See Kenneth R. Wright, "Ancestral Puebloan Water Handling," *LakeLine* (Winter 2008): 25–28; and Michael C. Meyer, *Water in the Hispanic Southwest: A Social and Legal History, 1550–1850* (Tucson: University of Arizona Press, 1996), 12.

21. Wright, "Ancestral Puebloan Water Handling," 24–26

22. Wright, "Ancestral Puebloan Water Handling," 26–28. See also Brian R. Billman, Patricia M. Lambert, and Banks L. Leonard. "Cannibalism, Warfare, and Drought in the Mesa Verde Region during the Twelfth Century A.D.," *American Antiquity* 65, no. 1 (2000): 145–174.

23. "Treaty of Peace, Friendship, Limits, and Settlement Between the United States of America and Mexican Republic," Feb. 2, 1848, *United States Statutes at Large* 9 (1848): 922.

24. Liping Zhu, *The Road to Chinese Exclusion: The Denver Riot, 1880 Election, and the Rise of the West* (Lawrence: University Press of Kansas, 2013), 12–13 and 16–17.

25. The homesteading law allowed American citizens to receive, virtually for free, fee simple title to 160 acres of land in exchange for five years of continued settlement and improvements to the land. *Homestead Act of 1862*, Public Law 37–64 *U.S. Statutes at Large* 12 (1862): 392 (repealed 1976).

26. Tom I. Romero II, "Uncertain Waters and Contested Lands: Excavating the Layers of Colorado's Legal Past," *University of Colorado Law Review* 73 (2002): 542.

27. For the move toward the riparian doctrine, see Act (November 5, 1861), *Colorado Session Laws* sec. 1: 67; Act (Aug. 15, 1862), *Colorado Session Laws* sec. 13: 44, 48.

28. For the Colorado legislature's early actions toward developing a theory of appropriation, see Act (March 11, 1864) *Colorado Session Laws*, sec. 32: 49, 58.

29. Colorado Constitution, art. 16, sec. 6.

30. Coffin v. Left Hand Ditch Co., 6 Colo. 443, 446 (1882).

31. *Coffin*, 6 Colo. at 446–447; see also *Yunker v. Nichols*, 1 Colo. 551, 553 (1872) (asserting that the "rules respecting the tenure of property must yield to the physical laws of nature . . . [i]n a dry and thirsty land" such as Colorado).

32. Pisani, *To Reclaim a Divided West*, 29–32.

33. See generally David Schorr, *The Colorado Doctrine: Water Rights, Corporations, and Distributive Justice on the American Frontier* (New Haven: Yale University Press, 2012). See also Romero, "Uncertain Waters," 540–541.

34. Donald Worster, *Rivers of Empire: Water, Aridity, and the Growth of the American West* (New York: Oxford University Press, 1985), 111.

35. Worster, *Rivers of Empire*, 114. See also Stephen C. McCaffrey, "The Harmon Doctrine One Hundred Years Later: Buried, Not Praised," *Natural Resources Journal* 36 (1996): 549, 550.

36. Pisani, "Reclamation and Social Engineering in the Progressive Era," *Agricultural History* 57, no. 1 (1983): 47–52; Worster, *Rivers of Empire*, 114, 120–123.

37. *Naturalization Act of 1790, U.S. Statutes at Large* 1 (1790): 103. Although the requirements for naturalization changed frequently, this basic prerequisite for citizenship would remain the same until 1952. See Ian Haney López, *White by Law: The Legal Construction of Race* (New York: New York University Press, 1996). After the Civil War and passage of the Fourteenth Amendment to the US Constitution, Congress amended the Nationality Act to extend the right to naturalize to "persons of African nativity or descent." As Mai Ngai documents, however, no one in Congress "seriously believed" that there would be appreciable immigration from Africa. Mai Ngai, *Impossible Subjects: Illegal Aliens and the Making of Modern America* (Princeton: Princeton University Press, 2004), 38. Those from the far east, however, posed unanticipated challenges to simple white/nonwhite categorizations in the law. See Doug Coulson, *Race, Nation, and Refuge: The Rhetoric of Race in Asian American Citizenship Cases* (Albany: State University of New York Press, 2017).

38. Tomás Almaguer, *Racial Fault Lines: The Historical Origins of White Supremacy in California* (Berkeley: University of California Press, 1994), 153.

39. Zhu, *The Road to Chinese Exclusion*, 16.

40. Zhu, *The Road to Chinese Exclusion*, 16. See also Lucy E. Salyer, *Laws as Harsh as Tigers: Chinese Immigrants and the Shaping of Modern Immigration*

Law (Chapel Hill: University of North Carolina Press, 1995). Emphasis added.

41. Almaguer, *Racial Fault Lines,* 153.
42. Almaguer, *Racial Fault Lines,* 154.
43. California Constitution, Article 19, sec. 1.
44. California Constitution, Article 19, sec. 2 and 3.
45. "Additional articles to the treaty between the United States of America and the Ta-Tsing Empire of June 18, 1858 (Burlingame Treaty)," July 28, 1868, *United States Statutes at Large* 16 (1868): 739; and In re Tiburcio Parrott, 1 F. 481 (C.C. Cal. 1880). See also Paul Kens, "Civil Liberties, Chinese Laborers, and Corporations," in *Law in the Western United States,* ed. Gordon Morris Bakken, 499 (Norman: University of Oklahoma Press, 2001).
46. Zhu, *The Road to Chinese Exclusion,* 268.
47. Pisani, "Reclamation and Social Engineering," 52; see also Boime, "Beating Plowshares into Swords," 27–53.
48. Donald Pisani, *From the Family Farm to Agribusiness: The Irrigation Crusade in California and the West, 1850–1931* (Berkeley: University of California Press, 1984). Of course, one of the irrigation crusade's chief proponents, William Smythe, "looked forward as well as backward" in envisioning a carefully planned community of family farms. Pisani, "Reclamation and Social Engineering," 50. See also Donald E. Worster, "Irrigation and Democracy in California: The Early Promise," *Pacific Historian* 28 (1984): 30; and David Schorr, "The First Water-Privatization Debate: Colorado Water Corporations in the Gilded Age," *Ecology Law Quarterly* 33, no. 2 (March 2006): 321–323.
49. According to the 1890 census, 25 percent of the West's population was foreign-born, as compared to 22.3 percent for the Northeast, 18.2 percent for the Midwest, and 2.7 percent for the South. Campbell Gibson and Emily Lennon, "Historical Census Statistics on the Foreign-born Population of the United States: 1850–1990," US Census Bureau, Population Division (February 1999).
50. Louis Windmuller, "Why Immigration Ought Not To Be Restricted," *New York Times,* December 30, 1892.
51. 57th Cong. 1st sess., *Congressional Record* (1902), 2283.
52. Pisani, "Reclamation and Social Engineering," 53; Rowley, *The Bureau of Reclamation,* 73–75.
53. *Official Proceedings of the Nineteenth Annual National Conference of Charities and Correction,* (June 1892).
54. *Official Proceedings of the Nineteenth Annual National Conference of Charities and Correction,* 10.
55. "Report of the Standing Committee on Immigration and Inter-State Migration," *Annual Conference of Charities and Correction* (June 23, 1892): 155, 157. As one historian succinctly observes, the immigration restrictions of the late nineteenth century revealed the fundamentally contradictory notion between fears of an "immigrant flood" of undesirables and the "immense economic

value of the immigrant labor supply" within immigration law and administration. Patrick Ettinger, *Imaginary Lines: Border Enforcement and the Origins of Undocumented Immigration, 1882–1930* (Austin: University of Texas Press, 2009): 35.

56. Reclamation Act of 1902, sec. 1093.
57. Whereas 7.3 million acres of land were irrigated in 1900, proponents of the law estimated that over 100 million acres could be irrigated in the West alone. Pisani, *Water and American Government*, 3–6. The act originally applied to Arizona, California, Colorado, Idaho, Kansas, Montana, Nebraska, Nevada, New Mexico, North Dakota, Oklahoma, Oregon, South Dakota, Utah, Washington, and Wyoming. Later, it was extended to Texas and other states.
58. "Great West Their Pride: Trans-Mississippi Congress Meets in Seattle," *Los Angeles Times*, August 19, 1903.
59. April Marleaux, *Sugar and Civilization: American Empire and the Cultural Politics of Sweetness* (Chapel Hill: University of North Carolina Press, 2015), 32.
60. Marleaux, *Sugar and Civilization*, 34.
61. *Official Proceedings of the Thirteenth National Irrigation Congress*, 262.
62. Charles Wood Eberlein, "Foreign Immigration and the States," *Pacific Monthly*, 16 (1906): 397.
63. Eberlein, "Foreign Immigration and the States," 398.
64. *Official Proceedings of the Thirteenth National Irrigation Congress*, 22.
65. *Official Proceedings of the Thirteenth National Irrigation Congress*, 22.
66. *Official Proceedings of the Thirteenth National Irrigation Congress*, 61–62.
67. *Official Proceedings of the Thirteenth National Irrigation Congress*, 62.
68. *Official Proceedings of the Thirteenth National Irrigation Congress*, 62.
69. *Official Proceedings of the Thirteenth National Irrigation Congress*, 252.
70. *Official Proceedings of the Thirteenth National Irrigation Congress*, 253 (emphasis added).
71. *Official Proceedings of the Thirteenth National Irrigation Congress*, 253–254.
72. Importantly, Wantland framed the "question" as one between the "character" of those immigrating to the East Coast from Europe, the Chinese on the West Coast, and emigration of "American" boys from the Midwest to Canada. *Official Proceedings of the Thirteenth National Irrigation Congress*, 260.
73. *Official Proceedings of the Thirteenth National Irrigation Congress*, 261.
74. *Official Proceedings of the Thirteenth National Irrigation Congress*, 260.
75. *Official Proceedings of the Thirteenth National Irrigation Congress*, 260–261.
76. *Official Proceedings of the Thirteenth National Irrigation Congress*, 261.
77. *Official Proceedings of the Thirteenth National Irrigation Congress*, 261–262.
78. Alva Adams, "Apples and Alfalfa" (1909), 3, Stephen H. Hart Library, Colorado History, Denver Colorado.
79. Adams, "Apples and Alfalfa," 6.
80. Adams, "Apples and Alfalfa," 3.

81. Adams, "Apples and Alfalfa," 6.

82. R. W. Roskelley, *Population Trends in Colorado 1860 to 1930: A Historical Perspective for Agricultural, Industrial, and Human Planning* (Colorado State College, 1940).

83. Bayard Taylor, *Colorado: A Summer Trip* (G. P. Putnam, 1867), 44.

84. Robert R. Crifisi, *A Land Made from Water: Appropriation and the Evolution of Colorado's Landscape, Ditches, and Water Institutions* (Boulder: University Press of Colorado, 2015), 46–49. Crifisi notes, "it is no wonder that farmers remain so possessive toward their water. Once the backbreaking process of digging ditches and establishing their homestead was complete, the experience was seared in their psyche, and the labor they expended serves as proof enough of their right to use their water and control their ditch." Indeed, the "Spanish and Indian origins of the ditch" soon faded into memory as new European "emigrants" to Colorado became "migrants" or "immigrants" as "Colorado was remade both in name and environment." Crifisi, *A Land Made from Water*, 49, 233.

85. Appellate Eaton's Br. 2, Wyatt v. Larimer & Weld Irrigation Co. 1892. Colorado Court of Appeals (in file of Supreme Court case no. 3117). Colorado State Archives. As quoted in Schorr, *The Colorado Doctrine*, 66–68.

86. "Do You Need a Change?" *Colorado Bureau of Immigration* (1905): 4, Stephen H. Hart Library, Colorado History, Denver, Colorado.

87. "Do You Need a Change?" 4.

88. Immigrants from Ireland, Germany, and England also made up a sizable portion of the foreign-born population in Colorado and Weld County during this era. Rubén Donato, *Mexicans and Hispanos in Colorado Schools and Communities, 1920–1960* (Albany: State University of New York Press, 2007), 29.

89. David Boyd, *Irrigation near Greeley, Colorado* (US Government Printing Office, 1897), 28–73 (detailing the physical geography and legal history of water rights in Greeley, Colorado); see also Michael Holleran, *Ditches and Canals in Colorado: Historic Context for Irrigation and Water Supply* (Colorado Center for Preservation Research, June 2005), 14.

90. The provisions for mutual ditch companies as well as a corresponding private right of condemnation for the purpose of ditch construction would become a part of the Colorado Constitution upon statehood in 1876: "All persons and corporations shall have the right-of-way across public, private, and corporate lands for the construction of ditches, canals, and flumes for the purpose of conveying water for domestic purposes, for the irrigation of lands, and for mining and manufacturing purposes, and for drainage, upon payment of just compensation." Colorado Constitution, art. 16, sec. 7. The larger legal and social history as well as a more nuanced understanding of water "distinguishing ownership of water by individuals and user-owned corporate bodies from control by investor-owned companies" is detailed in Schorr, "The First Privatization Debate," 358.

91. See generally Gregory Hobbs Jr., "Colorado Water Law: An Historical Overview," *Denver Water Law Review* 1, no. 1 (1997): 13–15.
92. William May, "The Great Western Sugarlands: The History of the Great Western Sugar Company and the Economic Development of the Great Plains" (PhD diss., University of Colorado, 1982), 378–380.
93. One farmer, in a familiar echo of Governor Adams, argued that "our conditions here are very favorable . . . it would be difficult for any place in the United States to show as a good a combination of soil, climate, water, fuel, cheap rates for transportation and home market for the product." "A Fruitful Field for Beet Culture," *The* (Denver) *Times*, November 5, 1899.
94. "Larger Sugar Beet Planting Is Announced," *Ft. Morgan Herald*, May 4, 1939. Indeed, prior to the Great Depression, sugar beets would become the greatest single source of agricultural income in the state, generating annual profits north of $20,000,000. Alvin T. Steinel, *History of Agriculture in Colorado: 1858–1926* (Colorado State Agricultural College, 1926), 307.
95. Eric Twitty, *Silver Wedge: The Sugar Beet Industry in Fort Collins*, SWCA Environmental Consultants (2003), 53.
96. May, "The Great Western Sugarlands," 380. See also "Italians to Work in Sugar Beet Fields," *Republican*, April 18, 1903.
97. Schorr, "The First Water-Privatization Debate," 325–326; see also Schorr, *The Colorado Doctrine*, 71.
98. Donato, *Mexicans and Hispanos in Colorado*, 29.
99. Donato, *Mexicans and Hispanos in Colorado*, 30; Roskelley, "Population Trends in Colorado," 48 ("Mexican immigrants totaling 13,144 outranked any other foreign-born group in 1930"). The census data used to compile table 5.1 reveals some of the challenges in categorizing in relation to citizenship as well as racial and ethnic identities of those living and working in Colorado's beet fields. For example, the 1930 census for the first and only time had a separate "Mexican" racial category. But in a subsequent report on agriculture in 1935 that included data on "farms, farm acreage and value by color," it designed "white" to include "Mexicans and Hindus" and "Colored" as "Negroes, Chinese, Japanese, and all other nonwhite race." US Bureau of Census, "Reports for States with Statistics for Counties and a Summary for the United States," vol. 2, part 3 (ca. 1935), 854–855. US Department of Agriculture, Census of Agriculture Historical Archive, http://agcensus.mannlib.cornell.edu/AgCensus/getVolumeOnePart.do?year=1935&part_id=770&number=41&title=Colorado.
100. Boime, "Beating Plowshares into Swords," 38. Elwood Mead's role in Colorado and his various roles as water booster and public servant, culminating in heading the Bureau of Reclamation from 1924 to his death in 1936, is detailed in Paul Conklin, "Vision of Elwood Mead," *Agricultural History* 34, no. 2 (1960): 88–97.
101. Representative of such attitudes are Remsen Crawford, "The Deportation of

Undesirable Aliens," *Current History* 30 (September 1929): 1080; Remsen Crawford, "The Menace of Mexican Immigration," *Current History* 31 (1930): 907. I draw upon and explore in greater detail such issues in Tom I. Romero II, "'A War to Keep Alien Labor Out of Colorado': The 'Mexican Menace' and Colorado's Depression-Era Militarization of Immigration Law and Policy," in Carissa Hessick and G. Jack Chin, eds., *Strange Neighbors: The Role of States in Immigration Policy* (New York: New York University Press, 2014).

102. The census tells a compelling story in this regard as 1900 was the first time a "colored" classification was used in tabulating census data for agriculture. Because the color line was strictly between African Americans and everyone else, most of the data was exclusive to the American South. US Bureau of Census, "Chapter IV—Farm Statistics by Color and Tenure of Farmer" (ca. 1923), 187. US Department of Agriculture, Census of Agriculture Historical Archive, http://usda.mannlib.cornell.edu/usda/AgCensusImages/1920/Farm_Statistics_By_Color_and_Tenure.pdf. Nevertheless, the census revealed that white ethnics (many foreign-born) owned or leased almost all of the irrigable farmland in Colorado and much of the American West. US Bureau of Census, "Chapter V—Farm Statistics by Race, Nativity, and Sex of Farmer" (ca. 1923), http://usda.mannlib.cornell.edu/usda/AgCensusImages/1920/Farm_Statistics_By_Race_Nativity_Sex.pdf.

103. "An Address by Thomas. F. Mahony, Problem of the Mexican Wage Earner," *The Catholic Conference on Industrial Problems*, Denver, Colorado, May 12, 1930.

104. Dennis Nodín Valdés, *Al Norte: Agricultural Workers in the Great Lakes Region, 1917–1970* (1991), 5.

105. Mahony, "Problem of the Mexican Wage Earner," 1, 4.

106. Mahony, "Problem of the Mexican Wage Earner," 4.

107. "Boys in the Beet Fields," *The* (Denver) *Republican*, March 30, 1904.

108. In the first decades of the twentieth century, Mexican immigrants were subject to federal immigration laws that applied to all immigrants, regardless of their country of origin. In 1924, Congress, as part of its sweeping restrictions on immigration, restricted immigration to only those persons "eligible for citizenship" while forming the border patrol to police almost exclusively the water-based US border with Mexico. The quota system also adopted by the Johnson-Reed Act excluded Mexico and Canada by deeming all persons immigrating from North America to be "white" as far as immigration policy was concerned. *Immigration Act of 1924*, Public Law 68–139 *U.S. Statutes at Large* 43 (1924): 153. For further detail on the applicability of immigration laws to Mexicans during this time, see Romero, "A War to Keep Alien Labor Out of Colorado," 67–72.

109. H. S. Varner, "The Mexican as a Farm Hand," *Through the Leaves*, June 1924, 339 (emphasis added).

110. Natalia Molina, "'In A Race All Their Own': The Quest to Make Mexicans

Ineligible for U.S. Citizenship," *Pacific Historical Review* 79 (2010): 171. See also David G. Gutiérrez, *Walls and Mirrors: Mexican Americans, Mexican Immigrants, and the Politics of Ethnicity* (Berkeley: University of California Press, 1995), 39–68.

111. Sarah Deutsch, *No Separate Refuge: Culture, Class, and Gender on an Anglo-Hispanic Frontier in the American Southwest, 1880–1940* (New York: Oxford University Press, 1987), 129.

112. Robert McLean, "Tightening the Mexican Border," *The Survey* 64 (April 1930): 28, 55.

113. Mahony, "Problem of the Mexican Wage Earner," 6.

114. Clara E. Rodríguez, *Changing Race: Latinos, the Census, and the History of Ethnicity in the United States* (New York: New York University Press, 2000): 83–84. Yet, even the legal categorization of Mexicans as white was contested. See Romero, "A War to Keep Alien Labor Out of Colorado," 71; Molina, "In a Race All Their Own," 175–187.

115. Mahony, "Problem of the Mexican Wage Earner," 129.

116. May, "The Great Western Sugarlands," 381–386.

117. Mahony, "Problem of the Mexican Wage Earner," 3. See also Valdés, *Al Norte*, 12–15.

118. According to one study of the Arkansas Valley in southeastern Colorado cited by Mahony, nearly 30 percent of the children died among a group of 140 families working in the sugar beet fields. Mahony, "Problem of the Mexican Wage Earner," 5.

119. Mahony, "Problem of the Mexican Wage Earner," 6.

120. Mahony, "Problem of the Mexican Wage Earner," 3.

121. Twitty, *The Silver Wedge*, 53.

122. Roskelley, "Population Trends in Colorado," 46.

123. May, "The Great Western Sugarlands," 401. For representative sugar company attitudes extolling the virtues of Mexican labor, see Varner, "The Mexican as a Farm Hand," 339; Jose Queralt-Mir, "Regarding Mexican Beet Workers," *Through the Leaves*, November 1923, 464–465 (article by Mexican consul to Denver giving "Man to Man" suggestions for treatment of Mexican field worker); "Colonizing Mexican Beet Workers," *Through the Leaves*, November 1923, 393–394.

124. "Colonizing Mexican Beet Workers," 415.

125. Donato, *Mexicans and Hispanos in Colorado*, 34. See also "Do Concessions to Beet Labor Pay?" March 1921, 135–136.

126. F. L. Cooper, "'Beet Shacks' v. Beet Houses," *Through the Leaves*, March 1920, 187–188.

127. Donato, *Mexicans and Hispanos in Colorado*, 34–35.

128. "Colonizing Mexican Beet Workers," 393–396; and Gregory T. Chase, "Hispanic Migration to Northeastern Colorado during the Nineteen Twenties:

Influences of Sugar Beet Agriculture" (master's thesis, University of Denver, 2011).

129. Camila Montoya, "Not A Sweet Deal: Mexican Migrant Workers in the Sugar Beet Farms of the Midwest and Mountain States, 1900–1930" (PhD diss., Michigan State University, 2000), 33.

130. Donato, *Mexicans and Hispanos in Colorado*, 33. Even when it attempted to help Mexicans climb the social ladder, however, racism was overt. Great Western sold lots and materials needed for construction of homes to Mexican families, which was peculiar as Mexicans in the area rarely were able to attain property ownership. Mexican laborers, however, needed to demonstrate to Great Western that they were "trustworthy and experienced beet workers" and also to present a recommendation by a supervisor as part of a vetting process that was required only of Mexicans. Donato, *Mexicans and Hispanos in Colorado*, 33.

131. May, "The Great Western Sugarlands," 401.

132. Donato, *Mexicans and Hispanos in Colorado*, 34. The rhetoric of illegality in relation to Mexicans is seen in contemporary accounts such as Robert McLean, "Tightening the Mexican Border," 28–29; Robert McLean, "The Mexican Return," *The Nation*, August 24, 1932, 165–166; Paul Taylor, "More Bars Against Mexicans," *The Survey* 64 (April 1930): 26–27. See generally Ngai, *Impossible Subjects*; Kelly Lytle Hernández, *Migra! A History of the U.S. Border Patrol* (Berkeley: University of California Press, 2010).

133. John Farnham, "Colorado Aliens Face Deportation," *New York Times*, March 31, 1935, E6; "Barricading Jobs: Troops Guard Colorado Borders to Keep Out the Indigent," *Literary Digest*, May 2, 1936, 5 (noting both of his parents as immigrants who naturalized); Edwin C. Johnson, March 2, 1936, Box 26916, Governor Edwin Carl Johnson Collection, Colorado State Archives, Denver, Colorado (lamenting the "evil alien menace").

134. Francis Wayne, "Colorado Aliens Will Be Deported," *Denver Post*, March 25, 1936, 1, 3.

135. Francis Wayne, "Aliens on Relief to Be Put in Camp," *Denver Post*, March 27, 1935, 1, 3; "Urges Deporting of Aliens," *New York Times*, March 28, 1935, 7.

136. See Romero, "A War to Keep Alien Labor Out of Colorado," 63–98.

137. C. J. Blanchard, "The Mentor: Reclaiming the Desert," *United States Bureau of Reclamation* 6, no. 17 (October 15, 1918), 4.

138. Romero, "A War to Keep Alien Labor Out of Colorado," 63–88; Hernández, *Migra!*, 90.

139. US Census Bureau, "Report on Agriculture by Irrigation in the Western Part of the United States at the Eleventh Census," (1894), US Department of Agriculture, Census of Agriculture Historical Archive, http://agcensus.mannlib .cornell.edu/AgCensus/censusParts.do?year=1890.

140. US Census Bureau, "Report on Agriculture by Irrigation."

141. US Census Bureau, "Thirteenth Census of the United States Taken in the Year 1910, Volume VI: Agriculture 1909 and 1910 Reports by States, with Statistics for Counties, Alabama-Montana," (1913), US Department of Agriculture, Census of Agriculture Historical Archive, http://usda.mannlib.cornell .edu/usda/AgCensusImages/1910/06/01/1833/41033898v6ch2.pdf.

142. US Census Bureau, "Fourteenth Census of the United States Taken in the Year 1920, vol. VI: Agriculture: Reports for States, with Statistics and Counties," (1922). One recent study notes that "until the 1920s, Colorado vied with California for the most irrigated acreage in the nation, and the Piedmont [Greeley area] possessed far and away the most irrigated acres within Colorado." Michael A. Weeks, "Industrializing a Landscape: Northern Colorado and the Making of Agriculture in the Twentieth Century" (PhD diss., University of Colorado–Boulder, 2016), 10.

143. Paul Taylor, "Mexican Migration and the 160-Acre Water Limitation," *California Law Review* 63, no. 3 (1975): 733; Gilbert C. Gonzalez and Raul A. Fernandez, *A Century of Chicano History: Empire, Nations and Migration* (London: Routledge, 2003), 128.

144. Taylor, "Mexican Migration and 160-Acre Limitation," 739–740 (noting that the "high tide" of immigration from Mexico did not lead to large-scale landownership for Mexican immigrants under the reclamation law.)

145. Worster, *Rivers of Empire*, 7.

146. Boime, "Beating Plowshares into Swords," 30.

6

Jurisdictional No Man's Land

Choctaws, Lawyers, and the Coal Question in Indian Territory

BRIAN FREHNER

Shortly after the Civil War ended, an ex-Confederate soldier from Tennessee killed an African American person and eluded authorities by fleeing westward to Indian Territory. Having served time in Ohio as a prisoner of war, Victor M. Locke refused to be captured again even after authorities shot him in the arm. After several days on the run, he was tired, hungry, and uncertain of his next move when he arrived at the Red River, the border between Texas and Indian Territory. There he met a ferry operator, an African American with whom he began to converse. A voice called to the black man from across the river, instructing him in the Choctaw language to transport the fugitive over the water. Locke found the language strange and asked the ferry operator many questions about Choctaw Indians and whether they were good people. Awaiting him on the other side of the river was a Choctaw man who looked upon Locke's Confederate uniform and told the ferry operator that he too had once worn such a uniform. The man welcomed Locke into his home, his wife dressed the gunshot wound, and the couple fed and housed him. Locke gradually regained his strength, began studying the Choctaw language, and married a three-quarter Choctaw woman; together they had a son, Victor M. Locke Jr., who would become politicized and serve as the Choctaw principal chief. The senior Locke made many friends among the Choctaw people, acquiring influence in tribal affairs, advising, counseling, and protecting them such that, to his way of thinking, he was "sort of a 'father to the Indians.'"[1]

Locke's story reveals how Indian Territory was both a literal and figurative borderlands environment. Borderland regions are those spaces on the edges of nations and empires where different people, ideas, cultures, and economies intermingle, and these interactions often create opportunities for some inhabitants and eliminate opportunities for others. People who recognize the fluid nature of overlapping and conflicting institutions and legal regimes such as tribal, state, and national laws and the different courts and jurisdictional venues may exploit the confusion to great advantage. Borderlands inhabitants exist within a jurisdictional no man's land, where the rule of law remains unclear, uncertain, and often unenforced. Such was the case in Indian Territory when Victor M. Locke arrived there in 1866 as a fugitive from the law and from justice. Like many people who entered into a borderlands region, Locke had escaped one legal regime and found opportunities in the confused tangle of jurisdictions created when the US government removed Native Americans and legally designated their homeland "Indian Territory." Although a white man, Locke found safe haven among Indian people who integrated him into their society and whose laws allowed him to find a wife and to have a son who rose to the ranks of Choctaw principal chief. Not everyone in a borderlands region fared so well. While Locke Sr. created opportunities for himself economically and politically by inserting himself into Choctaw tribal politics, others failed to capitalize on the shifting circumstances in borderlands regions and stood to lose economic and political power.

Oklahoma was a geographical space proscribed and referred to as Indian Territory, but the people who resided there prior to statehood lived within a highly ambiguous legal terrain.[2] Law constructed borders of citizenship between Native Americans and others. The most obvious and significant factors complicating citizenship for Native Americans originated from their forced relocation by the United States government and its unwillingness to recognize them as legal citizens until 1924. Once removed to Indian Territory in 1830, Choctaws disagreed among themselves as to who qualified for membership within their tribe. The attempt by federal bureaucrats to provide legal formulas to designate tribal citizenship further complicated who qualified as a citizen. Much of the confusion related to Choctaw tribal enrollment resulted from the question of who could receive royalty payments from communal coal resources. Whether incoming non-Indians held American citizenship status or not, their lack of tribal citizenship briefly prevented them from acquiring Indians' land and resources, but intermarriage

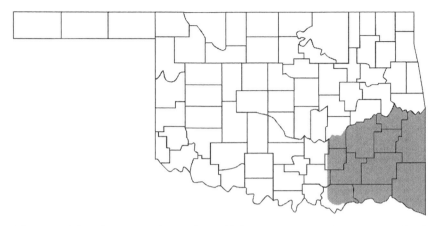

Figure 6.1. The Choctaw Nation within Oklahoma. Vector map by Scott Nazelrod via WikiMedia Commons.

presented a legal mechanism for many non-Indian men to acquire tribal citizenship and pursue their economic interests unencumbered. Thus, whoever could effectively navigate this legal borderland stood to gain a great deal of economic and political power.[3] The children of white and Choctaw couples emerged as another constituency of Indians who often saw issues involving economic and political affairs differently than their full-blood forebears, intensifying disputes among enrolled tribal members that sometimes erupted into violent factional battles for power. Locke was just one of many white people who entered into this borderlands environment and seized upon the incipient legal and economic regimes in order to build and consolidate his status and power within and among the Choctaw people.

The story of Indian removal and the subsequent incursion of white settlers into Indian Territory has long been told and appropriately characterized as a story of colonialism. This essay expands upon that story by considering how law, lawyers, and the legal system in this uniquely designated place aided and facilitated non-Indians to take possession of natural resources and how, in response, some Native people used the law to empower themselves and profit from coal resources. The Choctaws provide a case study of Native Americans who both suffered from the introduction of an alien legal regime and wielded significant influence by applying their own concepts of order and justice to federal law and hiring lawyers who sometimes exploited them and at other times effectively fought for and protected their interests. Law and capitalism worked together in a borderlands region and empowered settlers to exploit Indigenous people and their resources. Conversely, law and capitalism presented new forums that some Indigenous people entered into, learned, and embraced in order to reap new political, legal, and economic opportunities.

The history of law, Native Americans, and natural resources has received some scholarly attention. The manner and means by which non-Indians appropriated Indians' land and natural resource wealth from the Five Tribes has been told most thoroughly by Angie Debo in her classic account *And Still the Waters Run.* Debo provides extensive examples of the ambiguities and complexities of territorial, state, and national laws and how their manipulation, often by lawyers, resulted in exploitation of Native Americans in Indian Territory. While laws and lawyers appear in her account, rarely does she depict Indians themselves as legal actors who wielded the law in any way. Rather, her narrative reads more like an exposé and provides little theorizing or historicizing of legal context to show how law empowered or disempowered the people in her study. Most subsequent scholarship examining the introduction of capitalism to Indian Territory follows Debo's lead, casting Native people as helpless victims unable to function amidst the onslaught of a capitalist system based upon a legal regime Indians failed to comprehend.[4]

Other scholars have revised this interpretation somewhat by showing how Indians resisted federal efforts to impose allotment and functioned as legal actors when making agreements to rent or lease their land for mineral extraction. Although legally engaged, there were limits to the autonomy people experienced given the volatile fluctuations of the market economy.[5] As Clara Sue Kidwell has argued, the Choctaws demonstrated a great deal of legal power, as they "dogged the US government" to uphold treaty obligations, pled their cases in courts of law, and badgered congressmen to maintain moral standards with regard to their treaty rights.[6] The Choctaws attempted to assert their natural resource rights while working within a settler-established legal regime by using the dominant culture's legal principles "as both a shield and a sword in the battle for natural resource control and protection."[7] This perspective serves as a partial corrective to the gap in scholarship on the topic of Indians and the American economy by considering how they responded to capitalism. Furthermore, introducing "law" as one of the tools Indians wielded to resist and engage a capitalist regime may illuminate some of the political and moral dimensions of the settler-colonial origins of the United States.[8]

The major claim this study makes is that Choctaws who sold their land in an attempt to exercise legal control over coal resources hired lawyers to resist the efforts of federal officials and non-Choctaw trespassers who homogenized and proscribed tribal members legally, economically, politically, and racially. The notion that the United States created boundaries around Indigenous people and their land as part of a colonial effort, although accurate, depicts a static conception of politics and political relationships between Indigenous people and state power. The idea of fixed borders around land and people precludes the possibility that state, federal, and tribal power changed in meaning over time or in relationship to each other.[9] Rather than merely barriers between people and places, boundaries function as "sites of co-constitutive interaction" where people, governments, nations, and states compete to define political meanings of time, space, and identity.[10] Indigenous people may take advantage of such sites to constitute legal meaning and definitions by demanding rights and resources from the settler-state, thereby resisting homogenization and proscription and creating what one scholar has dubbed "the third space of sovereignty."[11] For the Choctaws and for other Indigenous people, the ability to define how their land was used constituted a key component of their identity and sovereignty. Land functioned as an economic and political asset that Choctaws and other Indians deployed to defend their sovereignty. For example, one Indigenous group repurchased land that it had once owned, effectively flipping "the story of Indigenous land on its head" and creating a narrative not of tribal *dispossession* but of tribal *possession*, or a history consisting of their struggle to reclaim lands that had once been their own.[12] The Choctaws underwent a similar struggle, not to repossess land they had lost but to force the federal government to sell tribally held lands that contained coal in order to generate sorely needed revenue for tribal members' survival. This decades-long struggle to secure compensation for redistributed land and resources constituted Choctaw members' resistance to American colonial rule.[13]

Resistance to the US government by Choctaws who favored allotment coalesced around the leadership of Victor M. Locke Jr., son of the escaped Confederate soldier described in the opening vignette. In his role as principal chief, Locke Jr. recognized that the Choctaws must wage a legal battle to assert their right to sell valuable coal lands and disburse the revenue to tribal members. He enlisted the aid of a savvy attorney and trusted childhood friend, Patrick Hurley, to argue on behalf of Choctaws in the courts and before Congress. A central component of the legal dispute over allotting

Choctaw coal lands involved challenges to the federal government, but Hurley and other lawyers also wrangled over legal questions of lineage and inheritance when Choctaws who remained in Mississippi also claimed allotments in Indian Territory.

One might impugn Hurley as one of the many lawyers to exploit Native Americans because he generated an annual salary of $5,000 for the legal services he performed, but such a judgment would be harsh. He was a white man who wielded the law not in his personal interest but to protect Choctaw people around whom he had been raised and in particular his friend, Locke Jr. Indeed, rather than stay in Oklahoma to generate money representing Native Americans, Hurley considered his victory in the Mississippi Choctaw case his last official act as lawyer for the Choctaw people. After declaring that nothing remained for him to do, Will Rogers reminded Hurley that one task remained: "You can stop the tide of Anglo-Saxon civilization at the borders of the Choctaw Nation."[14] Hurley's experiences interacting with Choctaw people and working for the tribe did not change his perspective on the law. Halting westward expansion, he responded, had never been his intention or desire. "I wasn't trying to stop that great, beautiful, indefinable, cruel thing called Anglo-Saxon civilization in its march to conquest," Hurley clarified, "I was just trying to retain a place within that civilization for the Choctaw people."[15] Like the Choctaws who hired him, Hurley knew that legal arguments would provide necessary weapons to combat the onslaught of Americans pouring into Indian Territory.

The law mattered greatly to Choctaws' lives and their ability to access their resources before and after Oklahoma statehood in 1907. During the time that the official designation of Indian Territory prevailed, the Commission to the Five Civilized Tribes, or "Dawes Commission," oversaw the creation and compilation of citizenship rolls, allotment of lands (wherein tribes relinquished titles to traditional lands and a portion of these were assigned to individual members), and distribution of assets to tribal members. Decisions regarding citizenship, however, could be appealed to federal courts, a legal maneuver that transferred power from commissioners into the hands of lawyers who could navigate the federal judicial system.[16] Therefore, tribes who hired lawyers to challenge decisions made by the Dawes Commission empowered themselves by winning cases that overruled commissioners' decisions on matters such as who qualified as a tribal member and who was entitled to receive tribal land and resources. Even after statehood in 1907, law and politics continued to complicate these issues among Choctaws because unallotted land, coal, asphalt, and timber remained to be claimed by the tribe and its citizens.[17]

Beneath approximately one-fifth of the state of Oklahoma resided coal deposits that generated a great deal of wealth beginning in the latter nineteenth century. Generally, coal exists in a large L shape that extends from Kansas southward into Oklahoma and eastward into lands once owned entirely by Choctaw Indians. Geologists working in the neighboring states of Arkansas, Texas, and Kansas conducted surveys looking for coal throughout the nineteenth century.[18] Noah Fields Drake worked for the Arkansas Geological Survey in 1896 and extensively investigated and mapped the geological conditions of deposits that existed in Indian Territory. Drake's reconnaissance revealed three separate structural and topographical formations, all of which spilled over into nearby states, but the majority of these three coal formations remained within Indian Territory. Mining generated millions of tons of coal and millions of dollars. By 1903, thirty-two companies produced more than three million tons of coal and that sum increased each year until 1906 when oil began replacing coal as a fuel source.[19] Choctaw and Chickasaw governments received $1,200,000 in coal royalties from 1872 to 1897, but this represented only a fraction of its worth.[20]

J. J. McAlester is the man most frequently credited with initiating coal mining in Indian Territory. He was living in Fort Smith, Arkansas, in 1865 when he saw the field notebook of a geologist who had worked as a member of a government surveying party before the Civil War. The geologist's notes indicated that coal deposits ran throughout the Choctaw Nation and prompted McAlester to consider relocating there to capitalize on the resource.[21] Legal impediments stood in his way. Trading lawfully in Indian Territory required a federal license and a permit from the Choctaw government.[22] McAlester eventually found his way to the Choctaw Nation by working as a teamster for a trading company and transporting merchandise. He remained in Indian Territory working as a clerk in a general merchandise store located near the intersection of the Texas and California Roads and the coal outcroppings he had seen on the geologist's map. News that surveyors had been scouting locations to build a railroad in the area prompted him to fill a wagon full of coal and transport it to the railroad's headquarters and persuade the company that tracks should pass near this fuel source, which he could supply in abundance. Sensing additional economic opportunities, McAlester purchased the interests of one of the partners in the trading firm where he worked and renamed the company McAlester and Hannaford.[23]

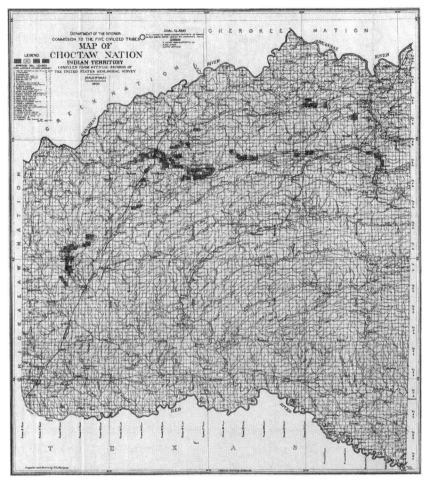

Figure 6.2. *Map of Choctaw Nation, Indian Territory: Compiled from Official Records of the United States Geological Survey.* R. L. Mcalpine and the United States Department of the Interior. Washington, DC: The Dept., 1900. Map. Retrieved from the Library of Congress, https://www.loc.gov/item/2007627519/ (accessed January 6, 2018).

The need for coal increased dramatically and a ready market presented itself when the Missouri, Kansas, and Texas Railroad reached the site of McAlester's store in 1872; the townsite was named after him.[24] Selling goods to passersby proved lucrative for McAlester, but the prize he sought most was Choctaw coal by which he might amass a fortune when the railroad was completed.

McAlester married Rebecca Burney, who was a Choctaw and sister to a politically powerful man who later became a Chickasaw chief. Marrying a Choctaw woman conferred Choctaw citizenship upon McAlester and others like him; such marriages presented important legal unions that enabled capitalist enterprises such as the coal and railroad industries to enter Indian Territory on an expanded scale.[25] Based upon an 1866 treaty, people who intermarried with Choctaws acquired the right to vote, hold office, sue and be sued, stand trial, and suffer punishment when found guilty.[26] The intermarriage of white, male entrepreneurs to women who had descended from politically powerful Choctaw families created new economic opportunities for some white and Indian people living in the Choctaw Nation. The Choctaw Constitution conferred to any citizen who located minerals ownership of that resource within a one-mile radius of the discovery. McAlester's marriage to Burney enabled him to transform his knowledge of coal outcrops into a large-scale enterprise called the Osage Coal and Mining Company that he parlayed into significant wealth and political power.[27] Non-Indians who controlled corporations used the law to conduct business and assert their rights in relation to Choctaws who controlled coal resources. The ability of white entrepreneurs to establish legal claims to coal through intermarriage represented the first step in a process that enabled the federal government to impose its jurisdiction in Indian Territory.[28]

McAlester represented one of thousands of non-Indians who poured into Indian Territory after the Civil War looking for land and economic opportunities. Although Indian Territory theoretically served as a perpetual home for Indigenous people removed from their traditional homelands, the redrawing and shrinking of its borders and the influx of Euro-Americans and African Americans rapidly changed the area's demographic makeup and economy. Commercial development grew rapidly as migrants sought land and resources that enabled them to develop profits from mining, railroads, cattle ranching, harvesting timber, and coal production. Although tribal governments required permits of noncitizens to enter the territory, the lure of profits prompted tens of thousands of migrants to ignore this provision along with other stipulations of tribal law.[29] By 1890, the federal census recorded 50,000 Native Americans, 19,000 African Americans, and 110,000 Euro-Americans living in Indian Territory. The percentage of Native Americans measured 28 percent but fell to 9 percent by statehood in 1907.[30] Not surprisingly, non-Indians favored efforts by the Dawes Commission to allot Indians' land because they believed allotment would present them with additional economic opportunities to buy land that remained once allotment had occurred.[31] For their part, federal officials and progressive reformers justified dissolving tribal government and imposing new laws and regulations as solutions to end the exploitation of Indians.[32] Angie Debo describes the Dawes Commission reports as "couched in a high moral tone rising to impassioned eloquence condemning the exploitation" and notes that they contained "glowing" language that explained the "deliverance" awaiting Native people from reforms federal planners hoped to implement. The reports emphasized "the great natural resources of the Indian Territory which were lying undeveloped."[33] Coal was just one of many resources non-Indians coveted, but it presented a particularly attractive allure because of its power to fuel other industries such as railroads that permitted economies of scale to grow.

The Civil War served as a catalyst to transform tribal economies and introduce capitalism into Indian Territory in the form of railroads. In retaliation against the Choctaws for allying with the Confederacy, the federal government voided antebellum treaties and crafted new ones that provided entrée to entrepreneurial endeavors. Soon, railroads bisected Indian Territory in perpendicular routes. By 1872, the Union Pacific, Southern Branch (later incorporated as the Missouri, Kansas, and Texas and known widely as the MK&T or "Katy") traversed Indian Territory in a north-south direction. By the 1890s, an east-west line ran from modern-day Tulsa to the western half of the state.[34] Railroads offended tribal governments from the moment they entered Indian Territory. They paid nothing for utilizing tribal lands, paid no taxes, and violated tribal laws by purchasing timber and stone from individuals rather than from tribal governments.[35] Congress had ordered that once allotment was complete, railroads would receive land grants to subsidize their construction costs. Thus, railroad interests became some of the most aggressive agitators calling for an end to tribal governments.[36] Railroads profited by building tracks and hauling commerce into and through Indian Territory, and they accelerated the growth of extractive industries such as coal, oil, and timber.[37] Even members of the Dawes Commission observed that "the railroad has been fatal to the old order of things" and that removing them would prove as difficult as "restoration of the tepee and the war dance."[38]

Despite their disregard for tribal autonomy and governance, railroad corporations presented opportunities for some enterprising Choctaws to engage in capitalism by signing contracts to supply building materials. The MK&T needed materials to construct bridges and tracks and some Choctaw citizens readily agreed to supply them, but in doing so they used communal resources for private gain. Capitalism instilled within some Choctaws an attitude of self-interestedness that the tribal council sought to regulate. The Choctaw council appointed a national agent to intervene in trade matters by negotiating contracts with Choctaw citizens to supply materials and making separate contracts with outside entities in need of timber and stone. With legal agreements in place, the Choctaw council could regulate trade and collect royalties on resources sold. To further protect its legal and financial interests, the council nullified contracts between Choctaw citizens and others, deemed anyone who traded outside its purview a "transgressor," and fined perpetrators $1,000 plus the cost of prosecution.[39] Ironically, railroad officials objected to Choctaw measures to regulate commerce; the general manager of the MK&T declared the prohibition of private contracts a violation of the "habits of civilization."[40]

In response to the development of a market economy based on railroads, coal, and an influx of white entrepreneurs, Choctaw leaders mobilized to control communal resources throughout the 1860s and 1870s.[41] The Choctaw National Council enacted a series of laws in 1873 to regulate coal production on its land. The laws addressed issues of royalty payments, duration of leases, the rights of noncitizens to lease, and penalties for those who failed to comply. They passed laws throughout the 1880s and 1890s to oversee and protect lands and resources, but the federal government and private citizens continued to gain control over their assets.[42] Factional infighting among Choctaws grew particularly intense during these decades and complicated their efforts to present a unified front or to formulate a clear legal strategy that prevented non-Choctaws from exploiting them.[43] Factionalism morphed into heated party rivalries, dramatically shaping Choctaw politics and often determining who was elected principal chief. Indeed, political strife grew so intense that sometimes Choctaws killed their political rivals.[44] Political divisiveness found its way into the courtroom and influenced the outcome of legal decisions. Economic status or political influence could determine how juries decided guilt or innocence even when adjudicating charges of murder and rape. Criminals often went free because of a close relationship with a tribal chief, council member, or intermarried affluent white man.[45] Thus, the law presented Choctaws with some recourse to control their lives individually and collectively but the confusion introduced by removal, territorial status, statehood, and questions of who qualified for US and tribal citizenship endlessly complicated the outcome of legal decisions.

During the time that the Dawes Commission attempted to impose allotment, lawyers and clients who enlisted their expertise could potentially amass great wealth in land and natural resources. Because several original members of the Dawes Commission had legal backgrounds, the process of allotment presented itself as ordered and governed by comprehensible rules. Even with capable lawyers involved, however, incalculable complications, conflicts, and disagreements arose and plagued the process of allotment.[46] The ensuing difficulties came to define allotment and underscored how fundamentally law mattered to accruing and maintaining economic power in this borderlands environment. Debo touches upon the vital role of the law when she states that the "battle for spoils" that occurred after 1920 was one of "contests between rival applicants and their attorneys for the opportunity of plundering the estates of wealthy Indians."[47] The numerous examples of exploitation Debo recounts in her narrative involve people who exploited the law for economic gain at the expense of Native Americans. Most notably, she recounts instances of white people who acquired legal guardianship over Native American minors in order to reap financial rewards by controlling the children's allotments. Debo's narrative falters, however, when she characterizes Indians as "helpless pawns in the game."[48] Certainly, many Native people may have felt helpless confronting an alien legal regime, but this interpretation alone fails to account for those who understood the law's power to transform their lives and protect their interests in courts and who hired lawyers to represent them.[49]

When Choctaws failed to enforce tribal laws amidst the onslaught of American settlement, they sought recourse by working with lawyers who knew how to operate more seamlessly within the US legal system. Choctaw tribal officials hired lawyers to protect their interests in local, state, and federal courts. Robert Owen played a particularly prominent role as a lawyer hired to protect Indian interests. He reported in 1886 how brazenly intruders stole from Indians and the inability of US laws to prevent this theft from occurring. Owen said that "the timber and coal thieves along the border say truly enough that there is no law to punish their trespass."[50] Borders demarcated Indian Territory but constrained Native Americans legally and liberated Euro-Americans to steal almost at will. Part Cherokee himself, Owen recognized how borders obscured legal jurisdictions and left Native American resources vulnerable. As subsequent passages will reveal, however, his Native American ancestry did not constrain his willingness to use knowledge of the law to profit mightily at the expense of Indian people. Unlike many of those who were exploited, Choctaws recognized the peculiar legal situation they confronted as a threat to their survival.

Oklahoma statehood did little to resolve the legal affairs of Choctaws. They still had unallotted assets in the form of timber, land, coal, and asphalt, but these resources remained under the control of the federal government and Choctaws could not access them in order to function as capitalists or as a sovereign nation.[51] Their economic situation, already strained prior to statehood, grew dire when the price of coal declined due to oil booms throughout Texas and Oklahoma that enabled petroleum to begin replacing coal as a fuel of choice. Still, the Choctaws needed profits from their coal deposits in order to survive, and they fashioned a legal strategy to advance their interests.

The legal status of Choctaw people and their lands transformed dramatically throughout the latter nineteenth and early twentieth centuries. Although firmly committed to allotting lands of the Choctaws and other tribes in Indian Territory, the federal government reserved approximately 445,000 acres of land containing coal and asphalt deposits for sale at a later date. Invoking language in their treaty contracts and relying upon their political skills, members of the Five Tribes astutely but only temporarily won exemption from the 1887 Dawes Act mandating allotment of their land.[52] The Dawes Commission applied relentless pressure, and in 1897 Choctaw and Chickasaw delegations conceded to the terms of the Atoka Agreement that allotted both tribes' land except that containing coal and asphalt deposits. The subsequent Curtis Act (1898) and its supplement (1902) exempted coal lands from allotment, or "segregated" them, and provided for their eventual sale. These so-called segregated coal lands soon became the object of great desire by Indians and non-Indians alike due to the mineral wealth they held, but their segregated condition meant that the federal government maintained ultimate control over their legal status. To generate royalties from their coal lands, the Choctaws needed the federal government to grant permission for their sale.

From the perspective of Principal Chief Victor Locke Jr., the federal government was moving too slowly in bringing about allotment, resulting in

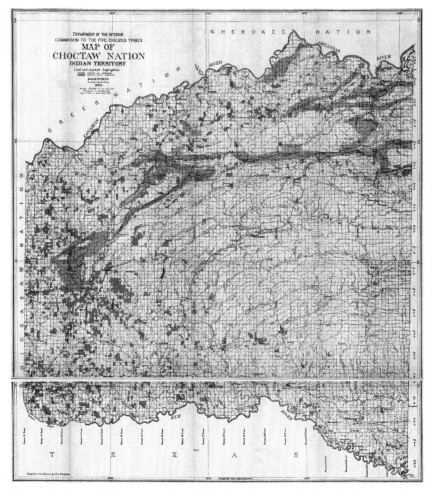

Figure 6.3. *Map of Choctaw Nation, Indian Territory, Coal and Asphalt Segregation.* R. L. Mcalpine and the United States Commission to the Five Civilized Tribes. Washington, DC: The Dept., 1903. Map. Retrieved from the Library of Congress, https://www.loc.gov/item/2007627494/ (accessed January 6, 2018).

lost revenue for deserving tribal members and precipitating political problems among different tribal factions. Locke advocated allotment and stated his position clearly: "I am in favor of the early allotment of the Indian's land. This should be done as soon as possible. Such delays as we are having now is hurtful to every interest."[53] He also advocated selling town lots because they "are valuable. The owners thereof made them so, and they should reap the benefits of their labor."[54] The failure of the government to act quickly led Locke to seek a lawyer who could protect tribal interests, and he found that man in his childhood friend.

Patrick J. Hurley was born in the Choctaw Nation, Indian Territory in 1883, worked in a coal mine throughout his childhood, and later served as legal counsel for the Choctaw Tribe before serving as an officer in the military and later as Secretary of War under President Herbert Hoover. Hurley's American mother met and wed his Irish immigrant father in San Antonio before the two joined the flood of non-Indians moving to Indian Territory in search of opportunities. Hurley's parents arrived in the Choctaw Nation and settled near McAlester where his father worked in the coal mines. At the age of eleven, Patrick joined his father as a laborer in the coal mines. With no formal education, Hurley continued working in the mines until the age of seventeen but saw an opportunity to escape the toil and traveled to the Creek Nation in northeastern Indian Territory. In Muskogee, he attended Indian University (currently Bacone College) and graduated with a degree in 1905. Hurley then went to Washington, DC, where he entered National University and received a law degree in 1905 at the age of twenty-five.[55] Hurley returned to Tulsa, Oklahoma, where he established a successful law practice that catered to the burgeoning oil industry, and in 1911 William Howard Taft appointed him national attorney for the Choctaw Nation.[56] US presidents appointed tribal attorneys at this time; Hurley's appointment resulted from his close contacts with the Choctaw people.

As a child Hurley befriended Locke and forged a lifelong friendship that would shape political and economic power within Indian Territory and particularly for the Choctaw people. Locke was born in Doaksville, Indian Territory, in 1876 to a white father, Victor M. Locke Sr., and a three-quarter Choctaw woman, Susan McKinney. Locke spoke English and Choctaw fluently, skills that enabled him to communicate across cultural divides and broker power among different factions of his tribe. At the age of thirty-four he became the youngest Choctaw principal chief, a position he held from 1910 to 1918.[57] Shortly after his appointment, Locke solicited his boyhood friend, Hurley, who was only twenty-eight years old at the time, to serve as the tribe's national attorney, a post he held from 1912 to 1917. Together, the two men sought to protect Choctaw economic interests and prevent the tribe's exploitation by non-Indians who had been settling in Indian Territory and Oklahoma and preying upon the assets of Native people. The influx of white settlers, land grafters, and lawyers who had successfully exploited Choctaws also disrupted tribal relations, pitting many tribal members against one another as they argued over how to prevent future losses of their land and power.

The experience of growing up in Indian Territory, knowing Indian people, and developing intimate friendships with Choctaws uniquely qualified Hurley later in life to represent their legal interests. Unlike his parents and many of the white people who moved to Indian Territory, Hurley was born and reared among Choctaw people, which presented opportunities to socialize, build relationships, and gain a sense of their culture many other whites did not possess. Hurley's parents rented their family home and land from a wealthy Choctaw leader, Benjamin Franklin Smallwood, who served as principal chief from 1888 to 1890. Smallwood arrived in Indian Territory as part of the Choctaw Trail of Tears, amassed a fortune, and built a plantation-style mansion complete with columns and veranda where well-dressed and distinguished people gathered to discuss pressing issues of the day. While Choctaws generally remained circumspect in social and intellectual exchanges with whites, Smallwood developed an affection for young Hurley and welcomed him into the mansion. The time that the boy spent in the Smallwood home provided a unique window into the Choctaws' culture and educated him about issues that concerned them. Hurley sat quietly and listened to adults recount stories of their ancestors' lives in Mississippi prior to removal, economic problems the tribe faced in Indian Territory, and political maneuvering at the tribal council.[58] These stories illustrated to Hurley the legacy of broken treaties and federal mismanagement that shaped Choctaws' relationships with each other and how they viewed encroachments by "land grabbing" whites.[59]

The issue of Mississippi Choctaws seeking enrollment and allotments in Indian Territory would not go away. The lure of profit emboldened lawyers in Mississippi to lobby their congressmen for legislation to reopen Choctaw rolls. A politician determined to make a name for himself, Pat Harrison, answered the call. In 1912, Harrison introduced a bill that argued Choctaws who elected to stay in Mississippi retained their rights as tribal citizens, did not have to relocate to Oklahoma, and were entitled to receive Choctaw lands. The bill further stipulated that lawyers representing claimants could enter into contract with the secretary of the interior to ensure payment of $2,080 for each successfully litigated case. Harrison argued his case before Congress by suggesting that Choctaw chieftain Pushmataha would have welcomed more legally enrolled tribal members were he alive: "He would

Figure 6.4. Patrick J. Hurley, 1929. Photograph. Retrieved from the Library of Congress, https://www.loc.gov/item/npc2007017171/ (accessed January 6, 2018).

appeal to his white father in yonder White House, to his brethren in Oklahoma, to his white friends in this Chamber, and say 'Give to the Mississippi Choctaws the rights guaranteed to them under the fourteenth article of the treaty of 1830.'"[60] Ironically, Harrison's imagining of Choctaw words constituted what one scholar has characterized as "the essence of Choctaw political identity" in the post-statehood era, that is, the continued appeal for treaty rights to the legislative, executive, and judicial branches of US government.[61] Choctaw sovereignty hinged on the tribe's ability to mobilize attorneys to advocate in their interests at each branch of government.

Hurley argued persuasively and successfully that Congress should not reopen tribal rolls and that the failure of the federal government to liquidate the Choctaws' coal, asphalt, and timber resources and to sell unallotted land incentivized attorneys and their clients who sought enrollment. Given the increasing frequency of fraudulent Choctaw citizenship claims, well-meaning congressman like Robert LaFollette repeatedly blocked attempts to sell the segregated coal lands in order to protect Choctaws and their property from further exploitation.[62] Attempts by progressive politicians to prevent the sale disregarded the 1902 agreement in which Choctaws expressed their desire to sell segregated coal lands and the government's promise to comply. Writing to Chief Locke, with a problem undoubtedly familiar to twenty-first-century tribal attorneys, Hurley complained that he frequently had to reeducate new politicians about the Choctaws' wishes to sell segregated coal lands after each election cycle when new members of Congress convened.[63] Various constituencies who favored or opposed sale of the segregated coal lands disputed its actual value. LaFollette estimated the value of segregated coal lands as high as $4.3 billion, but geologists working for the US and Oklahoma geological surveys estimated the value at somewhere between one to two million dollars.[64] According to Hurley, the segregated coal lands were worth a minimum of $35 million. Whatever their value, many Choctaws lived in severe poverty and their inability to profit from these lands denied them desperately needed income.

Complicating the effort by Chief Locke to allot these lands were factional divides among Choctaws that had befallen the tribe toward the end of the nineteenth century. Throughout the 1890s, factional divisions emerged within Choctaw politics between Progressives, who were mostly mixed-bloods favoring allotment, and Nationalists, who were Choctaw-speaking full-bloods opposing allotment.[65] Tensions flared between the two groups during a hotly contested election for principal chief in 1892, when Progressive candidate Wilson N. Jones captured a very slim margin of victory over Nationalist candidate Jacob Jackson. Upon taking office, Chief Jones moved quickly to fund and reconstitute a militia to oppose Nationalists who he described as "an armed mob unduly excited over supposed wrongs" (wrongs that led them to assassinate four Choctaw citizens; Jones said they had proclaimed "if necessary to carry out their nefarious designs, to murder all from the chief down").[66] Each faction charged the other with plots to murder political opponents.[67] When a circuit judge from a neighboring district requested that the chief apprehend a Nationalist-allied suspect, Chief Jones called upon the militia to seize and arrest the man, who sought protection at the home of Victor Locke Sr. Choctaw Nationalists unwaveringly trusted the elder Locke even though he was a white man whose citizenship stemmed from intermarriage, and he opened the doors of his home to approximately one hundred Nationalists who arrived to defend the suspect. During the armed conflict, known as the Locke-Jones War, one militia

Figure 6.5. INDIANS, AMERICAN. MAJ. VICTOR M. LOCKE, CHIEF OF THE CHOCTAW, 1916. Harris & Ewing, photographer. Photograph. Retrieved from the Library of Congress, https://www.loc.gov/item/hec2008005331/ (accessed January 6, 2018).

member was killed, several others wounded, and one of Locke's daughters was nearly killed. Although technically a legal action to apprehend a fugitive, the confrontation reflected the political differences that rippled throughout the Choctaw Nation over issues of allotment and allocations of economic and political power. The younger Locke was not present at the time of the violence, but his mother was prompted to call him home from school and the confrontation marked a turning point in his life. Both sides eventually surrendered, but negative sentiments remained and the threat of violence hovered over this uneasy peace. So pivotal was the violent episode in Locke's life that he cited the feud as the reason he entered into tribal politics.

By the time Locke became principal chief in 1910, the impending reality of Oklahoma's 1907 statehood had exacerbated disagreements among Choctaws and precipitated deeper divisions between Progressives and Nationalists as well as within each faction. As a youth, Locke absorbed much of his father's pro-Nationalist sentiment. He spent several months campaigning with his father's clan for Nationalist nominee Jacob Jackson for principal chief in 1892, who opposed allotment.[68] The approach of statehood, however, forced a schism between Locke Sr. and Locke Jr. over their political views and particularly over the issue of allotment.[69] Locke Jr. began to believe that allotment was inevitable, and he demonstrated a willingness to work with the federal government to ensure an effective transition of tribal lands from communal to private ownership. The views of Locke likely began to change while he served as private secretary to Green McCurtain, an avowed Progressive who was principal chief for three terms from 1896 to 1910 and participated in the Locke-Jones War, opposing Locke's father's faction. McCurtain commanded a group of armed men who demanded custody of the Nationalists implicated in murdering the four Progressives.[70] McCurtain's election to principal chief in 1896 occurred only because of the splintering of factions and increasing disarray of Choctaw tribal politics. He represented a wing of the Progressives, the Tuskahoma party, that favored negotiating with the Dawes Commission to ensure that allotment progressed as equitably and rapidly as possible, that land be equally divided among white and Indian citizens, and that freedmen receive allotments of forty acres. This was a highly unpopular political platform at the time, but he won the election because opponents of allotment divided their votes among three other candidates.[71] Locke may have begun to consider allotment as a viable alternative to the Choctaws' woes due to his service under McCurtain, but he remained strongly allied with the full-bloods who filled the ranks of the Nationalist faction.

Factionalism complicated Locke's tenure as principal chief, particularly when he allied with Hurley to use the courts as a vehicle to seek compensation for land the Choctaws and Chickasaws ceded. The so-called Leased

District encompassed a large tract of land in southwestern Indian Territory ceded to the federal government in an 1866 treaty.[72] The United States initially paid $300,000 for the land to establish reservations for other Native American tribes. The Choctaws and Chickasaws received nearly three million dollars in 1893 for the unallotted portion of the land, but Locke and Hurley saw the promise of additional financial gain through the courts.[73] As Hurley pursued the claim in 1911, so too did another group calling itself the Choctaw-Chickasaw Treaty Rights Association, which was created and guided by J. F. McMurray, a white man and lawyer who had been hired previously by the Choctaws to exclude petitioners from tribal rolls. McMurray had gained an infamous reputation as an Indian lawyer and in 1910 was the subject of a congressional investigation to determine whether he exploited his Native American clients with unjustifiably high contingency fees. A contest soon emerged between McMurray and Hurley and their respective Choctaw and Chickasaw clients when each lawyer submitted a memorial to Congress requesting additional payment for the Leased District.[74] The two memorials demonstrated the increasing willingness of Choctaws and Chickasaws to use litigation as a tool for seeking financial gain and showed how political conflicts divided the nations internally and against each other.[75] The law provided Native Americans with a tool to protect their interests but could just as easily become a wedge that kept tribes and factions from forging a consensus, leaving them vulnerable to exploitation.

Blood quantum had always influenced the degree of economic and political power people lost or accrued in Indian Territory, a point reinforced to Hurley while attending a meeting of the Choctaw-Chickasaw Treaty Rights Association in 1913. In his account of the experience, he reported to Locke that of the seventeen men present only two "had the appearance of being Indian." Hurley scrutinized each man's phenotype, including the Johnston brothers, who "of course are men of Indian blood but to all intents and purposes [are] white men." In a borderlands region where opportunities ebbed and flowed, blood quantum alone proved insufficient to determine "Indianness." Hurley's perusal of the remaining men left him uncertain about the "degree of blood" possessed by others, but he concluded that most were like attendee Dr. Miller, who was "an intermarried white citizen." Hurley's account of the proceedings to Locke were candid but fair: "I have no tangible facts to support my opinion, but from the attitude of these men I am convinced that they are more interested in the fee which Mr. McMurray thinks he will receive than they are in securing for the Choctaws and Chickasaw Indians payment for the leased district." Hurley conceded that he was "sure that there are many good men" who participated in the association but believed they are "unconsciously being used" and that they "are allowing themselves to be the means of putting McMurray in position to collect another enormous fee from the Choctaw and Chickasaw Nations for services that he has never and will never render for the Nation."[76] Blood quantum mattered for those living in Indian Territory, but its meaning could become obscured when the stakes rose to claim, in this case, economic and legal power.

Meanings and perceptions shifted in a borderlands region, and the people who exploited jurisdictional confusion stood to make great economic and political gains. Enterprising opportunists, like Owen and McMurray, made large sums of money charging exorbitant legal fees that came at the expense of Indian people's wealth. The issue of preserving Native Americans' potential for prosperity became ever more pressing as the federal government imposed allotment on Indian Territory. Enterprising people who could find their way onto tribal rolls often stood to receive an economic windfall, and enterprising lawyers who could facilitate tribal enrollment potentially gained even more. Determining who was an Indian became a lucrative enterprise for many lawyers.

Meanwhile, Choctaws' efforts to profit by selling the segregated coal lands remained mired in litigation and jurisdictional disputes throughout the first half of the twentieth century. In 1904, Choctaw leaders convinced the US government to sell unleased coal lands in 960-acre tracts, but the Department of the Interior deemed the sealed bids that were submitted too low and rejected them all. Two years later, the federal government withdrew all of the segregated lands from sale until their leases expired. The state of Oklahoma attempted to purchase the lands in 1907, but the deal never transpired. Surface rights to the land began being sold in 1912, but Choctaws retained subsurface rights to coal and asphalt deposits. The US Congress approved an act to begin selling coal deposits at public auctions in 1918, but leased tracts sold at a higher rate than unleased tracts. By 1930, Choctaws and Chickasaws retained approximately 375,000 acres of the segregated coal lands. Not until 1947 did the federal government offer $8.5 million for the segregated coal lands, which the Choctaws and Chickasaws accepted and distributed to tribal members and to heirs of deceased enrollees. By this time, however, the economic value of coal had dropped precipitously as oil had become the preferred fuel for many sectors of the economy.

Notes

1. Locke recounted these details to O. L. Blanche, who was a mixed-race Choctaw. Blanche related these and other details of Locke's life in an oral history: Blanche, O. L. "Interview with O. L. Blanche regarding Victor Locke." Indian-Pioneer Papers, Western History Collection, University of Oklahoma, Norman, Oklahoma. May 21, 1937, https://digital.libraries.ou.edu/cdm/ref/collection/indian pp/id/62 (accessed June 16, 2017).

2. Mary L. Dudziak and Leti Volpp, introduction, "Legal Borderlands: Law and the Construction of American Borders," *American Quarterly* 57, no. 3 (September 2005): 596.

3. Discussed below, the history of intermarriage as a means of dispossession is featured in Lauren L. Basson, *White Enough To Be American? Race Mixing, Indigenous People, and the Boundaries of State and Nation* (Chapel Hill: University of North Carolina Press, 2008); Bethany Ruth Berger, "After Pocahontas: Indian Women and the Law, 1830 to 1934," *American Indian Law Review* 21, no. 1 (1997), 1–62; Katrina Jagodinsky, *Legal Codes and Talking Trees: Indigenous Women's Sovereignty in the Sonoran and Puget Sound Borderlands, 1854–1946* (New Haven: Yale University Press, 2016); Peggy Pascoe, *What Comes Naturally: Miscegenation Law and the Making of Race in America* (New York: Oxford University Press, 2009).

4. Angie Debo, *And Still the Waters Run: The Betrayal of the Five Civilized Tribes* (Princeton: Princeton University Press, 1973). See Donald Lee Fixico, *The Invasion of Indian Country in the Twentieth Century: American Capitalism and Tribal Natural Resources* (Niwot: University Press of Colorado, 1998); H. Craig Miner, *The Corporation and the Indian: Tribal Sovereignty and Industrial Civilization in Indian Territory, 1865–1907*, new ed. (Norman: University of Oklahoma Press, 1989).

5. David A. Chang, *The Color of the Land: Race, Nation, and the Politics of Landownership in Oklahoma, 1832–1929* (Chapel Hill: University of North Carolina Press, 2010), 144–148.

6. Clara Sue Kidwell, *The Choctaws in Oklahoma: From Tribe to Nation, 1855–1970*, American Indian Law and Policy Series (Norman: University of Oklahoma Press, 2007), xvii.

7. Benjamin A. Kahn, "Sword or Submission?: American Indian Natural Resource Claims Settlement Legislation," *American Indian Law Review* 37, no. 1 (2012–2013).

8. Alexandra Harmon, Colleen M. O'Neill, and Paul C. Rosier, "Interwoven Economic Histories: American Indians in a Capitalist America," *Journal of American History* (2011): 699. For a penetrating account of the diverse choices Choctaws made prior to Oklahoma statehood, see Devon Abbott Mihesuah, *Choctaw Crime and Punishment, 1884–1907* (Norman: University of Oklahoma Press, 2009); Alexandra Harmon, *Rich Indians: Native People and the*

Problem of Wealth in American History (Chapel Hill: University of North Carolina Press, 2013).

9. Kevin Bruyneel, *The Third Space of Sovereignty: The Postcolonial Politics of U.S.-Indigenous Relations* (Minneapolis and London: University of Minnesota Press, 2007), xii.

10. Bruyneel, *Third Space of Sovereignty*, xix.

11. Bruyneel, *Third Space of Sovereignty*, xvii.

12. This is the central idea articulated in an insightful new study of the Meskwaki Nation. Eric Steven Zimmer, "Red Earth Nation: Environment and Sovereignty in Modern Meskwaki History" (PhD diss., University of Iowa, 2016), 13.

13. Robert A. Williams, *The American Indian in Western Legal Thought: The Discourses of Conquest* (New York: Oxford University Press, 1990).

14. Cited in Don Lohbeck, *Patrick J. Hurley* (Chicago: Henry Regnery, 1956), 60.

15. Lohbeck, *Patrick J. Hurley*.

16. Jeffrey Burton, *Indian Territory and the United States, 1866–1906: Courts, Government, and the Movement for Oklahoma Statehood* (Norman: University of Oklahoma Press, 1995), xiii.

17. Kidwell, *Choctaws in Oklahoma*, 193.

18. Noah Fields Drake, "A Geological Reconnaissance of the Coal Fields of Indian Territory," *Proceedings of the American Philosophical Society* 36, no. 156 (1897): 329.

19. I. C. Gunning, *When Coal Was King: Coal Mining in the Choctaw Nation* (Eastern Oklahoma Historical Society, 1975), 16–17.

20. Oliver Knight, "An Oklahoma Indian Trader as a Frontiersman of Commerce," *Journal of Southern History* 23, no. 2 (1957): 215.

21. Knight, "Oklahoma Indian Trader," 203.

22. Knight, "Oklahoma Indian Trader," 205.

23. Kidwell, *Choctaws in Oklahoma*, 103.

24. Muriel H. Wright, *Our Oklahoma* (Guthrie, OK: Co-Operative Publishing Company, 1939), 224.

25. Conferring tribal citizenship onto non-Indian men who married Choctaw women signified a remarkable departure from American marriage and citizenship practices, which in this period bestowed American citizenship on the noncitizen wives of American men and divested American citizenship of women who married noncitizen men. See Nancy F. Cott, "Marriage and Women's Citizenship in the United States, 1830–1934," *American Historical Review* 103, no. 5 (December 1998), 1440–1474. Gender historians might consider whether these intermarriages bore similarities to earlier fur trade unions chronicled in the works of Jennifer S. H. Brown, *Strangers in Blood: Fur Trade Company Families in Indian Country* (Vancouver: University of British Columbia Press, 1980); Andrew Graybill, *The Red and the White: An American Family Saga* (New York: W. W. Norton, 2013); Anne F. Hyde, *Empires, Nations and Families: A History of the North American West, 1800–1860* (Lincoln: University of

Nebraska Press, 2011); Sylvia Van Kirk, *Many Tender Ties: Women in Fur-trade Society, 1670–1870* (Norman: University of Oklahoma Press, 1983).

26. Mihesuah, *Choctaw Crime and Punishment*, 66.

27. Kidwell, *Choctaws in Oklahoma*, 103. See Kidwell, 103–105, for other examples of white men whose marriages to Choctaw women consolidated their interests in the coal industry. See also Danney Goble, *Progressive Oklahoma: The Making of a New Kind of State*, 1st ed. (Norman: University of Oklahoma Press, 1980), 62–63.

28. Kidwell, *Choctaws in Oklahoma*. Kidwell makes this same point but does not emphasize the legal nature of this power dynamic.

29. For a discussion of the many ways in which non-Indians discounted tribal jurisdiction in Indian Territory and other parts of Indian Country in this same time period, see Sydney L. Harring, *White Man's Law: Native People in Nineteenth-Century Canadian Jurisprudence* (Toronto: University of Toronto Press, 1998).

30. Goble, *Progressive Oklahoma*, 66.

31. Kent Carter, *The Dawes Commission and the Allotment of the Five Civilized Tribes, 1893–1914* (Orem, Utah: Ancestry.com, 1999), 181.

32. C. Joseph Genetin-Pilawa, *Crooked Paths to Allotment: The Fight Over Federal Indian Policy after the Civil War* (Chapel Hill: University of North Carolina Press, 2012); Rose Stremlau, *Sustaining the Cherokee Family: Kinship and the Allotment of an Indigenous Nation* (Chapel Hill: University of North Carolina Press, 2011).

33. Debo, *And Still the Waters Run*, 24.

34. Goble, *Progressive Oklahoma*, 58. For further discussion of the exploitation of Native Americans by railroads, see Richard White, *Railroaded: The Transcontinentals and the Making of Modern America* (New York: W. W. Norton, 2011).

35. Angie Debo, *The Rise and Fall of the Choctaw Republic*, 2d ed. (Norman: University of Oklahoma Press, 1961), 118.

36. Goble, *Progressive Oklahoma*, 58.

37. Sandra L. Failman-Silva, "Tribal Land to Private Land: A Century of Oklahoma Choctaw Timberland Alienation from the 1880s to the 1980s," *Journal of Forest History* 32, no. 4 (1988): 193.

38. Records of the Bureau of Indian Affairs, Record Group 75, Records of the Five Civilized Tribes Agency, National Archives, Southwest Region, entry 37, annual report, 1895, 69; Cited in Carter, *The Dawes Commission and the Allotment of the Five Civilized Tribes, 1893–1914*, 181.

39. Kidwell, *Choctaws in Oklahoma*, 107.

40. Robert S. Stevens to F. A. Walker, MK&T, Sedalia, Missouri, February 12, 1873, reel 180, frame 831, Office of Indian Affairs, Letters Received; as cited in Kidwell, *Choctaws in Oklahoma*, 107–108.

41. Kidwell, *Choctaws in Oklahoma*, xvii.

42. Failman-Silva, "Tribal Land to Private Land," 195.

43. Mihesuah, *Choctaw Crime and Punishment*, 5.

44. Mihesuah, *Choctaw Crime and Punishment*, 10.

45. Mihesuah, *Choctaw Crime and Punishment*, 11.

46. Robert L. Williams, "Tams Bixby, 1855–1922," *Chronicles of Oklahoma* 19, no. 3 (1941): 207.

47. Debo, *And Still the Waters Run*, 318.

48. Debo, *And Still the Waters Run*, 318.

49. Katrina Jagodinsky, "'In Family Way': Guarding Indigenous Women's Children in Washington Territory," *American Indian Quarterly* 37, no. 2 (Spring 2013): 160–177.

50. Commissioner of Indian Affairs, annual report, 1886, 158.

51. Kidwell, *Choctaws in Oklahoma.*

52. Tanis C. Thorne, *The World's Richest Indian: The Scandal over Jackson Barnett's Oil Fortune* (New York: Oxford University Press, 2003).

53. Victor M. Locke, "An Interview with V. M. Locke," *The South McAlester Capital*, February 1, 1900, Victor M. Locke Collection, Western History Collection, University of Oklahoma, Norman, Oklahoma.

54. Locke, "Interview with V. M. Locke."

55. Parker La Moore, *"Pat" Hurley: The Story of an American* (New York: Brewer, Warren, and Putnam, 1932), 24–29.

56. Fred L. Borch, "From Cowboy and Tribal Lawyer to Judge Advocate and Secretary of War: The Remarkable Career of Patrick J. Hurley," *The Army Lawyer*, March (2014).

57. "Doaksville," Oklahoma Historical Society, http://www.okhistory.org/sites/ftdoaksville?full (accessed January 22, 2017).

58. Lohbeck, *Patrick J. Hurley*, 24.

59. Lohbeck, *Patrick J. Hurley*, 24.

60. "The Mississippi Choctaw," speech of Hon. Pat Harrison of Mississippi in the House of Representatives, December 12, 1912 (Washington, DC, 1912), Choctaw Nation Collection, Western History Collection, University of Oklahoma, Norman, Oklahoma; cited in Kidwell, *Choctaws in Oklahoma*, 198. See also William Sidney Coker, "Pat Harrison's Efforts to Reopen the Choctaw Citizenship Rolls," *Southern Quarterly* 3 (October 1964), 36–61.

61. Kidwell, *Choctaws in Oklahoma*, 198.

62. Kidwell, *Choctaws in Oklahoma*, 202.

63. Patrick Hurley to Victor Locke, May 28, 1912, folder 1, box 12, Patrick Hurley Collection, Western History Collection, University of Oklahoma, Norman, Oklahoma.

64. Charles N. Gould, "Coal," *Oklahoma Geological Survey Bulletin No. 1*, Preliminary Report on the Mineral Resources of Oklahoma (Norman: Oklahoma Geological Survey, 1908), 11.

65. Debo, *Rise and Fall of the Choctaw Republic*, 255–268.

66. October 13, 1892, *Indian Citizen*; as cited in Mihesuah, *Choctaw Crime and Punishment*, 129.

67. Debo, *Rise and Fall of the Choctaw Republic*, 168.
68. Interview with Colonel Victor M. Locke, October 25, 1937, by Amelia F. Harris, 5. Indian-Pioneer Papers, Western History Collection, University of Oklahoma, Norman, Oklahoma. https://digital.libraries.ou.edu/cdm/ref/collection/indianpp/id/37 (accessed June 1, 2017).
69. Vance H. Trimble, *Choctaw Kisses, Bullets and Blood* (Wilmington, Delaware: Market Tech, 2007), 151.
70. Debo, *Rise and Fall of the Choctaw Republic*, 171.
71. Historical assessments of McCurtain's political career are mixed, but as one historian said, McCurtain held a "statesmanlike grasp of the problems confronting his people," and "[it is] doubtful whether any other citizen of the Choctaw Nation could have carried through the unpopular policy of relinquishing the tribal institutions." Debo, *Rise and Fall of the Choctaw Republic*, 255–256.
72. John D. May, "Leased District," Oklahoma Historical Society. Encyclopedia of Oklahoma History and Culture, http://www.okhistory.org/publications/enc/entry.php?entry=LE002 (accessed June 15, 2017).
73. Choctaws submitted a claim on this matter as early as 1910 but received no response. Hurley adroitly employed the legal tactic of getting the request referred to the US Court of Claims for adjudication. By the early twentieth century, federal courts had begun a trend of considering Indian claims as issues of federal policy rather than legal rights and referred them to Congress. Kidwell, *Choctaws in Oklahoma*, 204.
74. Kidwell, *Choctaws in Oklahoma*, 202–204.
75. Kidwell, *Choctaws in Oklahoma*, 203.
76. Patrick J. Hurley to Victor M. Locke Jr., January 1, 1913, folder 2, box 18, Patrick J. Hurley Collection, Western History Collection, University of Oklahoma, Norman, Oklahoma.

Part III
Legal Borderlands of Justice and Reform

7

The Courtroom as Legal Borderland

Colonial Encounters between Western and
Indigenous Legal Tradition in the Courts of the
Alaska District, 1902–1903

Andrea Geiger

On November 3, 1902, the United States Commissioners' Court in Juneau,
Alaska, issued a criminal complaint charging five Indigenous men with murder. According to the complaint, Kee-tee-ish, Koh-suk-dake, and Kluni-ish,
also known as Moses, Benjamin, and John Smith, had "willfully, feloniously
and unlawfully" caused the death of George Smalley, whose Tlingit name
was Kol-ketch-ish, by "purposely and of deliberate and premeditated malice" taking him by canoe to a remote location in late October, tying his
hands, and holding him without food or water for eight days, causing him
to die as they were returning to the village of Hoonah.[1] One month later,
on December 3, a grand jury indicted the three young men who had taken
Kol-ketch-ish to Sea Point and had denied him food and water. Also indicted were two elders, Kui-da-qua (Jeremiah King) and Che-ha-te (Aaron
Sharp), who allegedly directed the three younger men to impose this sanction on Kol-ketch-ish in order to force him to release another member of
their community, known as Archie, from an illness they believed Kol-ketch-
ish had caused.[2] The trials that followed provide a glimpse of the encounter
between Western and Indigenous legal culture and tradition in the colonial
courtroom.

My examination of the courtroom as a legal and cultural borderland and
site of colonial contact draws on understandings of Indigenous law articulated by Canadian legal historians John Borrows and Val Napoleon, who

have examined encounters between Western and Indigenous legal tradition in the Canadian courts. Borrows reminds us that, like the oral traditions that are a key constituent of Indigenous bodies of law, the common law tradition at the heart of both British and American legal practice is also rooted in storytelling. This parallel, in turn, creates spaces that allow for the incorporation of Indigenous legal tradition into bodies of law that have historically been regarded purely as artifacts of Western tradition, such as the body of federal law that delineates Indigenous rights in both Canada and the United States, as demonstrated by recent rulings of the Supreme Court of Canada directing its lower courts to take Indigenous oral traditions into account in determining the existence of Aboriginal title in Canada.[3]

Exported to and imposed upon Alaska's Indigenous peoples in the wake of the purchase of Russian interests in Alaska by the United States in 1867, the criminal law framework applied in these cases would not appear to create parallel openings for the integration of Indigenous law.[4] There is no question, as Sidney Harring and others have observed, that US criminal law was proactively used as an instrument of colonialism and as a means to suppress Indigenous rights and cultural practices in Alaska. Harring, however, sees Tlingit and US law as operating in entirely separate spheres and always in opposition, resulting, finally, in the "imposition of U.S. law over the Tlingit and the corresponding destruction of Tlingit law."[5] In contrast, Napoleon reminds us not only that Western and Indigenous law are concerned with addressing similar types of harms but that the displacement of Indigenous law does not mean that it disappeared.[6] Nor did a "legal vacuum" exist in Alaska prior to the introduction of colonial law, as some scholars have assumed.[7] Indeed, the very fact that Indigenous law was effectively displaced in many areas arguably makes it all the more important to notice instances where it factored into decision-making processes.

As in Canada, a parallel common law tradition that contemplated the jury's weighing of oral evidence created a space in US courtrooms—here, in Alaska—where, I argue, encounters between these two separate legal cultures could take place. At such moments, courtrooms could become— however briefly—spaces not just of colonial oppression but also of cultural encounter that allowed for the meeting and integration of elements of both Western and Indigenous legal tradition, even if only at a local level or in the context of a given case. If only at particular times and in particular places, such as the preterritorial phase in Alaska that provides the context here, the courtroom itself could function as a borderland where separate and distinct worldviews and legal traditions converged, forcing participants in the process being acted out on that stage, Indigenous and non-Indigenous alike, to negotiate the interface between two separate ways of understanding law and justice. These negotiations created the courtroom as a legal borderland. As Mary Dudziak and Leti Volpp explain, although legal borderlands also constitute "physical zones where . . . the 'territorial and legal limits of [nation states] are . . . negotiated,'" legal borderlands such as those I explore here "function not as literal physical spaces but as contact zones between ideas, as spaces of ideological ambiguity that can open up new possibilities of both repression and liberation"—like geographical borderland regions, legal borderlands also constitute "interstitial zones of hybridization" that are often transient and unstable.[8]

Despite their marked differences, Western and Indigenous legal traditions, Borrows and Napoleon point out, are more compatible than is often recognized. Most legal orders, Indigenous and non-Indigenous alike, Napoleon argues, seek to address problems that are universal in nature in order to ensure, to the best of their ability, "community safety, fairness, and accountability."[9] To focus only on the coercive use of law, even in criminal cases such as those considered here, is to miss both points of convergence and moments of negotiation. Refusing to see Western law as anything but a tool of colonial oppression also causes us to miss more subtle encounters and intersections between these separate legal traditions, as well as moments when Indigenous people—far too often victimized though they were in and by the courts—spoke their truth so clearly that, in so doing, even in an alien and coercive environment, they were able to influence and help shape judicial decisions that might otherwise have produced a different result.

This case study examines the five linked cases that stemmed from the indictment of Kee-tee-ish, Koh-suk-dake, Kluni-ish, Kui-da-qua, and Che-ha-te for murder in the death of Kol-ketch-ish.[10] Although the records are not complete, the documents that have been preserved, including the jury instructions proposed by defense counsel and refused or accepted by the judge, give us access both to the arguments made by counsel and the reasoning of the judge.[11] Statements made by four of the defendants to the grand jury in response to the charges against them also provide access to their thinking and concerns at the time of the underlying events, as well as the cultural and political pressures brought to bear on Indigenous communities in the context of the times.[12] Far from complete though these glimpses are, they nevertheless tell a far more complicated story about ways in which members of both Indigenous and settler societies negotiated the divide between two separate legal and cultural traditions than we might expect, and they are deserving of further study.

All of the Indigenous defendants spoke through interpreters whose names, for the most part, do not appear in the record—their very ability to serve as translators itself a product of the encounter between settler-colonial and Indigenous society.[13] These interpreters played a key role in facilitating the exchanges that made it possible for the courtroom to function as a legal borderland. Those who served in this capacity, Richard and Nora Marks Dauenhauer observe, "existed on the margins of Native and colonial society."[14] Interpreters, in short, were quintessential borderlands people who occupied, both literally and figuratively, the transient and interstitial spaces between settler and Indigenous societies. The written record here, like most others of the period, was produced by non-Indigenous administrators or court clerks based on translations of the Indigenous witnesses' statements provided by interpreters. Although we do not have direct access to the witnesses' voices, this does not mean that their voices are not indirectly reflected in records that we do have. As Richard White reminds us, in at least some cases, Indigenous voices can be discerned through the careful application of "traditional historical practice: close reading, evaluation, and contextualization of the records," that takes into account how, where, when, for what purpose, and by whom each source was produced.[15]

The United States did not establish a system of territorial courts in Alaska until 1884. During the decades that followed the acquisition of Russian interests in Alaska by the United States in 1867, the administration of US law in Alaska was left first to the US military and, after 1877, primarily to customs officials in the area, until Congress passed the Organic Act of 1884, which established a formal district court system in Alaska. By December 1902, when the cases here were heard, Congress had established three separate judicial districts in Alaska, presided over by just four federal judges, including the First District centered in Juneau where these cases were brought.[16] Combining the functions that both federal and state courts served elsewhere, Alaska's district court system was still developing at the time the cases under discussion here were heard, raising questions regarding the scope of the courts' jurisdiction and whether constitutional guarantees applied in the Alaska district the same way as they did elsewhere in the United States.[17]

Figure 7.1. Courthouse, Juneau, Alaska. Alaska State Library, Louise Carey McConnel Collection, ca. 1908–1912, ASL-P104–004.

Located on Alaska's southeastern panhandle, Juneau was incorporated in 1900 with a population of just 1,864 and named the capital of Alaska that year.[18] Built on the shore of the Gastineau channel across from Douglas Island, the rocky slopes of the mountains that soar almost four thousand feet above Juneau drop precipitously down into the sea and, then as now, cut off road access to other parts of Alaska. After Juneau's original courthouse was destroyed in a fire in 1898, a new courthouse that towered over the surrounding buildings was later built by the shore. Clearly intended to exemplify the power and majesty of the court, it was not yet in operation when the cases discussed here were heard in late 1902 but is nevertheless indicative of how colonial-settler society imagined the role of the federal courts at the time.[19]

The village of Hoonah (*Xunaa*), in turn, where all but one of the Indigenous participants in these cases were born and lived their entire lives, is an ancient Tlingit village. Situated at the northern end of Chichagof Island on the shore of an arm of Icy Strait across from Glacier Bay to the northwest, *Xunaa* refers to a dwelling place in the "lee of the north wind."[20] This and other Indigenous names for all of these places reflect the nature both of

Figure 7.2. The village of Hoonah (*Xunaa*), a Tlingit community at the northern end of Chichagof Island, Alaska, during the early twentieth century. Alaska State Library Place File, Photographs, ASL-P01–4182.

the harsh climate and the stark but intensely beautiful landscape, shaped by the dense forests that line the rocky coasts of the islands that make up the archipelago of which Chichagof Island is a part. Great distances divide the human settlements in this region, Indigenous and non-Indigenous alike. Although the northern coast of Chichagof Island lies just forty miles west of Juneau, traveling there by water even today entails a far longer journey still.[21] To reach Juneau by water, one must make one's way from Hoonah southeast along Icy Strait to Chatham Strait, turn sharply north to navigate around the northern tip of Admiralty Island, and then head south again along Stephens Passage before branching off into Gastineau Channel where Juneau is located across from Douglas Island.[22]

Indictment

The events that gave rise to these cases are best presented through the statements of the four defendants who chose to address the grand jury, after the US commissioner overseeing the process explained that they had a right to provide any explanation they thought would "tend to [their] exculpation" at the conclusion of the government's case.[23] Although Tlingit elder Kui-da-qua declined to address the grand jury,[24] each of the three younger defendants, Kee-tee-ish, Koh-suk-dake, and Kluni-ish, chose to make a statement, as did the elder Che-ha-te, whose account contradicted that of the younger men in some respects.[25]

According to Kee-tee-ish, Koh-suk-dake, and Kluni-ish, Kui-da-qua, an elder and chief, had visited a member of their community known as Archie during the last week of October 1902 because Archie was so ill that he had begun to cough up blood.[26] Archie reportedly told Kui-da-qua that he had dreamed that it was George Smalley (Kol-ketch-ish) who had made him ill. Kol-ketch-ish, he alleged, was a witch who was working with two others to kill him. Archie told Kui-da-qua that, in an effort to address what he understood to be the cause of his illness, he had paid Kol-ketch-ish "some money, some blankets and a shot gun to free him from [his illness] and save his life." His condition, however, had not improved. In response to Archie's account, the three young men reported, Kui-da-qua gave Archie permission to "tie that boy up." Archie, however, refused, explaining that the government might come after him and declaring that he was "afraid of the law" and "afraid of the government."[27] Both Kui-da-qua and Che-ha-te, another elder who, according to the three young men, had arrived as this conversation was taking place, sought to reassure Archie. Che-ha-te, they testified, told Archie that he also had his permission to tie up Kol-ketch-ish, suggesting that this would help him get better and noting that he was "giv[ing] [him his] brother."[28] When Archie again refused based on his fear that the US government would sanction him if he tied up Kol-ketch-ish, Che-ha-te reportedly told the three younger men to do this for him. Kee-tee-ish added that when he expressed concern that he did not know how to tie someone's hands for this purpose, Kui-da-qua showed him how to cross his wrists and tie the cords. Kui-da-qua then instructed Kee-tee-ish, Koh-suk-dake, and Kluni-ish to take Kol-ketch-ish by canoe to Sea Point, about a day's journey away, and to keep him tied up and deny him both food and water for eight days before they returned on the ninth day. Koh-suk-dake and Kluni-ish told the grand jury that they untied Kol-ketch-ish after three days but gave him no more food as instructed.[29] On the evening of the eighth day, they left Sea Point by canoe and arrived at Hoonah the following morning, only to find that Kol-ketch-ish had died as they neared the village. After arriving at Hoonah, the three young men carried the body of Kol-ketch-ish up to Archie's house, where they were met by a member of their community known as David Lawrence, who asked what they had done to Kol-ketch-ish. Koh-suk-dake and Kluni-ish concurred in the regret felt by Kee-tee-ish, reflected in his statement to the grand jury: "I trembled in my mind when David asked me what we did to that boy. I thought of how Smalley [Kol-ketch-ish] looked when he died. . . . I did not think he was going to die."[30]

Che-ha-te's statement to the grand jury differed from that of the three younger men in key respects. He denied that he believed in witches and insisted that he had not instructed them to tie up Kol-ketch-ish or to deny him food and water. He had also visited Archie, he testified, but on an earlier Saturday and not on the day that they tied him up. He was aware of Archie's illness, Che-ha-te said, and knew of Archie's dream and the payment he said he had made to Kol-ketch-ish to ask him to release him from his illness. Although Che-ha-te insisted he did not believe in witches, however, he did believe that Kol-ketch-ish had a propensity to do evil and explained that he had warned "Smalley not to do so many evil things." As examples of the evil he believed Kol-ketch-ish had done, Che-ha-te said that he had "first . . . joined the Greek [Orthodox] Church, then . . . the Presbyterian Church, [and then] the Salvation Army." Che-ha-te also testified that he had reminded Kol-ketch-ish "not to talk about witches" given that "the Government and the judge had told him not to say anything about a witch." Archie, he reported, knew that he, Che-ha-te, was "ashamed" by talk about witchcraft—regularly invoked by settler society as evidence of the purport-edly uncivilized nature of Alaska natives.[31] Che-ha-te said that Archie had reassured him, telling him that once he had recovered from his illness, they would turn Kol-ketch-ish over to the government and leave him in its care.[32]

Trial

The cases of the three younger men went to trial during the week of December 18 and concluded on December 24, each heard by a different jury whose members met "qualifications based on race, gender, age, language, and citizenship" as they applied in that time and place.[33] Jury instructions proffered by defense counsel for Kee-tee-ish, Koh-suk-dake, and Kluni-ish—ultimately refused by the judge though they were—provide insight into the way defense counsel J. F. Maloney argued his clients' cases. In each case, he questioned whether the defendant had intended that Kol-ketch-ish die, arguing that each of his clients lacked the mens rea, or criminal intent, required as a necessary element of the crime of murder. The first proffered instruction would have told the jury that they should find Kee-tee-ish not guilty if he acted based on "an honest though mistaken belief that [his action] was lawful."[34] In that case, the proposed instruction would have provided, the act did not constitute a crime. The same was true if defendants had acted based on the "belief that the said Smalley [Kol-ketch-ish] was causing the death or serious sickness of another Indian named Archer; and that in order to save Archer from death, it was necessary to tie [him] up in a secluded place for a period of eight days." Defense counsel thus proposed that the jury be instructed that if they found beyond a reasonable doubt that the defendants had acted "for the sole purpose of saving the life, or curing said Archer, and not with the intent or purpose of killing or injuring the deceased," they should enter a verdict of not guilty on the charge of murder.[35]

Defense counsel argued that rather than being motivated by malice or an intent that Kol-ketch-ish die, his clients' real purpose had been to save Archie's life. The lack of mens rea required to convict his clients of murder, he argued in effect, was demonstrated by the fact that each had acted on the instruction of an elder according to the legal and cultural tradition of their own community. Maloney likened his clients' actions to those of "a physician [who] may through gross ignorance, perform an operation on a patient that kills; yet if he is exercising his best skill, and judgment, for the patient'[s] benefit, he is not guilty of a crime." Their cases could also be equated, he argued, to one where a person "through an honest mistake administer[s] a deadly poison, believing it to be a wholesome medicine." This, he urged, would constitute not a crime but "a misadventure" and best described the consequences of his clients' actions.[36]

Judge Melville C. Brown refused the jury instructions proffered by defense counsel that would have required the jury to acquit if they found that the defendants had acted in accordance with the dictates of Indigenous law and custom, and denied motions for a directed verdict based on this reasoning.[37] But the instructions Judge Brown did give suggest that he was influenced by defense counsel's argument that his clients lacked the mens rea needed to permit the jury to find them guilty of murder, all but directing a verdict on the lesser included charge of manslaughter based on the facts of the case. Although jury instructions typically function only to instruct members of the jury with regard to the law they are to apply and generally avoid detailed discussion of the underlying facts, given that it is the jury's task to determine the facts and to apply the law to those facts, the instructions Judge Brown gave the juries engaged in a detailed discussion of the

Figure 7.3. A decade before he was appointed federal judge for the District of Alaska in 1900, Melville C. Brown chaired Wyoming's constitutional convention. Studio portrait of Melville C. Brown, ca. 1889, NEG #1489, Photograph Collection, Wyoming State Archives, Department of State Parks and Cultural Resources.

facts adduced at trial and applied the legal tests for manslaughter and unlawful homicide directly to those facts.

In Instruction No. 2 given in *U.S. v. Kluni-ish*, for example, Judge Brown explained that "unlawful homicide may be committed in many ways," including "forcibly taking a person and confining him in some out-of-the-way place where he is exposed to cold, deprived of food, and otherwise injured, until he perish from such injury, exposure and starvation." The judge added:

If such act is done with intent . . . that he should so remain until he die, then the homicide would be murder. But if such tying up, deprivation of food and exposure was intended as a punishment for some offence, imaginary or otherwise[,] that the person so deprived of liberty had committed against those that tied him, and it was not intended that he should be left to remain until he died, but for a time only as a punishment and to be released before death, the person so depriving him of liberty, and food, would not be guilty of murder because of the lack of intention to take life. *Even if the person dies* [italicized portion hand-written by the judge on the typed jury instruction].[38]

Judge Brown, in short, not only adopted but described in more exacting detail still the mens rea defense argued by counsel. The judge's express direction that the jury could find that the defendants' actions were intended as a sanction for a separate offence, recognized as such under the tenets of Indigenous law, directly reflects the meeting of Western and Indigenous legal traditions. Judge Brown also applied this standard to the evidence adduced at trial, once again directing the jury's attention to the Indigenous legal framework that jury members were permitted to find explained the defendants' actions:

Under the evidence in this case, it not appearing that there was any intention on the part of the defendant and others to confine the deceased until he should die, but for a time only, as a punishment for some fancied wrong or to aid in the restoration of health to some other person as was believed by the parties, and that the deceased was to be released before death ensued, you cannot find him guilty of murder in any degree. The *highest* offence of which the defendant can be found guilty under the evidence in this case is the crime of manslaughter as defined in these instructions; and then only when you find the facts constituting the offence are proved beyond all reasonable doubt.[39]

Even if jury members did not believe that Kol-ketch-ish caused Archie's illness nor that it was possible for the sanction imposed on Kol-ketch-ish to cure Archie of his illness, the jury was to consider the fact that the young men who had tied Kol-ketch-ish up did believe this and meant only to coerce him into releasing Archie from his illness, negating the required element of mens rea necessary to convict any individual of murder.

Based on Judge Brown's instructions, the juries convicted Kee-tee-ish, Koh-suk-dake, and Kluni-ish not of murder but of manslaughter. Judge Brown sentenced each of the three young men to four years at McNeil Island Penitentiary in Washington State.[40] He also denied motions submitted without argument by defense counsel asking him to set aside the jury's verdict and to grant a new trial on the ground, in each case, that the evidence adduced at trial was "wholly insufficient to justify and support the verdict" of manslaughter, and "for errors of law occurring at the trial and excepted to by the defendant and particularly shown in the Bill of Exceptions."[41]

Although Judge Brown refused to grant motions for a new trial in any of these cases, the fact remains that his instructions to the jury all but ensured that none of the defendants would be convicted of murder. The instructions he gave not only spoke directly to the encounter between Indigenous and Western legal tradition that unfolded in his courtroom but also were, in effect, a product of both. Although the criminal law ultimately prevailed in each of these cases, the harshness of the judgments that might have been rendered under its tenets alone was tempered by its encounter with Indigenous law as communicated to the judge by the defendants in explaining their reasons for their actions.

The Elders

The cases of elders Kui-da-qua and Che-ha-te had a different outcome. Unlike the three younger men, Kui-da-qua and Che-ha-te were accused not of directly causing the death of Kol-ketch-ish but of advising the three younger men to act in a manner that caused his death. They were charged, in short, as accessories before the fact. Kui-da-qua and Che-ha-te were represented not by J. F. Maloney but by W. E. Crews. Che-ha-te's case did not proceed to trial in December 1902 at the time the other defendants were tried; based on the evidence adduced at those trials, it appears that the prosecutor became concerned that he lacked the evidence needed to prove that Che-ha-te was in Hoonah on the Saturday that Kol-ketch-ish was tied up and taken to Sea Point.[42] Kui-da-qua's case did go to trial in December 1902. At his trial, the government called as witnesses only Kee-tee-ish and Kluni-ish, whose testimony likely mirrored that which they gave earlier to the grand jury. Defense counsel, in contrast, called a total of ten witnesses, including both Che-ha-te and Kui-da-qua's wife, as well as Kui-da-qua himself, to testify on his behalf.[43]

As in the cases of Kee-tee-ish, Koh-suk-dake, and Kluni-ish, Judge Brown once again instructed the jury to take into account the dictates of Indigenous legal tradition in determining whether the defendant, Kui-da-qua, should be convicted of murder or manslaughter, or acquitted altogether, repeating almost verbatim the language of the instructions given in the cases of the three younger men.[44] As long as Kui-da-qua had not intended that Kol-ketch-ish "be so held, tied up and deprived of food and water until he should die, and that such death was not to have been reasonably expected from the beginning though death ensued from these causes, [he] would not be guilty of murder, but of *voluntary* manslaughter."[45]

Based on these instructions, the jury found Kui-da-qua guilty of manslaughter. But in contrast to his decision in the cases of the three younger men, Judge Brown agreed to set aside the jury's verdict and grant the defense motion for a new trial, setting it for the May term.[46] By May, however, the new prosecutor, John J. Boyce, who had replaced Robert A. Friedrich as US Attorney in the interim, was no longer interested in taking the case to trial. Instead, he moved on his own initiative to dismiss all charges against both Kui-da-qua and Che-ha-te, both of whom he described as "advanced in age and controlling in influence." Boyce explained that Archie had died of tuberculosis in April 1903 and noted that, at the time of the events that led to the death of Kol-ketch-ish, Archie was "in the last stages of consumption, . . . afflicted with hemorrhages, and . . . bleeding from the lungs."[47] Both motions to dismiss accepted as fact the assertions made by Che-ha-te in his original statement to the grand jury. These facts, Boyce reported, had been the subject of further investigation prior to the start of the May term. Boyce had concluded, based on that investigation, that Archie himself bore the "chief responsibility" for setting in motion the events that led to the death of Kol-ketch-ish. It was Archie himself, Boyce declared, who had "initiated the idea of appealing to a long established custom among the Indian tribes for exorcising witches when any member of the tribe had any sickness, which was believed to originate from the arts and wiles of witches."[48] "Prior to the arrival of the white man," he added, it had been customary to assume that someone who was ill was "possessed of a witch" and that the remedy was to tie up and starve the witch for some nine days. This remedy, Boyce observed, "rarely resulted fatally, but after this exercise, the member of the tribe who had been bewitched, was supposed to be free from the influence and the witch destroyed or driven out." "Tying up," he noted, was also the remedy "for any mental defect or eccentricity, which in this age is deemed to be considered the result of insanity, craziness, or any defectiveness of intellect."⁴⁹

Kui-da-qua, Boyce noted, had been "convicted of manslaughter on the theory that he was an accessory before the fact," but he no longer believed it likely that the evidence would support a conviction if the case was retried. In fact, he added, "a verdict of guilty again rendered in this cause ought not to be sustained as a matter of law under the facts of the case." It was therefore his own opinion that the case against Kui-da-qua should be dismissed in the interest of justice.⁵⁰ This was all the more true of the case against Che-ha-te, the US Attorney argued. Based on the evidence adduced at the trials of the other four defendants, he had concluded not only that Che-ha-te "was not active, influential or prominent in advising" the three younger men to withhold food and water from Kol-ketch-ish but that he was not even present in Hoonah on the day Kol-ketch-ish was tied up and taken to Sea Point. Che-ha-te "could not be regarded in any sense as an active participator" in those events and, for that reason, justice required that the case against him also be dismissed.⁵¹ Judge Brown agreed with the US Attorney that "a verdict of guilty ought not to be sustained as a matter of law under the facts of [either] case" and granted the motions to dismiss both cases "in furtherance of justice." Both elders, well along in years and highly regarded in their community, were free to go.⁵²

The Meeting of Western and Indigenous Legal Tradition

It is not possible to explain the outcomes in these cases by reference to Western legal tradition alone; consideration of Indigenous law and culture is also required to understand and explain both the defendants' motivation and the decisions made by judge and jury. Because the final outcome in each of these cases was a product of the meeting of these two separate legal traditions, treating either one as operating in isolation and unaffected by the other leaves us with an incomplete understanding of the proceedings and the ultimate result in each of these cases.

In drawing attention to this convergence, my purpose is not to deny the disruptive impact of colonialism or to ignore the many ways in which law served as a tool to impose the will of the colonizer on Indigenous people. There is no question, as Harring has argued, that the attitudes of a majority of judges and officers of the court in Alaska and elsewhere in the United States were informed by an abiding belief in the superiority of their own legal tradition and a determination to suppress Indigenous practices with which they disagreed.[53] Here, as elsewhere, the power and "majesty" of the court would have been very much in evidence, reflected not only in the building constructed to house the legal process that unfolded within its walls but in the rituals that framed each step of the court proceedings, as well as in its material accoutrements—from the judge's judicial robes to the raised bench that allowed him to look down upon the defendants.[54] As Melinda Harm Benson notes, all "legal systems and processes have their own incantations that must be uttered, acts that must be performed, and conditions that must be present" for cases to proceed.[55] Majesty, to the extent that it expressed itself in such rituals or in symbolic visual or even aural forms such as the call to order or the striking of the judge's gavel, was a language with which the Tlingit individuals who appeared before the court would not have been unfamiliar. Rituals and symbolic elements, both material and aural, also aided in establishing the authority of the Tlingit shamans "responsible for maintaining the well-being of [their] communit[ies] . . . and insuring spiritual harmony."[56]

Critical though it is to recognize and acknowledge the disruptive impact of colonialism, a singular or exclusive focus on the coercive power of the courts alone can obscure more subtle encounters or negotiations where Indigenous people influenced the courts by insisting on their own worldview to a degree that forced the courts to take their perspectives into account at more abstract levels. To notice only the actions of the colonizing power is to miss instances where—even as the web of colonial law enforcement tightened and extended its reach across Alaska—Indigenous people spoke their truth to power and wrote their own stories into the record in ways important to them.[57] Mediated though their voices were by their own lawyers and the interpreters who translated their statements, the fact remains that the Indigenous defendants in these cases articulated their own understanding of the underlying events, insisting that their actions were justified based on their own legal traditions. That they retained control of their own stories is apparent even in that most coercive of legal proceedings: the criminal case.

We hear the voices of the Indigenous defendants in the statements they made to the grand jury, as well as indirectly in the proposed instructions filed by their attorney that would have directed the juries to acquit them if the jurors believed "their action was lawful or necessary to prevent another's death."[58] "Lawful" here, of course, meant "lawful" within the context of Indigenous legal tradition. Although Judge Brown was not willing to direct an acquittal on this ground, he applied substantially the same standard in the jury instructions he did give, all but directing a verdict of not guilty on the murder charge if jury members believed that the tying up of Kol-ketch-ish had itself been intended as a sanction based on Indigenous legal precepts. Not only did his instructions to the jury engage elements of both Western and Indigenous law, but the incorporation of Indigenous legal tenets tempered what would have been a far harsher result had the outcome in these cases been based on the application of Western legal principles alone. A finding that the defendants' actions were justified based on Indigenous law and motivated by the belief, rooted in the cultural traditions of their community, that their actions would save the life of a very ill man, served to negate the element of intent or mens rea required under criminal law. We miss such moments when we focus only on the coercive use of power in the courts, as we do the efforts made by both sides to negotiate and even accommodate a system of law with which they were unfamiliar.

We also miss the fact, as noted above, that Indigenous and Western legal traditions are not always at odds with one another.[59] Here, within the context of both legal orders, permission was not direction, evidence mattered, and the fact that a death, tragic as it was, was unintended was deserving of recognition. All bodies of law, Borrows and Napoleon remind us, evolve over time as they respond to changing conditions and "cross-cutting influences," and Indigenous legal traditions are no more static than those of the West.[60] As understandings of the sources of illness and disease changed in recent centuries, all legal orders developed new ways of assigning responsibility for injuries deemed to have been caused deliberately or through negligence. Indeed, there is evidence that Tlingit law itself was in transition at the time of these trials. That the traditional sanction imposed here did not contemplate the death of the individual whose hands were tied, as may sometimes have been the case in earlier times, is reflected not just in the defendants' statements that they did not think Kol-ketch-ish would die but also in David Lawrence's reported shock on learning that Kol-ketch-ish had died and his question to Kee-tee-ish asking what they had done to him.[61]

The cases were brought at a time when this north Pacific borderlands region had already undergone a series of profound changes over the course of several centuries due to the arrival of non-Indigenous peoples, starting with the Russians who first colonized Alaska.[62] The prior impact of the US judicial system is evident here in Archie's reluctance to tie up Kol-ketch-ish himself for fear that he would be punished by federal officials and the courts,

Figure 7.4. Studio portrait of Skoon-doo-oo yak (Skundoo), a Tlingit shaman who was tried in Juneau in 1895 and sentenced to three years' imprisonment in an earlier prosecution involving the death of an alleged witch. Alaska State Library, Case and Draper Photographs 1898–1920. ASL-PCA-39-488.

even though he clearly believed that this would free him from his illness.[63] It is also evident in Che-ha-te's report that a judge told Kol-ketch-ish not to talk about witches or, presumably, witchcraft, suggesting that Kol-ketch-ish had previously come into contact with the federal justice system in Alaska.[64] It may also be that word of earlier prosecutions by US authorities in Alaska during the 1880s and 1890s that targeted shamans accused of imposing traditional sanctions on individuals identified as "witches" had also reached those at Hoonah, remote though this community was.[65] The Tlingit, Rosita

Worl reports, regarded it as deeply ironic that "Western authorities protected the witches," whom the Tlingit regarded as "practitioners of evil," but prosecuted the "shamans . . . responsible for the general welfare of the Tlingit."[66]

The broader contours of the cultural clash that framed the encounters in the courtroom are reflected in Che-ha-te's perception that Kol-ketch-ish's evident interest in the various Christian denominations—Russian Orthodox, Protestant, and Salvation Army—that had built churches in Hoonah was indicative, in and of itself, of a propensity to do evil deeds.[67] It is also reflected in Archie's reported conviction that the US government would want to take custody of Kol-ketch-ish once he, Archie, had been cured of the lung condition he believed Kol-ketch-ish had caused. Although Archie himself was unwilling to participate in imposing that penalty on Kol-ketch-ish because he wanted to avoid the government sanction he feared would follow, his statement reveals that he believed that the penalty imposed on Kol-ketch-ish—tying him up with cords and denying him food and water—would make him well again. So certain was he of cause and effect that he also apparently believed that the US government would want to prosecute Kol-ketch-ish for having caused him harm once he was released from his illness. Ironically, if Kol-ketch-ish did in fact accept the payment Archie reportedly gave him, he may unwittingly have contributed to the events that later brought about his death by reinforcing Archie's belief that it was he who had made him ill.[68]

That none of the Indigenous individuals at the center of these cases negotiated the clash of cultures that followed the US acquisition of Russian interests in Alaska in the same way is reflected in the varied strategies adopted by the Tlingit participants—whether as victim, defendants, or witnesses—to navigate the broader cultural clash that framed their lives, from Kol-ketch-ish's exploration of non-Indigenous religious tradition by joining various Christian churches; to the embrace of traditional Tlingit remedies and determined defiance of US government officials by the three younger men; to Archie's careful negotiation of that cultural borderland, tinged as it was with anxiety and fear of federal sanctions even as he turned to Indigenous cultural practices to heal his illness. Archie's complex response to the encounter between Indigenous and Western worldviews in itself demonstrates the limits of the power of the US judicial system: although the threat of prosecution made Archie reluctant to act on his belief that Kol-ketch-ish had caused his illness, it had not persuaded him that disease could not be caused by witchcraft. The federal courts may have had the power to coerce certain kinds of behavior but the exercise of judicial power, even in its most extreme manifestation, was not necessarily enough to convince those who appeared before the courts to change their underlying beliefs or ways of understanding the world.[69]

That the non-Indigenous participants in these events also responded in a range of ways to the broader cultural clash that followed US colonization of Alaska is demonstrated, in turn, by one US Attorney's willingness to dismiss charges that another intended to pursue, as well as by the notably distinct attitudes reflected in the actions of the US commissioner who oversaw the indictment of the defendants and the non-Indigenous lawyers who represented those defendants—as well as by Judge Brown's willingness to hear and take into account both the oral evidence of the defendants and the Indigenous legal framework within which they had acted. Judge Brown's approach, taken together with his instructions to the jury and his decisions, on the prosecutor's recommendation, to dismiss the charges against the elders Kui-da-qua and Che-ha-te, raises the question of how we are to understand his actions given the pattern of prosecution directed by federal authorities in Alaska against those who continued to practice shamanic traditions. Equally as important as demonstrations of majesty in establishing the authority of the courts, Hay argues, was the exercise of mercy. Mercy, he contends, served to reinforce the rule of law by creating the illusion that those who dispensed it were "men of compassion and magnanimity," which was critical "to maintain[ing] the fabric of obedience, gratitude and deference" to a judicial system that existed only to serve the interests of the powerful.[70] Hay's claim that mercy is ultimately an expression of self-interest was rebutted by John Langbein, who, after engaging in a careful analysis of the evidence on which Hay based his claim, concluded that far from being "arbitrary and self-interested," the discretion exercised in the context of the judicial system that existed in England during the eighteenth century in fact "turned on the good-faith consideration of factors with which ethical decision-makers ought to have been concerned."[71] While the federal court system that existed in Alaska during the early twentieth century was distinguishable on any number of grounds, since principles developed by the English courts had been incorporated into US law, the arguments advanced by Hay and Langbein, taken together, provide a useful framework for analyzing the exercise of discretion in these cases. Their perspectives are best understood as points along a continuum where the elements that come into focus depend, in part, on scale. I would argue that in analyzing a given exercise of "mercy," it is important not to conflate legitimate observations about the way in which a court system as a whole operated in any given context with the individual motivations of any given individual judge. The latter may well have engaged in "good-faith consideration of factors with which ethical decision-makers ought to [be] concerned" but nevertheless may have contributed, inadvertently though it may be, to the reinforcement of a system that served to sustain the interests of, here, the colonizing power.[72]

In the context of criminal cases, "mercy" refers not to "pity or forgiveness" but to the equitable power of the courts, which provides judges with a mechanism that can be used to mitigate unfairness that might result from a strict or literal reading of the law.[73] Although Judge Brown took the unusual step of laying out the facts when he instructed the jury, his instructions to the jury are best understood as an exercise not of mercy but of justice, given that his directions engaged the elements of the charged crimes as set out by statute.[74] His decisions to set aside the jury's verdict in Kui-da-qua's case the first time it was tried and, subsequently, to dismiss the cases against both elders, however, were clear exercises of his power in equity. We have no way of knowing just where along the continuum articulated by Hay and Langbein his motivation lay. Worth noting, however, is that both Judge Brown and the prosecutor who moved for dismissal cited as the reason for that dismissal their belief that there was not enough evidence to sustain a conviction, which imposes on an ethical decision-maker the obligation not to proceed with a case.

Important to remember, as well, so that we do not mistake the practice prosecuted here as representative of all aspects of Tlingit culture, is that remedies such as that which led to the death of Kol-ketch-ish constituted just one element of a rich and complex cultural tradition. A majority of the federal court cases that targeted Indigenous cultural practices in Alaska involved extreme examples or, as here, instances where the intended outcome had gone awry. Newspapers tended to emphasize the most extreme sanctions imposed on those identified as witches, no doubt because such accounts sold more copies even as they reassured readers of the superiority of their own culture, expressly marking Indigenous legal traditions as primitive and implicitly justifying the imposition of Western legal proscriptions.[75] This tendency toward lurid exaggeration and callous disregard for facts before, and even after, they were objectively determined was also reflected in the earliest reports of the incident that occurred in Hoonah. Citing the

Record-Miner, the *Alaskan* reported on November 8, 1902, the same day that the original indictments were issued, "the news that a murder was committed at Hoonah village last Saturday. It was a horrible affair and the victim must have suffered great agony. The victim was accused of witchcraft, and according to ancient Indian custom was executed."[76]

Harsh as the penalty imposed on Kol-ketch-ish was, eight days' confinement pales in comparison to the four years of imprisonment imposed on Kee-tee-ish, Koh-suk-dake, and Kluni-ish—penalties that were further exacerbated by their removal to a place they had never been, nearly a thousand miles away on McNeil Island, Washington, where Indigenous prisoners also died unintended deaths of tuberculosis and other diseases.[77] Their incarceration in a distant place represents an integral stage in the evolution of the carceral state described by Kelly Lytle Hernández in this volume.

The fact remains that even though Kee-tee-ish, Koh-suk-dake, and Kluni-ish bore the brunt of the judgments rendered in these prosecutions, their having acted in accordance with Indigenous legal tradition served as a mitigating factor that resulted in their being convicted not of murder but of manslaughter. The meeting of Western and Indigenous legal traditions in these cases demonstrates, as the editors of this volume argue, that the West was indeed "a place of many overlapping legal borderlands rather than a lawless place."[78] Located in a borderland that was itself the product of a series of efforts made by Western powers to assert control over an area where the Tlingit had lived for many centuries, the courtroom functioned as a borderland where the coming together of two separate legal traditions produced outcomes that would not have been possible had they been determined by the tenets of either system of law alone.

Notes

I am grateful to the editors and to Tom Romero and all the participants in this volume for their thoughtful comments, as well as to archivists and librarians at the Alaska State Archives, Alaska State Court Law Library, Juneau-Douglas City Museum, Alaska State Library–Historical Collection, the Seattle branch of the National Archives and Records Administration and, although it has unfortunately since been closed, its Anchorage branch, for their help in tracking down key photographs and materials.

1. *United States of America v. Moses (Kee-tee-ish), Benjamin (Koh-suk-dake), John Smith (Klune-ish) [sic], Jeremiah King [Kui-da-qua], and Aaron Sharp [Che-ha-te]*, Record Group 21, National Archives and Records Administration, box 10

(Juneau Criminal Cases), case no. 344 (US District Court, Alaska, District I, 1902); *U.S. v. Kluni-ish, alias John Smith*, case no. 347 (US District Court, Alaska, District I, 1902). The spelling of the defendants' names varies from one document to another. In citing cases, I use the spelling used in the original caption of the case; to refer to individuals in this essay, I adopt the spelling used by the defense counsel, who is most likely to have been acquainted with his client's preference in this regard.

2. *U.S. v. Moses, et al.*

3. John Borrows, *Recovering Canada: The Resurgence of Indigenous Law* (Toronto: University of Toronto Press, 2002), 14–15. Like John Borrows, Val Napoleon, and Emily Snyder, I regard both systems of law as playing a similar role in ordering social relations in the communities where they were applied and deserving of equal consideration. See Emily Snyder, "Indigenous Feminist Legal Theory," *Canadian Journal of Women and the Law* 26 (2014): 365–401, 367–368 and n. 6, citing Val Napoleon, "Ayook: Gitksan Legal Order, Law and Legal Theory" (PhD diss., University of Victoria, 2009), 1–2. See also Snyder, 382–383. As used in Canada, "Aboriginal law" refers to the body of law that pertains to the rights of Indigenous people under state law in Canada, whereas "Indigenous law" refers to those bodies of law rooted in the customs and practices of Indigenous peoples themselves. Borrows, *Recovering Canada*, 4. I use "Western legal tradition" as shorthand to refer generally to British and American bodies of law imposed following the colonization of North America. Key cases where the Supreme Court of Canada held that Indigenous oral tradition should be taken into account in determining Aboriginal title include *Delgamuukw v. British Columbia* (1997) 3 S.C.R. 1010 and *Tsilhqot'in Nation v. British Columbia* (2014) 2 S.C.R. 257.

4. The 1867 treaty between Russia and the United States failed to address the status of Alaska's Indigenous peoples, stating only that what it characterized as its "uncivilized tribes [would] be subject to such laws and regulations as the United States may, from time to time, adopt in regard to aboriginal tribes in that country." Donald Fixico, ed., *Treaties with American Indians: An Encyclopedia of Rights, Conflicts, and Sovereignty* (Santa Barbara: ABC-CLIO, 2008), 195, quoting *Treaty concerning the Cession of the Russian Possessions in North America by his Majesty the Emperor of all the Russias to the United States of America*; concluded March 30, 1867; ratified by the United States, May 28, 1867; exchanged June 20, 1867; proclaimed by the United States, June 20, 1867 (15 Stat. 539). As Donald Fixico explains, under its terms, the United States "neither formally recognized, categorized, nor compensated any native Alaskan Eskimos or Indians, only referring to them as 'uncivilized' tribes under the control of Congress." Donald Fixico, ed., *Treaties with American Indians: An Encyclopedia of Rights, Conflicts, and Sovereignty* (Santa Barbara: ABC-CLIO, 2008), 195. By 1902, when the cases here arose, the federal courts had declared that "Alaska was not Indian country" and that federal Indian law doctrine and

rulings such as that in *Crow Dog's Case*, which had held that US criminal jurisdiction did not extend to Indian Country, did not apply. See Sidney L. Harring, *Crow Dog's Case: American Indian Sovereignty, Tribal Law, and United States Law in the Nineteenth Century* (Cambridge: Cambridge University Press, 1994), 213, 219–220, citing *Kie v. United States*, 27 F. 351 (C.C.D.Or. 1886). In *Kie v. United States*, federal district court judge Matthew P. Deady, based in Portland, Oregon, distinguished *Ex Parte Crow Dog* on the ground that *Ex Parte Crow Dog* had arisen "in Dakota, a territory acquired from France in 1803, while the anomalous condition of Alaska was not probably considered by the court." *Kie v. United States*, 27 F. at 353 citing *Ex parte Crow Dog*, 109 U.S. 556 (1883), 561–562. Also a factor creating uncertainty as to Alaska's status was the fact that it was first organized as a department (1867–1884), then as a district (1884–1912), and, only in 1912, as a territory in the absence of any intention, until then, that it eventually become a state. Claus-M. Naske and Herman E. Slotnick, *Alaska: A History*, 3rd ed. (Norman: University of Oklahoma Press, 2011), 219; Mary Alice Cook, "Manifest Opportunity: The Alaska Purchase as a Bridge between United States Expansion and Imperialism," *Alaska History* 26, no. 1 (Spring 2011). Given the terms of the 1867 US treaty with Russia, its failure to account for Alaska's Indigenous peoples, and Alaska's status as a district, it was assumed that the same bodies of federal law that applied to other residents also applied to Alaska's Indigenous peoples and that they were not entitled to any of the special protections that applied to Indigenous peoples in the continental United States. Harring, *Crow Dog's Case*, 213. These are both factors that distinguish the cases here from those arising along the US-Canada border on the Great Plains during the same period that Jeff Shepherd analyzes elsewhere in this volume.

5. Harring, *Crow Dog's Case*, 233, 236, 243. Given Harring's focus on the coercive use of criminal law, he does not examine moments when more nuanced encounters such as those described in this essay took place.

6. See, e.g., Napoleon, "What Is Indigenous Law? A Small Discussion (University of Victoria, School of Law, Indigenous Law Research Unit, n.d.), 5, noting that "Indigenous law exists, it has not gone anywhere . . . but there are also serious gaps where some Indigenous law[s] have been undermined, distorted, or lost." See also Napoleon, "Recovering Indigenous Legal Systems and Governance," Singing a New Song Conference, Victoria, BC, April 26–27, 2013, and see generally Borrows, *Canada's Indigenous Constitution* (Toronto: University of Toronto Press, 2010).

7. See, e.g., Michael Schwaiger, "Salmon, Sage-brush, and Safaris: Alaska's Territorial Judicial System and the Adventures of the Floating Court, 1901–1915," 26 *Alaska Law Review* 97 (2009): 101–102 (section entitled "Filling the Legal Vacuum").

8. Mary L. Dudziak and Leti Volpp, introduction, "Legal Borderlands: Law and the Construction of American Borders," *American Quarterly* 57, no. 3 (September

2005): 593–610, 595–596, 602. Although Dudziak and Volpp note the integral role played by state law in producing sovereign boundaries, they stop short of applying the same framework to Indigenous legal systems.

9. Borrows, *Recovering Canada*, 8, noting that "many Indigenous and non-Indigenous legal principles can be consistent and coexist without conflict." See also Napoleon, "What Is Indigenous Law?" 3 and 5.

10. *U.S. v. Kee-tee-ish; U.S. v. (Koh-suk-dake*, case no. 349; *U.S. v. Klune-ish*, case no. 347; *U.S. v. Kui-da-qua*, case no. 348; *U.S. v. Aaron Sharp* [Che-ha-te], case no. 350, RG 21, National Archives and Records Administration, box 10 (Juneau Criminal Cases) (US District Court, District I, 1902–1903).

11. Proposed jury instructions submitted by counsel to a judge articulate each side's arguments regarding the law that the judge should instruct the jury to apply to the evidence adduced at trial. Jury instructions can thus be read "backwards" to understand both the nature of that evidence and the arguments made by counsel for each side regarding the legal principles that should guide the decisions of both judge and jury. Notations that proposed jury instructions were refused indicate that the judge disagreed with counsel's argument regarding the applicable law or characterization of it. The jury instructions actually given by the judge to the jury, in turn, reveal his or her own understanding of both the case and the law to be applied.

12. Among the documents not included in the record, for example, are transcripts of the evidence given at trial, although the nature of some of that evidence can be inferred from other documents.

13. Richard Dauenhauer and Nora Marks Dauenhauer note that the interpreters were "often unnamed in the histories that depended so much on their skills," also the case here. See Richard Dauenhauer and Nora Marks Dauenhauer, "The Interpreter as Contact Point: Avoiding Collisions in Tlingit America," in John Sutton Lutz, ed., *Myth and Memory: Stories of Indigenous-European Contact* (Vancouver: University of British Columbia Press, 2007), 160–206; 160.

14. Dauenhauer and Dauenhauer, "The Interpreter as Contact Point," 160.

15. Richard White, "Indian Peoples and the Natural World: Asking the Right Questions," in Donald L. Fixico, ed., *Rethinking American Indian History* (Albuquerque: University of New Mexico Press, 1997), 87–100; 92.

16. Naske and Slotnick, *Alaska: A History*, 102, 115–117, 407 (appendix C). The population of Alaska had doubled during the 1890s from 32,052 in 1890 to 63,592 in 1900, resulting in a dramatic demographic shift that rendered the Tlingit "a minority in their own land." Naske and Slotnick, 409 (appendix E, for population figures); Harring, *Crow Dog's Case*, 237 (for quote). See also Schwaiger, "Salmon, Sage-Brush, and Safaris," 102.

17. See, e.g., *U.S. v. Rasmussen*, 25 S. Ct. 514, 49 L. Ed. 862 (1905), considering whether "Alaska ha[d] been incorporated into the United States, as a part thereof, or [was] simply held . . . as a possession or dependency" and determining that, because it had been incorporated into the United States, the constitutional

guarantees applicable in other parts of the United States also applied in Alaska, including the Sixth Amendment, which Congress had waived to permit a jury of just six to sit in misdemeanor cases. This was not an issue that arose in the cases under discussion here, however, since they involved felony and not misdemeanor charges. See also my note 4 above.

18. *Encyclopædia Britannica*, academic.eb.com/levels/collegiate/article/Juneau/44 153 (accessed June 1, 2017).

19. "Majesty" is Douglas Hay's term for physical and material demonstrations of the power of the courts. See Douglas Hay, "Property, Authority and the Criminal Law," in Douglas Hay, Peter Linebaugh, John G. Rule, E. P. Thompson, and Cal Winslow, *Albion's Fatal Tree: Crime and Society in Eighteenth-Century England* (London: Verso, 1975), 36. Hay's thesis and the material elements at play in the cases under discussion here are addressed in greater detail in the final section of this essay. See my notes 70 to 74 below and accompanying text.

20. Thomas F. Thornton, ed., *Haa Léelk'w Hás Aaní Saax'ú: Our Grandparents' Names on the Land* (Juneau and Seattle: Sealaska Heritage Institute and University of Washington Press, 2012), 27, 45.

21. Hoonah Indian Association, http://www.fhwa.dot.gov/tribal/tribalprgm/govts /hoonah.htm (accessed July 30, 2016). Although the pleadings in these cases describe Hoonah as located just "25 miles west of Juneau, Alaska," the Hoonah Indian Association states that the distance from Juneau to Hoonah, the largest and most populous Tlingit community today, is forty miles.

22. In the sections that follow, I endeavor to let the record speak for itself. Although I summarize the evidence and highlight key aspects of the proceedings, I have avoided inserting my own observations in an effort to permit, to the extent it is possible to do so, the voices of the participants to be heard. My own analysis and reflections follow in the final section of this essay.

23. *U.S. v. Moses, et al.*, Hiram H. Folsom, US commissioner and ex-officio justice of the peace, certifications dated November 8, 1902. The defendants were informed that they were "at liberty to waive making a statement," but each was warned that if he did address the grand jury, his statement "might be given in evidence against him in his trial." *U.S. v. Moses, et al.*

24. There is no way to know what Kui-da-qua's decision not to address the jury signified. It may have been an expression of reluctance to recognize the grand jury as a legitimate authority or it may have been a decision taken on the advice of counsel since he was only indirectly implicated in the case but could not deny that he was present at the time that the decision to sanction Kol-ketch-ish was made, in contrast to Che-ha-te. The fact that Kui-da-qua later testified at his own trial suggests that it may have been the latter.

25. *U.S. v. Moses, et al.*, Hiram H. Folsom, Certifications dated November 8, 1902. The defendants spoke through an interpreter who used their English names. I choose to use their Tlingit names because the record appears to reflect that this was their preference. The one exception involves the individual who was ill; he

is referred to only as Archie (or Archer) in the record even though he was also Tlingit. The deceased, Kol-ketch-ish, is often referred to as George Smalley in the record; with no way to know what he would have preferred, I have chosen to use his Tlingit name both to acknowledge his status as a member of the community and because his Tlingit name was carefully written in by hand on a number of court documents, suggesting that using it was identified as important as the cases proceeded.

26. *U.S. v. Moses, et al.*, Statements of Moses (Kes-tu-ish), Benjamin (Koh-suk-dake), and John Smith (Klune-ish), dated November 8, 1902. All four described themselves as hunters and/or fishers and were uncertain of their age. The three younger men stated that they were born in Hoonah and had lived there all their lives; Che-ha-te stated that he was born at Hudson Bay and had lived there most of his life. *U.S. v. Moses, et al.*

27. *U.S. v. Moses, et al.*, statements of Moses (Kes-tu-ish), Benjamin (Koh-suk-dake), and John Smith (Klune-ish) dated November 8, 1902.

28. *U.S. v. Moses, et al.* Given Che-ha-te's reported statement that he was giving Archie his brother, it appears that Che-ha-te may have been related to Kol-ketch-ish.

29. *U.S. v. Moses, et al.*, statements of Moses (Kes-tu-ish), Benjamin (Koh-suk-dake), and John Smith (Klune-ish) dated November 8, 1902 (while Koh-suk-dake referred only to food, Klune-ish stated that they denied Kol-ketch-ish both food and water for the entire eight days).

30. *U.S. v. Moses, et al.*, statements of Moses (Kes-tu-ish), Benjamin (Koh-suk-dake), and John Smith (Klune-ish), dated November 8, 1902. Both Benjamin and John Smith stated that they concurred with all that Moses had said. David Lawrence's Tlingit name is not provided in the existing record; he was among the witnesses called by the federal government at trial.

31. For examples of texts that cited a belief in witchcraft as evidence of the "uncivilized" nature of Indigenous people in Alaska, see my note 61 below.

32. *U.S. v. Moses, et al.*, statement of Aaron Sharp (Che-ha-te), dated November 8, 1902. Another factor that seemingly informed the actions of the defendants was their belief that Kol-ketch-ish had also caused the death of Che-ha-te's wife, but Che-ha-te himself denied that his wife was dead and called the veracity of the younger men into question. *U.S. v. Moses, et al.* Although the translator referred to the "Greek Church," this was likely intended as a reference to the Russian Orthodox Church.

33. *U.S. v. Kee-tee-ish*, case no. 344; *U.S. v. Kluni-ish*, case no. 347; Schwaiger, "Salmon, Sage-Brush, and Safaris," 125 (for quote).

34. *U.S. v. Kee-tee-ish*, case no. 344; *U.S. v. Kluni-ish*, case no. 347 (unnumbered jury instructions marked "refused" by Judge M. C. Brown). The three younger defendants were represented by J. F. Maloney of Maloney & Cobb, in contrast to the elders, Kui-da-qua and Che-ha-te, who were represented by W. E. Crews. Among the witnesses called by the government at the trial of the younger

defendants were Archie, Mrs. Archie, and David Lawrence. *U.S. v. Kee-tee-ish*, witness certification form. Witnesses called at the trial of Kluni-ish included Dr. Lilian C. Irwin, a physician who lived in Juneau between 1899 and 1906 with her husband, George M. Irwin. *U.S. v. Kluni-ish*, case no. 347, document entitled "Trial" naming jurors and witnesses called at trial. Other than Dr. Lilian Irwin (whose obituary appears in the *Alaska Sportsman* in October 1962), jurors and witnesses alike left little trace in the historical record other than their role or appearance in these cases, no doubt itself a reflection of how very transient Alaska's non-Indigenous population was at the time.

35. *U.S. v. Kee-tee-ish*, case no. 344 (unnumbered jury instructions marked "refused" by Judge Brown). The same or substantially similar instructions were also proffered by defense counsel in *U.S. v. Kluni-ish*, case no. 347. In determining whether the defendant was guilty of murder, Maloney argued in this case, the jury should be permitted to take into account their "ignorant and barbarous condition . . . for which he is not responsible [as well as] the superstitions of which he may be the victim." *U.S. v. Kluni-ish*. There is no way to know whether this statement reflected Maloney's own attitude or whether it was an appeal to what he believed to be the prejudices of the jury.

36. *U.S. v. Kee-tee-ish* case no. 344; *U.S. v. Kluni-ish*, case no. 347 (unnumbered jury instruction marked "refused" by Judge Brown).

37. See, e.g., *U.S. v. Kluni-ish*, case no. 347; *U.S. v. Koh-suk-dake*, case no. 349 (jury instructions and directed verdict form marked "refused" and signed by Judge Brown). Melville C. Brown had served as the first mayor of Laramie, Wyoming, and chaired Wyoming's constitutional convention before being appointed a federal judge for the district of Alaska in 1900. He moved to Seattle in 1904 and then back to Laramie, Wyoming, where he practiced law until his death in 1928. Evangeline Atwood and Robert N. DeArmond, *Who's Who in Alaskan Politics: A Biographical Dictionary of Alaskan Political Personalities* (Portland: Binford & Mort for the Alaska Historical Commission, 1977), 11. Brown became a vocal supporter of women's suffrage. See, e.g., "Record of Progress of Suffragettes," *Vancouver Daily World*, July 21, 1906.

38. *U.S. v. Kluni-ish*, case no. 347, Jury Instruction no. 2. In addition to the handwritten portion of the instruction (rendered in italics), the judge added, "If . . . the deceased Smalley was . . . confined in some out of the way place where he was exposed to *inclement weather*, deprived of food, and otherwise injured by being tied until he perished from such injury, exposure and starvation, or if he perished shortly after being released from such confinement, though death had not been intended by the defendant and others acting with him . . . you should find him guilty of manslaughter."

39. *U.S. v. Kluni-ish*, case no. 347, Jury Instruction no. 2. The jury was also instructed that if they had "a reasonable doubt as to whether the death of said Smalley was caused by such tying up and starving then [they] must acquit." Instruction no. 6. Other instructions given to the jury included standard instructions on

reasonable doubt, circumstantial evidence, that it was the government and not the defendant that had the burden of proof, and that members of the jury were "the sole judges of the credibility of witnesses, and the weight to be given to the testimony of each and all of them." The sets of jury instructions given in the remaining cases are not as complete as those in *U.S. v. Kluni-ish*, but those that are included are the same or substantially similar, e.g., Instruction no. 6 and the reasonable doubt instruction.

40. *U.S. v. Kee-tee-ish; U.S. v. Kluni-ish; U.S. v. Koh-suk-dake* (sentencing documents).

41. See, e.g., *U.S. v. Kluni-ish*, Motion and Order. Unfortunately, the Bills of Exceptions in these cases were not preserved so there is no way to know what legal errors defense counsel believed the court had made.

42. *U.S. v. Aaron Sharp*, case no. 350, Motion to Dismiss. The prosecutor's concern is consistent with Che-ha-te's own statement before the grand jury that although he had visited Archie while he was ill, he had done so on an earlier Saturday and not on the Saturday when Kol-ketch-ish was taken to Sea Point and tied up. See *U.S. v. Moses, et al.*, Statement of Aaron Sharp (Che-ha-te), dated November 8, 1902.

43. *U.S. v. Kui-da-qua*, case no. 349, list of witnesses. Unfortunately, there is no record of the testimony of these witnesses at trial, either because it was not transcribed in the first place or because any record that was created was not preserved.

44. Because it was undisputed that Kui-da-qua was not present at Sea Point, he could only be convicted if found to have been an accessory to the crime. "An accessory," the judge explained, "is one who stands by and aids, abets, or assists; or who . . . hath advised, encouraged, aided, or abetted the perpetration of the crime charged." But they could convict the defendant as an accessory only if they found that the underlying crime constituted voluntary manslaughter. If they found that the underlying crime was involuntary manslaughter, "there are no accessories to such a crime." If they found that "the defendant did not advise, counsel, or direct" the younger men to treat Kol-ketch-ish as they did but "merely permitted them to do in this respect as they pleased," and did not direct them to do so, they were to acquit. *U.S. v. Kui-da-qua*, case no. 348, jury instructions.

45. *U.S. v. Kui-da-qua*, case no. 348, jury instructions (italicized word handwritten by judge on typed copy of jury instruction). Except for the addition of the word "voluntary," Judge Brown made only minor grammatical changes to the typed instructions and did not add the handwritten phrase "even if the person dies" as on the instructions given in the earlier cases. Compare, for example, *U.S. v. Kui-da-qua*, case no. 348, with *U.S. v. Kluni-ish*, case no. 347, Instruction no. 2.

46. *U.S. v. Kui-da-qua*, case no. 348, Verdict and Motion to Dismiss.

47. *U.S. v. Kui-da-qua*, case no. 348; *U.S. v. Aaron Sharp*, case no. 350, Motions to Dismiss. Robert A. Friedrich, who had served as US Attorney in Alaska for a

number of years, died suddenly on December 31, 1902, just a week after the tri-als of the three younger men ended, as a result of ptomaine or food poisoning. See "Arctic Honors to the Dead: Body of General R. A. Friedrich Arrives on Puebla To-Day," *San Francisco Call*, January 17, 1903.

48. *U.S. v. Kui-da-qua*, case no. 348; *U.S. v. Aaron Sharp*, case no. 350, Motions to Dismiss.

49. *U.S. v. Kui-da-qua*, case no. 348; *U.S. v. Aaron Sharp*, case no. 350, Motions to Dismiss. For examples of ethnographic accounts that describe these practices, see my note 61 below.

50. *U.S. v. Kui-da-qua*, Motion to Dismiss.

51. *U.S. v. Aaron Sharp*, case no. 350, Motion to Dismiss.

52. *U.S. v. Kui-da-qua*, case no. 348; *U.S. v. Aaron Sharp*, case no. 350, Orders Granting Motions to Dismiss.

53. See, e.g., Harring, *Crow Dog's Case*, 223–224, 233, 243.

54. Hay, "Property, Authority, and the Criminal Law," 27–28. In this seminal es-say, Douglas Hay identified "majesty" or the role of spectacle as a key element in establishing the authority of the courts in eighteenth-century England, to-gether with "justice" and "mercy." Hay, "Property, Authority, and the Criminal Law," 17–63.

55. Melinda Harm Benson, "Rules of Engagement: The Spatiality of Judicial Re-view," in Irus Braverman, Nicholas Blomley, David Delaney, and Alexandre (Sandy) Kedar, eds., *The Expanding Spaces of Law: A Timely Legal Geography* (Redwood City: Stanford Law Books, an imprint of Stanford University Press, 2014), 215. Although Benson makes her observation in the context of analyzing recent cases filed in US courts, the same is true in other contexts including many Indigenous legal traditions.

56. See, for example, the descriptions of masks and regalia, ceremonial objects, rat-tles, or drums, in the accounts of winter rituals, initiation, and curing ceremonies cited by Rosita Worl, an anthropologist who is herself Tlingit and the president of the Sealaska Heritage Institute. Rosita Worl, "The *Ixt'*: Tlingit Shamanism," in *Celebration 2000: Restoring Balance through Culture* (Juneau: Sealaska Heri-tage Foundation, 2000), 167–169, at 161. Worl explains that dealing with those identified as witches was just one of a shaman's responsibilities. Other respon-sibilities included "serving [clan members] as military advisor," "locat[ing] clan members who had been lost on hunting or trading ventures, retriev[ing] lost and stolen items, . . . communicat[ing] with . . . relatives who were absent from the village," "assur[ing] success in hunting and fishing activities by locating wild-life," and "predicting the arrival of these animals." Worl, "The *Ixt'*: Tlingit Sha-manism," 161.

57. The process, as I see it, is not unlike that described by James (Sákéj) Youngblood Henderson in his essay "Post-Colonial Ledger Drawings: Legal Reform," in which he describes the drawings Indigenous people made of their own experi-ences in the ledger books they were provided, rather than using them to practice

writing and arithmetic. See James (Sákéj) Youngblood Henderson, "Post-Colonial Ledger Drawings: Legal Reform," in Marie Battiste, ed., *Reclaiming Indigenous Voice and Vision* (Vancouver: University of British Columbia Press, 2000), 162.

58. See my note 34 above and accompanying text.

59. See my note 9 above and accompanying text, citing Borrows, *Recovering Canada*, 8; Napoleon, "Recovering Indigenous Legal Systems and Governance."

60. Borrows, *Canada's Indigenous Constitution*, 59; Val Napoleon, "Thinking About Indigenous Legal Orders," in R. Provost and C. Sheppard, eds., *Dialogues on Human Rights and Legal Pluralism* (Dordrecht: Springer, 2013), 229–245, 232 ("Law is never static, but rather, lives in each new context.").

61. See my note 30 above and accompanying text. For accounts of Tlingit traditions related to witchcraft, see Aurel Krause, *The Tlingit Indians: Observations of an Indigenous People of Southeast Alaska 1881–1882*, trans. Erna Gunther (Seattle: University of Washington Press, 1956) (original edition, *Die Tlinkit-Indianer*, published in Germany in 1885), 250; George Thornton Emmons, *The Tlingit Indians* (New York and Vancouver, BC: Douglas & McIntyre for the American Museum of Natural History, 1991) (original typescript prepared in 1888), 398–412; Anatolii Kamenskii, *Tlingit Indians of Alaska* (1906), 118 (reprinted by the University of Alaska Press, 1985); Livingston F. Jones, *A Study of the Thlingets of Alaska* (New York: Fleming H. Revell, 1914) (first reprinting, Johnson Reprint Corporation, 1970, *Landmarks in Anthropology* series, ed. Weston La Barre), 154, 156–158. Worl explains that "suspected witches were tortured until they confessed their guilt" and that "in most cases, the torture resulted in the witch's death." Worl, "The *Ixt'*: Tlingit Shamanism," 162. Western legal tradition in both Europe and the Americas long condoned similar practices. *The Law Times* reported in 1901 that the law making witchcraft punishable by death in England was repealed only in 1736 and in Ireland only in 1821. The last death in England to result from torture intended to determine whether an accused individual was a witch is reported to have occurred in 1712. *The Law Times*, vol. 112 (November 9, 1901), 24.

62. For a detailed account of Russia's occupation of the region, see, e.g., Naske and Slotnick, *Alaska: A History*, 33–95.

63. See my note 27 above and accompanying text.

64. See my note 30 above and accompanying text. To date I have not been able to locate a record of this encounter. It may be that Kol-ketch-ish was not a named party in an earlier case but was called as a witness whose name may or may not have been accurately recorded, if at all.

65. Although the elders brought before the court in these cases were not identified as shamans, Worl explains that "many lay Tlingit besides the shaman were involved historically in shamanic practices" or *íxt'*. Worl, "The *Ixt'*: Tlingit Shamanism," 170. For a detailed discussion of earlier prosecutions involving

allegations of witchcraft, see Harring, *Crow Dog's Case*, 241–245. Many of those convicted were incarcerated in distant penitentiaries.

66. Worl, "The *Ixt'*: Tlingit Shamanism," 159, 171.

67. For a detailed discussion of the colonial encounter between Christianity and Tlingit shamanism, see Sergei Kan, "Shamanism and Christianity: Modern-Day Tlingit Elders Look at the Past," *Ethnohistory* 32, no. 4 (Fall 1991): 363–387.

68. See my note 27 above and accompanying text.

69. As Hay notes, it may be that what those in authority "interpreted as deference and gratitude of the poor was in fact conscious deception. Perhaps the ordinary Englishman played the role assigned to him, but was never convinced by the play." Hay, "Property, Authority, and the Criminal Law," 54. The same might well be true of the Indigenous defendants brought before the colonial courts.

70. Hay, "Property, Authority, and the Criminal Law," 48–49. As Carolyn Strange observes, "mercy is exercised by those empowered to be merciless, should they opt to be so," with the result that "those who appeal for mercy are necessarily *at* the mercy of power-holders." Carolyn Strange, ed., *Qualities of Mercy: Justice, Punishment, and Discretion* (Vancouver: University of British Columbia Press, 1996), 5. Tina Loo analyzes cases that raise cultural defenses, one of which involved the death of an alleged witch in nineteenth-century British Columbia. Loo's analysis, however, stops short of engaging the elements of the charged crime, leading her to conclude that "culture was [not] a matter of fact or law—that is, it was not a matter for juries or even judges to decide." Tina Loo, "Savage Mercy: Native Culture and the Modification of Capital Punishment in Nineteenth-Century British Columbia," in Strange, ed., *Qualities of Mercy*, 115. Unclear is whether Loo would have reached this conclusion had she engaged the elements of the charged crime and/or had access to documents equivalent to those analyzed here.

71. John H. Langbein, "Albion's Fatal Flaws," *Past and Present* 98 (1983): 97–120, at 120.

72. Langbein, "Albion's Fatal Flaws," 120 (for text of quote).

73. Strange, *Qualities of Mercy*, 3, 5.

74. See Hay, "Property, Authority, and the Criminal Law," 32–33, for a description of "justice."

75. Harring, *Crow Dog's Case*, 223–224, 243. For accounts by early ethnographers see my note 61 above.

76. "Murder at Hoonah: An Indian Accused of Witchcraft Was Put to Death," *The Alaskan*, November 8, 1902. A report issued one week later offered a more accurate statement of the underlying facts consistent with the statements given by the defendants to the grand jury. *The Alaskan*, November 15, 1902. The tendency of newspapers to exaggerate is also reflected in the report published in the *Morning Oregonian* on November 19, 1902. "Five Hoonah Indians are in jail at Juneau, Alaska, charged with murdering one of their tribe, George Smalley,

whom they accused of witchcraft. Two of the older Indians ordered three men to take Smalley into the woods, tie him to a tree and leave him for eight days. Smalley died on the ninth day as he was being brought home." *Morning Oregonian*, November 19, 1902. In fact, there was no evidence that Smalley was tied to a tree and the evidence reflected that he was tied up for just three days and not eight.

77. Deaths due to tuberculosis and other diseases that occurred in McNeil Island penitentiary were presumably no more intended by prison administrators than was that of Kol-ketch-ish. See generally National Archives and Records Administration, RG 129.8, Records of the Bureau of Prisons, McNeil Island Case Files, 1881–1981.

78. Katrina Jagodinsky and Pablo Mitchell, "Laying Down the Law: Critical Legal Histories of the North American West," Call for Papers, May 2015. A Joint Symposium Sponsored by the William P. Clements Center for Southwest Studies at Southern Methodist University and the University of Nebraska–Lincoln's History Department and Center for Great Plains Studies.

8

Reforming Deportees

Imprisonment and Immigration Control during the 1930s

KELLY LYTLE HERNÁNDEZ

In October 1930, the nation's leading prison reformers attended a conference in Louisville, Kentucky. For four days and nights, they debated how to improve US jails and prisons, but all agreed that the fundamental purpose of imprisonment was not punishment. It was rehabilitation. The prison administrators gathered in Louisville focused their discussions on how to prepare the imprisoned to "re-enter society and be a good citizen."[1] As Sanford Bates, a giant among the reformers and director of the US Bureau of Prisons liked to put it: "The man who is in prison today was on the street yesterday and will be on the street again tomorrow."[2] With this in mind, the reformers left the 1930 Louisville conference determined to institutionalize the principles of rehabilitation and reentry for the nation's imprisoned.

But as the prison reform movement took off during the 1930s, an increasing number of federal prisoners were Mexican immigrants. Most had been convicted of unlawfully crossing the US-Mexico border and were scheduled to be deported from the country at the end of their sentence. If, as the reformers believed, imprisonment was a project of rehabilitation and reentry into US society, what was the function of imprisoning Mexican deportees?[3] This essay examines how, during the 1930s, the prison reform movement took a turn in the US-Mexico borderlands where the Bureau of Prisons designed programs to deport Mexican nationals rather than reincorporate US citizens.

Falling in the gap between prison history and immigration history in the United States, this story about the making and meaning of Mexican immigrant imprisonment during the 1930s has never before been told. Immigration historians study immigration control.[4] Crime and punishment historians do not; they study imprisonment. Immigration historians do not study imprisonment.[5] In turn, imprisonment as a means of immigration control has largely slipped through the cracks and chasms of historical inquiry.[6] This essay reaches across the analytical divide to lay the foundation for a hub of historical inquiry at the crossroads of incarceration within the United States and deportation from the United States, and in particular explores the intersection of prison reform and immigration control in the US-Mexico borderlands during the 1930s.

For this volume on Western legal history, this essay examines a particularly Western turn in the prison reform movement, which, in the federal prisons of the US-Mexico borderlands, incorporated the demands of US immigration control by preparing Mexicans for deportation rather than reentry. It also documents an early carceral turn in the US immigration regime while opening a Western window onto the rise of incarceration in the United States. What we learn by looking through a Western window onto the carceral landscape is that efforts to control entry into the United States is a key dynamic in the history of imprisonment within the United States.

The reformers themselves left few of the familiar historical flags to alert us to the intersection of incarceration and immigration control that emerged within the federal penal system during the 1930s. They said little in public and issued few reports about the rising number of Mexican immigrants serving time in federal prisons. They said even less about the shadow system of imprisonment they built across the borderlands to prepare Mexican prisoners for deportation. However, the archives of the US Bureau of Prisons are crammed with evidence. In particular, Sanford Bates and his band of reformers at the bureau advanced immigration control by developing programs specifically designed to imprison and rehabilitate Mexico's unlawful border crossers.

Federal Prison Reform

In 1930, Congress funded a massive expansion of the federal penal system. Since the early 1900s, a blizzard of federal laws had dramatically increased the size of the federal prison population. In particular, the aggressive prosecutions of the Mann Act, which made it a felony to transport a woman or girl across state lines "for the purpose of prostitution or debauchery, or for any other immoral purpose" and the Volstead Act, which ignited the Prohibition era by banning the production, sale, and transport of alcoholic beverages, more than tripled the federal prison population, but the number of federal prisons had remained virtually unchanged since the 1890s. Under pressure from prison reformers to end severe overcrowding in federal prisons, Congress established the Bureau of Prisons in May 1930 and authorized funds to build new jails and prisons across the country.[7]

Appointed director of the new Bureau of Prisons, Sanford Bates coordinated the construction of more than six new federal prisons and jails between 1930 and 1938. He also handpicked a cadre of experienced prison reformers to join him at the bureau. Among them were James Bennett, Lowell Bixby, and Austin MacCormick. Together, they did more than build prisons: they seeded the principles of rehabilitation and reentry in the growing federal prison system.

Prior to the reformers' ascent within the Bureau of Prisons, wardens at federal prisons harshly disciplined recalcitrant, rebellious, or noncompliant inmates. They hung them by their thumbs, whipped their backsides into mangled pallets of flesh, shackled them to posts, or starved them in dark, dank, and infested dungeons.[8] But the reformers believed that such tactics only broke men's bodies and minds and failed to rebuild them again. Most significantly, such punishments only prepared the imprisoned to live in an authoritarian regime, failing to prepare them to live as citizens imbued with rights and responsibilities.[9] Of course, some US citizens did live under violent authoritarian regimes. The citizenship rights of African Americans, for example, were violently denied in Southern states.[10] But the prison reformers of the 1930s imagined the federal prisoner as white and male. And with white men in mind, the prison reformers vowed to end corporeal punishment.

When Bates became the first director of the Bureau of Prisons, he made good on the reformers' promise to end corporeal punishment in US prisons. He immediately prohibited beatings, whippings, and all forms of physical punishment in all federal prisons. "The days of the lash, the water cure, the paddle, the rack, and the torture chamber have gone from our American prisons," he later reflected.[11] Bates also ordered wardens to end solitary confinement. Solitary confinement, he explained, locked humans in "living tomb[s]" and rendered them "unfit . . . to live again with other human beings."[12]

In place of corporeal punishment and solitary confinement, Bates developed a clear set of privileges for all prisoners and advised wardens to grant and revoke privileges according to an inmate's behavior and compliance with prison programs and rules. Privileges included the opportunity to make purchases at the prison commissary, send letters to family and friends, spend time in the library, and get extra time on the prison yard. He listed the privileges in a rulebook distributed to wardens, guards, and every person imprisoned at a federal prison.

While Bates issued new disciplinary codes for the Bureau of Prisons, James Bennett and Austin MacCormick reformed the bureau's education system. According to Bennett, prison education needed to provide vocational and academic training that prepared prisoners to "fit" into society.[13] "We want him [the imprisoned] to conform to the social order," explained Bennett at the 1930 Louisville gathering of prison reformers. "It is the function of the prison, the function of prison education, to aid [the prisoner] to reach that state of mind where he wishes to fit in, to find the place in which he is most competent to fit, and to increase his competence in life."[14] Bennett advocated for a wide range of courses in history, geography, government, and civics to teach prisoners about society and social structure. The curriculum was tailored for the "American citizen," in particular, namely, white men expected to remain in the United States and return to full franchise when released from prison. History courses focused on British colonial America and the American Revolution. The geography courses focused on the US states.[15] The government courses reviewed the three branches of government. It was a set of political and social development courses designed for the Bureau of Prison's largest population during the 1930s: white men.

It was Lovell Bixby's primary job to ready the bodies of imprisoned white men returning to US streets and society. Indeed, in an era when social and political competence was often measured by physical fitness, it was Bixby's job to redesign the bureau's nutritional program. He closely watched the daily provisions for each prison, detailing that the imprisoned needed a balanced diet of meat, vegetables, fats, starches, and so on. He also increased the caloric intake for each prisoner and supervised the development of culinary programs that provided more diverse and healthful options, believing that strong bodies made better workers and fitter citizens.[16]

With these changes and more, the men charged with leading the Bureau of Prisons during the 1930s advanced the era's principles of penal reform. Their operating logic was to make the federal prison system into a pathway to life beyond bars within the United States. To this end, they developed a range of new programs and practices that prepared the imprisoned for reentry into society. The rise of Mexican immigrant imprisonment forced them to adjust their plans.

The Crime of Unlawful Entry

At the turn of the twentieth century, few Mexicans immigrated to the United States. At the time, the effects of foreign investment, industrialization, and land privatization were just beginning to be felt. In the United States, the seasonal industries that demanded a massive and migrating supply of casual labor were just beginning to grow. The basic economic foundation of mass migration between Mexico and the United States—that is, uprooted and underemployed Mexican laborers providing low-wage work for seasonal industries in the western United States—was still in its infancy. But by the 1920s, the foundations of mass migration had matured and tens of thousands of Mexicans crossed the border each year. By 1929, 10 percent of the Mexican population lived in the United States.[17]

For many Anglo Americans, the rise of Mexican immigration to the United States was one of the most divisive topics of the 1920s. In a decade now remembered as the "Tribal Twenties"—a time when the KKK was resurrected, Jim Crow came of age, and public intellectuals preached the science of eugenics—many in Congress worried that Mexican immigration degraded the nation's racial stock. Mexicans, they argued, were "mongrels" and "racially unsuited" to American citizenship.[18] Mexican immigration, it followed, had to stop. Throughout the 1920s, the opponents of Mexican immigration to the United States—popularly known as the Nativists—proposed legislation to greatly reduce the number of Mexicans allowed to enter the country each year. At a time when an estimated one hundred thousand Mexicans crossed the border annually, the Nativists demanded that no more than a few hundred Mexicans be allowed to enter the country each year. They wanted to cut the tide of Mexican immigration to a trickle.

Employers across the southwestern United States vehemently challenged the Nativists' proposals. Western industries, they testified, were "dependent" upon Mexican labor. Further, they promised, "The Mexican is a 'homer.' Like the pigeon he goes home to roost."[19] Like "birds of passage," Western employers explained, Mexicans would always return home, never settling, never remaining north of the border. On the promise that Mexicans in the United States would always labor, leave, and never live north of the

border, employers in the West successfully defeated the Nativists' proposals to place a numerical cap on Mexican immigration to the United States.

Yet, by the close of the decade, the promises made by Western employers
were wearing thin. Defying their employers' hopes, Mexicans increasingly
settled within the United States. They bought homes, started businesses, got
married, had children, joined parishes, and buried their dead. Building what
many have described as MexAmerica and becoming, as George Sánchez has
argued, Mexican American, Mexicans in the United States were busy making full and permanent lives for themselves and their children north of the
border.[20]

Monitoring the rise of MexAmerica, Nativists in Congress continued to
charge employers in the West with recklessly courting Anglo America's racial doom at its southern border. They demanded that a limit be placed on
the number of Mexicans allowed to enter the country each year. Western
employers still fiercely objected.[21] "We need the labor," they roared back at
the Nativists in Congress. Amid the escalating conflict, a senator from Dixie
proposed a compromise.

Senator Coleman Livingston Blease hailed from the hills of South Carolina. According to one biographer, Blease was a proud and unreconstructed
white supremacist touched by a strain of "Negro-phobia that knew no
bounds."[22] He entered Congress in 1925 committed, above all else, to protecting white supremacy. In 1929, as the dueling interests of the Tribal Twenties tussled over the future of Mexican immigration to the United States, it
was Senator Blease who proposed a way forward.[23]

According to US immigration officials, Mexicans made nearly one million authorized border crossings into the United States during the 1920s.
Many others, however, did not register for legal entry. They evaded the expense and inconvenience of legal entry and, instead, surreptitiously crossed
the border along its many desolate stretches between ports of entry. With
Nativists and employers unable to agree on the number of Mexicans allowed to legally enter the country each year, Senator Blease shifted the conversation to stopping unauthorized immigration from Mexico.

Citing the large number of unauthorized border crossings made by
Mexicans, Senator Blease suggested criminalizing unlawful entry into the
United States. According to Blease's bill, "unlawfully entering the country"
would be a misdemeanor and unlawfully returning to the United States after deportation would be a felony. As written, the proposal would impact

any immigrant who unlawfully entered the United States, but it was taken up in Congress as a measure to control and punish unlawful Mexican immigrants in particular.[24] To this, the Western agribusinessmen registered no protest. The criminalization of unlawful entry only strengthened their hand in their everyday labor relations with Mexican immigrant workers. So on March 4, 1929, Congress passed Blease's bill. Given the elusively simple title, the Immigration Act of March 4, 1929, Blease's bill dramatically altered the story of imprisonment in the United States, especially in the US-Mexico borderlands.

With stunning precision, the criminalization of unlawful entry caged thousands of Mexico's proverbial birds of passage. Within one year, US Attorneys prosecuted 7,001 cases of unlawful entry.[25] By the end of the decade, they had prosecuted more than 44,000 cases. Taking custody of all persons sentenced to prison on federal immigration charges, the Bureau of Prisons reported that Mexicans never constituted fewer than 84.6 percent of all immigration prisoners. Some years, Mexicans constituted 99 percent of all immigration prisoners.[26] By the end of the 1930s, tens of thousands of Mexicans had been arrested, charged, prosecuted, and imprisoned for unlawfully entering the United States. With 71 percent of all Mexican federal prisoners charged with immigration crimes, no other federal crime—not prohibition, not drug laws, and neither prostitution nor the Mann Act—sent more Mexicans to federal prison during the 1930s.[27] And, throughout the entire federal penal system, only liquor crimes created more prisoners than unlawful entry during the 1930s.

Mexican authorities protested the imprisonment of Mexico's unauthorized border crossers. Led by Enrique Santibañez, the Mexican Consul in San Antonio, Mexican consuls in the borderlands visited jails and prisons, taking an informal census of the number of Mexicans behind bars. They reported back stories of jail cells crammed with Mexican prisoners charged with or convicted for unlawful entry. Before the first year of the new law's implementation was complete, Santibañez was predicting that, to cage Mexico's unlawful border crossers, the US government would have to build new jails.[28] He was correct.

When Congress established the Bureau of Prisons in 1930, the federal government operated no prison or jail facilities in the US-Mexico border region. For decades, the US attorney general's office had simply reimbursed county sheriffs one dollar per person per day to confine federal prisoners in the region. But Blease's law demanded an expansion of the federal prison system in the US-Mexico border region. One of the first of the new federal prisons to be planned and built after the establishment of the Bureau of Prisons in 1930 was the La Tuna Detention Facility. Located just outside of El Paso, Texas, La Tuna was built to imprison the large number of Mexicans sentenced to prison for unlawful entry to the United States.

La Tuna Prison: "A Little Different from Any Other"

La Tuna opened on April 29, 1932. It was a sprawling prison farm with a maximum inmate capacity of 420 inmates, making La Tuna a carceral facility with an official inmate capacity nearly as large as Fort Leavenworth, McNeil Island, and the Atlanta Penitentiary. Established to absorb the sudden boom in federal imprisonment that the criminalization of unlawful entry created, La Tuna was a major addition to the federal prison system. Within three months of its opening, the first warden at La Tuna, Texas-born borderlander Thomas B. White, reported that the prison's inmate capacity would soon be breached. He promised to "tak[e] on a little more than capacity," by transforming the chapel into a dormitory, pushing inmate capacity to five hundred prisoners.[29] Still, by the beginning of 1933, La Tuna regularly exceeded capacity, averaging more than five hundred prisoners daily. Some of the prisoners at La Tuna were transfers from other federal facilities. But a roving 90 to 97 percent of all inmates at La Tuna were Mexicans convicted on immigration charges.[30] As intended, La Tuna was a large borderland prison established to imprison Mexican immigrants for unlawful entry into the United States.

Federal prison authorities immediately recognized the first of the borderlands' emerging archipelago of Mexican deportee imprisonment centers as unique within the federal prison system. As Warden White put it, "Our situation is a little different from any other."[31] The differences in imprisoning Mexican deportees impacted all decisions made regarding inmate care and management at the new federal prisons in the borderlands.

Within the first months of operation at La Tuna, the chief clerk at the prison reported, "the Mexican population requires a different distribution of foods from that in the other institutions."[32] Acknowledging that prisoners at La Tuna were eating substantially less than the bureau's upgraded nutritional ration, he argued that "our prisoners are at least 90 percent

Mexicans and they are used to a very light diet."[33] He advocated establishing "somewhat different standards" for feeding prisoners at La Tuna.[34] Reviewing the clerk's report from La Tuna, A. H. MacCormick agreed, supporting different nutritional standards for La Tuna's prisoners. "It seems to me," he explained, "that it will be wise for you to experiment a little with the standard ration in view of the large percentage of Mexicans in your population. I know how accustomed most of them are to a diet consisting largely of beans."[35] Tweaking the federal prison menu and its nutritional standards to accommodate "the Mexican population we have here," MacCormick approved "somewhat different standards" for Mexicans imprisoned at La Tuna.[36] But the nutritional program at La Tuna was just the first hint that prison reformers were making accommodations to imprison Mexican deportees in the borderlands.

Education was a cornerstone of penal reform during the 1930s. The reformers believed that few lawbreakers were biologically inclined toward crime. Rather, they believed that lawbreakers lacked the appropriate social and technical skills to make a living and live within the law. Reformers imagined prison as an institution where lawbreakers would become citizens by acquiring new skills and deepening their education. Imprisoning deportees raised new questions about education within the federal penal system.

"Obviously we do not want to waste any time teaching Mexicans who are to be deported how to read and write English," wrote MacCormick the year after La Tuna opened.[37] He asked his reformer colleagues, "What can be done in the way of education with the particular type of men you have?" Given the large number of Mexican deportees imprisoned there, he acknowledged, "your problem will undoubtedly differ from that of every other institution in our service."[38] Moreover, MacCormick wondered how education could advance the return of Mexicans to Mexico and reduce their recidivism in the years ahead. "Perhaps if we make them more familiar with the traditions and possibilities of their own country it will do something to cut down the 'illegal entries,'" replied Lovell Bixby.[39] MacCormick liked the idea. By 1933, the reformers had revised the literacy courses at La Tuna to "teach them to read and write in their own language."[40] The Bureau of Prisons also developed social studies courses at La Tuna that focused on the "geography and culture of Mexico."[41] The objective was to prepare Mexican citizens to return to Mexico, and to stay there. In other words, the reformers altered the education program at La Tuna to advance immigration control.

Warden White, a former Texas Ranger and Bureau of Investigation agent in the US-Mexico borderlands, chafed at the reformers' ideas and programs. On the matter of educating Mexican prisoners, he saw no point in it. "A Mexican only thinks of today. The future and its consequences are no worry of his," he once explained to Director Bates.[42] When all the reformers' efforts proved to have little effect—unlawful entries continued and many men returned to La Tuna several times within the first few years of the prison's operation—White delighted at Bates's request for help. "Our present program for them is not rigorous enough to have a deterrent value," Bates wrote to Warden White in January 1936. "Perhaps we even need to inject some of the Alcatraz type of discipline and routine."[43]

These were words White had longed to hear. "In connection with some sort of program suitable to deal with the large number of Mexican immigration cases here. . . . I am very glad indeed that you wrote me about this and opened the door to suggestions, for I have felt a long time need for some sort of better plan. . . . What to do to put a check has always been a problem," explained White, who considered himself, a borderlander, more the expert on Mexican immigration than Bates, a Boston Brahmin. To date, White admitted, he had already begun to "have as few privileges and as rigorous discipline as I could get by your instructions on." But he had done so quietly until Bates asked for help, after which White recommended nothing but hard labor and harsh discipline for Mexican prisoners. "I think the best plan is a good dose of work, putting in as many hours as possible each day, with as many days as the week has, every day in the year, Sunday, the only exception. . . . I would rule out the exercise periods that you suggested, for that would be too much like sport for some of the continuous 'border jumpers.' . . . Work is the pain they get. . . . If this is put across like I believe we can, there won't be much time for any more educational work than what we carry on now. This sort of program I believe will have the best deterrent effect."[44]

Bates approved the plan.[45] He also approved alternative disciplinary methods. Warden White literally threw out the reformers' rulebook and wrote his own, a pamphlet outlining few privileges and lots of work for Mexico's immigration prisoners.[46] "While confined to this institution, prisoners will have no need for anything which is not furnished by the Government," began his pamphlet. If an inmate's family or friends sent money or packages to the prison, White promised that guards would reject the delivery. White also informed the men at La Tuna that they were banned from sending more than one letter monthly. White's pamphlet detailed that inmates at La Tuna were prohibited from "boisterous and noisy behavior." "Loud noises, such as whistling, singing, slamming of doors, etc." were all forbidden at La Tuna. No play or privileges were due to them because, according to White's pamphlet, "work is our principal objective" at La Tuna.[47]

White's pamphlet, which spilled little ink on privileges, detailed the prison's strict work regime. All inmates were to "rise promptly" at the sound of the morning bell and, "without delay," "fall in line" for breakfast, followed by a day's work on the prison farm, milking cows, building roads, tending fields of beans and vegetables, and canning fruit. Only the "old" or "crippled" would be allowed to sit idly in their cells. At the end of the day's work, White's pamphlet instructed inmates to "retire promptly and maintain silence."[48]

The men at La Tuna did not abide Warden White's rules and often broke them. When they did, White used disciplinary tactics shunned by the reformers. "You have punished men for skylarking, throwing pillows, unnecessary noise, etc. and you have apparently locked them up for several days," wrote Bates when he received some of the first disciplinary reports from La Tuna.[49] "I realize, of course, the necessity for your maintaining an orderly institution and the need for preserving respectful discipline . . . but I must confess that it seems to me as though you ought to be able to burn up some the playful energy of the Mexicans in some way other than locking them up. Why not take them out to the yard, walk them around, or give them an additional dose of work, or possibly take away their yard privileges?" Bates suggested.[50] But Warden White defended his "long list of solitary confinement cases."[51] "I don't think that our numbers punished are too many after taking into consideration the fact that 85 percent of our population consists of men coming from the wilds of Mexico, where they are their own choosers as to their law and order and haven't the remotest idea as to good conduct."[52] Solitary confinement, argued White, was a "simple remedy" for people from the "wilds of Mexico." "I believe that if you will abide with us in our problems . . . that in time we can better satisfy you that the situation is not as serious as you seem to think."[53] Bates considered White's defense and backed down, agreeing to "mak[e] due allowances for the character of the inmates you have to handle."[54] He issued a similar break from policy for another facility designed to imprison Mexican deportees, Tucson Prison Camp #10. Both breaks set aside the rehabilitation ideal and resurrected hard labor and harsh discipline for Mexican prisoners.

Tucson Prison Camp #10

When La Tuna breached its capacity in early 1933, Sanford Bates asked the assistant director of the Bureau of Prisons, James V. Bennett, to quickly find a place to hold more prisoners. Bennett took an expedition into southern Arizona, promising to find a "sufficiently isolated place to camp some of your Mexican friends."[55] On a twenty-five-mile trek that wound across the desert and up into the Santa Catalina Mountains, Bennett searched until he found a spot in a small desert clearing at the base of the mountains where prisoners could be housed in tents and put to work building a new road. He named the site after the nearest town, calling the roughshod facility Tucson Prison Camp #10.

Opened in the summer of 1933, Tucson Prison Camp #10 was a minimum-security convict labor camp. From the quickly assembled base camp filled with canvas tents and work tools, prisoners were to build a road up, through, and across the mountains to a little town named Oracle, where local residents had hopes of building a health resort. As James Bennett explained after his survey of the area, "the chief purpose of the road is to open up a recreational area for the residents of Tucson so they can escape the heat of the lower country during the hot summer months."[56]

The first warden assigned to the Tucson camp was James Gaffney, who had worked at a prison in Alabama prior to his appointment in the Arizona borderlands. With Gaffney worked five to six guards. Sent hundreds of immigration prisoners from La Tuna and across the Arizona and New Mexico borderlands, Warden Gaffney and the guards supervised the inmates as they blasted a road into the rocky mountainside that burst from the boiling landscape of the Arizona borderlands. The work progressed at Tucson, but Gaffney soon described Mexican immigration offenders as a "thorn in our side."[57] As he and others acknowledged, a "considerable" number of Mexican immigration offenders escaped from the Tucson prison camp.[58] More than forty inmates, for example, almost all of them Mexican deportees, fled the camp in the summer of 1933.[59] According to Gaffney, the escapes from the Tucson camp "ruined my escape record of which I was very proud over in Alabama."[60] Trying to explain the camp's high escape rate, Warden Gaffney described the escapees as "young Mexicans, with very few brains, if any."[61] Bates concurred, describing escapees from Tucson as "ignorant Mexicans."[62] But the archival record suggests that an intelligent assessment of camp conditions prompted mass escapes from Tucson.

Within the camp's first year of operation, there were multiple injuries
and two inmates died while working on the mountain road. A truck the
inmates were riding in rolled off the road and down the mountainside, land-
ing roof-first some three hundred feet below. "This job is extremely dangerous and let no one tell you differently," explained Warden Gaffney, but he
took few measures to mediate "the dangers that exist." "Always jump, and
jump quick" when vehicles begin to roll, he advised the inmates.[63] Although
escapees from the prison camp left no traces of their motives, it is easy to
believe that the camp's dangerous labor conditions influenced their decisions to leave. Tucson, after all, was a minimum-security camp. The guards
did not carry guns, significantly reducing the immediate risk of attempted
escape.

But, if recaptured, escapees faced serious consequences. Judges, for their
part, often sentenced escapees to serve additional time after completion of
their original term. For example, Francisco Valdez, inmate #95 at the Tucson
Prison Camp, was originally sentenced to serve fourteen months for unlawful entry. After Francisco's failed escape from the Tucson camp, a judge
sentenced him to serve ten additional months. By the time Francisco was
released, he had served more than two years in prison.[64]

But Warden Gaffney, a man with experience in the southern penal system, also devised punishments to be meted out at the camp. "There is a place
of punishment called 'the hole,'" reported one reviewer of Tucson Prison
Camp #10. Either a wooden box or, more likely, a hole dug into the ground,
"the hole" was a box covered by a 1 x 4 steel grate. "To be confined in it
for several days is quite severe punishment and in hot weather comes very
near inhumane," explained the reviewer.[65] For shirking work or trying to
mail complaints to Gaffney's supervisors, Gaffney had men placed in "the
hole."[66] There, they wasted for days without water, food, or a toilet.

By 1930, US prison reformers were widely committed to the principles of
rehabilitation and reentry into Anglo-American, middle-class society, and
they led some of the nation's largest prison systems. Among them were Sanford Bates and the cohort of men he hired to build the US Bureau of Prisons.
But as Mexican imprisonment began to soar during the 1930s, demands for
immigration control pushed Bates and the reformers at the Bureau of Prisons to adjust their rehabilitation ideals. In particular, the reformers established new prisons and designed special diets, programs, and punishments
for Mexican men and prepared them for deportation to Mexico rather than

reentry into the United States. Indeed, deportation deeply shaped the rise of the federal penal system in the US-Mexico borderlands.

Notes

1. *Proceedings of the 60th Annual Conference of the American Prison Association* (Louisville, Kentucky, 1930), 15.
2. Sanford Bates, *Prisons and Beyond* (New York: Macmillan, 1938), 108. See also "Father of Modern Penology," *San Quentin News*, February 11, 1972.
3. Natalia Molina, *Fit to Be Citizens? Public Health and Race in Los Angeles, 1879–1939* (Berkeley: University of California Press, 2006); Natalia Molina, "In a Race All Their Own: The Quest to Make Mexicans Ineligible for U.S. Citizenship," *Pacific Historical Review* 79, no. 2 (May 2010): 167–201; Kelly Lytle Hernández, *City of Inmates: Conquest, Rebellion, and the Rise of Human Caging in Los Angeles* (Chapel Hill: University of North Carolina Press, 2017).
4. Several leading histories of US immigration control are: Torrie Hester, *Deportation: The Origins of U.S. Policy* (Philadelphia: University of Pennsylvania Press, 2017); Deidre Moloney, *National Insecurities: Immigrants and U.S. Deportation Policy since 1882* (Chapel Hill: University of North Carolina Press, 2012); Erika Lee, *At America's Gates: Chinese Immigration during the Exclusion Era, 1882–1943* (Chapel Hill: University of North Carolina Press, 2004); Mae Ngai, *Impossible Subjects: Illegal Aliens and the Making of Modern America* (Princeton: Princeton University Press, 2004).
5. Several leading histories of crime and punishment in the United States include: Norval Morris and David J. Rothman, eds., *The Oxford History of the Prison: The Practice of Punishment in Western Society* (New York: Oxford University Press, 1997); Heather Anne Thompson, "Why Mass Incarceration Matters: Rethinking Crisis, Decline, and Transformation in Postwar American History," *Journal of American History* 97, no. 3 (December 2010): 703–734; Elizabeth Hinton, *From the War on Poverty to the War on Crime: The Making of Mass Incarceration in America* (Cambridge: Harvard University Press, 2016); Rebecca McLennan, *The Crisis of Imprisonment: Protest, Politics, and the Making of an American Penal State, 1776–1941* (New York: Cambridge University Press, 2008).
6. Other fields of inquiry, however, have begun to jointly study mass incarceration and mass deportation while legal scholars have developed the field of "crimmigration studies." See Jenna Loyd, Matt Mitchelson, and Andrew Burridge, eds., *Beyond Walls and Cages: Prisons, Borders, and Global Crisis* (Athens: University of Georgia Press, 2012); David Hernández, "Pursuant to Deportation: Latinos and Immigrant Detention," *Latino Studies* 6, no. 1 (2008): 35–63; Juliet Stumpft, "The Crimmigration Crisis: Immigrants, Crime, and Sovereign Power," *American University Law Review* 56, no. 2 (December 2006).

7. Paul W. Keve, *Prisons and the American Conscience: A History of U.S. Federal Corrections* (Carbondale: Southern Illinois University Press, 1991), 18–50.

8. Blake McKelvey, *American Prisons: A History of Good Intentions* (Montclair: Patterson Smith, 1977), 184–189, 199–203.

9. Bates, *Prisons and Beyond*, 176–202. McKelvey, *American Prisons*, 299–321.

10. Douglas Blackmon, *Slavery by Another Name: The Re-Enslavement of Black Americans from the Civil War to World War II* (New York: Random House, 2008); Mary Ellen Curtin, *Black Prisoners and Their World: Alabama, 1865–1900* (Charlottesville: University Press of Virginia, 2000); Sarah Haley, *No Mercy Here: Gender, Punishment, and the Making of Jim Crow Modernity* (Chapel Hill: University of North Carolina Press, 2016); Talitha Le Fleuria, *Chained in Silence: Black Women and Convict Labor in the New South* (Chapel Hill: University of North Carolina Press, 2016); Alex Lichtenstein, *Twice the Work of Free Labor: The Political Economy of Convict Labor in the New South* (New York: Verso, 1996); Matthew J. Mancini, *One Dies, Get Another: Convict Leasing in the American South, 1866–1928* (Columbia: University of South Carolina Press, 1996); David Oshinsky, *Worse than Slavery: Parchman Farm and the Ordeal of Jim Crow Justice* (New York: Free Press, 1996); Robert Perkinson, *Texas Tough: The Rise of America's Prison Empire* (New York: Metropolitan, 2010).

11. Bates, *Prisons and Beyond*, 177.

12. Bates, *Prisons and Beyond*, 87.

13. *Proceedings of the 60th Annual Conference of the American Prison Association*, 37.

14. *Proceedings of the 60th Annual Conference of the American Prison Association.*

15. *Proceedings of the 60th Annual Conference of the American Prison Association*, 38.

16. "First Month of Food at La Tuna," report dated June 14, 1932, Class 4 Files, File 4-35-1-29, Record Group 129, Bureau of Prisons, National Archives and Records Administration–College Park (hereafter cited as NARA–College Park).

17. Mark Reisler, *By the Sweat of Their Brow: Mexican Immigrant Labor in the United States, 1900–1940* (Westport, CT: Greenwood, 1977).

18. For the racialization of Mexicans during the 1920s congressional hearings, see Ngai, *Impossible Subjects*, 56–90; Mark Reisler, "Always the Laborer, Never the Citizen: Anglo Perceptions of the Mexican Immigrant during the 1920s," *Pacific Historical Review* 45, no. 2 (May 1976): 231–254; and Molina, "In a Race All Their Own," 167–201.

19. Testimony of S. Parker Frisselle, *Seasonal Agricultural Laborers from Mexico*, 69th Congress, 1st Session (Washington, DC: GPO, 1926), 7.

20. Douglas Monroy, *Rebirth: Mexican Los Angeles from the Great Migration to the Great Depression* (Berkeley: University of California Press, 1999); George J. Sánchez, *Becoming Mexican American: Ethnicity, Culture, and Identity in Chicano Los Angeles, 1900–1945* (New York: Oxford University Press, 1995).

21. The US secretary of state tried to bridge the impasse by ordering consular representatives in Mexico to reduce the number of visas they approved. Without visas, Mexicans could not legally enter the country.

22. Kenneth Wayne Mixon, "The Senatorial Career of Coleman Bleaser" (master's thesis, University of South Carolina, 1967), 5. See also Stephen Kantrowitz, *Ben Tillman and the Reconstruction of White Supremacy* (Chapel Hill: University of North Carolina Press, 2000).

23. The secretary of labor actually wrote the bill and worked with Blease to have it introduced in Congress.

24. Congressional Record, 70th Congress, 2nd Session, vol. 70, pt 4, pages 3619/20.

25. US Attorney General Annual Report FY 1930, 37.

26. US Bureau of Prisons, *Federal Offenders*, FYs 1931–1936

27. "Total Mexicans Received from Courts into Jails by Offense," in US Bureau of Prisons, *Federal Offenders*, FYs 1931–1936.

28. Enrique Santibañez, *Ensayo acerca de la inmigración Mexicana en los Estados Unidos* (San Antonio: Clegg, 1930), 81.

29. October 7, 1932, Warden White to Director Bates. Class 4 Files, File 4-35-3-46, RG 170, NARA–College Park. For note that chapel was transformed into dormitory see, 1935 La Tuna Annual Inspection, Class 4 Files, File 4-35-3-29, RG 129, NARA–College Park.

30. Monthly Reports from La Tuna, September to December 1932. Class 4 Files, File 3-35-3-13, RG 129, NARA–College Park. *Los Angeles Times*, "Federal Prison Plans Speeded," March 22, 1931.

31. March 21, 1933, Warden White to Director Bates, Bureau of Prisons. Class 4 Files, File 3-35-3-14, RG 129, NARA–College Park.

32. La Tuna Report for November 1932. Class 4 Files, File 4-35-1-29, RG 129, NARA–College Park.

33. June 14, 1932, Chief Clerk L. O. Mills to Director Bates. Class 4 Files, File 4-35-1-29, RG 129, NARA–College Park.

34. La Tuna Report for November 1932. Class 4 Files, File 4-35-1-29, RG 129, NARA–College Park.

35. June 22, 1932, A. H. MacCormick to Warden White. Class 4 Files, File 4-35-1-29, RG 129, NARA–College Park.

36. "The Mexican population we have here" is from a letter dated July 16, 1932, Warden White to Director Bates. Class 4 Files, File 4-35-1-29, RG 129, NARA–College Park. "Somewhat different standards," La Tuna Report for November 1932. Class 4 Files, File 4-35-1-29, RG 129, NARA–College Park.

37. August 25, 1933, A. H. MacCormick to Warden White. Class 4 Files, File 4-35-3-27, RG 129, NARA–College Park.

38. August 25, 1933, A. H. MacCormick to Warden White.

39. November 15, 1935, F. Lovell Bixby, Attention Mr. Hicks letter to Warden White. Class 4 Files, File 4-35-3-27, RG 129, NARA–College Park.

40. August 25, 1933, A. H. MacCormick to Warden White. Class 4 Files, File 4-35-3-27, RG 129, NARA–College Park.

41. November 15, 1935, F. Lovell Bixby to Warden Hicks. Class 4 Files, File 4-35-3-27, RG 129, NARA–College Park.

42. January 9, 1936, Warden White to Director Bates. Class 4 Files, File 4-35-3-27, RG 129, NARA–College Park.
43. January 3, 1936, Director Bates to Warden White. Class 4 Files, File 4-35-3-38, RG 129, NARA–College Park.
44. January 9, 1936, Warden White to Director Bates. Class 4 Files, File 4-35-3-27, RG 129, NARA–College Park.
45. January 20, 1936, Director Bates to Warden White regarding Mexican Immigration Cases. Class 4 Files, File 4-35-3-27, RG 129, NARA–College Park.
46. March 21, 1933, T. B. White to Director, Bureau of Prisons. Class 4 Files, File 3-35-3-14, RG 129, NARA–College Park. See also La Tuna Rule Book, Class 4 Files, File 3-35-3-14, RG 129, NARA–College Park.
47. La Tuna Rule Book, Class 4 Files, File 3-35-3-14, RG 129, NARA–College Park.
48. March 21, 1933, Warden White to Sanford Bates. Class 4 Files, File 3-35-3-14, RG 129, NARA–College Park. See also La Tuna Rule Book, Class 4 Files, File 3-35-3-14, RG 129, NARA–College Park.
49. September 6, 1933, Director Bates to Warden White. Class 4 Files, File 4-35-3-49, RG 170, NARA–College Park.
50. September 6, 1933, Director Bates to Warden White.
51. November 1, 1933, Warden White to Director Bates. Class 4 Files, File 4-35-3-49, RG 170, NARA–College Park.
52. March 21, 1933, T. B. White to Director Bates. Class 4 Files, File 4-35-3-14, RG 129, NARA–College Park.
53. March 21, 1933, T. B. White to Director Bates.
54. November 6, 1933, Director Bates to Warden White. Class 4 Files, File 4-35-3-49, RG 129, NARA–College Park.
55. March 27, 1933, Asst. Dir. Bennett to Warden White. Class 4 Files, File 4-35-3-29, RG 129, NARA–College Park.
56. Asst. Dir. Bennett to Director Bates. Class 4 Files, File 4-35-3-29, RG 129, NARA–College Park.
57. October 23, 1934, Warden Gaffney to Director Bates. Class 4 Files, File 4-31-4-1, RG 129, NARA–College Park.
58. October 23, 1934, Warden Gaffney to Dir. Bates.
59. List of Escapees from Tucson Prison Camp #10 dated January 1934. Class 4 Files, File 4-31-11-0, RG 129, NARA–College Park.
60. October 5, 1933, Warden Gaffney to W. T. Hammack, Asst. Dir. of the US Bureau of Prisons. Class 4 Files, File 4-31-3-11, RG 129, NARA–College Park.
61. June 24, 1933, James B. Gaffney to Asst. Dir. Bennett. Class 4 Files, File 4-31-3-11, RG 129, NARA–College Park.
62. January 24, 1934, Dir. Bates to Asst. Dir. Bennett. Class 4 Files, File 4-31-11-0, RG 129, NARA–College Park.
63. October 23, 1934, Warden Gaffney to Dir. Bates. Class 4 Files, File 4-31-4-1, RG 129, NARA–College Park.

64. December 21, 1933, Warden Gaffney to Dir. Bates. Class 4 Files, File 4-35-3-46, RG 129, NARA–College Park.

65. 1936 Annual Report, Tucson Prison Camp. Class 4 Files, File 4-31-3-29, RG 129, NARA–College Park.

66. May 6, 1936, Dir. Bates to Warden Gaffney. Class 4 Files, File 4-31-3-29, RG 129, NARA–College Park.

9

The Specter of Compensation

Mexican Claims against the United States, 1923–1941

ALLISON POWERS USECHE

On the morning of October 8, 1922, Ricardo Chaboya and five other workers staged a sit-down strike while building a San Diego road for the California Construction Company. Chaboya, a thirty-nine-year-old man from the Mexican state of Guanajuato, had been laid off two days prior and demanded pay for his time worked. The others sought a raise from $4.50 to $5 per day. Superintendent J. L. Heath arrived on the scene, and eyewitness accounts offer three distinct versions of the events that transpired. Ramón Miranda, Antonio González, and Jesús Granados testified that Heath attacked Chaboya, striking him on the head with a shovel and producing an injury that led to his death.[1] Foreman C. R. Sear conceded that Heath had dealt the fatal blow but suggested that Chaboya instigated the fight by agitating for a strike and insulting the superintendent with language "no white man would take from anybody."[2] Finally, Heath insisted that he struck his former employee to protect himself from a knife that never materialized during the police investigation.[3] The coroner's inquest found Heath not guilty by reason of self-defense, and the county court judge did not initiate a criminal case concerning Chaboya's death.[4]

Altercations like the struggle between Ricardo Chaboya and J. L. Heath were not uncommon during the first decades of the twentieth century in the American West. Historians have long recognized the role of racialized violence in concentrating political and economic power in the region during its protracted incorporation into the United States.[5] Ricardo Chaboya's story was not particularly unusual, but what happened next remains largely absent from the historiography of the region. Chaboya's sister Maximina filed a claim against the US government before the US-Mexico Claims Commission, an international tribunal formed in 1923 to address grievances accumulated between the two states. She argued that by allowing her brother's murder to go unpunished, the United States had violated international legal norms concerning the protection of life and property. And she was not alone. Hundreds of Mexican nationals filed similar claims for relatives who had been killed, injured, or unjustly incarcerated while residing in the United States.

These now-forgotten claims placed the workings of the American justice system under scrutiny at a moment when foreign policymakers sought to institutionalize the US model of private property rights as an international legal standard to be emulated across the globe. This chapter explains how cases like those of Maximina Chaboya posed an unanticipated challenge to a mode of foreign policymaking premised on the exemplarity of the US legal system. By considering how Mexican claims against the United States government transformed an institution designed to project American power abroad into a referendum on the legitimacy of the US political economy, the chapter offers a new explanation for the "turn to nonintervention" in US foreign relations during the era of the Good Neighbor Policy.

An international tribunal may have seemed an unlikely place for Maximina Chaboya to seek justice during the 1920s. Throughout the nineteenth and early twentieth centuries, bilateral arbitrations tended to favor the interests of powerful, capital exporting, and creditor nations along with their nationals.[6] They often concerned investment disputes arising from legislation or court decisions that curtailed the profits of foreign investors.[7] The US-Mexico Claims Commission seemed set to continue this trend. The tribunal was created in response to the 1910–1920 Mexican Revolution, for the express purpose of compensating American property owners for losses resulting from the war and its aftermath. Given the roughly one billion dollars of US investments in Mexico on the eve of the revolution, the State Department was concerned with the redistributive impulses of the 1917 Mexican Constitution, which offered social and labor rights unmatched in the Americas.[8] Foreign investors were particularly alarmed by the implications of the Mexican Constitution's Article 27 because it laid the groundwork for agrarian reform and resource nationalization through government expropriations.

President Warren G. Harding demanded the creation of a new claims settlement tribunal to award compensation for losses to American property owners as a condition of his recognition of the new postrevolutionary Mexican state. President Álvaro Obregón complied, and on September 8, 1923, the United States and Mexico created the General Claims Commission.

The tribunal was designed, like other arbitrations of its kind, to depoliticize injustices suffered by foreign nationals through the mechanism of monetary compensation. Three judges—one American, one Mexican, and one neutral—would decide which claimants deserved compensation for "losses or damages suffered by persons or their property" incurred at the hands of the foreign government.[9] These judges based their rulings on the Law of Nations and in particular on the "standard of civilization": an uncodified set of norms concerning protections for life and property. The standard provided the conceptual foundation for nineteenth- and early twentieth-century international law. Its contents were determined through the writings of international jurists, the decisions of international tribunals, and the actions of states deemed civilized. The United States was at the time accustomed to the assumption that its legal system upheld and even embodied the standard of civilization. In demanding the formation of a claims settlement tribunal in 1923, the State Department appealed to the standard not only to secure compensation for existing American property holders in Mexico but also to shore up an international legal regime that would dissuade other nations from pursuing similar redistributive projects. Secretary of State Charles Evans Hughes directed US representatives at the meetings convened to outline the terms of the Claims Commission to "conserve and strengthen the rules of international conduct" so as to protect the right to private property abroad.[10]

The US-Mexico Claims Commission then seemed poised to limit the redistributive impulse of the Mexican Revolution by securing under international law the right to market-value compensation for expropriated property. However, unlike the postrevolutionary claims commissions created between Mexico and other nations including France, Germany, Italy, Great Britain, Spain, and Japan, this one fell apart. Its collapse stemmed from one crucial difference in structure: the US-Mexico arbitration allowed not only claims of American citizens against Mexico but also cases brought by Mexican citizens against the US government. Given that the previous Claims Commission established between the two nations in 1868 had resulted in a

$4 million dollar debt from Mexico to the United States, the State Department did see significant reason for concern in allowing the tribunal to consider claims from both states.[11]

But after a long-drawn-out period of pleadings, the two governments dissolved the commission in 1937 with three thousand individual cases remaining unresolved. As a result of the privately negotiated lump sum settlement that replaced the tribunal, Mexico paid only a small fraction of the amount of compensation originally demanded by the United States. Historians and legal scholars have attributed the collapse of the Claims Commission to the inherent inefficiency of this form of arbitration, to new military exigencies of World War II, and to the noninterventionist commitments of the Good Neighbor Policy.[12] This chapter offers an additional explanation for the transformation in foreign policy orientation: the United States abandoned the Claims Commission, suspending its hard-line stance against land and resource nationalization in the absence of full compensation, in part because of cases like those of Maximina Chaboya.

Mexican claims against the US government for treatment of its nationals abroad formed a crucial component of the diplomatic struggles between the two nations over the limits of the Good Neighbor Policy's commitment to sovereign equality and nonintervention during the decades following the Mexican Revolution. Although financially far outweighed by the compensation demanded by US property owners from the Mexican government, these cases threatened to challenge a key conceptual and institutional framework through which the State Department articulated its foreign policy of investment protection—one premised on the presumed superiority of the US legal system and enacted through the mechanism of international claims settlement.

Representatives of the Mexican Ministry of Foreign Relations knew that Mexico faced millions of dollars of American claims for expropriated property. Any cases against the US government then held the potential to chip away at some of this looming debt. Ministry of Foreign Relations lawyers recognized that cases like those of Ricardo Chaboya could not monetarily match the amount claimed by American investors concerning loss of profits for mines, railroads, or haciendas. They nonetheless used these incidents to challenge the US government's insistence that its system of private property rights represented the international standard to be met by civilized states. A 1925 report to the Mexican agent in charge of general claims found:

There are many claims that having a similar cause can be presented before the General Commission, where the immense series of murders committed in the United States, many of which are unpunished for the only reason that the murderers were North Americans and the victims Mexicans, would most probably cause a shocking impression. In my concept, this impression will favor the claims presented for this cause, especially if they are carefully prepared and appropriately presented.[13]

Beginning in 1923, government lawyers including Oscar Rabasa, Benito Flores, Roberto Córdova, Eduardo Suárez, and Bartolomé Carvajal y Rosas scoured consular records for potential claims. They did not have to look far. Episodes of violence against individuals of Mexican origin or descent in the United States had produced decades of mounting protest. Reports to local consuls, the efforts of voluntary organizations such as the Sociedad Honorífica Mexicana, and demonstrations in front of American embassies had produced vast paper trails that provided evidence of misconduct among American law enforcement agents. The Ministry of Foreign Relations then used Spanish-language newspapers in the United States to publish calls for additional claimants.[14]

The large response to this call for claims shaped the terms of the cases Mexico could bring against the United States not only by increasing their numbers but also by providing insight into their significance. In a letter to Mexican agent Benito Flores, Adelfa Delgado explained that her father *fue muerto por robarle su trabajo*—was killed in order to steal the products of his labor.[15] Ramón Delgado, a seventy-year-old cotton sharecropper from Coahuila, had been shot and killed by his landlord during a dispute over the terms of their labor contract for a Yancey, Texas, plantation. Observations like Adelfa Delgado's suggested that the murder of Mexican nationals was not a series of isolated incidents but instead a structural feature of the political economy of the American West. The Mexican lawyers who translated these testimonies into litigation then argued that the failure to prosecute cases concerning the death of Mexican nationals demonstrated that the US legal process systematically failed to adhere to the protections for life and property mandated by the standard of civilization.

The United States presented roughly 2,800 claims for almost $514 million before the General Claims Commission, while Mexico advanced 836 claims against the United States for $245 million.[16] Although many of these cases concerned lands taken in violation of the Treaty of Guadalupe Hidalgo—a

topic historians Rodolfo de la Garza and Karl Schmitt have explored—
hundreds concerned far more recent incidents in which the US legal system
had failed to adequately protect the lives of Mexican nationals.[17] These "denial of justice" claims raised the question of how to determine state responsibility for the actions of law enforcement officials and private citizens. A
denial of justice was a mechanism that one state could use to hold another
accountable for treatment of its nationals that did not adhere to international
law. A cornerstone of the law of diplomatic protection of persons and their
property held that sovereign powers were obligated to protect the interests
of their subjects abroad and could demand recourse when their citizens' international legal rights were violated by a foreign government. While often
invoked in regard to investment disputes, the concept could also be used to
consider instances of homicide and personal injury.[18] Throughout the nineteenth and early twentieth centuries, the United States in particular tended
to take a denial of justice involving investment protections much more seriously than a breach of contract or unpaid bonds, even if the financial stakes
involved were comparable, due to the fact that this kind of case posed more
of a perceived ideological threat to the protection of private property under
international law.[19]

Disagreements over the meaning of a denial of justice began with an early
case that came before the General Claims Commission: *The United Mexican
States on behalf of Teodoro García and María Apolinar Garza v. The United
States of America*, decided in 1926. In their majority opinion, neutral and
Mexican commissioners Cornelius van Vollenhoven and Genaro Fernán-
dez MacGregor ruled that the United States had violated international law
when President Woodrow Wilson pardoned an army lieutenant who had
shot and killed nine-year-old Concepción García, while she and her family
were crossing the Rio Grande on April 8, 1919.[20] The Mexican memorial for
the case urged the tribunal to address the problem of how to deal with state
actions such as the pardon "which while they assuredly comply with constitutional requirements, nonetheless transgress the Law of Nations . . . the
principles of Universal Justice accepted by all Nations and which therefore
are a part of International Law."[21] The Mexican and neutral commissioners
ruled that the actions of the US government had fallen below accepted standards for civilized states."[22] As international legal writer Edwin Borchard
noted at the time, this was the first time an international claims commission
had attempted to outline in detail the elements of "an international standard concerning the taking of human life."[23] The dissenting commissioner

on the case, American Fred Nielsen, admitted that "whether the United States is so liable must, in my opinion, be ascertained by a determination of the question whether American law sanctions an act that outrages ordinary standards of civilization."[24] He rejected, however, the outcome of the decision—a $2,000 award for the claimants—citing a lack of evidence as to what kinds of violence the standard of civilization actually prohibited.

Rulings like the *García and Garza* decision threatened to destabilize the presumption that the US legal system operated as an exemplar to be emulated at a moment when the putative superiority of this system served as the key justification for US foreign policymaking. And the case was only one of hundreds that Mexican nationals brought against the US government through the Claims Commission regarding their treatment at the hands of US law enforcement and military agents. The Claims Commission considered cases of mass violence that will be familiar to historians of the American West, if not in their international dimensions. Some sets of pleadings were filed as omnibus claims, such as those stemming from the El Porvenir Massacre of 1918, in which Texas Rangers attacked and summarily executed fifteen unarmed men of Mexican descent on a ranch owned by Manuel Morales.[25] Another set of claims stemmed from the infamous Bisbee Deportation of 1917, where armed vigilantes led by local police imprisoned over one thousand Arizona copper miners in railroad boxcars and "deported" them to the Sonoran desert in response to a strike by the Industrial Workers of the World (IWW).[26] Beyond explicit instances of police and military violence, many more cases concerned the everyday coercion that enforced a racialized system of labor exploitation. Mexican lawyers suggested that episodes of unpunished violence were sanctioned by the American state when Mexican laborers were driven out of town under threat of violence just before the harvest or were murdered after refusing to accept their working conditions.[27]

Lawyers for the Mexican Ministry of Foreign Relations argued that the sheer number of jury acquittals or grand jury decisions not to indict when it came to Mexican nationals killed or injured by white Americans could "not be explained otherwise than by race hatred, very well exemplified as among the Americans in Texas and those Mexicans who are so unfortunate as to venture to contribute their quota to the labor of that region." The racially partial conduct of the American authorities, they concluded, "was not conformable to the general principles of international law, and even less so to the general principles of justice and of equity which are now invoked."[28]

Defending a justice system that allowed this kind of widespread violence and labor coercion to take place, they suggested, "would be to sanction a social regime much below international standards, in which human life would absolutely depend on the bloodthirsty instincts of such officers who by their attitude demonstrate that for them human life has no value."[29]

While the proceedings of the tribunal remained private until the judges issued their decisions, it became increasingly difficult for the federal government to ignore the ongoing problem of state violence against Mexican nationals as the issue took on an increasingly public character during the 1930s. In the midst of violent repressions of labor organizing across industries coupled with repatriation drives that swept up Mexican citizens and US citizens alike in mass deportations, one case of police violence in particular captured the attention of the media, the government, and the public.

On the evening of June 7, 1931, Emilio Cortés Rubio and Manuel García Gómez were fatally shot by Deputy Sheriff William Guess after being pulled over on Highway 77 in Ardmore, Oklahoma—an oil town not far from the Texas border. The incident might have produced a brief flurry of diplomatic notes before being filed away in State Department and Ministry of Foreign Relations archives. But one of the victims happened to be the nephew of Mexican president Pascual Ortiz Rubio. The young men had been traveling home to Mexico from the colleges they attended in Kansas. As a result of their social status, the incident generated extensive press coverage and increased protests against the treatment of Mexicans at the hands of US law enforcement officials. Once the victims' identity became known, American authorities recognized that they had a problem. The governor of Oklahoma sent an urgent telegram to the county attorney of Ardmore, entreating him to tread carefully. "Owing to the standing of the Mexicans and the international aspect with a neighboring republic," Governor William H. Murray explained, "it is essential that you make thorough, complete and unprejudiced investigation."[30] His request did not change the fact that all but one member of the local jury that considered the case were members of the Ku Klux Klan, who found Guess not guilty by reason of self-defense.[31] American ambassador to Mexico J. Reuben Clark Jr. expressed immediate concern that the incident was further straining international relations between the United States and Mexico.[32]

The press response to the "Ardmore incident" demonstrates that debates as to whether or not the US justice system adhered to the standard of civilization were not limited to the realm of high diplomacy but also permeated popular understandings of violence against Mexican nationals in the United States during the 1930s. A June 10, 1931, editorial in *La Prensa* speculated,

> If the authorities act in such a manner—although now, because of the social position of the victims, excuses, etc., are fabricated—what can be expected of the rest of the Americans, above all with regard to Mexicans in humble circumstances? Certainly, one may rest assured that because the youths shot down were Mexicans, the Yankee police had no hesitation in venting their fury upon them with an idiotic idea of "racial superiority" and that if the victims had been some Hernandez or Lopez instead of kin to the President of the Mexican nations, these events would have passed by unnoticed, simply constituting one more example of hatred towards us, and the assassin police would have remained pompous in their classical impunity.[33]

El Gráfico similarly questioned, "If this happens when it is a case of victims who were well known, assassinated in scandalous circumstances, what must it be when unknown Mexican workingmen are assassinated."[34] The *Excelsior* called the case "a typical one of DENIAL of JUSTICE" and called on the Ministry of Foreign Relations to intervene.[35] *El Universal Gráfico* quoted a recent article by William Randolph Hearst to suggest that "we Mexicans should be convinced that the neighboring country is not a civilized one, and that consequently we should not send children, women, or even men to that country, because they can not hope to find culture in a country where it does not exist."[36] The article concluded, "There can be no doubt that the machinery of justice functions badly, very badly, in Yankeeland."[37]

Ambassador to Mexico J. Reuben Clark sent to the State Department a number of cases "for possible assistance" in the matter, including several decided by the General Claims Commission in favor of the United States.[38] But the problem was, he explained, "while in the popular opinion in the United States Mexico is held to be a persistent offender under international law when it comes to the apprehension and conviction of murderers of American citizens in Mexico, the files of the Department do not support that opinion to any great extent."[39] Combing through the department records after 1925, he had found "but one case where it could be charged properly that there had been an absolute denial of justice in this respect."[40]

Clark then "urgently recommend[ed]" that the president ask Congress to appropriate a large sum of money to pay as compensation to Mexico for the Ardmore affair, explaining that this would making pending negotiations over the future of the US-Mexico Claims Commission easier for the State Department to manage.[41] Secretary of State Henry Stimson apprised Congress of the situation, and the "McReynolds bill" was passed on February 22, 1933, authorizing payment of $30,000 to the Mexican government for the incident as an "act of grace" without legal obligation.

While this payment helped to ease diplomatic relations with Mexico, the ongoing cases being heard before the General Claims Commission made growing tensions between the two administrations more acute. The Ardmore murders had produced extensive press coverage of a problem that was long-standing and ongoing in the United States. The hundreds of cases filed against the US government suggested that the police shooting on Highway 77 was far from an isolated incident. US State Department attorney Bert Hunt, who was in charge of defending the US government before the tribunal, expressed increasing concern at the volume and content of cases accumulating against the United States on the tribunal's docket. In 1935, Hunt wrote a series of reports urging the State Department to direct more funds and legal expertise toward the Mexican Claims Committee. Requesting an emergency congressional appropriation bill to fund his work, Hunt explained, "There has never been, to my knowledge, an arbitration in this country anything like the present proportions, which has been successfully completed in anything like the amount of time available to this Agency." Referencing the nearly eight hundred remaining claims against the US government, Hunt concluded, "I cannot overemphasize the fact that now, for the first time, the Agency is confronted with the immediate necessity of defending this Government against Mexican claims, totaling $245,000,000." If said congressional appropriation was not forthcoming, he warned, he would not take responsibility for the outcome of the arbitration.[42]

Hunt was not alone in his concern that the outcome of Claims Commission might not favor the United States. In a memo about the effects of the tribunal for the future of Mexico penned for the secretary of foreign relations, Mexican ambassador to the United States Fernando González Roa expressed confidence that cases documenting lack of adequate legal protections for Mexican nationals residing in the United States were working to destabilize the interpretative authority of the State Department over the contents of the standard of civilization. In doing so, the ambassador suggested, Mexico was effectively undermining the "extremely conservative concept of property" that the United States sought to promote in its foreign relations, thereby paving the way for a new interpretation of the "principles universally sanctioned by international law and that form the norms of conduct between civilized nations."[43]

Hunt and his attorneys at the State Department, including Benjamin Oehlert Jr., Benedict English, Edward Metzler, and H. M. Bishop, recognized that many of the cases brought against the United States would indeed be difficult to defend. But rather than concede defeat, they hedged their legal argument that decedents like Ricardo Chaboya had been killed in self-defense by questioning whether the homicide, personal injury, and incarceration cases in question had generated enough monetary value to merit consideration before an international arbitration tribunal. The lawyers tasked with defending claims against the US government overwhelmingly premised their arguments on two related points: lack of calculable damages and loss of nationality.

Because the US-Mexico Claims Commission was an arbitral tribunal, the question of whether a denial of justice had occurred under international law remained bound up with the issue of whether the market value of the loss of life or earning power could be calculated. A core tenet of arbitration stipulated that claimants would receive awards based on the pecuniary value of their damages. The commissioners worked out a detailed formula for calculating the value of losses due to death, injury, or false imprisonment that included age, earning capacity, probability of increase in earning capacity, relationship to claimant, extent of contributions made toward support of claimant, expenses incurred, mental anguish caused by death, and insurance.[44]

The US agency for the Claims Commission used this calculation formula as a strategy to avoid the legal question of whether a denial of justice had occurred by arguing that claims should be dismissed on the technicality of market value calculation alone. Hunt and his fellow attorneys repeatedly insisted that even if a denial of justice had taken place, the compensation owed would be negligible because the decedents had not earned enough money, or had not earned their money in legitimate ways, for their deaths to have a significant financial impact on their relatives.

In most cases, the United States argued that the decedent's wages had been so low that they could not realistically have contributed significant financial support to their families. In his reply brief for the case of the wrongful killing of Murcio Arredondo by police officers at his home in Mexía, Texas, after Arredondo had reported the officers' attempt to lynch his son to the local Mexican consul, Bert Hunt suggested, "It hardly requires demonstration that, according to all accepted mortality tables, a man of 68 years of age has very nearly reached the twilight of his life expectancy, and certainly the vast majority of persons fortunate enough to arrive at such an age retire from active participation in business affairs . . . his legally calculable prospective earnings would have been negligible indeed."[45]

The US agency further insisted that claimants and their relatives had not been engaged in legitimate forms of labor but instead in criminal activities. Benedict English and H. M. Bishop fell back on the argument that the decedents had been bandits, smugglers, or generally "bad men"—a contention that doubled to support the claim of self-defense in the majority of the ranger and police murder cases. Santos Rivera, for example, according to the US reply brief for the case, "had no trade or occupation; his living was earned at gambling . . . he never worked at all, that is at honest labor."[46] In their answer to the claim of Luis Amezquita Gomar, who had been murdered by a police officer affiliated with the Ku Klux Klan on the pretext of searching for moonshine, Bert Hunt suggested that the decedent's earnings could not be calculated because he was a "notorious bootlegger."[47] In regard to the case of Quirino Cano, who American immigration inspectors shot and killed while he was crossing the Rio Grande, Hunt insisted that "any attempt to calculate damages could be no more than a mere guess as to how long he might succeed in carrying on his illegal traffic and as to what portion of his undetermined receipts from such criminal activities were devoted to the support of the claimant."[48]

State Department attorneys suggested that the claimants' lack of productive economic activity had not only deprived their labor capacity of calculable value but had also resulted in the loss of their Mexican nationality during their residency abroad. Hunt argued that the vast majority of claimants against the US government had lost their Mexican nationality and, as stateless individuals, could not appeal to international law for redress. There were two principal ways he attempted to establish that Mexican claimants had become stateless. The first concerned the marital status of the claimants, many of whom were women claiming compensation as the wives, daughters, and sisters of parties injured or killed in the United States. Historians have demonstrated that women in the United States were particularly vulnerable to statelessness during the interwar years, as their nationality followed that of their husbands.[49] This work has focused on the problem of women who were denaturalized from their US citizenship through marriage to foreigners. The State Department's response to Mexican claims reveals another dimension of the federal government's invocation of statelessness to meet its political goals during the same period. The US agency argued that claimants were stateless not by revoking their US citizenship but by challenging their Mexican nationality. Lawyers for the United States suggested that because the claimants could not provide documentation concerning the nationality of their husbands, they could not establish their own statuses as Mexican citizens.[50] In the *Chaboya* case, the US agency mistakenly treated Maximina as though she were the decedent's wife, when she was actually his sister. But overall the strategy was effective at limiting the number of cases that could be brought against the United States. Many who filed claims concerning their husbands had trouble obtaining the necessary paperwork to establish their nationality due to the destruction of birth and baptismal records during the Mexican Revolution and the lack of documentation needed to travel across the US-Mexico border prior to the Johnson-Reed Immigration Act of 1924.

The second strategy the United States used to cast Mexican claimants as stateless individuals more explicitly concerned the question of commercial personhood. Hunt argued that most claimants had lost their Mexican citizenship because they had resided for too long in the United States without engaging in legitimate economic pursuits. To prove this assertion, he regularly cited chapter I, article 2 of the May 28, 1886, Mexican law of Alienship and Naturalization, which stipulated: "The following are aliens: Those absent from the Republic without permission or commission from the Government, excepting in order to prosecute their studies, or in the interests of the public, or for the establishment of trade or industry, or in the practice of a profession, who allow ten years to elapse without asking permission to prolong their absence."[51]

Hunt proposed that this provision was automatic in its operation. A lack of Mexican government records, bolstered by the fact that claimants by definition had to demonstrate that they relied financially on their deceased relatives in order to advance a claim, paved the way for the United States to argue that both decedents and claimants had lost their Mexican nationality in almost every single denial of justice case pleaded in 1935 or after. While the Mexican agency also maintained that certain claimants were not US citizens, the contents and scale of their respective arguments differed dramatically. Mexico only invoked a loss of nationality in regard to a handful of claims, whereas the United States invoked it in hundreds of cases. Furthermore, Mexican lawyers suggested that certain claimants had lost their US nationality by acquiring a new one, whereas their American counterparts predicated their assertions on the concept of statelessness.

Denationalization was a concerted strategy of the US agency evidenced not only by its regularity but also through correspondence. Bert Hunt routinely sent letters to employers and public officials from the towns where claimants lived seeking evidence "desired for the purpose of showing that the several claimants were not Mexican nationals at the time this claim was filed in 1925, or that they [had] since lost their Mexican nationality."[52] So frequently did US lawyers attempt to denationalize Mexican claimants, Roberto Córdova and Alfredo del Valle Gomez observed that it had become "systemic for the Agency of the United States to deny the established nationality of the claimants."[53] Oscar Rabasa further argued that "by accepting the thesis of the United States it would be materially impossible to prove the Mexican nationality of the claimants, because that theory of the Agency of the United States, concerning which the attention of the Honorable Commissioners is respectfully called, can be summed up thus: to deny in all cases the proof of the nationality of Mexican Claimants, whatever that proof may be."[54]

Because the legal mechanism of compensation necessitated explicit articulation of which forms of life and labor produce economic value, claimants were able to challenge the legal doctrines and economic models judges used to assign awards by demonstrating that the supposedly independent variables used to calculate compensation—wages, life expectancy, and citizenship status—were themselves the result of structural injustices perpetuated by the US legal system in violation of international norms. Mexican lawyers instead suggested that "because the fact that the deceased did not enjoy a great income does not imply that the claimants might not have sustained material damages, because, being poor people, any circumstance directly injuring their economic status, was of great importance, and precisely on account of their humble position they had to feel the loss of the head of the family, since the wife was left destitute with the children and in the worst economic conditions which she had to confront in her struggle for life."[55] Furthermore, they pointed to the exploitative labor conditions throughout the United States and within Texas in particular, where the majority of these claims originated, to argue that wages were not a just gauge of compensation. In the case of Bernabé Garcia, who was shot and killed by a deputy sheriff in a saloon near Donna, Texas, Rabasa suggested the problematic nature of a compensatory mechanism that based its awards on wages that were unjustly suppressed through violence in the first place. He argued that it was not enough to award a claim "based on the rate of wages of a minimum character of such Mexican day laborers, established in Texas, and, in general, in the South of the United States."[56]

These protracted disputes over seemingly given legal facts concerning the earning power and citizenship status of claimants significantly prolonged the pleadings process of the US-Mexico Claims Commission. The volume of briefs, counterarguments, motions to dismiss, and requests for additional evidence attached to each case became too much for either agency to keep up with. In 1936, Mexico and the United States restructured the tribunal so that two new commissioners—Oscar Underwood and Benito Flores—could examine the existing pleadings to efficiently rule on the hundreds of remaining cases to be decided.

The stakes of the outcome of the tribunal had never been higher. Early negotiations between the United States and Mexico following the revolution—particularly the 1923 Bucareli conference and 1928 Calles-Morrow agreement—had promised to protect most American property owners in Mexico from outright expropriation. This commitment dissolved with the 1934 election of Mexican president Lázaro Cárdenas, who represented a radical departure from the policies of his predecessors with regard to the control of foreign capital over the Mexican economy. Cárdenas gave teeth to the redistributive impulses of the 1917 Constitution beginning with a series of agrarian land expropriations in 1936 and culminating in his decision to nationalize the Mexican oil industry in 1938.[57]

The State Department expressed increasing concern to Mexican ambassador Francisco Castillo Nájera over the direction of the Cárdenas administration. His politics threatened not only to impinge on foreign investments in Mexico but also to challenge domestic labor structures in the United States. These fears seemed realized when in March 1936, Mexican consul at Laredo Juan E. Richer was reported to have presided over a labor meeting "called for the purpose of organizing a labor union composed of all laborers of the Mexican race whether born in the United States or Mexico"[58] American government officials quickly responded with outrage, criticizing the consul for overstepping the limitations of his rights and duties as a diplomat posted abroad and thereby upending the international rules of diplomatic relations. It did not help matters that Richer was quoted as having stated that he was present at the meeting at the explicit instruction of his government, as part of a larger project of "organizing the laborers against inroads and encroachments of capitalism" in which "the Laboring class must act and resolve their social conquests."[59]

Assistant Secretary of State Benjamin Sumner Welles warned Castillo Nájera of potential "grave consequences" if the Mexican president did not stop his consuls from intervening in matters of domestic politics, registering particular outrage at the idea that a consul would attempt to use his nationals "as instruments of class struggle."[60] He urged the Mexican president, ambassador, and consul to promise to limit themselves to the traditional role under international law to protect Mexican nationals.[61] But as the proceedings of the Claims Commission had amply demonstrated, the question of protecting the lives and property of nationals abroad could not be fully disentangled from the problem of securing better labor conditions in the United States. It was precisely this problem that Underwood and Flores confronted in their consideration of outstanding claims.

Given that cases concerning US investors represented the financial bulk of the remaining cases to be considered before the commission, it is striking that Underwood and Flores called their initial meetings in Mexico City primarily "to discuss general principles, particularly with regard to death cases and citizenship."[62] When they met in Washington to begin appraising cases, they again started with the homicide claims.[63] As Underwood found, "acts of violence by police officers had been the most fruitful source of ill-will between the nationals of our two countries."[64] The transcripts of their meetings demonstrate that the majority of their discussions remained centered on how to determine state responsibility for acts of violence, what constituted legitimate acts of self-defense, and how to establish evidence of nationality—precisely the questions that had been raised by both agencies in the context of Mexican denial of justice claims against the United States. In the end, Underwood and Flores agreed on the validity of only 110 cases.[65] The remaining claims they either agreed to disallow, disagreed on, or did not have a chance to discuss.

As a result, the General Claims Commission closed its doors in 1937 with thousands of cases left undecided. The two governments worked toward reaching a "global settlement" that would include general claims as well as outstanding agrarian and oil claims generated in response to the more recent expropriations enacted under the Cárdenas administration. The Mexican Ministry of Foreign Relations depicted early negotiations over a global settlement as a victory for Mexico on the global stage. A 1938 report stated that Mexico had "continued consolidating its international reputation in accordance with the principles that serve to guide the governments emanating from the Revolution."[66] In the last diplomatic note issued by Mexico before the settlement was finalized, minister of foreign affairs Eduardo Hay wrote to the secretary of state, Cordell Hull, that since the General Claims Commission had not yet assessed all outstanding claims, it was "not known which of the two countries is going to turn out to be the creditor and which one the debtor."[67] While the amount of money claimed by the United States far exceeded that claimed by Mexico, the ongoing disputes over Mexican cases against the US government made it difficult for the United States to use the Claims Commission as an instrument to protect an interpretation of property rights favorable to US foreign investors throughout the Americas.

The appraisals of Flores and Underwood, though never officially published as rulings by the tribunal, shaped the terms of the lump settlement that replaced the Claims Commission's mandate to individually adjudicate all cases. Their findings were not made available to Congress or the public but were used to calculate the amount of money the United States owed to Mexico.[68] Ultimately, Underwood confessed to Secretary of State Hull that he had been "forced to the conclusion that present events and the developments of the times are such that conditions are not yet ripe for a full and free arbitration of these matters between Mexico and the United States."[69]

The lump settlement agreement, finalized in 1941 under the Manuel Ávila Camacho administration, marked an unprecedented victory for Mexico in which the United States effectively underwrote a "token payment" from Mexico for expropriated property.[70] When American politicians, constituents, and the media caught wind of the settlement negotiations, many were indignant. One newspaper asked if Mexico had "Pulled a Fast One" on the United States.[71] The *New York Times* emphasized "the importance of the precedent that would be set if the United States Treasury, in effect, were to finance the Mexican expropriation of American property at a time when other Latin American States have expropriated or are tempted to expropriate foreign capital."[72] Contemporary legal scholar Herbert W. Briggs instead noted in the *American Journal of International Law*, "While it might thus appear that the United States Government is financing the payment of claims by Mexico, the international responsibility of Mexico to pay for damage to American nationals has been accepted."[73] This focus on the Claims Commission as an institution that protected the rights of foreign investors from the threat of resource nationalization has largely been reproduced in subsequent legal and historical scholarship. It is a narrative that obscures the struggles that took place during the tenure of the tribunal, over the kinds of property rights—in life and labor, as well as real estate—that international law would recognize and protect.

Before it was shuttered, the US-Mexico Claims Commission considered a series of legal battles over not only the legality of resource nationalization but also the role of legal institutions in promoting racialized models of economic coercion in the American West. As demonstrated through cases like those of Ricardo Chaboya, the question of labor coercion as a function of state violence became a fundamental problem that the United States and Mexico confronted during the pleadings of the Claims Commission and then eschewed when the tribunal dissolved. As a result of this settlement, Mexico avoided paying the majority of compensation initially demanded by American investors, while the United States prevented the precedent of an arbitral tribunal ruling that its justice system violated international legal norms. Nonetheless, the questions of state violence that the tribunal considered played an important if subtle role in determining how the Good Neighbor Policy's putative commitments to nonintervention and sovereign equality would actually be implemented in the presence of a major threat to American financial interests abroad.

The majority of the Mexican claimants who brought cases before the Claims Commission never saw the justice they sought or the compensation they demanded. Adelfa Delgado de la Garza's final letter to the Mexican secretary of foreign relations is particularly revealing. "Realizing by reading the newspaper that the Claims Commission has already ended," she wrote to Bartolomé Carvajal y Rosas in 1931,

> I want you to tell me why you did not let me know on time for me to pursue other options. Look, they killed my father, they robbed him of all of the products of his labor, ninety acres of cultivated cotton and corn; and given that these "Gringos" are so afraid of the idea of theft, how is it possible that they murdered and stole from my father, and that despite his obvious guilt this "Gringo" P. S. Childress (as the murderer is named), that they [the commission] have not ruled on my claim?[74]

If the Mexican secretary of foreign relations pursued no further legal action against the US government in this matter, Delgado de la Garza threatened, she would be forced to make a claim against the Mexican government.[75] But she would continue to wait. The Mexican government promised to pay claimants "when the treasury permitted."[76] In 1955, over five hundred claimants formed an organization to demand their outstanding compensation.[77] They were not successful, and the organization dissolved as individual claimants continued to seek remedies through the Mexican Treasury.[78] When a group of claimants filed a lawsuit in the US District Court for Washington, DC, in 1983, the case was dismissed for lack of jurisdiction.[79]

This chapter has considered how the Mexican and US federal governments used the claims advanced by their legal subjects to promote their respective political economic systems through the process of international arbitration. It has argued that Mexican claims against the United States transformed an institutional framework designed to project United States power abroad into an unexpected site of contestation over the legitimacy of the American justice system. The United States invoked arbitration to challenge the ability of the Mexican government to nationalize property in land and resources. The Mexican agency instead sought to destabilize the authority of the State Department to interpret the contents of international law by suggesting that the United States engaged in its own model of illegal wealth redistribution by allowing forms of racial violence and labor coercion that violated the standard of civilization.

In the end, the US-Mexico Claims Commission did not fully endorse either model of property rights. But the competing visions of international law proposed during the fifteen-year tenure of the tribunal were not without consequence. If the terms of the global settlement obscured from the international legal record a moment when arbitral judges actively considered how police violence and economic coercion operated as forms of wealth distribution for which states might be held responsible under international law, Mexican claims against the United States challenged the ability of the State Department to invoke the standard of civilization to justify interventions abroad. In doing so, they prompted foreign policymakers to develop new legal concepts and institutions to promote US interests across the Americas and beyond.

When Ricardo Chaboya was murdered at the San Diego construction site, the local coroner's jury determined that his killer had acted in self-defense. Before an international tribunal a decade later, judges concluded that if Chaboya's family deserved compensation, it would be calculated through wages that he had been protesting on the day he died. When witnesses risked their own safety to report what they had seen to their local Mexican consul, they formed part of a diverse range of claimants from San Diego, California, to San Sebastian, Texas, who challenged the assumption that the American justice system offered exemplary protections for life and property.

Cases like those of Ricardo Chaboya illuminate the rise and fall of a forgotten vision of international legal order. International tribunals ultimately became forums for punishing spectacular atrocity rather than for promoting collective welfare. International law has now largely bifurcated into distinct institutions designed to address physical violence on the one hand and wealth distribution on the other. But these developments were not foregone conclusions. The records of the US-Mexico General Claims Commission reveal visions of a world in which grand jury decisions could be held accountable to review by international tribunals, racial wage differentials represented a form of expropriation that required compensation, and the specter of lawlessness could be invoked to reveal that the American justice system fell short of the standard of civilization it was thought to embody. The political battles, labor actions, and press coverage that shaped the terms of the US-Mexico Claims Commission demonstrate the ways international legal disputes have naturalized—but also disrupted—accepted assumptions about the legitimacy of wealth distribution and political power in the American West.

Notes

1. Oscar Rabasa and Vicente Sánchez Gavito Jr., Brief of The United Mexican States on behalf of Maximina Chaboya v. The United States of America, Claim No. 539, 8; General Claims Commission, Mexican Claims Against U.S., Dockets 538–539; box 39, Folder Pleadings; Records of Boundary and Claims Commissions and Arbitrations, Record Group 76; National Archives and Records Administration—College Park, MD (hereafter cited as NARA–College Park).

2. J. Reuben Clark Jr. and Charles Kerr, Answer of the United States in the Case of The United Mexican States on behalf of Maximina Chaboya v. The United States of America, Docket No. 539, Annex 1, 6; General Claims Commission, Mexican Claims Against U.S. Dockets 538–539; box 39, Folder Pleadings; Records of Boundary and Claims Commissions and Arbitrations, Record Group 76, NARA–College Park.

3. Oscar Rabasa and Vicente Sánchez Gavito Jr., Brief of The United Mexican States on behalf of Maximina Chaboya v. The United States of America, 8.

4. Oscar Rabasa and Vicente Sánchez Gavito Jr., Brief of The United Mexican States on behalf of Maximina Chaboya v. The United States of America, 2.

5. See in particular David Montejano, *Anglos and Mexicans in the Making of Texas, 1836–1986* (Austin: University of Texas Press, 1987); Linda Gordon, *The Great Arizona Orphan Abduction* (Cambridge: Harvard University Press, 1999); María Montoya, *Translating Property: The Maxwell Land Grant and the Conflict over Land in the American West, 1840–1900* (Berkeley: University of California Press, 2002); Benjamin Johnson, *Revolution in Texas: How a Forgotten Rebellion and Its Bloody Suppression Turned Mexicans into Americans* (New Haven: Yale University Press, 2003); Zaragosa Vargas, *Labor Rights Are Civil Rights: Mexican American Workers in Twentieth-Century America* (Princeton: Princeton University Press, 2005); Katherine Benton-Cohen, *Borderline Americans: Racial Division and Labor War in the Arizona Borderlands* (Cambridge: Harvard University Press, 2009); and William D. Carrigan and Clive Webb, *Forgotten Dead: Mob Violence Against Mexicans in the United States, 1848–1928* (Oxford: Oxford University Press, 2013).

6. Benjamin Coates, "Transatlantic Advocates: American International Law and U.S. Foreign Relations, 1898–1919" (PhD diss., Columbia University, 2010): 228.

7. See Jan Paulsson, *Denial of Justice in International Law* (Cambridge: Cambridge University Press, 2005); Kate Miles, *The Origins of International Investment Law: Empire, the Environment, and the Safeguarding of Capital* (Cambridge: Cambridge University Press, 2013); and Martins Paparinskis, *The International Minimum Standard and Fair and Equitable Treatment* (Oxford: Oxford University Press, 2013). Remedios Gómez Arnau, in *México y la protección de sus nacionales en Estados Unidos* (Mexico City: Centro de Investigaciones sobre Estados Unidos de América, Universidad Nacional Autónoma de México, 1990), 127–128, demonstrates the importance of local consuls in Mexico's attempt to protect the rights of its nationals in the late nineteenth and early twentieth centuries. While the book mentions the Claims Commission in the context of US investments in Mexico, it does not examine the denial of justice claims Mexico brought against the United States.

8. Alan Knight, *U.S.-Mexico Relations, 1910–1940: An Interpretation* (La Jolla: Center for U.S.-Mexican Studies, University of California, San Diego, 1987), 21.

9. Article I, United States–Mexico General Claims Convention of September 8, 1923.

10. Robert Freeman Smith, "Estados Unidos y la Revolución Mexicana, 1921–1950," in *Mitos en las relaciones México Estados Unidos* (Mexico City: Secretaría de Relaciones Exteriores: Fondo de Cultura Económica, 1994), 216.

11. John Dwyer, *The Agrarian Dispute: The Expropriation of American Owned Rural Land in Post-Revolutionary Mexico* (Durham, NC: Duke University Press, 2008), 268.

12. See Noel Maurer, *The Empire Trap: The Rise and Fall of U.S. Intervention to Protect American Property Overseas, 1893–2013* (Princeton: Princeton

University Press, 2013) for the argument that 1938 marked the "end of empire" when the American government did not force Mexico to pay compensation for most of the oil expropriated from American companies. In *The Agrarian Dispute*, John Dwyer explains the favorable terms of the 1941 Global Settlement for Mexico as arising out of Cárdenas' diplomacy, but does not mention the denial of justice cases that came before the US-Mexico General Claims Commission. George Herring, in *From Colony to Superpower: U.S. Foreign Relations Since 1776* (New York: Oxford University Press, 2008), explains the late 1930s "turn to nonintervention" in American foreign policy in terms of large-scale ideological and strategic shifts in global politics.

13. Expediente VI-73/242(72:73)/81, Reclamante: Alejandra Andrade de Carrillo, 1925; Fondo Reclamaciones; Archivo Histórico Genaro Estrada de la Secretaría de Relaciones Exteriores de México, Mexico City.

14. Rodolfo O. de la Garza and Karl Schmitt, "Texas Land Grants and Chicano-Mexican Relations: A Case Study," *Latin American Research Review* 21, no. 1 (1986): 127.

15. Adelfa Delgado de la Garza to Benito Flores, 8 de agosto de 1930; Expediente VI.73/242(72:73)/115, Reclamante: Adelfa, Dorotea, Cecilia y Amada Delgado; Fondo Reclamaciones; Archivo Histórico Genaro Estrada de la Secretaría de Relaciones Exteriores de México, Mexico City.

16. de la Garza and Schmitt, "Texas Land Grants and Chicano-Mexican Relations," 126–127.

17. I consider here only Mexican claims against the United States originating in US territory. Many more claims came from the Mexican side of the US-Mexico border and from Vera Cruz during the US invasion and occupation in 1914. There were initially many more than three hundred claims like these brought before the tribunal, but for the purposes of expediency, the Mexican government grouped similar cases into omnibus claims.

18. Miles, *Origins of International Law*, 52.

19. Miles, *Origins of International Law*, 52.

20. Teodoro García and M. A. Garza (United Mexican States) v. United States of America, December 3, 1926, dissenting opinion by American Commissioner, undated, in *United Nations, Reports of International Arbitral Awards, General Claims Commission (Agreement of Sept. 8, 1923) (United Mexican States, United States of America)*, vol. 4 (2006): 119–134.

21. Por María Apolinar Garza, que no sabe firmar: Manuel Montemayor; Por Teodoro García, que no sabe firmar: Pablo C. Ornelas; signed, Benito Flores, Memorial of The United Mexican States on behalf of Teodoro García and María Apolinar Garza v. The United States of America, Docket No. 292, 4; General Claims Commission, Mexican Claims Against U.S. Dockets 290-293, box 5, Folder Docket 292 Pleadings; US and Mexico General Claims Commission; RG 76, NARA–College Park.

22. Fred Nielsen, dissenting opinion in the case of Teodoro García and M. A. Garza

(United Mexican States) v. United States of America, December 3, 1926. Dissenting opinion by American Commissioner, undated in *United Nations, Reports of International Arbitral Awards, General Claims Commission (Agreement of Sept. 8, 1923) (United Mexican States, United States of America)*, vol. 4 (2006): 123.

23. Edwin Borchard, "Important Decisions of the Mixed Claims Commission United States and Mexico," *American Journal of International Law* 21, no. 3 (July 1927): 519.

24. Fred Nielsen, dissenting opinion in the case of Teodoro García and M. A. Garza (United Mexican States) v. United States of America, December 3, 1926. Dissenting opinion by American Commissioner, undated in *United Nations, Reports of International Arbitral Awards, General Claims Commission (Agreement of Sept. 8, 1923) (United Mexican States, United States of America)*, vol. 4 (2006): 127.

25. Oscar Rabasa, The United Mexican States on behalf of Concepción Carrasco de González, Jesús García, Victoria Jiménez de García, Librada M. Jacquez, Eulalia González, Juana Bonilla, Rita Jacquez, Severiano Morales, Alejandro Nieves, Francisca Morales, Pablo Jiménez y Luis Jiménez, U.S. Dockets 561, 655, 873, 1081, 1040, 1041, and 3040, 17–18; General Claims Commission, Mexican Claims Against U.S. Docket 561; box 51, Folder Pleadings; Records of Boundary and Claims Commissions and Arbitrations, Record Group 76, NARA–College Park.

26. Oscar Rabasa and Guillermo E. Tamayo, Alegato de Los Estados Unidos Mexicanos en nombre de Francisco C. Lopez, contra Los Estados Unidos de América, Reclamación número 2914, 18; General Claims Commission, Mexican Claims Against U.S. Dockets 2912–2914; box 182, Folder Docket 2914 Pleadings; Records of Boundary and Claims Commissions and Arbitrations, Record Group 76, NARA–College Park. For discussion of Bisbee Deportation, see Katherine Benton-Cohen, *Borderline Americans,* and Christopher Capozzola, *Uncle Sam Wants You: World War I and the Making of the Modern American Citizen* (New York: Oxford University Press, 2008), 125–131.

27. Memorial, The United Mexican States on behalf of Jesus Barajas Robles v. The United States of America, 1; General Claims Commission, Mexican Claims Against U.S. Dockets 371–372; box 29 Folder Docket No. 372; RG 76; NARA–College Park. See also Oscar Rabasa and Román Cabello Jr., Brief of The United Mexican States on behalf of María de Jesus Facundo de García and Guillermo Ortiz v. The United States of America, Claim Nos. 2902 and 450, September 23, 1935, 3; General Claims Commission, Mexican Claims Against U.S. Dockets 2901–2903; box 108, Folder Pleadings; RG 76; NARA–College Park.

28. Angela Ibarra Vda. de Gómez and Benito Flores, Memorial of The United Mexican States on behalf of Angela Ibarra de Gómez and her children Guadalupe, Pedro, Delfina, Genaro, Braulio, Román Juliana, Reynaldo and Gilberto Gómez v. the United States of America, Docket No. 536, July 19, 1925, 2–3; box 37

Folder Pleadings; General Claims Commission, Mexican Claims Against U.S. Dockets 534–536; RG 76, NARA–College Park.

29. Oscar Rabasa and Jose S. Gallástegui, Brief of The United Mexican States on behalf of Angela Ibarra widow of Gómez and her children, Docket No. 536. October 19, 1935, 4–5; box 37, Folder Docket 536 Pleadings; General Claims Commission, Mexican Claims Against U.S. Dockets 534-536; RG 76, NARA–College Park.

30. Telegram from William H. Murray to County Attorney of Ardmore, Oklahoma, June 8, 1931; Enclosure in William H. Murray to Cordell Hull, December 5, 1934; Department of State Decimal File 411.12 Gomez and Rubio/138; box 1882; Department of State Decimal File 1930–39 From 411.12 Gomez & Rubio/65 to 140; box 1882; RG 59, NARA–College Park.

31. William H. Murray to Cordell Hull, December 5, 1934, 2; Department of State Decimal File 411.12 Gomez and Rubio/138; box 1882; RG 59 Department of State Decimal File 1930–39 From 411.12 Gomez & Rubio/65 to 140; RG 59, NARA–College Park.

32. J. Reuben Clark Jr. to Secretary of State, June 15, 1931, 1; Department of State Decimal File 411.12 Gomez and Rubio/25; box 1882; Department of State Decimal File 1930–39 From 411.12 Gomez & Rubio/65 to 140; RG 59, NARA–College Park.

33. Enclosure 13: *La Prensa,* June 10, 1931 Editorial: "The Mexicans in Yankee Land," 2 in J. Reuben Clark Jr. to Henry L. Stimson, June 11, 1931; Department of State Decimal File 411.12 Gomez and Rubio/29; box 1882; Department of State Decimal File 1930–39 From 411.12 Gomez & Rubio/65 to 140; RG 59, NARA–College Park.

34. "The Famous Gringo Justice," *El Gráfico,* November 23, 1931; Enclosure in J. Reuben Clark Jr. to Henry L. Stimson, December 1, 1931, 2; Department of State Decimal File 411.12 Gomez and Rubio/89; Department of State Decimal File 1930–39 From 411.12 Gomez & Rubio/65 to 140; RG 59, NARA–College Park.

35. Enclosure 2: "Oklahoma Justice," *Excelsior,* November 24, 1941, 4; Enclosure in J. Reuben Clark Jr. to Henry L. Stimson, December 1, 1931; Department of State Decimal File 411.12 Gomez and Rubio/89; box 1882; Department of State Decimal File 1930–39 From 411.12 Gomez & Rubio/65 to 140; RG 59, NARA–College Park.

36. "A Handful of Gold in Exchange for their Blood!," *El Universal,* December 5, 1931, 1; Enclosure in J. Reuben Clark Jr. to Henry L. Stimson, December 7, 1931; Department of State Decimal File 411.12 Gomez and Rubio/92; box 1882; Department of State Decimal File 1930–39 From 411.12 Gomez & Rubio/65 to 140; RG 59, NARA–College Park.

37. J. Reuben Clark Jr. to Henry L. Stimson, December 7, 1931, 4.

38. J. Reuben Clark Jr. to Henry L. Stimson, December 1, 1931; Department of State Decimal File 411.12 Gomez & Rubio/85; box 1882; Department of State

Decimal File 1930–39 From 411.12 Gomez & Rubio/65 to 140; RG 59, NARA–College Park.

39. Green Hackworth, "Memorandum In Re Payment to Mexican Relatives of Victims of Ardmore Shooting Affray," April 11, 1932, 1; Department of State Decimal File 411.12 Gomez and Rubio/98; box 1882; Department of State Decimal File 1930–39 From 411.12 Gomez & Rubio/65 to 140; RG 59, NARA–College Park.

40. Hackworth, "Memorandum In re Payment to Mexican Relatives of Victims of Ardmore Shooting Affray," 1–2.

41. Hackworth, "Memorandum In re Payment to Mexican Relatives of Victims of Ardmore Shooting Affray," 2.

42. Bert Hunt to The Mexican Claims Committee, February 20, 1935; Department of State Decimal File 411.12 P/951; box 1885; Department of State Decimal File 1930–39 From 411.12 P/769 to 951; RG 59, NARA–College Park.

43. Fernando González Roa, "Effects of the Convention for the Future of Mexico," April 5, 1933, 21–27; Expediente 21, Legajo 1, Inventario 2473, Fojas 4–5; González Roa, Relaciones México; Archivo Plutarco Elías Calles; Fidecomeiso Archivos Plutarco Elías Calles y Fernando Torreblanca, Mexico City.

44. Oscar Underwood, "Memorandum on Measure of Damages," 1; box 1, Untitled Folder; Appraisals of Claims by Commissioner Underwood; US and Mexico General Claims Commission, 1924–37; RG 76, NARA–College Park.

45. Bert L. Hunt, B. H. Oehlert Jr., and B. M. English, Reply Brief of the United States, Docket No. 1025, The United Mexican States on behalf of Genaro Arredondo y Guadalupe Méndez viuda de Arredondo and their children, Genaro, Eleuterio, Emilio, Nemesio, Estefano and Antonio v. The United States of America, 18; box 112, Folder Pleadings; General Claims Commission, Mexican Claims Against U.S. Dockets 1023–1025; RG 76, NARA–College Park.

46. Bert L. Hunt, Benjamin H. Oehlert Jr., and Benedict M. English, Reply Brief of The United Mexican States on behalf of Virginia Estrada Viuda de Rivera, Santos, Flavio and Alicia Rivera. v. The United States of America, Docket No. 344, 79; box 25, Folder Docket 344 Pleadings; General Claims Commission, Mexican Claims Against U.S. Dockets 433–367; RG 76, NARA–College Park.

47. Bert L. Hunt, Answer of the United States in the case of The United Mexican States on behalf of Cecilia Buzo vda. de Amezquita v. The United States of America, Docket No. 1032, 5; box 104, Folder Docket 1032 Pleadings; General Claims Commission, Mexican Claims Against U.S. Dockets 1030–1033; RG 76, NARA–College Park.

48. Bert L. Hunt and Benjamin H. Oehlert Jr., Reply Brief of the United States in the case of The United Mexican States on behalf of Soledad García vda. de Cano v. The United States of America, Docket No. 558, 25–26; box 49, Folder Docket 558 Pleadings; General Claims Commission, Mexican Claims Against U.S. Dockets 557–558; RG 76, NARA–College Park.

49. See for example Linda Kerber, "Toward a History of Statelessness in America,"

in Mary L. Dudziak and Leti Volpp, eds., *Legal Borderlands: Law and the Construction of American Borders* (Baltimore: Johns Hopkins Press, 2006), 135; Patrick Weil, *The Sovereign Citizen: Denaturalization and the Origins of the American Republic* (Philadelphia: University of Pennsylvania Press, 2013).

50. Oscar Rabasa and Indalecio Sánchez Gavito, Mexican Counter-Brief in the case of The United Mexican States on behalf of Maximina Chaboya v. The United States of America, Docket 539, 4; box 39, Folder Docket 539 Pleadings; General Claims Commission, Mexican Claims Against U.S. Dockets 538–539; RG 76, NARA–College Park.

51. Oscar Rabasa and Indalecio Sánchez Gavito, Mexican Counter-Brief in the case of The United Mexican States on behalf of Maximina Chaboya v. The United States of America, Docket 539.

52. Bert L. Hunt to Frank H. Crockett, Inspector in Charge, United States Immigration Service, Laredo, Texas, September 25, 1935, 3; box 23, Folder Docket 323 Correspondence; General Claims Commission, Mexican Claims Against U.S. Docket 323; RG 76, NARA–College Park.

53. Roberto Córdova and Alfredo del Valle Gomez, Brief of The United Mexican States on behalf of Juan Ortiz Cavazos, Irineo Villanueva and Luisa Villanueva (Filed in the Memorandum in the name of Juan Ortiz Cavazos) v. The United States of America, Docket 2920, September 2, 1936, 7; box 185, Folder Docket 2920 Pleadings; General Claims Commission, Mexican Claims Against U.S. Dockets 2919–2921; RG 76, NARA–College Park.

54. Oscar Rabasa and J. Costas Enríquez, Brief of The United Mexican States on behalf of Cayetano L. González v. The United States of America, Docket No. 2928, November 30, 1935, 7–8; box 189, Folder Docket No. 2928 Pleadings; General Claims Commission, Mexican Claims Against U.S., Dockets 2927–2929; RG 76, NARA–College Park.

55. Roberto Córdova and Oscar Treviño Ríos, Counter Brief, The United Mexican States on behalf of Genaro Arredondo, Guadalupe Mendea vda. de Arredondo, and Genaro, Eleuterio, Emilio, Nemesio, Estefano and Antonio Arredondo, v. The United States of America, Docket No. 1025, nd., 37; box 112, Folder Pleadings; General Claims Commission, Mexican Claims Against U.S. Dockets 1023–1025; RG 76, NARA–College Park.

56. Brief of The United Mexican States on behalf of Florencia Saenz, widow of García, Octaviano García, América García, Rosa Estela García and M. Concepción Garcia v. The United States of America, Docket No. 223, 10; box 1, Folder Docket 223 Pleadings; General Claims Commission, Mexican Claims Against U.S. Dockets 212–223; RG 76, NARA–College Park.

57. Lorenzo Meyer, *Mexico and the United States in the Oil Controversy, 1917–1942* (Austin: University of Texas Press, 1977).

58. Phineas Nell to Francisco Castillo Nájera, March 20, 1936, 1; Incidente Cónsules Mexicanos en Texas," Leg. 21; APFCN 120; Archivo Histórico Genaro Estrada de la Secretaría de Relaciones Exteriores, Mexico City.

59. Nell to Castillo Nájera, March 20, 1936, 2.
60. Francisco Castillo Nájera to Lázaro Cárdenas, March 20, 1936, 1–3; Incidentes Cónsules en Texas, Leg. 21 APFCN 120; Archivo Histórico Genaro Estrada de la Secretaría de Relaciones Exteriores, Mexico City.
61. Castillo Nájera to Cárdenas, March 20, 1936, 9.
62. Oscar W. Underwood Jr. and Benito Flores, Conferences in Mexico April 3–7, 1936, Narrative Report, 3, April 3, 1936; box 1; International Claims Commissions. US and Mexican Claims Commissions; US and Mexico General Claims Commission 1924–37; Narrative Reports of Underwood-Flores Meetings, April 3, 1936–March 19, 1937; RG 76, NARA–College Park.
63. Oscar W. Underwood Jr. and Benito Flores, Conferences in Mexico Commencing February 6, 1937, February 6, 1937; box 1, folder 5; International Claims Commissions, US and Mexican Claims Commissions, US and Mexico General Claims Commission 1924–37; Narrative Reports of Underwood-Flores Meetings, April 3, 1936–March 19, 1937; RG 76, NARA–College Park.
64. Underwood Flores Narrative Report, April 4, 1936, 7–8.
65. Oscar W. Underwood Jr. and Benito Flores, Conferences in Mexico Narrative Reports, box 1; International Claims Commissions; US and Mexican Claims Commissions; US and Mexico General Claims Commission 1924–37; Narrative Reports of Underwood-Flores Meetings, April 3, 1936–March 19, 1937; RG 76, NARA–College Park.
66. "Informe Presidencial Secretaría de Relaciones Exteriores," 36–37; SRE III/033.2 36–37/1 Memoria de la Secretaria, 1937; Datos del Depto. para la . . . Mem. 9633 de la O. M. Informe de las labores de la "Sección de Asuntos Americanos" en el mes de agosto de 1938; Archivo Histórico Genaro Estrada de la Secretaría de Relaciones Exteriores, Mexico City.
67. "Text of Mexico's Note to U.S. Rejecting Proposal for Arbitration of Claims in Oil Property Expropriation," *New York Herald Tribune,* May 5, 1940, 37. Eduardo Hay to Josephus Daniels, May 1, 1940.
68. Herbert W. Briggs, "The Settlement of Mexican Claims Act of 1942," *American Journal of International Law* 37, no. 2 (April 1943): 225.
69. Bert Hunt to Cordell Hull, "Agent's Report, American-Mexican Claims Arbitration, 1934–1937," vol. 1, Decisions Docs 23–380, June 9, 1938, 2–3; Department of State Decimal File 511/12/, Declassified Authority State Letter 1/11/72; vol. 1, box 1877; Department of State Decimal File 1930-39 From 411.12/2665 F.W. To 411.12/2690; RG 59, NARA–College Park.
70. Dwyer, *The Agrarian Dispute,* 260.
71. E. M. Ainsworth, "Has Mexico Pulled a Fast One?" *Los Angeles Times,* December 13, 1938.
72. Harold Callender, "British Skeptical of Mexican Deal," *New York Times,* September 7, 1941, 24.
73. Briggs, "The Settlement of Mexican Claims Act of 1942," 222.
74. Adelfa Delgado de la Garza to Bartolomé Carbajal y Rosas, August 26, 1931.

SRE Expediente VI.73/242(72:73)/115. VI.73(G)/242(72.73)1959–648, Reclamante: Adelfa, Dorotea, Cecilia y Amada Delgado, 1925; Fondo Reclamaciones; Archivo Histórico Genaro Estrada de la Secretaría de Relaciones Exteriores, Mexico City.
75. Delgado de la Garza to Carbajal y Rosas, August 26, 1931.
76. de la Garza and Schmitt, "Texas Land Grants and Chicano-Mexican Relations," 132.
77. de la Garza and Schmitt, "Texas Land Grants and Chicano-Mexican Relations," 132.
78. de la Garza and Schmitt, "Texas Land Grants and Chicano-Mexican Relations," 133.
79. de la Garza and Schmitt, "Texas Land Grants and Chicano-Mexican Relations," 134.

10

Negotiating Race

The Legal Borderlands of Court-Ordered Desegregation in Denver, Colorado

DANIELLE R. OLDEN

"What do you do when you cannot document his ancestry?" It was a seemingly simple inquiry, but one with a complicated past and far-reaching ramifications. Naomi Bradford, a woman who identified as part Hispano and part Navajo, posed the question to the Denver Board of Education in November 1974, seven months after the US District Court in Denver had ordered system-wide desegregation of the city's public schools. The ultimate goal of the desegregation plan was racial balance among the district's five racial groups. This meant, of course, that before individual students could be placed in the plan, they had to be racially classified by school officials. Bradford's question about documenting ancestry was only the beginning. She asked further, "Can an individual demand to be classified as minority because of dark skin? Can a person of mixed ancestry switch from one racial classification to another? Does a married Anglo woman who bears a Spanish surname qualify to be Hispano?"[1] Her questions, and their implications, concerned school board members. They also revealed a troubling reality. Court-ordered school desegregation plans were vulnerable not only because they were politically contentious but also because the very basis of these plans, racial classification, was a historically fraught process. Denver parents opposed to "forced busing" discovered that this gave them a way to challenge the legitimacy of the court's order. Because race was so difficult to pin down, they implied, any plan that relied on racial categorization was invalid. Such logic was extended to support their larger claim, that court-ordered desegregation plans were unconstitutional and un-American.

This episode was only one of many similar instances in Denver that demonstrate the precariousness of court-ordered desegregation, one of the most powerful weapons deployed in the struggle for equitable education for all children. Combined, they raise unsettling questions about racial formation, the power of resistance to school desegregation mandates, and the ability of the courts to right civil rights wrongs. Although seminal civil rights victories like the 1954 *Brown v. Board of Education of Topeka* decision and the 1964 Civil Rights Act are celebrated as moments when the metaphorical borders of the nation expanded and its legal institutions finally were made to recognize the equality of all people, the structures that maintained white hegemony were remarkably resilient. Denver's school desegregation battle, litigated in the nation's highest court but implemented within a specific local context, is a case study into how the law can lead to a denial of justice. Like Allison Powers Useche's contribution to this volume, this essay further interrogates the culpability of the US legal system in maintaining structures of racial inequity.

As the first "Northern" school desegregation case heard by the US Supreme Court, *Keyes v. School District No. 1* (1973) set an important legal precedent. But it also reveals important lessons about processes that reworked ideas about race and equality in the post–civil rights period. In this essay I employ the concept of legal borderlands in two ways in order to examine the shifting legal landscape beneath civil rights efforts in the 1970s. First, my examination of *Keyes* enables me to interrogate the racial borderlands that complicated the litigation and implementation of the court's desegregation plan. As scholars of legal borderlands have illustrated, borderlands can and often do function not as physical spaces but "as contact zones between ideas, as spaces of ideological ambiguity that can open up new possibilities for both repression and liberation."[2] As people tried to articulate, negotiate, and adjudicate racial identity, they brought to the surface debates about racial identity and the legal boundaries of racial categories. In Denver the battle over school desegregation was not only about the constitutionality of court-ordered desegregation in a city that had never mandated segregated schools, the pros and cons of busing, or the social upheaval and violence that accompanied integration; it was also about the meaning and application of race itself. How these debates were resolved had consequences for the city's children, families, and communities. Yet my study of the road to resolution, rocky as it was, unmasks not just the fluidity of racial identity but also the political utility of racial uncertainty in civil rights legal battles.

By the 1970s racial identity trials were a phenomenon of the past. With no racial restrictions on immigration, naturalization, marriage, or other rights of citizenship, there was no need to litigate race in order to enforce exclusion.[3] In the post–civil rights period, however, determining race for the purpose of inclusion became an important political battleground. Recent civil rights legislation, Great Society programs, and the courts provided new avenues for people of color to claim the benefits of full American citizenship, but these claims did not go uncontested, particularly if the claimants were racially ambiguous. Who could claim "minority" status?[4] How would "race" be determined and who would determine it? With so much at stake in *Keyes*, race became one of the primary weapons of desegregation foes who used the uncertainty inherent to racial classification as a way to challenge not only the extent of court-ordered desegregation plans but also their very legitimacy.

The second way I engage the concept of legal borderlands is temporal. I argue that the two decades following the 1964 Civil Rights Act represent a temporal borderland that lay between two different legal racial regimes. Under the pre-1964 regime the nation's legal institutions were tasked with determining race in order to uphold racial distinctions in the law.[5] A prohibition against marriage between a black man and a white woman could not be enforced unless some legal actor—a county clerk or marriage bureau office worker, in this case—concluded that the man was indeed black and the women was indeed white. Yet these bodies were remarkably inconsistent in how they determined race, particularly when it came to deciding the racial positioning of people marked as not clearly black or clearly white. Jurists, policymakers, and state bureaucrats could utilize evidence from science, social science, common sense, and the law, in addition to appearance and performance, in order to legitimize their decisions.[6] This was true even when the courts contradicted themselves. In *Ozawa v. United States* (1922), for example, the Supreme Court ruled that a Japanese petitioner was not eligible for naturalization because he was not white. Invoking both science and common knowledge justifications, the Court held that "the words 'white person' were meant to indicate only a person of what is popularly known as the Caucasian race."[7] Here science, whose experts had determined that "Caucasian" was one of the world's great races, and popular perceptions of race worked together to deny Ozawa was white and to make him therefore ineligible for naturalization.

Just a few months later, however, the court rejected scientific rationales for racial categories and, by default, its own racial logic. In *United States v. Bhagat Singh Thind* (1923), the justices determined that a man born in Punjab, India, was not racially eligible for citizenship even though, according to anthropological understandings of race, Indians were Caucasian. While scientific evidence proved that Ozawa was nonwhite because he was not Caucasian, Thind was denied whiteness *in spite of* the fact that science defined him as Caucasian. Rather than science, the court relied on common knowledge, stating that he was not white in the "popular sense of the word."[8] The malleability and contingency of race, as this example reveals, is what made it so powerful a tool of exclusion. This was particularly evident in the West, where racial diversity had always shaped understandings of race, as well as the laws, policies, and ordinances that policed the boundaries of inclusion.[9] Racial categorization, therefore, was a crucial technology in the maintenance of white supremacy.

In the post-1964 regime, color-blind racial ideology came to define the possibilities and limitations of antidiscrimination law by providing the intellectual framework for a new judicial interpretation of the US Constitution. It also provided a useful discourse for ordinary Americans opposed to civil rights but who desired a more neutral, less overtly racist language for expressing their hostility. By the mid-1980s color-blind racial ideology had become the dominant mode of expressing this opposition.[10] Between roughly the mid-1960s and the mid-1980s, the temporal borderland, political and legal struggles over the reach of the Fourteenth Amendment, and debates over the methods of civil rights enforcement created the perfect breeding ground for new forms of massive resistance to take shape. Of course, race-neutral or color-blind arguments against integration had been used for decades. Even in the South, as middle- and upper-class whites fled the cities for the suburbs, their arguments in favor of racial exclusivity shifted from supporting racial segregation to advocating individual rights for property owners.[11] But in the post–civil rights period, as the federal government took on a larger role in enforcing desegregation, race-neutral logic took on new meaning, ultimately transforming how many people and the courts interpreted the Fourteenth Amendment's Equal Protection Clause. Today legal scholars maintain that color-blind constitutionalism—simply, the belief that the US Constitution prohibits the government from classifying people on the basis of race—is rooted in its adherents' reading of the *Brown* decision.[12] While *Brown* laid the legal precedent by invalidating racial segregation, it was subsequent civil rights battles that laid the political groundwork for this interpretation to gain dominance among jurists and lay people alike.[13]

A close interrogation of this period reveals the on-the-ground processes that made the transition between legal discrimination and color-blind constitutionalism so effective. "In borderland spaces," argue Mary Dudziak and Leti Volpp, "we can see what the law *does* in American history and American culture."[14] We can unpack the ways in which legal norms and practices contribute to both formal and informal structures of racial subordination. In the post-1964 temporal borderland, before the law could fully develop the rules and parameters of a new legal racial regime, the rules and parameters of the old regime were reimagined for a new sociolegal context. The porousness of race, once a requirement for the continued legitimacy of legal racial exclusions, now played an important part in the race work unfolding in the post-1964 period. As *Ozawa* and *Thind* demonstrate, racial classification was not a newly ambiguous or contingent process. It was just that its *purpose* had changed. Now its malleability was no longer an open secret, used under the guise of popular, scientific, or legal legitimacy. Its flexibility was the very characteristic of race utilized by anti-integrationists in the name of fairness, transparency, and individualism. Before the courts could articulate fully a color-blind reading of the US Constitution, a diverse group of officials, pundits, and ordinary people helped pave the way by invoking the old logics of race for a new, nefarious purpose: obstructing civil rights.[15]

Like the pre-1964 period, moreover, the existence of people marked as not clearly white and not clearly black made racial classification all the more useful. In Denver the multiracial character of the case presented several avenues of opposition to the court's desegregation order. Mexican Americans not only joined those who supported integration efforts but also challenged the plan in large numbers.[16] Although their objectives for doing so often differed from those of whites, they frequently adopted the same rhetoric and tactics. Some, like Naomi Bradford, challenged the school district's racialization of their children in order to point out the absurdity, as they saw it, of an integration plan that required racial balance. An examination of Mexican American racial and political subjectivities during this period contributes to a fuller understanding of the evolution of color-blind racial ideology.

By using legal borderlands as a framework for my examination of the case, I show that implementation of the 1974 court-ordered desegregation plan was complicated by the simple fact that Denver's school population was multiracial. Neither the judicial system nor the local school district was prepared to sort through the nuances of racial identity in the development of an acceptable program for desegregation. Part of the problem was that legal doctrine did not provide easy answers. Challenging school segregation in the courts, at least as it related to racial discrimination, had been framed in black and white terms. Not surprisingly, the objective of dismantling segregated schools in the South was a part of the much bigger project of eliminating Jim Crow in all areas of American life. *Brown*, which dealt with so-called de jure segregated black schools, became the foundation for future desegregation efforts. When civil rights activists began to challenge segregated education in northern cities, deep divides emerged over *Brown*'s applicability in cases of so-called de facto segregation.[17] For the most part, however, the issue was debated and litigated by people who assumed they were talking about integration between blacks and whites.[18]

The multiracial composition of Denver's school district, like those of other cities in the West, created new challenges for the courts as they adjudicated school segregation cases.[19] In many of these districts school officials tried to maintain all-white schools as much as possible, while still maintaining the posture of race-neutrality. This meant, in practice, that many schools had student bodies that were racially diverse but had few white students. Thus one of the questions brought before the courts was the applicability of *Brown* to situations that looked quite different from *Brown* and its progeny. In fact, as civil rights activists considered the possibility of bringing a lawsuit against the Denver schools for its discriminatory practices in 1956, they were confounded by the matrix of practices the district employed to ensure segregation. "This is a subtle type of discrimination that is difficult to put your finger on," NAACP lawyer Sam Menin explained, "but we know it exists."[20] By 1969 the problem had become acute. Without a precedent on which to rely, the plaintiffs' attorneys in *Keyes* had to develop a new legal strategy in order to prove that the Denver school district was segregating students. As I show elsewhere, they grouped Mexican American and black students into one "minority" category and juxtaposed them with "Anglo" students to create an Anglo/minority binary. Employing this racial construction, the plaintiffs argued that the district had adopted policies that maintained majority Anglo schools and majority minority schools, which was a violation of *Brown*.[21]

Not only was proving segregation difficult but so was developing and implementing a desegregation remedy once segregation was found. There were familiar debates, such as the question of whether the Constitution required desegregation—the removal of racial qualifications for school attendance, or integration—and some level of racial balance. But there was also uncharted territory. What did desegregation look like in a district that was not split along black and white lines? How could the courts balance interests among groups while still staying true to school desegregation doctrine? There were, of course, no clear answers. How the drama unfolded tells us a lot about how ideas regarding race, equal opportunity, and educational equity were shaped by the law and, in turn, how these ideas shaped the law.

By the mid-1970s federal courts had determined that racial balance was the primary remedy for segregated schools. That is, they ordered desegregation plans that tried to spread children throughout the district so that the racial makeup of each school mirrored, as closely as possible, the racial composition of the city. Prior to *Keyes*, the Supreme Court had never ruled on a school segregation case that included a plaintiff class composed of three racial groups: whites, blacks, and Mexican Americans. Denver's school district at the time the court ruled was approximately 66 percent white, 14 percent black, and 20 percent Mexican American.[22] By the end of the decade, the district was about 41 percent white, 23 percent black, and 31 percent Mexican American.[23] These demographics made the case different from previous cases heard by the nation's highest court. One of the central questions before the justices was whether or not you could group black and Mexican American students into one "minority" category for the purpose of proving segregation. They had to decide, in other words, whether Mexican Americans were white or nonwhite.

This debate emerged several times during the district court trial. The defendants, in fact, implicitly raised this question when they disputed the plaintiffs' construction of Mexican Americans as "minority." Their attorneys took issue especially with the fact that the plaintiffs grouped Mexican Americans and blacks into one racial category. They did so with good reason. By grouping them with black students, the plaintiffs positioned Mexican Americans closer to blackness than whiteness. In the post–1964 Civil Rights Act period, it made legal sense to compare them to blacks, who were viewed as the prime beneficiaries of civil rights legislation. Yet prior to this moment in school desegregation litigation, lawyers representing Mexicans and Mexican Americans had consistently argued that they were white. Because school officials could not segregate white children from "other white" children, they argued, districts that did segregate persons of

Mexican descent were in violation of the law. In multiple cases, the courts agreed.[24] It was not until the late 1960s that Mexican American civil rights attorneys began to challenge school segregation by invoking *Brown*. That is, they did not claim racial discrimination in these cases until well after *Brown* had outlawed "separate but equal" in the nation's public schools.[25] The US Census Bureau, moreover, consistently racialized Mexicans and Mexican Americans as white, with the exception of 1930 when a separate "Mexican" category was established.[26] With both judicial and bureaucratic backing, Mexican Americans were able to claim a fragile whiteness even if their lived realities defied such an identification.

Such long-standing legal support for Mexican American whiteness provided a solid basis for the defense to challenge the Anglo/minority binary. If they could prove that the plaintiffs' racial thinking was flawed, they could disrupt their entire legal argument. The racial identity of Mexican Americans, therefore, was central to the outcome of the litigation. Their precarious position somewhere in the borderlands between white and black made them critical to the maintenance of Denver's segregated school system and, at the same time, a threat to its survival. As legal historian Ariela Gross argues, Mexican Americans wore a "Caucasian cloak" that could be thrust upon them or removed at any moment. They wore the cloak—they were white— when it helped the state maintain the racial status quo. It came off, however, when it served to maintain the racial subjugation of Mexican Americans.[27] School districts in Texas, for example, had been using Mexican Americans to maintain segregated schools in the face of increasing federal pressure to meet *Brown*'s mandate. By arguing that they were white, school officials were able to insist they had desegregated when in reality they had merely found a way to maintain segregation. Black and Mexican American students were placed in the same schools and white students remained in their own schools.[28] In those very same districts white Texans made it clear that they believed that most Mexican Americans were a part of an inferior race.

In Denver the same racial flip-flopping served the school district's segregation efforts. There were areas of the city that were predominantly Mexican American, just as there were neighborhoods that were mostly black or mostly white. But there were also areas that were more mixed, and Mexican Americans were, compared to blacks, more residentially dispersed. With such housing demographics, creating and maintaining segregated schools while still appearing race-neutral meant that school officials needed to think creatively. Particularly in the city's central neighborhoods, Denver Public

Schools (DPS) administrators gerrymandered school attendance boundaries so as to maintain as much separation between white and other students as possible. They also bused white students in overcrowded schools to other white schools that were further away than many minority schools. When minority schools became overcrowded, they simply constructed mobile classroom units rather than bus minority students to nearby white schools. In short, school officials manufactured racial imbalance. When the plaintiffs provided evidence that suggested their actions were discriminatory, one of the ways the school district defended itself was by questioning the racialization of Mexican Americans as minority. Schools in the core city area could not be segregated, they implied, because there were near equal numbers of white students, both Anglos and Mexican Americans, and black students enrolled.[29]

The defense was only partially successful. On March 21, 1970, district court judge William E. Doyle ruled that DPS was guilty of de jure segregation in northeast Denver schools, where the city's black population was concentrated. As to the plaintiffs' Anglo/minority binary argument, however, Judge Doyle was unconvinced. While Mexican American and black Denverites had similar experiences and histories of prejudice and discrimination, he indicated that he did not believe combining the two groups was allowable under federal antidiscrimination law. In his opinion he wrote, "Whether it is permissible to add the numbers of the two groups together and lump them into a single minority category for purposes of classification as a segregated school remains a problem and a question."[30] By rejecting this argument he denied that school officials maintained segregation in other areas of the city. Many schools in the central city area, for example, did not have a predominance of black or Mexican American pupils. Rather, these students attended school together, often with few Anglo students.

Both the plaintiffs and the defendants appealed the decision to the Tenth Circuit Court of Appeals, which, in large part, confirmed Judge Doyle's decision. When the case finally made its way to the US Supreme Court in 1972, it became the first "Northern" school desegregation case heard by the court. Often missing from discussions on the significance of *Keyes*, however, is the centrality of Mexican Americans to the litigation and the important role of racial identity, of policing the borders of racial identity, in the implementation of the court-ordered desegregation plan. On June 21, 1973, the court ruled that Mexican Americans were "an identifiable class," more akin to blacks than whites. The justices thus granted approval to the plaintiffs' Anglo/minority approach, noting, "in the Southwest, Hispanos and Negroes have a great many things in common."[31] Their decision forced *Keyes* back to the district court in Denver, where Judge Doyle ruled DPS a dual school system and ordered system-wide desegregation.[32]

Among Denver residents the Supreme Court's ruling on Mexican American racial identity became a pivotal part of public debate because it so dramatically altered the ramifications of the case. Under Judge Doyle's original ruling, only northeast Denver schools were affected. Now many more schools potentially could be segregated and many more students might have to be involved in a desegregation remedy. The *Denver Post* staff editorialized that it was strange the justices would make such a decision when, from what they could see, most Mexican Americans in the city did not seem to favor integration. The editor admitted that Mexican American children often experienced the same educational inequities as black children. But he insisted that "most Hispanos in Denver—the articulate ones at least—apparently do not want their children to have the same degree of school integration sought by most blacks."[33] While this editorial ignored the diversity of opinions within the Mexican American community, it did highlight both the significance of Mexican Americans to the case and their lack of consensus over the issue of busing for racial balance, even after the Supreme Court ruled.

This story is absent from our understanding of post-1964 civil rights history. Historians have examined school desegregation battles and the fear of "forced busing" in the urban North as important aspects of shifting political sensibilities during the 1970s, but they have missed an important part of this story by eliding the experiences and contributions of Latinas/os.[34] Where did they stand in these debates? How did they contribute to or challenge the emerging discourse of color blindness? How did their very existence shape civil rights opponents' resistance strategies? Affirmative action, which was often a part of school desegregation plans—it was in Denver—and busing for racial balance were the two issues that most ignited the opposition of liberals and conservatives alike. Their rejection of race-conscious remedies helped nurture a budding anticlassification form of color blindness, what Ian Haney López calls "reactionary color blindness."[35] As a strategy of resistance to civil rights remedies, hostility to racial classification has proven an effective method. It uses the language of antiracism to argue against race-consciousness. The Colorado State Board of Education's brief of amicus curiae, for example, argued that race-consciousness was a violation of the principle established in *Brown* because it perpetuated the same racism that motivated classifying students by race during the Jim Crow era.[36] While Haney López applies the term to legal doctrine, it is also a useful way to understand how regular people shifted their thinking on civil rights. Examining the post–civil rights period with Latinas/os in mind sheds new light on how this transition occurred. In the temporal borderlands between the passage of the 1964 Civil Rights Act, which ended legal segregation, and the "post-1980s rearticulation of antiracism into color blindness," questions over Latino/a racial identity helped grassroots opponents of race-conscious policies like court-ordered racial balance plans chart out new forms of resistance.[37]

It also was during this period that Mexican Americans began to shift their own civil rights strategies away from legal whiteness arguments to racial discrimination arguments. From a litigation standpoint it made sense to shift strategies because Mexican American civil rights attorneys were operating in a new legal regime, brought on by the passage of the 1964 Civil Rights Act. Legal segregation was over and the federal government now offered protections against discrimination. This landmark piece of legislation, notes historian Nancy MacLean, "enabled Mexican Americans to embrace nonwhite identity without assuming the risk involved when discrimination was legal."[38] But the transition was complicated, as both the courts and various state bureaucracies struggled to determine whether or not Latinas/os were meant to be the beneficiaries of antidiscrimination law, whether they *wanted* to be beneficiaries, and how to determine whether one was indeed a racial minority.

Mexican Americans, in fact, took an array of positions on their racial and cultural identities, and they did not agree on the issue of court-ordered racial balance, particularly when it threatened their attempts to secure bilingual and bicultural education programs. In 1968 and 1969, when desegregation plans first were being debated by school officials, the diversity of opinions on the proposed plans was on full display. Members of the Crusade for Justice, a local Chicana/o empowerment organization, interrupted a packed school board meeting to proclaim their opposition to any desegregation plan that shuffled students around the city but did nothing to address the educational needs of Mexican American students. Integration, argued their leader Corky Gonzales, was "a misleading proposition in regards to solving the problems imposed upon the children of the Mexican American segment of this society."[39] Rather than the integration schemes being deliberated by the district, the Crusade emphasized Chicana/o community control of Chicana/o schools. At the same time the newly formed Congress of Hispanic Educators (CHE) underscored the importance of an integrated educational setting for Mexican American children. Members recognized that desegregation was not the only solution to the plethora of problems Mexican Americans faced in the Denver schools, but they believed it was a critical component.[40] In school board meetings and community gatherings Mexican American parents, too, displayed ambivalence on the subject of desegregation and busing, with some supporting the goal of integration and others insisting it was not necessary for achieving the kind of educational reforms they sought for their children.[41] This ambivalence was reflected in a 1972 study of "Spanish-surnamed" Denverites by a group of social work students at the University of Denver. Though their sample was small, their study indicated that there was no consensus among Mexican Americans when it came to desegregation and busing. In fact, there appears to have been a significant amount of uncertainty. There was more agreement, however, about the need for bilingual education.[42]

Finally, when Mexican American students walked out of their schools in the middle of citywide debates over the merits of various desegregation plans in 1969, they revealed their particular dissatisfaction with the educational experiences they had in Denver schools. Their list of demands, submitted to school officials, included calls for greater representation, courses that taught Mexican American history and culture, and pedagogical changes that recognized students' diverse backgrounds and learning needs. While they recognized a number of problems with the way teachers and administrators engaged with them, they did not articulate a demand for racial balance in their schools.[43] Their vision of educational equality differed in critical ways from that being advocated by integration proponents.

With the Supreme Court's decision final and a large number of Mexican Americans about to become a part of the integration plan, the CHE decided it was time to ensure Mexican American children were being represented in the case. Having tried for years to convince school officials of the need for the kinds of programs Mexican American students demanded, members obtained legal counsel with the Mexican American Legal Defense and Educational Fund (MALDEF) and intervened in the case.[44] They sided with the plaintiffs, arguing that integration was necessary to guarantee equal educational opportunity but that so were other educational reforms. Once again, bilingual-bicultural educational programs were their top priority. In order to make their claims, they insisted that Mexican Americans were a part of a distinct race, separate from both blacks and whites. As students with "inalienable racial characteristics," Mexican Americans had unique educational needs that racial balance alone would not provide.[45] In early 1974 Judge Doyle granted their petition and MALDEF attorneys became the official representatives of Denver's Mexican American community in the case.

Even though the Supreme Court had determined Mexican Americans were an identifiable class under the Fourteenth Amendment and MALDEF was pursuing their interests as a distinct racial group, the racial wrangling that had been a feature of the litigation since the beginning actually intensified. The Denver public had been debating the issue of desegregation and racial balance for several years. Starting in 1974, however, some parents and other residents began to challenge court-ordered racial balance by disputing the validity of racial categorization. As a form of resistance to Judge Doyle's district-wide plan, challenges to racial categorization took several forms, and Mexican Americans were often at the center. First, desegregation opponents protested the very notion that each student's race had to be documented by the school district and used to determine their school assignment. How could this be legal, they asked, when the Colorado Constitution forbid this very act? Title IV of the 1964 Civil Rights Act, moreover, explicitly rejected racial balance remedies. Nolan Winsett, president of the anti-integration group Citizens Association for Neighborhood Schools (CANS), consistently made this argument.[46]

Second, anti-integrationists criticized the process of racialization. Before school officials could begin to develop a plan, they had to make sure each student's race was officially recorded. DPS practice had long depended on teacher observation of students to determine their race and this continued during the desegregation era. Sometimes they utilized surname and/or language. Often, marking children's race encompassed several of these practices, particularly when there was some question about their racial identity. DPS parent Marguerite Cardova complained to school board members that teacher observation was fraught with "many inaccuracies brought about by color of skin, hair, and eyes and the sound of the name."[47] Lila Lewis, demonstrating Cardova's point, presented board members with pictures of each of her four children and asked them if they could identify the race to which they belonged. Her point was that her children's racial identity could be easily mistaken. Because they had varying skin shades and facial features, they were inconsistently racialized by the school district. When she asked for documentation from the schools, officials sent her a letter that named two of her children as "Hispano" and two of them as "Other," even though all four children had the same parents and the same last name. She told the board that there were thousands of students just like her children who were being incorrectly classified.[48] Because racial identity was so uncertain, these parents implied, it was not a solid basis upon which to base a desegregation plan that would shift thousands of students to other schools.

This objection to the process of racialization led to the third manner in which anti-integrationists utilized anticlassification arguments. Racial identities were in fact so difficult to pin down that only parents could identify their child's true race. If racial balance was going to go forward, parents had *a right* to name their child's race. "No one could state with any degree of accuracy," insisted Robert Weaver, "the ethnicity or race of a child except the mother or father."[49] Several parents, concerned about how their mixed-race children were being classified by the district, demanded that parents be sent a survey that would allow them to designate officially their child's race. If they found that school officials had misclassified them, moreover, they should be allowed to change it. Taking this argument a step further, some parents argued for the inclusion of a "mixed-race" category, which would represent more accurately the thousands of "half and half" students in the district. As Lila Lewis explained after she showed her children's photos to school board members, "neither Judge Doyle nor the Board had the right to designate which ethnic background her own children must belong to."[50] Recognizing the ambiguity of racial categories gave parents the ability to claim a particular status in order to manipulate their child's placement in the district's scheme to create racial balance.

Once the court approved a plan to allow children to stay in their neighborhood schools if their presence contributed to racial balance at that school, the district was inundated with demands from parents that they be able to choose their child's race.[51] As a result the district had to ask Judge Doyle to define minority categories. If some pupils are going to be exempt from busing, DPS wrote in its Motion for Modification and Clarification, "it is necessary that certain standards be established for determining whether a child is a minority child for these purposes."[52] At a court conference in June, Judge Doyle addressed the defendants' request:

> Now, as to what constitutes a minority child, my thinking throughout, as I said at the other hearing, was to follow the School District

Staff's categories as a Black or Chicano and Oriental and American Indian. And I said that I was not going to measure and add up the percentage of parentage. If a person claims to be a minority child, why, that's the end of it as far as I am concerned.[53]

He seemed hesitant to issue more concrete definitions, assuming that it was not necessary for the district to successfully implement his desegregation plan. From the perspective of the defendants, who had to deal with the day-to-day execution of the plan, the court needed to issue specific guidelines for determining who qualified as a minority child and which racial classification they belonged to. By June the district had already heard from many parents on the question of racial definitions and expected more to follow. Already antagonistic toward the court's plan, school officials now had to navigate the complicated terrain of the racial borderlands that existed in the ideological space between black and white.

The plaintiffs, too, were concerned about the ways in which racial ambiguity was being used to pick apart the desegregation plan. Gordon Greiner, their lead attorney, was particularly concerned about two possible scenarios. First, he wondered about students with "a Chicano parent and an Anglo parent." How would they be classified? The fact that several parents with Mexican American children kept insisting on a mixed-race category had to have influenced his preoccupation with this issue. As outspoken opponents of the court's order, what did these parents stand to gain from the creation of such a category? And how would "mixed-race" fit into the plaintiffs' Anglo/minority argument that had won over the Supreme Court? Greiner had to have considered the possibility that a mixed-race category could jeopardize any plan for racial balance, and could give the district a way of appealing Judge Doyle's ruling that DPS was a dual system. He worried also that white parents might try to claim minority status for their children in order to remain in their neighborhood school.[54]

That so much time was spent on these issues reveals the precarious nature of court-ordered school desegregation and of legal remedies for civil rights violations more generally. Such remedies relied on racial categorization, yet the process of racially identifying students was much more complicated than many in the legal community were willing to address. Greiner's strategy in court, moreover, reinforced a strict racial divide between "Anglos" and "minorities" that was impossible to police. The long history of racial mixing wrought by the colonization of North America, first by Europeans and then by Americans, made identifying "Indians" and "Hispanos" particularly problematic.[55]

To address these questions Judge Doyle finally issued an order that dictated four minority categories for the district to use: "American Indian," "Oriental," "black," and "Hispano." He also laid out the process whereby school officials would assign racial classifications. The district was to continue its normal practice, teacher observation, unless a parent claimed their child's race was incorrectly documented. In that case the parent could fill out an affidavit with the correct race, which the district would then recognize. As per a request made by Gordon Greiner, probably in order to monitor the number of parents changing their child's race in an attempt to exempt them from the desegregation plan, Judge Doyle also ordered that the school administration keep track of these affidavits and file periodic reports to the court on the usage of this process.[56] Greiner's concerns about the demands for a mixed-race category and the use of these new racial affidavits indicate that he was suspicious of the emerging anticlassification arguments being used by anti-integration advocates.

His suspicions soon proved justified. Within a matter of months parents of DPS students had filed two hundred affidavits requesting that their child's race be changed. Although this was less than one percent of the entire district, two hundred students was not an insignificant number when one considers the delicate racial balancing the court was trying to achieve with its plan.[57] By October a controversy over racial classification had erupted in southwest Denver, where several of the most vocal opponents of the desegregation plan lived. Using the official racial classification affidavit, fifty-seven parents of children at Johnson Elementary School changed their child's race, claiming they had been identified mistakenly as Anglo when they were American Indian. Angered at "being used" in the city's busing controversy, local American Indians protested the false Indian claims in a meeting with school officials. "When more than fifty people file affidavits that they are Indian in 1974," noted Manson Garreaux, director of the Denver Indian Center, "it looks like people are playing at being Indian again." In fact, reports showed that there had been no American Indian children at Johnson in the previous three years.[58] James O'Hara, DPS executive director of pupil services, noted that at the time the disputed Johnson claims were brought to the district's attention, officials had already approved 148 Indian affidavits and were processing twenty more. Without any specific directions for approving parents' assertions of Indianness, O'Hara said they were accepting all of them "at face value."[59] Already aware of the ways in which the desegregation plan's challengers were implementing anticlassification arguments, district administrators' lack of attention to the manipulation of the affidavit system reveals the expediency of such tactics. On a practical level, with legal options running out for school officials, legitimizing parents' concerns about the ambiguity of racial identity proved a useful way to disrupt implementation of Judge Doyle's plan.

One parent, more than any other, led the way. Naomi Bradford was the mother of three DPS children, a resident of southwest Denver, president of the Johnson School Parent Teacher Association (PTA), a CANS member, and a future Denver school board member. Her questioning about racial classification procedures, which opened this essay, is only one example of her constant work to dismantle court-ordered school desegregation. She and her husband, Ronald Bradford, spoke at nearly every school board meeting and public hearing to denounce racial balance as unconstitutional and unworkable. Her leadership in the crusade against "forced busing" was so well regarded that in 1975 she was elected by Denver residents to the DPS Board of Education, where she spent several years doing everything in her power to stall implementation of Judge Doyle's plan and limit its effectiveness.[60]

In many ways Bradford fit the mold of other Americans "caught in the middle," a part of a group that President Nixon famously named the "Silent Majority."[61] But she and others like her, Mexican Americans who found radical civil rights activism distasteful and un-American, also introduced new dynamics to the conservative consensus over civil rights in the 1970s.[62] Her activism as a parent and then as a school board member reverberated with populist sentiment. "I was a peace-loving PTA president whose biggest delight in life was setting up PTA functions," she reported. "I was no activist. But I had to set it all aside to roll up my sleeves and fight for neighborhood schools."[63] Bradford's conservatism, particularly her antagonism toward court-ordered desegregation, must be analyzed within the context of the larger debate over civil rights remedies in the post–civil rights period. Her work to dismantle integration was deeply racialized, not only because she sometimes utilized overtly racist language in her tirades against fellow school board members and supported the project of systemic educational inequity but also because she took advantage of the confusion the racial borderlands presented.[64] Moreover, the fact that she was Mexican American gave her a useful way of deflecting accusations that she was an anti-integrationist and complaints that she did nothing for the Mexican American community.[65]

A focus on the legal borderlands of court-ordered desegregation reveals the significant role that Mexican Americans played in the transformation of American politics in the 1970s. Their new "minority" status gave them credibility when it came to talking about civil rights issues, but many of them resented being grouped into the "minority" category. Some, like Naomi Bradford, joined the growing conservative movement. Some Mexican Americans, frustrated at their inability to win the reforms *they* wanted, ended up adopting many of the same arguments and rhetoric of their white conservative counterparts.

Whether Bradford came up with the idea to claim her children were American Indian is not certain. What is clear, however, is that she was PTA president of the school at the center of the controversy and she frequently served as a spokesperson for their efforts. Once the high number of claims coming from parents in southwest Denver was investigated and Bradford was questioned about her claim to an Indian identity, she explained that although she was not a member of the tribe, she was Navajo. According to an interview she later gave a local newspaper, her mother was "Navajo and Hispano," and her father was "part Indian." While her politics persuaded others to lump her in with white anti-integrationists, she told the reporter, "Anyone who looks at me can tell I'm either Hispanic or Indian."[66] At other times she spoke of being "one-fourth Navajo," indicating that she viewed race as a matter of blood (see figure 10.1). On the one hand, Bradford's understanding of her racial identity embodied the spirit of *mestizaje* that was so central to the racial politics of the Chicana/o movement. She recognized that her ancestors were both indigenous and European, and she saw no contradiction in identifying as "Mexican," "Hispano," and "American Indian" at different points in her life. By claiming her Navajo ancestry, in fact, she did precisely what movement activists encouraged: she reclaimed her indigenous roots. On the other hand, one of her motivations for claiming particular identities was her desire to disrupt Judge Doyle's plan for racial balance. In claiming to be American Indian in the fall of 1974, she was not just trying to exempt her own children from being bused to another school. She was trying to prove that racial classification was an unfair, and ultimately unconstitutional, process for disseminating benefits like quality public education and jobs.

The reason so many parents had not identified their children as American

Figure 10.1. Naomi Bradford and family, 1978, photographer unknown, *Rocky Mountain News* Records, WH2129, photo box 33. Naomi and Ronald Bradford with their three children (*from left to right*): Rhonda, Joan, and Ralph, four years after Judge William E. Doyle ordered district-wide desegregation of the Denver public schools. Photo courtesy of the Western History Collection, Denver Public Library.

Indian before, Bradford argued, was because there was no need to racially classify them before court-ordered desegregation.[67] That is, there was no advantage parents like her could gain from being a minority prior to the court order. The Supreme Court's decision in *Keyes* that Mexican Americans were nonwhite, followed by the district court's order for district-wide desegregation dramatically altered the racial identity claims of hundreds of individual Denver residents. The law, in this space of ambiguity, produced new racial guidelines for people to follow in their pursuit of material benefits. That so many parents tried to manipulate the system forced Judge Doyle to take further action to define racial categories. While he previously had ordered that parents' claims of racial identity would stand, in the case of American Indians he now said that parents must be able to prove they had a "substantial" amount of "Indian blood"—perhaps 50 percent, he suggested. American Indians present at a meeting with DPS immediately protested such a recommendation, as they had a right to name their own community members. As Indian educator Bill Roberts explained to school officials, this was an important right of sovereignty.[68] Nonetheless, Judge Doyle ordered that any parent who had filed an affidavit claiming an American Indian identity for their child now had to refile with proof they qualified to be Indian.[69]

With this order the court was telling Denver parents that they had to "prove" their children's race in order for them to be classified as minority students. Anti-integrationists caused this disruption to the implementation of the desegregation plan and forced a federal judge to return to the norms of decades past, when racial determination trials determined one's access to full US citizenship. At the same time, federal law had always treated American Indians differently, and there was a long history of federal imposition on their sovereign right to name the members of their communities.[70] This conflict between civil rights and sovereignty is yet another aspect of the legal borderlands of court-ordered desegregation that demonstrates how difficult it is for the law to account for all of the complexities that go along with dismantling racialized systems of oppression.[71] In this sense the civil rights victories of the previous decade were not dramatic breaks with the past, as they are often understood. Rather, these victories brought on a period of legal, social, and cultural uncertainty, a borderlands space that helped reshape but did not eradicate legal exclusions based on race.

Many of the parents who had submitted American Indian affidavits chose not to resubmit and their children were reclassified as whatever category they had been the previous year. Several others, however, remained defiant by refusing to file another affidavit. Thirty families, including the Bradfords, wrote a joint letter to DPS that demanded more concrete definitions of all racial groups, not just American Indians. They argued that demanding proof of Indianness, while not requiring it for those claiming other racial identities, was unfair. If their children were not allowed to be American Indian, the parents asked, then how would they be classified?[72] A couple of days later these parents appeared before a school board public hearing to air their grievances. Based on the personal details they reported, it is clear that many of the families were mixed-race, with one parent being Mexican American. Betty McClain and Donna Thorberg protested the practice of teacher observation and use of surname to determine race. McClain, like Lila Lewis before her, presented photographs of her children as

Figure 10.2. "Dr. Doyle's Bureau of Indian Authenticity," by John P. Trevor, 1974. The cartoon is a comment on racial classification for "busing" purposes. Trevor criticizes the notion that parents of Johnson schoolchildren could claim their children were American Indian—he also notes that the school PTA (under Naomi Bradford) was leading the charge—*and* the idea that the courts could somehow confirm a person's ethnicity. Cartoon courtesy of the Western History Collection, Denver Public Library (call number 2015.024 ART).

evidence of the district's inability to correctly classify each child. She noted their dark skin and hair and told board members they were "half Spanish." Despite this, teachers had documented them "as Anglo because their father was Anglo" (see figure 10.2).[73]

Thorberg's family dynamics were even more complicated. She explained that her two eldest children, whose last name was McBride, had been classified as "Other" by school officials while her youngest child, whose last name was Romero, had been classified as "Hispano." Consequently, her "Hispano" child was exempted from busing while her two "Other" children were bused to another school. She claimed this had created a negative environment in her home because her children recognized that their different school assignments were based on "skin color." In an attempt to unify her home and prevent "permanent psychological division" in her family, she said that she filed American Indian affidavits for the two older children "rightfully claiming their Indian blood."[74] The DPS boardroom may not have been a court of law, but Thorberg's proclamation that her children possessed "Indian blood" and her insistence that they be classified as American Indian sounded a lot like the testimony heard in racial determination trials of the pre-1964 period. On a pragmatic level, sending one's children to two different schools based on perceptions of their race must have seemed ridiculous to parents like her, and perhaps even caused real hardships. On an ideological level, pointing this out was a potent political strategy in the battle against civil rights.

Parent after parent whose American Indian affidavits had been denied spoke on these hardships. In nearly all of their comments, moreover, they protested their loss of authority to identify their own race in a way that preserved the racial status quo, and expressed frustration with school administrators and Judge Doyle for questioning their motivations in filing their affidavits. One demanded to know, "Does [my] skin have to be black, brown, yellow, etc. before the public officials feel [I] could be discriminated against?" Another parent resented that her claim had been rejected by the district and she accused Judge Doyle of calling her and her parents liars. Both of her grandparents, she said, had been "born on a Cherokee Indian Reservation in Kentucky."[75]

When Naomi Bradford rose to speak again, it was clear to school board members that something had gone terribly wrong with the racial affidavit process. Bradford suggested that the court had given parents, particularly those with children who had some amount of Mexican American ancestry, no recourse for proving their race. "Since the court made it impossible to qualify as Indian," she told board members, "some considered claiming Spanish ancestry, but had no assurance this would not be met with the same opposition."[76] With this point she revealed the true motivations of this group of parents. If their goal was simply to get their own children exempt from busing, they easily could have claimed they were Hispano. DPS attorney Richard Cockrell, in fact, confirmed for them that such a claim would have been accepted.[77] Rather, they wielded racial ambiguity as a weapon in the battle to take down court-ordered desegregation. Bradford's close working relationship with fellow CANS member Nolan Winsett further suggests this possibility. Although he once admitted to a reporter that he exaggerated his "Indian blood," Winsett publically identified as a Cherokee Indian in order to illustrate, he explained, "the absurdities of the Denver

School Board's effort to classify all its students by race."[78] By so forcefully pursuing the American Indian strategy, they highlighted a centuries' long problem—the fluidity of race—in a modern, civil rights context, and revealed vulnerabilities in remedial law.

That this emerged as a tactic of anti-integration activists reveals color-blind ideology in formation. "People don't know about the ethnic business," Lila Lewis told the *Denver Post*, "so we told them."[79] Her cynical description of racial classification as the "ethnic business" demonstrates that she and fellow CANS activists had already grasped onto the anticlassification rhetoric that now dominates color-blind approaches to attacking race-conscious civil rights remedies. Their focus on mixed-race children, moreover, indicates that anti-integration activists in the 1970s had already learned an important lesson of the post–civil rights period. As Peggy Pascoe compellingly argues, *Loving v. Virginia* (1967) played a central role in the conservative reworking of color blindness by removing, once and for all, racial qualifications for marriage. Interracial marriage and, in particular, the increasing births of mixed-race children were proof that the United States had finally moved beyond race.[80] Opponents of court-ordered desegregation in Denver used the presence of mixed-race children to point out irregularities in the school district's process of racial classification, thus raising critical questions about the practicality and legality of racial balance schemes.[81]

More than sixty years after the Supreme Court declared racial segregation in the nation's schools unconstitutional, schools around the nation remain deeply segregated. According to the Civil Rights Project at UCLA, Latinas/os are the most racially isolated in the nation and, increasingly, blacks and Latinas/os attend classes together in segregated schools.[82] Legal efforts to remedy this inequality have, over the course of the last several decades, been set back by the judicial triumph of color-blind constitutionalism. In *Parents Involved in Community Schools v. Seattle School District No. 1* (2007), for example, the Supreme Court debated the constitutionality of race-based school assignment programs in Seattle, Washington, and Louisville, Kentucky. Arguing that these policies were beneficial for students and helped delay resegregation, the school districts tried to *defend* race-conscious approaches to education. Based on its anticlassification reading of *Brown*, the Supreme Court rejected their argument. "Before *Brown*," Chief Justice John Roberts wrote in the majority opinion, "schoolchildren were told where they could and could not go to school based on the color of their skin. The school districts in these cases have not carried the heavy burden of demonstrating that we should allow this once again—even for very different reasons." Trying to remedy school segregation, a Fourteenth Amendment violation, was not an excuse to violate the Constitution, according to the color-blind logic of the court's majority. Driving home the point, Chief Justice Roberts famously concluded, "The way to stop discriminating on the basis of race is to stop discriminating on the basis of race."[83]

It is a remarkable turn of events, though perhaps not surprising given the persistence and continuity of racial hegemony in the United States, always constructed, in part, through the law. While the courts were critical to the advancement of racial equality in the second half of the twentieth century, by the early twenty-first century color-blind jurisprudence had helped transform school desegregation doctrine into a tool of inequity. Legal remedies, therefore, are often no remedy at all. The central mechanism of this conversion was racial classification. Many people who believe in integration in principal are easily convinced that race-consciousness in the name of implementing a civil rights remedy is just as racist as the Jim Crow system of racial segregation. Such logic isn't new, as this examination of the temporal borderlands reveals. One Denver parent told the US Commission on Civil Rights that he originally was in favor of busing for racial balance because he believed all children should get an equal education. The process of racial classification, however, changed his mind. "The main reason I am against busing is the concept of categorizing children by their appearance or family names," he reported to the commission. "This concept in its totality defeats the entire purpose of desegregation."[84] If he followed school board meeting news, he surely would have been aware of the racial theatrics that seemed to play out monthly.

By closely examining the legal borderlands of court-ordered school desegregation in Denver we can see how anticlassification arguments began to take shape, even over the course of the litigation itself, as anti-integrationists experimented with different strategies. Although these efforts may not have forced a dramatic change to the desegregation plan ordered by Judge William Doyle, they did force the school district and the court to grapple with the day-to-day implementation of the plan. More significantly, these developments affected the ways in which many people, legal actors and ordinary people alike, understood and became politicized by school desegregation. Over time, as they struggled to make sense of the transformations brought on by court-ordered school desegregation and other prescriptions for civil rights violations, their efforts to limit the effectiveness of legal remedies took many forms. The most effective and consequential of these tactics rested on appeals to a post–civil rights society in which race no longer mattered. Analyzing this important period between roughly the mid-1960s and the mid-1980s as a temporal borderland, moreover, allows for a closer examination of the messy, multiracial nature of racial formation and civil rights political mobilization that developed in-between two different legal racial regimes. In the post–civil rights period the purpose of racial classification changed, but its mechanisms remained the same. At the same time Mexican American civil rights lawyers were leaving behind decades of legal efforts to achieve full integration for a new strategy that became viable only after major civil rights legislation formally ended legal discrimination based on race. No longer dependent on claims to "other-whiteness," their transition to a "distinct race" argument complicated civil rights litigation and enforcement, particularly in cases with more than one nonwhite group. In *Keyes* the Supreme Court settled the issue by approving the Anglo/minority binary constructed by the plaintiffs, thereby affirming Mexican American nonwhiteness. At the ground level, however, this decision had little impact on the ways in which ordinary people self-identified and viewed the civil rights debates happening all around them. By interrogating Mexican Americans' diverse political and racial subjectivities during this crucial period and the roles they played in civil rights battles, we can begin to unpack a more nuanced history of color-blind racial formation in post–civil rights America.

Notes

1. Minutes, Denver Board of Education Meeting, November 14, 1974, 4.
2. Mary L. Dudziak and Leti Volpp, introduction, "Legal Borderlands: Law and the Construction of American Borders," *American Quarterly* 57, no. 3 (September 2005): 596. See the essays in this special issue of *American Quarterly* for examples of legal borderlands scholarship.
3. On litigating racial identity, see Ian Haney López, *White by Law: The Legal Construction of Race*, rev. ed. (New York: New York University Press, 2006); Ariela J. Gross, *What Blood Won't Tell: A History of Race on Trial in America* (Cambridge: Harvard University Press, 2008); Peggy Pascoe, *What Comes Naturally: Miscegenation Law and the Making of Race in America* (Oxford: Oxford University Press, 2009), part II.
4. For a wider discussion of the policy debates and decisions that shaped federal recognition of different "minority" groups, see John D. Skrentny, *The Minority Rights Revolution* (Cambridge: Harvard University Press, 2004). An important

critique of Skrentny is Kevin R. Johnson, review of *The Minority Rights Revo-lution*, by John D. Skrentny, *American Journal of Legal History* 47, no. 3 (July 2005): 315–317.

5. Legal institutions included not just courts but various state bodies as well. See, for example, Peggy Pascoe, "Seeing Like a Racial State," chapter 5 in *What Comes Naturally*; Natalia Molina, *How Race Is Made in America: Immigration, Citizenship, and the Historical Power of Racial Scripts* (Berkeley: University of California Press, 2014).

6. Gross, *What Blood Won't Tell*.

7. Ozawa v. United States, 260 U.S. 178, 197 (1922).

8. United States v. Bhagat Singh Thind, 261 U.S. 204, 209 (1923). On the racial ra-tionales utilized in *Ozawa* and *Thind*, see Haney López, *White by Law*, 56–77.

9. The literature here is voluminous. See, for example, Patricia Nelson Limerick, *The Legacy of Conquest: The Unbroken Past of the American West* (New York: W. W. Norton, 1987); George J. Sánchez, *Becoming Mexican American: Eth-nicity, Culture, and Identity in Chicano Los Angeles, 1900–1945* (New York: Oxford University Press, 1993); Tomás Almaguer, *Racial Fault Lines: The Historical Origins of White Supremacy in California* (Berkeley: University of California Press, 1994); Neil Foley, *The White Scourge: Mexicans, Blacks, and Poor Whites in Texas Cotton Culture* (Berkeley: University of California Press, 1997); Erika Lee, *At America's Gates: Chinese Immigration during the Exclu-sion Era, 1882–1943* (Chapel Hill: University of North Carolina Press, 2003); Mae M. Ngai, *Impossible Subjects: Illegal Aliens and the Making of Modern America* (Princeton: Princeton University Press, 2004); Pablo Mitchell, *Coyote Nation: Sexuality, Race, and Conquest in Modernizing New Mexico, 1880–1920* (Chicago: University of Chicago Press, 2005); Natalia Molina, *Fit to Be Citi-zens? Public Health and Race in Los Angeles, 1879–1939* (Berkeley: University of California Press, 2006); Mark Brilliant, *The Color of America Has Changed: How Racial Diversity Shaped Civil Rights Reform in California, 1941–1978* (New York: Oxford University Press, 2010); Nayan Shah, *Stranger Intimacy: Contesting Race, Sexuality, and the Law in the North American West* (Berkeley: University of California Press, 2012).

10. For a concise discussion of the emergence of color-blind discourse in American politics and its different phases, see Michael Omi and Howard Winant, *Racial Formation in the United States*, 3rd ed. (New York: Routledge, 2015), 211–221. See generally Eduardo Bonilla-Silva, *Racism without Racists: Color-blind Rac-ism and the Persistence of Racial Inequality in America*, 4th ed. (Lanham, MD: Rowman & Littlefield, 2013).

11. Kevin M. Kruse, *White Flight: Atlanta and the Making of Modern Conservatism* (Princeton: Princeton University Press, 2005). See chapter 3, "From Commu-nity to Individuality: Race, Residence, and Segregationist Ideology."

12. Neil Gotanda, "A Critique of 'Our Constitution is Color-Blind,'" *Stanford Law Review* 44, no. 1 (November 1991): 1–68; Ian F. Haney López, "'A Nation

of Minorities': Race, Ethnicity, and Reactionary Colorblindness," *Stanford Law Review* 59, no. 4 (2007): 985–1064; Christopher W. Schmidt, "*Brown* and the Colorblind Constitution," *Cornell Law Review* 94, no. 1 (2008): 203–238.

13. Reva B. Siegel shows that "the anticlassification principle as we understand it today is the artifact of political struggles over *Brown*'s implementation," in "Equality Talk: Antisubordination and Anticlassification Values in Constitutional Struggles over *Brown*," *Harvard Law Review* 117, no. 5 (March 2004): 1475.

14. Dudziak and Volpp, introduction, "Legal Borderlands," 595, emphasis original.

15. Supreme Court justices had utilized color-blind logic in several decisions since the late nineteenth century, particularly after the 1954 *Brown* decision. But the adherents of color-blind constitutionalism had not yet developed a sophisticated case for it, nor had a plurality on the matter been reached. The first judicial statement in support of color-blind constitutionalism was in Justice John Marshall Harlan's dissent in *Plessy v. Ferguson* (1896), in which he famously wrote, "Our Constitution is color-blind, and neither knows nor tolerates classes among citizens." 163 U.S. 537, 559 (1896) (Harlan, J., dissenting). According to legal scholar Neil Gotanda, "Though aspects of color-blind constitutionalism can be traced to pre–Civil War debates, the modern concept developed after the passage of the Thirteenth, Fourteenth, and Fifteenth Amendments and matured in 1955 in *Brown v. Board of Education*." "A Critique of 'Our Constitution is Color-Blind,'" *Stanford Law Review* 44, no. 1 (November 1991): 2. For a detailed history of the court's rationale in *Brown*, and the justices' thinking on the constitutionality of racial classification, see Schmidt, "*Brown* and the Colorblind Constitution."

16. In his examination of Mexican Americans and school desegregation in Houston, Guadalupe San Miguel Jr. argues that Mexican Americans challenged the district's racialization of them as white and mobilized in response. But their activism is framed only as a part of the larger Chicana/o Movement. *Brown, Not White: School Integration and the Chicano Movement in Houston* (College Station: Texas A&M University Press, 2005).

17. Ansley T. Erickson demonstrates that the de jure/de facto divide is not only not a useful way of understanding the ways in which school segregation is constructed through state action but also actually obscures those processes. Erickson, *Making the Unequal Metropolis: School Desegregation and Its Limits* (Chicago: University of Chicago Press, 2016).

18. Although Mexican American civil rights lawyers had been filing lawsuits against school districts in the Southwest that segregated Mexican and Mexican American children since 1930, none of these lawyers argued that the discrimination faced by these students was racial. Rather, they argued that Mexicans and Mexican Americans were white and could not legally be separated from "other white" children. See Steven H. Wilson, "*Brown* Over 'Other White': Mexican Americans' Legal Arguments and Litigation Strategy in School Desegregation

Lawsuits," *Law and History Review* 21, no. 1 (Spring 2003); Neil Foley, "Over the Rainbow: *Hernandez v. Texas, Brown v. Board of Education,* and *Black v. Brown,*" in Michael A. Olivas, ed., *"Colored Men" and "Hombres Aquí":* Hernandez v. Texas *and the Emergence of Mexican-American Lawyering* (Houston: Arte Público, University of Houston Press, 2006), 111–122.

19. Tom I. Romero II argues that the complex, multiracial character of the US West provided fertile ground for many of the most important legal battles dealing with race and equality. "The 'Tri-Ethnic' Dilemma: Race, Equality, and the Fourteenth Amendment in the American West," *Temple Political & Civil Rights Law Review* 13, no. 2 (Spring 2004): 818. In general, see Brilliant, *The Color of America Has Changed.*

20. "ACLU Holds Off on Race Suit," *Denver Post,* October 30, 1956, 15, cited in Tom I. Romero II, "Our Selma Is Here: The Political and Legal Struggle for Educational Equality in Denver, Colorado, and Multiracial Conundrums in American Jurisprudence," *Seattle Journal for Social Justice* 3, no. 1 (Fall/Winter 2004): 85. These practices, including the selection of new school building sites, gerrymandering school attendance boundaries, the creation of optional attendance zones, the use of mobile classroom buildings, busing, and the use of a limited open enrollment plan, helped school officials maintain segregation.

21. Danielle R. Olden, "Becoming Minority: Mexican Americans, Race, and the Legal Struggle for Educational Equity in Denver, Colorado," *Western Historical Quarterly* 48, no. 1 (Spring 2017): 43–66.

22. Wilfred Keyes et al. v. School District No. 1, Denver, Colorado, et al., 413 U.S. 189 (1973), 195.

23. Ethnic Distribution of Students in DPS by Year (1975–1984), Addendum to Brief for Defendants-Appellants, *Keyes v. School Dist. No. 1,* U.S. Court of Appeals for the Tenth Circuit, March 10, 1988, 43, box 20, U.S. Court of Appeals, 10th Circuit, RG 276, National Archives and Records Administration (NARA), Denver, CO.

24. See Del Rio ISD v. Salvatierra, 33 S. W. 2d 790 (Tex. Civ. App., 1930); Mendez v. Westminster School Dist., 64 F. Supp. 544 (S.D. Cal., 1946); Delgado v. Bastrop ISD, Civ. No. 388 (unreported: W.D. Tex., June 15, 1948); Hernandez v. Driscoll Consolidated ISD, Civil Action 1384, U.S. District Court for the Southern District of Texas (S.D. Tex., 1957), Corpus Christi Division. The published opinion appears in *Race Relations Law Reporter* 2 (S.D. Tex., 1957), 329.

25. On the "other white" legal strategy, see Wilson, *"Brown* Over 'Other White,'" 150–173. At roughly the same time that *Keyes* was filed, lawyers for the plaintiffs in *Cisneros v. Corpus Christi Independent School District* also argued that Mexican Americans were racial minorities and they grouped them with black students in order to prove segregation in the district. Cisneros v. Corpus Christi ISD, 324 F. Supp. 599 (S.D. Tex. 1970).

26. Clara E. Rodríguez, *Changing Race: Latinos, the Census and the History of Ethnicity* (New York: New York University Press, 2000).

27. Ariela J. Gross, "'The Caucasian Cloak': Mexican Americans and the Politics of Whiteness in the Twentieth-Century Southwest," *Georgetown Law Journal* 95, no. 2 (Jan. 2007): 337–392.

28. Guadalupe San Miguel Jr., *"Let All of Them Take Heed": Mexican Americans and the Campaign for Educational Equality in Texas, 1910–1981* (Austin: University of Texas Press, 1987), 175–177; Wilson, *"Brown* Over 'Other White,'" 178.

29. Several times throughout the district court trial, attorneys for the school district questioned the plaintiffs' witnesses about why they defined Mexican Americans as minority. Court Transcript, February 2–20, 1970, *Keyes v. School District No. 1*, 413 U.S. 189 (1973), appendix, vol. 2, filed April 14, 1972, *U.S. Supreme Court Records and Briefs, 1832–1978*, Gale, Cengage Learning, The Ohio State University Moritz Law Library, http://galenet.galegroup.com.proxy.lib.ohio-state.edu/servlet/SCRB?uid=0&srchtp=a&ste=14&rcn=DW3903021824. I expand upon some of these courtroom instances in Olden, "Becoming Minority," 58–63.

30. Keyes v. School Dist. No. 1, 313 F. Supp. 61, 69 (1970).

31. Keyes v. School Dist. No. 1, 413 U.S. 189, 197–198 (1973).

32. Keyes v. School Dist. No. 1, 368 F. Supp. 207 (D. Colo. 1973); Keyes v. School Dist. No. 1, 380 F. Supp. 673 (D. Colo. 1974).

33. "Supreme Court Has Spoken," *Denver Post*, June 24, 1973. In testimony before the US Commission on Civil Rights, Colorado state legislator Ruben Valdez stated that, from his perspective, most Mexican Americans were not really concerned with the desegregation issue until the Supreme Court ruled that they should be included in the desegregation plan. United States Commission on Civil Rights, *Hearing Before the United States Commission on Civil Rights: Hearing Held in Denver, Colorado*, February 17–19, 1976 (Washington: Commission, 1977), 111–112.

34. A recent special issue of the *Journal of Urban History*, "Rethinking the Boston 'Busing Crisis,'" edited by Matthew Delmont and Jeanne Theoharis, demonstrates that historians must begin to address this historiographical gap. It includes an article that examines Latinas/os' responses to the desegregation plan in Boston, whereas previous histories of this important case have neglected this part of the story. Tatiana M. F. Cruz, "'We Took 'Em On': The Latino Movement for Educational Justice in Boston, 1965–1980," *Journal of Urban History* 43, no. 2 (2017): 235–255.

35. Haney López, "A Nation of Minorities," 988.

36. Brief of Amicus Curiae, Colorado State Board of Education, *Keyes v. School Dist. No. 1*, Combined Nos. 74-1349, 74-1350, and 74-1351, United States Court of Appeals for the Tenth Circuit, September 6, 1974, 23–24, folder 3, box 18, Keyes (Wilfred) v. Denver School District Collection, Accession 1 (1963–86), University of Colorado at Boulder Libraries (hereafter Keyes Collection).

37. Omi and Winant, *Racial Formation*, 262.

38. Nancy MacLean, "The Civil Rights Act and the Transformation of Mexican American Identity and Politics," *Berkeley La Raza Law Journal* 18 (2007): 127. Also see Wilson, "*Brown* Over 'Other White.'"

39. Charles Carter, "Integration Plan Talks Disrupted," *Denver Post*, October 27, 1968; "Chicano 'Socks It' to the School Board," *El Gallo* 2 (December 1968): 3.

40. Memorandum, "Recommendation for Enhancing the Educational Process for Hispano Students in the Denver Public Schools," January 7, 1969, 1, box 1, Congress of Hispanic Educators Collection, WH2334, Denver Public Library Western History and Genealogy Department (hereafter DPL-WHG). An informal survey of Mexican American teachers conducted by the CHE demonstrated that they almost unanimously supported desegregation. Art Branscombe, "Valdez Puts Hispano Goals on Scales," *Denver Post*, April 4, 1976, 20.

41. Minutes, Denver Board of Education Meetings, 1969–1974; Alan Cunningham, "Hispano Push for Unity to Effect School Change," *Rocky Mountain News* (Denver, CO), March 24, 1969. One west side community member—Denver's west side was predominantly Mexican American—expressed both pro- and anti-integration viewpoints. Germaine Aragon, letter to the editor, *West Side Recorder* 6, no. 2 (June 1969): 2; Germaine Aragon, letter to the editor, *West Side Recorder* 7, no. 11 (April 1971): 3.

42. Rudolph F. Castro et al., "The Problem of Racism: An Attitudinal Study of the Spanish-Surnamed," (MSW thesis, University of Denver, 1972), 135–140.

43. Westside Action Ministry, "Supplement" *West Side Recorder* 5 (March 1969), insert. For more on the school walkouts, see "Racist West High Teacher Must Go," *El Gallo* 2 (March 1969): 4; Christine Marín, *A Spokesman of the Mexican American Movement: Rodolfo "Corky" Gonzales and the Fight for Chicano Liberation, 1966–1972* (San Francisco, 1977); Ernesto B. Vigil, *The Crusade for Justice: Chicano Militancy and the Government's War on Dissent* (Madison: University of Wisconsin Press, 1999), 80–95. Chicano school walkouts, also called blowouts, occurred throughout the nation in the late 1960s. See Mario T. García and Sal Castro, *Blowout! Sal Castro and the Chicano Struggle for Educational Justice* (Chapel Hill: University of North Carolina Press, 2011).

44. MALDEF, Motion to Intervene as Parties Plaintiffs, *Keyes v. School District No. 1*, January 4, 1974, no. 47, book 1, box 25, Keyes Collection. This was not the CHE's first attempt to make school officials comply with federal civil rights law as it pertained to Mexican American students. In 1971 representatives from several Mexican American community organizations, including the CHE, sent a letter to the Office for Civil Rights in the Department of Health, Education, and Welfare (HEW), charging DPS with "noncompliance of equal educational opportunities for the Chicano child." Thomas P. Martinez et al. to Stan Pottinger, April 21, 1971, box 1, Congress of Hispanic Educators Collection.

45. MALDEF, Memorandum in Support of Motion to Intervene as Parties Plaintiffs, *Keyes v. School District No. 1*, n.d., ca. January 1974, no. 49, book 1, box 25, Keyes Collection.

46. Elaine Nathanson, "Winsett: Mr. Anti-Busing Steps Toward the Ballot," *Straight Creek Journal*, July 2–9, 1974, 6. Article IX, Section 8 of the Civil Rights Act of 1964 read, "'Desegregation' means the assignment of students to public schools and within such schools without regard to their race, color, religion, or national origin, but 'desegregation' shall not mean the assignment of students to public schools in order to overcome racial imbalance." Civil Rights Act of 1964, Pub. L. No. 88–352, 78 Stat. 241 (1964). I follow Matthew Delmont's rejection of terms like "antibusing activist" because such terms obscure the extent to which these individuals actually opposed desegregation. Instead, I use descriptors like "anti-integrationist" or "desegregation opponent." Matthew F. Delmont, *Why Busing Failed: Race, Media, and the National Resistance to School Desegregation* (Berkeley: University of California Press, 2016), 1–6.

47. Minutes, Denver Board of Education Meeting, April 18, 1974, 12.

48. Minutes, Denver Board of Education Meeting, April 18, 1974, 9.

49. Minutes, Denver Board of Education Meeting, November 14, 1974, 12.

50. Minutes, Denver Board of Education Meeting, April 18, 1974, 9.

51. Reporter's Transcript, Conference, *Keyes v. School Dist. No. 1*, U.S. District Court for the District of Colorado, June 10, 1974, folder 6, box 17, Keyes Collection.

52. Defendants' Motion for Modification and Clarification of Judgment and Decree, *Keyes v. School Dist. No. 1*, April 17, 1974, no. 32, book 3, box 25, Keyes Collection.

53. Reporter's Transcript, Conference, *Keyes v. School Dist. No. 1*, U.S. District Court for the District of Colorado, June 10, 1974, folder 6, box 17, Keyes Collection.

54. Reporter's Transcript, Conference, *Keyes v. School Dist. No. 1*, U.S. District Court for the District of Colorado, June 10, 1974, folder 6, box 17, Keyes Collection.

55. Martha Menchaca, *Recovering History, Constructing Race: The Indian, Black, and White Roots of Mexican Americans* (Austin: University of Texas Press, 2002); Laura E. Gómez, *Manifest Destinies: The Making of the Mexican American Race* (New York: New York University Press, 2008).

56. Order, Judge William E. Doyle, *Keyes v. School Dist. No. 1*, U.S. District Court for the District of Colorado, June 19, 1974, no. 30, book 3, box 25, Keyes Collection.

57. Minutes, Denver Board of Education Meeting, August 8, 1974, 26. As of September 1974, the total student population of the district was 79,670. Minutes, Denver Board of Education Meeting, November 21, 1974, 25.

58. Jane Earle, "Denver Indians Protest 'Being Used' by Parents to Avoid Busing," *Denver Post*, October 3, 1974, 2. Claiming to have Indian blood, as well as performing Indian-ness, has a long and contested history in the United States. See Philip J. Deloria, *Playing Indian* (New Haven: Yale University Press, 1998).

59. Jane Earle, "New School Affidavits Sought," *Denver Post*, October 23, 1974, 4.

60. "Rockwell, Bradford Win Seats on School Board," *Rocky Mountain News* (Denver, CO), May 21, 1975, 5.

61. Bradford explained that her community was "caught in the middle," too poor to own a home and belong to a homeowners' association but not poor enough to qualify for federal subsidies. Art Branscombe, "Early Poverty Molded Board Member," *Denver Post*, October 19, 1975, 24.

62. While Bradford was a grassroots activist, she positioned herself in opposition to the Chicana/o movement. "I reject the term Chicano," she explained. "To me, that's a political term. The only people who'll call themselves Chicanos are political activists. . . . I'm not a part of that radical element." Branscombe, "Early Poverty Molded Board Member." On the Silent Majority and the rise of conservatism in the postwar period, see Lisa McGirr, *Suburban Warriors: The Origins of the New American Right* (Princeton: Princeton University Press, 2001); Matthew Lassiter, *The Silent Majority: Suburban Politics in the Sunbelt South* (Princeton: Princeton University Press, 2006); Kruse, *White Flight.*

63. "Bradford Solidly Supports 'Neighborhood Schools,'" *Rocky Mountain News* (Denver, CO), May 14, 1981, 73.

64. According to school board member Omar Blair, Bradford used racist language in public forums on more than one occasion, calling Blair "a black s.o.b." and Bernard Valdez (another board member) "a wetback." Mitch Geller, "The Real Naomi Bradford," *Denver Magazine* 7, no. 1 (December 1976): 44–45, quote on 44.

65. Bradford's firm rejection of bilingual-bicultural education often made her the target of Mexican American educational organizations and activists. Tom Rees, "Chicanos Angered by Bilingual Criticism," *Rocky Mountain News* (Denver, CO), July 16, 1975, 6; "Bradford Solidly Supports 'Neighborhood Schools,'" *Rocky Mountain News* (Denver, CO), May 14, 1981, 73.

66. "Bradford Solidly Supports 'Neighborhood Schools,'" 73. In another interview she told the *Denver Post*'s education editor, "I've been called a Mexican all my life." Branscombe, "Early Poverty Molded Board Member," 24.

67. Jane Earle, "School, Indian Impasse Declared," *Denver Post*, November 10, 1974, 51.

68. Jane Earle, "Denver Indians Protest 'Being Used,'" 2.

69. In his order, Judge Doyle wrote, "An Indian means any individual who 1. Is a member of a tribe, band, or other organized group of Indians, including those tribes, bands, or groups terminated since 1940 and those recognized now or in the future by the State in which they reside, or who is a descendant, in the first or second degree, of any such member, or 2. Is considered by the Secretary of the Interior to be an Indian for any purpose or 3. Is an Eskimo or Aleut or other Alaskan Native, or 4. Is determined to be an Indian under regulations promulgated by the Commissioner [of education], after consultation with the National Advisory Council on Indian Education." Judge William E. Doyle, Order, *Keyes. v. School Dist. No. 1*, October 4, 1974, no. 52, book 1, box 26, Keyes

Collection. This continued to be a problem for the school district and the court. In April 1975 the court had to go even further to establish rules for the "American Indian" classification. Judge Doyle ordered that any parent who filed an affidavit claiming their child was American Indian would undergo an investigation that would be conducted by the Parents Committee formed under the Indian Education Act of Title IV. Judge William E. Doyle, Supplemental Order, *Keyes v. School Dist. No. 1*, April 25, 1975, no. 68, book 1, box 26, Keyes Collection.

70. Alexandra Harmon, "Tribal Enrollment Councils: Lessons on Law and Indian Identity," *Western Historical Quarterly* 32, no. 2 (2001): 175–201; Eva Marie Garroutte, "The Racial Formation of American Indians: Negotiating Legitimate Identities within Tribal and Federal Law," *American Indian Quarterly* 25, no. 2 (2001): 224–239; Circe Strum, *Blood Politics: Race, Culture, and Identity in the Cherokee Nation of Oklahoma* (Berkeley: University of California Press, 2002); and Mark Edwin Miller, *Claiming Tribal Identity: The Five Tribes and the Politics of Federal Acknowledgment* (Norman: University of Oklahoma Press, 2013).

71. For a more detailed examination of the conflict between civil rights discourse and indigenous fights for sovereignty, see Circe Strum, "Race, Sovereignty, and Civil Rights: Understanding the Cherokee Freedman Controversy," *Cultural Anthropology* 29, no. 3 (2014): 575–598.

72. Jane Earle, "School, Indian Impasse Declared," 51.

73. Minutes, Board of Education Meeting, November 14, 1974, 13.

74. Minutes, Denver Board of Education Meeting, November 14, 1974, 13–14.

75. Minutes, Denver Board of Education Meeting, November 14, 1974.

76. Minutes, Denver Board of Education Meeting, November 14, 1974, 14–15, quote on 14.

77. Minutes, Denver Board of Education Meeting, November 14, 1974, 16.

78. Elaine Nathanson, "Winsett: Mr. Anti-Busing Steps Toward the Ballot," *Straight Creek Journal*, July 2–9, 1974, 6.

79. Jane Earle, "Denver Indians Protest 'Being Used,'" 2.

80. Pascoe, *What Comes Naturally*, 301–306.

81. Legal scholar Tanya Katerí Hernández argues that the contemporary Mixed Category Movement's fixation on a mixed-race category for the US Census and their use of multiracial discourse actually supports color-blind jurisprudence by inadvertently implying that race is an individual, cultural category, rather than a sociopolitical one. "'Multiracial' Discourse: Racial Classifications in an Era of Color-Blind Jurisprudence," *Maryland Law Review* 57, no. 1 (1998): 97–173. Also see Joel Perlmann and Mary C. Waters, eds., *The New Race Question: How the Census Counts Multiracial Individuals* (New York: Russell Sage Foundation, 2005).

82. Gary Orfield and Erica Frankenberg, *Brown at 60: Great Progress, a Long Retreat and an Uncertain Future*, The Civil Rights Project (Los Angeles: University of California–Los Angeles, 2014), 2.

83. Parents Involved in Community Schools v. Seattle School Dist. No. 1, 551 U.S. 701, 747–748 (2007) (plurality opinion).

84. U.S. Commission on Civil Rights, *Hearing Before the United States Commission on Civil Rights: Hearing Held in Denver, Colorado*, 477–478.

Sarah Deer is a citizen of the Muscogee (Creek) Nation of Oklahoma. She was named a MacArthur Fellow in 2014. Currently a professor at the University of Kansas, Deer is also the chief justice for the Prairie Island Indian Community Court of Appeals. She is the author of *The Beginning and End of Rape: Confronting Sexual Violence in Native America* (University of Minnesota Press, 2015) and several books on tribal law.

Brian Frehner is an associate professor of history at the University of Missouri–Kansas City. He is author of *Finding Oil: The Nature of Petroleum Geology, 1859–1920* (2011) and coeditor of *Indians and Energy: Exploitation and Opportunity in the American Southwest* (2010).

Andrea Geiger is an associate professor of history at Simon Fraser University and the author of the prize-winning book *Subverting Exclusion: Transpacific Encounters with Race, Caste, and Borders, 1885–1928* (2011). Before turning to history, she served as a reservation attorney for the Confederated Tribes of the Colville Reservation and as a law clerk for judges at both the federal trial court and the state court of appeals for Washington State.

Alicia Gutierrez-Romine is an assistant professor of history at La Sierra University. She is the author of the forthcoming book *From Back Alley to the Border: Criminal Abortion in California, 1920–1969*.

Kelly Lytle Hernández is a professor of history and African American studies at the University of California, Los Angeles. She is the author of *Migra! A History of the U.S. Border Patrol* (2010) and *City of Inmates: Conquest, Rebellion, and the Rise of Human Caging in Los Angeles, 1771–1965* (2017).

Katrina Jagodinsky is an associate professor of history at the University of Nebraska–Lincoln and author of the prize-winning book *Legal Codes and Talking Trees: Indigenous Women's Sovereignty in the Sonoran and Puget Sound Borderlands, 1854–1946* (Yale University Press, 2016). She has earned article prizes in Western legal history from the Western History Association and is a William Nelson Cromwell Legal History Fellowship recipient and former fellow of the Clements Center for Southwest Studies at Southern Methodist University.

Pablo Mitchell is a professor of history and comparative American studies at Oberlin College. He is the author of *Understanding Latino History:*

Excavating the Past, Examining the Present (2018), *West of Sex: Making Mexican America, 1900–1930* (2012), and *Coyote Nation: Sexuality, Race, and Conquest in Modernizing New Mexico, 1880–1920* (2005).

Danielle R. Olden is an assistant professor of history at the University of Utah and a 2018 National Endowment for the Humanities Fellow. She is completing her first book, *Racial Uncertainties: Mexican Americans, School Desegregation, and the Making of Race in Post–Civil Rights America.*

Tom I. Romero II is an associate professor of law and affiliated faculty in the Department of History at the University of Denver. He has published numerous articles and book chapters on racial formation in the legal history of education, immigration, land use, state constitutions, water law, and jurisprudence in the American West. Romero was also a Legal History Fellow at the University of Colorado's Center of the American West.

Jeffrey P. Shepherd is an associate professor of history at the University of Texas at El Paso and author of *We Are an Indian Nation: A History of the Hualapai People* (University of Arizona Press, 2010). He is also a coeditor, with Myla Vicenti Carpio, of the University of Arizona book series Critical Issues in Indigenous Studies. He teaches classes and conducts research in Western, Borderlands, and environmental history, as well as Native American and Indigenous studies.

Allison Powers Useche is an assistant professor of history at Texas Tech University. She received her PhD from Columbia University, where her dissertation, "Settlement Colonialism: Compensatory Justice in United States Expansion, 1903–1941," received the Bancroft Award for American History and Diplomacy. From 2017–2018, she was a Past and Present Postdoctoral Fellow at the University of London's Institute of Historical Research.

Dana Elizabeth Weiner is an associate professor of history at Wilfrid Laurier University and author of *Race and Rights: Fighting Slavery and Prejudice in the Old Northwest, 1830–1870* (Northern Illinois University Press, 2013). Her work also appears in *People of African Descent: Rethinking Struggles for Recognition and Empowerment,* edited by Behnaz Mirzai and Bonny Ibhawoh (Africa World Press, 2018).

INDEX

Numbers followed by *f* or *t* refer to pages with figures or tables, respectively.